The Red Sox
in the Playoffs

Also by Joshua R. Pahigian

*Spring Training Handbook:
A Comprehensive Guide to the Ballparks of the
Grapefruit and Cactus Leagues* (McFarland, 2005)

Why I Hate the Yankees (2005)

The Ultimate Baseball Road-Trip (2004)

The Red Sox in the Playoffs

A Postseason History, 1903–2005

Joshua R. Pahigian

McFarland & Company, Inc., Publishers
Jefferson, North Carolina, and London

LIBRARY OF CONGRESS CATALOGUING-IN-PUBLICATION DATA

Josh Pahigian.
The Red Sox in the playoffs : a postseason history, 1903–2005 / Joshua R. Pahigian.
p.   cm.
Includes bibliographical references and index.

ISBN-13: 978-0-7864-2778-9
ISBN-10: 0-7864-2778-7
(softcover : 50# alkaline paper) ∞

1. Boston Red Sox (Baseball team) — History — 20th century.
2. World Series (Baseball) — History — 20th century.   I. Title.
GV875.B62R385   2006   796.357'640974461 — dc22   2006028310

British Library cataloguing data are available

©2006 Joshua R. Pahigian. All rights reserved

*No part of this book may be reproduced or transmitted in any form
or by any means, electronic or mechanical, including photocopying
or recording, or by any information storage and retrieval system,
without permission in writing from the publisher.*

Cover photograph: Bobby Doerr, Ted Williams and Dom DiMaggio
(Boston Public Library, Prints Division)

Manufactured in the United States of America

*McFarland & Company, Inc., Publishers
Box 611, Jefferson, North Carolina 28640
www.mcfarlandpub.com*

Table of Contents

Introduction 1

Chapter 1. **1903** 3
Chapter 2. **1912** 17
Chapter 3. **1915** 29
Chapter 4. **1916** 40
Chapter 5. **1918** 51
Chapter 6. **1946** 63
Chapter 7. **1948** 78
Chapter 8. **1967** 85
Chapter 9. **1975** 99
Chapter 10. **1978** 115

Chapter 11. **1986** 120
Chapter 12. **1988** 137
Chapter 13. **1990** 146
Chapter 14. **1995** 155
Chapter 15. **1998** 162
Chapter 16. **1999** 170
Chapter 17. **2003** 183
Chapter 18. **2004** 198
Chapter 19. **2005** 216

Appendix I: Regular Season Results 223
Appendix II: Postseason Results 226
Appendix III: Postseason Statistics 232
Chapter Notes 265
Bibliography 271
Index 273

Introduction

As is the case with most writers and the subject matter they spend their time exploring, this project was born of my own personal interest in this topic. As a lifelong Boston Red Sox fan I have had the opportunity to wince, grimace, and pace my way through more than half of the playoff and World Series games in the team's history. Yet, it recently occurred to me that my knowledge of the team's postseason exploits was not as complete as it could be. Like many fans, I possessed only a cursory knowledge of the team's five world championships between 1903 and 1918. Sure, I knew that in 1903 the Boston Americans had won the first modern World Series, that Cy Young had been a member of the squad, and that the home games had been played at the Huntington Avenue Grounds. And I knew that Babe Ruth had pitched the Red Sox to a pair of wins in the 1918 World Series, which stood for 86 years as the team's most recent championship. But beyond these highlights, I knew very little else about the most glorious stretch of Boston baseball history. In fact, I knew virtually nothing about the World Series of 1912, 1915 and 1916.

While my knowledge of the 1946, 1948 and 1967 seasons was somewhat more complete, it was based solely on the bits and pieces of information — some accurate, some exaggerated, some simply incorrect — ingrained in the collective psyches of members of today's Red Sox Nation. I knew that Pesky had allegedly "held the ball" in 1946, for example, allowing the Cardinals' Enos Slaughter to race home with the series' winning run. But I had no idea how the Red Sox had arrived at such a critical juncture in the seventh game, or whether the half-century old accusation was true.

Although I had, as stated, suffered through the team's more recent postseason contests, my memory had been rather selective in retaining the high points and low points of each series, while forgetting many other important moments. Naturally I remembered that the ball had gone through Buckner's legs in 1986. And like any real Red Sox fan I remembered that Calvin Schiraldi and Bob Stanley had already blown a two run lead by the time the gimpy first baseman made the gaffe. And I remembered that there had still been Game Seven to play. But how much did I really remember about that seventh game? The series had ended, in my mind, as soon as Ray Knight leapt into the arms of his teammates to score the winning run in Game Six. Similarly, I remembered Bucky Dent's home run in 1978 and Tony Pena's in 1995, and Pedro Martinez's heroics against the Indians in 1999, but my grasp of the details preceding and following these defining moments in the life of any Red Sox fan needed more than just a little refreshing.

I set out to write this book with the intent of enhancing my own working knowledge of each and every championship and near-championship campaign in Red Sox history. And to that extent I have succeeded. It is my hope that the pages that follow will provide readers with the same depth of understanding that I now possess. I must admit that writing this book would not have been psychologically possible for me had the Red Sox not mitigated so much anguish with their remarkable World Series victory in 2004. For that I will always be grateful. The release from the burden I had carried like all Boston fans freed me to revisit many moments I would not have previously chosen to explore, and in the process of doing so, I discovered many fond memories that would have otherwise been lost to me forever.

As source material, I reviewed video footage of the games whenever possible. I also relied heavily on the period accounts of the sportswriters of each era, and on the narratives penned by other authors. As you will see, the book offers a chapter treating each year in which the Red Sox appeared in the playoffs. Although major league baseball considers the one-game playoffs of 1946 and 1978 to be extensions of those years' regular seasons, I have included these in the book, since they were, in fact, played after the completion of the regular slate of games. Each chapter begins with a review of how the team qualified for the playoffs, noting significant roster moves, regular season games, and other happenings that contributed to the team's success. Next is a short synopsis of the team's postseason exploits in the focus year, followed by a game-by-game rendering of each playoff or World Series contest. Appendices at the end of the book provide relevant statistical information.

Boston, and in fact all of New England, seems to buzz with a special kind of excitement during those magical summers when the Red Sox vie for baseball's highest seat. This book is dedicated to the loyal men and women who support the team in good times and in bad.

CHAPTER 1

The Regular Season: 91–47

The 1903 World Series between Boston and Pittsburgh represented the first postseason meeting of the regular season champions of the fledgling American League and the venerable National League. The series is therefore regarded as the first modern World Series, although the term "World Series" had been used as early as 1884 when the Providence Grays of the National League met the New York Mets of the American Association in a best-of-five game series.

In the last two decades of the nineteenth century, baseball had continued to evolve so that by 1903, the third year of the American League's existence, the game resembled the one familiar to Americans in the twenty-first century. Amidst an atmosphere of fierce competition for fan loyalty between the two rival leagues, the American League followed the National League's lead and amended its rules in 1903 to begin counting foul balls as strikes, which is today regarded as one of the last major evolutionary steps necessary to modernizing the game. Still, baseball had much growing up to do, despite its widespread popularity. Years would pass before such modern staples of the game arrived as the lively ball, uniform numbers, webbed gloves, concrete and steel stadiums, dugouts, and relief pitchers.

After years as an NL city, a new Boston team was a charter member of the AL in 1901. The team, which would not adopt the name "Red Sox" until 1907, was originally known by an array of nicknames that included the Pilgrims, Plymouth Rocks, Somersets (for owner Charles Somers) and Puritans. But Boston writers most often referred to the new team as the Americans, a shorthand that distinguished them from the city's better-established National League club, the Beaneaters or Nationals.* The team played on a parcel of land in South Boston known as the Huntington Avenue Grounds, where the city had previously hosted fairs and circuses. A wooden ballpark sat on the plot, just across a set of railroad tracks from the South End Grounds, home of the NL's Beaneaters, the franchise from which the current Atlanta Braves descended.

After the advent of the American League, which placed competing franchises in National League cities, it became increasingly common to identify league affiliation when referring to clubs. It became commonplace, for a time, to read about the Philadelphia Americans (Athletics) or the New York Nationals (Giants). The fact that many teams were not then strongly associated with nicknames meant that there was relatively little risk of confusion or resentment on the part of the reader.

Three players from the Beaneaters jumped to the city's AL franchise in 1901, and played important roles in establishing the new team as the hottest ticket in town. Chief among the trio was third baseman Jimmy Collins who was lured to the Americans by the promise of a $10,000 salary and the title of team captain, akin to the term "manager" used today. Hard-hitting center fielder Chick Stahl and right-handed pitcher Bill Dinneen also fled the Beaneaters for the Americans.

The new team posted winning records in both 1901 and 1902, finishing second and third, respectively, while outdrawing the Beaneaters at the box office. The Americans team that headed north from spring training in Macon, Georgia in April of 1903 was essentially the same unit that had finished six and a half games behind Connie Mack's Philadelphia A's in 1902, with a record of 77–60. The only significant change was the addition of 36-year-old Marlboro, Massachusetts, native Charley Farrell, who supplanted catcher Lou Criger behind the plate. Farrell had played for the NL's Brooklyn team the year before.

In addition to Farrell, the 1903 Americans fielded three other native New Englanders in their starting nine. There was George "Candy" LaChance of Waterbury, Connecticut, second baseman Hobe Ferris of Providence, Rhode Island, and five-foot, five-inch shortstop Freddy Parent of Sanford, Maine. In addition to Collins, the club's top hitters were left fielder Patsy Dougherty, who had hit .342 as a rookie in 1902, and right fielder Buck Freeman, who had set the single season home run record in 1899, belting 25 dingers for Washington, a record that stood until Babe Ruth swatted 29 long balls for the Red Sox in 1919.

The team's strength coming out of spring training was clearly its pitching staff, led by 36-year-old Cy Young, who had won 32 games the year before, and Dinneen, who had won 21. George Winter, Norman Gibson and Tom Hughes were expected to compete for the number-three spot in the rotation. The quintet went on to start all but one of the team's regular season games and to pitch all but eight of the team's 1255 innings. Nick Altrock was the only other pitcher to play for the 1903 Red Sox, making one early season start before finishing the season in Chicago.

In a special season preview, *Boston Globe* sports editor Tim Murnane forecasted great things for the Americans' pitching staff in 1903. "Cy Young is burning them in as fast as ever," he wrote. "Billy Dinneen is in better shape than for many seasons... George Winters, who was down to 80 pounds last summer during his sickness, now weighs nearly double that... Gibson is a medium-sized, well-built fellow with fine control and a cool head... Tom Hughes looks good... Collins will have a marvelous string of pitchers."[1]

On April 20, the season opened with a split-admission double-header against the A's at the Huntington Avenue Grounds. The Americans won the morning tilt, 9–4, behind Young, but lost the afternoon affair, 10–7. A crowd of 19,282 fans turned out for the second game, the biggest assembly ever to watch a baseball game in Boston. The Americans and A's then traveled to Philadelphia where the Americans dropped the first two games of a three-game series to fall to 1–3 on the season.

The team struggled through the first month. After losing 6–4 to the St. Louis Browns on May 22, Boston's record stood at 13–14. And worse, Farrell, who was hitting a team-best .404, suffered a broken leg while sliding into second base. Criger, who had served as Young's personal catcher when the two played together in Cleveland and St. Louis, moved into the starting role behind the plate and the team's fortunes quickly improved. The Americans were 15–15 on May 28 when they began an 11-game win streak with a 5–4 win over Washington. Boston moved into first place on June 1, downing New York, 8–2, behind two two-run homers by Freeman and a complete game effort from Hughes. The pitcher known as "Long Tom" was solidifying his place as the team's third starter.

The Americans won 19 of 26 games in June and stood at 38–22 through the first two and a half months. They began July with a dramatic 1–0 win in Chicago, as Young pitched 10 shutout innings and drove in the winning run with a double against Pat Flaherty.

On the Fourth of July, Boston swept a pair of games from St. Louis, winning 4–1 and 2–0. Fans fired pistols into the air to celebrate good plays. The Americans' fans were not only well armed but fanatical, as a contingent known as the Royal Rooters, led by legendary Boston barkeep Mike "Nuf Ced" McGreevey, was notorious for rattling opposing players with incessant chants and banter.

Boston was on its way to winning the American League by a tidy 14½ games over runner-up Philadelphia. But the prospect of a postseason series against the top National League team was hardly guaranteed. Talk of a championship series first surfaced on September 1, when *The Globe* ran a short article that stated, "Henry Killilea, owner of the Boston club, will meet Barney Dreyfuss, owner of the Pittsburgh club of the National League, in a few days, and endeavor to arrange for a series of games this fall between the winning teams of the two major leagues, and play for the championship of the United States."[2]

During the next three weeks the two owners haggled over a number of issues that needed to be settled to facilitate a championship series, not the least of which was how to divide the gate receipts from the games. While the generous Dreyfuss was willing to give 100 percent of the profits to the players, Killilea, a Milwaukee lawyer who visited Boston infrequently, wanted to offer the players 50 percent. Further complicating matters, the Boston players were only under contract with the team through September 30, while the Pirates were signed on until October 15.

Much uncertainty still surrounded the possibility of a series between the top AL and top NL teams when Boston clinched the AL pennant on September 16 with a 14–7 win over Cleveland. Hughes earned the win, while Stahl went 5–5, improving the Americans to 72–57, and opening an 11½ game lead over the second-place Cleveland Spiders with 11 games to play.

Finally, on September 26 official word came that Boston and Pittsburgh (spelled here the modern way, although there was in fact no "h" in the city's name as of yet) would play a postseason series, consisting of the best-of-nine games. The players would receive 60 percent of the profits, while the team owners would split the remaining 40 percent. The agreement further stipulated that only players who had played for their teams prior to September 1 would be eligible for the series, and that the first three games would be played in Boston, the fourth through seventh in Pittsburgh, and eighth and ninth in Boston.

The Americans concluded the regular season with a double-header sweep of the Browns on September 28, to finish 91–47. The Americans led the AL in batting average (.272), runs (708), triples (113) and home runs (48). Freeman finished with a .287 average, 20 triples, and league-leading totals of 13 home runs and 104 RBI, while Dougherty led the AL in hits with 195 and runs with 107, and batted .331. Collins (.296, 17 triples, 5 HR, 72 RBI) and Parent (.304, 17 triples, 4 HR, 80 RBI) were also top performers. The five-man pitching staff placed first in ERA (2.57), opponents' batting average (.242), and shutouts (20). The ageless Young finished 28–9 with a 2.08 ERA and a league-leading 34 complete games. Old Uncle Cyrus also batted .321 in 137 at-bats. Dinneen (21–13, 2.26), Hughes (20–7, 2.57), Gibson (13–9, 3.19) and Winter (9–8, 3.08) were all excellent on the mound, or "in the box," to use the jargon of the day.

The Postseason: 5–3

In an era when many still considered the NL the only real "major league," most prognosticators agreed that the Americans were slight favorites entering the series only because the NL team was beset by injuries. Pittsburgh had been as dominant in the NL as Boston had in the AL, posting a 91–49 record and leading the circuit in runs (793), triples (110) and home runs (34) and finishing second in batting average (.286). Shortstop Honus Wagner led the league with a .355 average and 19 triples, while also driving in 101 runs, while Pirates captain Fred Clarke finished second in the NL with a .351 average, and Ginger Beaumont led the circuit with 209 hits, while batting .341.

Despite losing ace Jack Chesbro to the AL before the season, the Pirates still finished second in the NL in ERA in 1903, allowing just 2.91 earned runs per game. Sam Leever filled the void left by Chesbro, going 25–7 with a league-best 2.06 ERA, while Deacon Phillippe (25–9, 2.43) and Ed Doheny (16–8, 3.19) were also reliable starters.

The Pirates knew they would be without the services of Doheny, though, as they rode the rails to Boston. The lefthander was in a Pittsburgh mental institution after suffering what would turn out to be a career-ending mental breakdown in mid–September. Leever would pitch in the series, but would be ineffective due to a shoulder injury suffered while trapshooting clay pigeons a few weeks before the series. Wagner and third baseman Tommy Leach also played through lingering injuries in the series.

The Pirates jumped out to a three-games-to-one lead as their only healthy starter, Phillippe, started three of the first four games. More than a century later, Phillippe still holds World Series records for his five starts, five decisions, and 44 innings pitched in the series. After a slow start, Boston came back to win four straight games and claim the championship. Dinneen emerged as the hero, winning three of his four starts, including two shutouts, while Young claimed Boston's other two victories. The pair of aces combined to pitch 69 of 71 innings for the Americans in the series.

The Royal Rooters also rose to a new level of national prominence in the series, as many Boston fans traveled to Pittsburgh to harass the Pirates in their own Exposition Park. Throughout the series, fans in both ballparks were allowed to stand on the outfield lawn once the bleachers and grandstands had filled. The masses stood behind rope barriers, between the outfield fence and the outfielders, necessitating special ground rules that mandated any ball hit in the crowd should be ruled a double or triple, depending on the size and depth of the crowd each day. Although the Americans clinched the series with a Game Eight victory in Boston, many of the Royal Rooters were not on hand to witness the finale due to a ticket controversy that saw speculators, or "scalpers" as they are called today, mysteriously acquire several thousand tickets. The scandal was one of the main reasons AL president Ban Johnson pressured Killilea to sell his interests in the Americans after the season. *Boston Globe* magnate Charles Taylor bought the team.

1903 World Series: Americans 5, Pirates 3

Game 1: Pirates 7, Americans 3

	1	2	3	4	5	6	7	8	9	R	H	E
Pittsburgh	4	0	1	1	0	0	1	0	0	7	12	2
Boston	0	0	0	0	0	0	2	0	1	3	6	4

Chapter 1. 1903

The Americans and Pirates pose for a joint photograph. (Courtesy of the Boston Public Library, Print Department)

WP   Deacon Phillippe
LP   Cy Young

On a Thursday afternoon, an overflow crowd in excess of 16,000 fans mobbed the Huntington Avenue Grounds to watch Cy Young pitch the biggest game of his already illustrious career. Baseball's first World Series was about to get under way, and Boston was abuzz with excitement. The jubilance of the home fans didn't last long though, as Phillippe shut down the Americans, and the Boston defense stumbled behind Young, making four errors.

Before the game, the Pirates' Leach boldly predicted a win, telling reporters, "I think we have it all over [Boston]. I don't see how we can lose."[3] The third baseman backed up his bravado with a 4-for-5 performance that included two triples, and Pittsburgh won easily.

The Pirates scored four runs in the top of the first, doing all of the damage after two were out. Leach started the rally, stroking a two-out ground rule triple into the throng that stood just behind Freeman in right field. Wagner then laced a single to left to plate the game's first run, then stole second base, and moved to third when Ferris couldn't handle a groundball by Kitty Bransfield, who was safe at first. On Young's first pitch to Claude Ritchey,

Bransfield broke for second. Criger came out of his crouch and fired an errant throw into center field, allowing Wagner to trot home from third with the second run, as Bransfield took third. After Ritchey walked and stole second, Jimmy Sebring singled to score both runners for a 4–0 lead.

Young allowed single runs in the third, fourth and seventh, while the Americans didn't break through against Phillippe until they scored twice in the seventh on back-to-back triples by Freeman and Parent, and a sacrifice fly by LaChance. A Wagner error led to Boston's third run in the ninth.

Phillippe was the star of the day, using an assortment of breaking pitches to scatter six hits and strike out ten in a complete game effort. Every Boston starter struck out at least once, except Freeman.

Game 2: Americans 3, Pirates 0

	1	2	3	4	5	6	7	8	9	R	H	E
Pittsburgh	0	0	0	0	0	0	0	0	0	0	3	2
Boston	2	0	0	0	0	1	0	0	X	3	9	0

WP   Bill Dinneen
LP   Sam Leever

Big Bill Dinneen drew the start for Boston the next day, while Pittsburgh sent the ailing Leever to the box. Boston owner Killilea was in attendance, having traveled by rail overnight from Milwaukee to watch the game.

For the second day in a row, the only runs the victors would need crossed the plate in the first inning. Boston scored a pair against Leever in the bottom of the first and rode the right arm of Dinneen to victory.

Boston leadoff hitter Dougherty shared the spotlight with Dinneen, going 3-for-4 with a pair of solo homers.

Dougherty got things started, drilling Leever's very first offering to the deepest part of the ballpark in right-center, more than 500 feet from home plate. The previous day, the hit might have been a ground-rule triple, but a noticeably smaller crowd of about 9,000 fans had turned out for the second game, freeing up space in centerfield. By the time Beaumont retrieved the ball and relayed it to the infield, Dougherty had crossed the plate. Stahl followed with a one-out double to center, and scored on Freeman's single, giving Boston a 2–0 lead.

Clarke lifted the sore-armed Leever after the first inning, handing the ball over to rookie Bucky Veil who had appeared in just 12 regular season games. The 22-year-old pitched well, limiting Boston to just one run over the final seven innings. Despite the fine effort, Veil did not appear again in the series, and made just one start for the Pirates in 1904 before disappearing from organized baseball.

In the sixth inning, Dougherty hit his second homer. This one left the yard, sailing over the fence just inside the left field foul pole and touching down on Huntington Avenue. The clout represented the second ball all season to clear the left field fence, which was 350 feet from the plate. These were the only two home runs Boston would hit in the 1903 World Series.

Dinneen, who had pitched six shutouts in 34 regular season starts, was masterful. He allowed only four balls to leave the infield—three singles, and a fly out to center—while surrendering three hits and two walks and striking out 11.

Fans swarmed the Huntington Avenue Grounds before Game 3 of the World Series. (Courtesy of the Boston Public Library, Print Department)

GAME 3: PIRATES, 4, AMERICANS 2

	1	2	3	4	5	6	7	8	9	R	H	E
Pittsburgh	0	1	2	0	0	0	0	1	0	4	7	0
Boston	0	0	0	1	0	0	0	1	0	2	4	2

WP Deacon Phillippe
LP Tom Hughes

Saturday's third game attracted the largest crowd of the series, and certainly the largest crowd ever to watch a baseball game in Boston. Although the official attendance was announced at 18,801, the Boston ticket office refused to turn away any potential paying customer and an estimated 30,000 fans packed the ballpark. A full hour before the 3:00 PM start, the crowd on the field had already broken through the roped off boundaries and crept all the way to where the outfield grass met the infield dirt, surrounding the infield six people deep, and preventing the teams from completing their pre-game drills. The undermanned Boston police staff eventually managed to corral the fans back into the outfield extremities, beating them back with rubber fire hoses. Nonetheless, the crowd

Jimmy Collins at the Huntington Avenue Grounds. (Courtesy of the Boston Public Library, Print Department)

would play an important role in determining the outcome of the game. The ropes in the outfield had been brought in 75 feet closer to the infield than where they were during Game One, and the two captains agreed that balls hit into the crowd would be ruled doubles, not triples.

Phillippe started on just one day of rest for Pittsburgh, which even in this era was unusual, while Hughes started for Boston.

After a scoreless first inning, Boston was snake-bitten by the crowd in both halves of the second. After Hughes retired the first two Pirates in the opening frame, Ritchey lofted a high fly ball to left field. Under ordinary circumstances, Dougherty would have settled under the ball to record the third out, but with so many fans on the field, he ran out of room and the ball dropped into the masses for a double. After Sebring walked, Pirate catcher Ed Phelps dumped a hit in front of Stahl in center to put Pittsburgh ahead 1–0. The crowd had the inverse effect in the bottom of the frame, taking a Boston run off the scoreboard when LaChance blasted a drive over the crowd in left-center with two outs. The ball landed just short of the fence. Under ordinary circumstances, the hit would have likely been an inside-the-park home run, but because it had cleared the ropes but fallen short of Huntington Avenue, it was declared a double. The next hitter, Ferris, grounded out, stranding the potential tying run at third.

The presence of the crowd benefited the Pirates again in the third inning when Beaumont led off with a walk and Clarke followed with another cheap double. Leach singled to score Beaumont, making the score 2–0 and putting runners on first and third with still no outs. Collins decided he had seen enough of Hughes. The captain brought Young into the game in relief, and although the right-hander allowed Clarke to score, he pitched the final seven innings while allowing just a single run in the eighth. This begged the question, of course, why didn't Collins just start Young in the first place if he was willing to wear him out in a losing effort?

Phillippe was every bit as good as he'd been in the first game, and maybe better, holding Boston to just four hits and two runs over nine innings. He struck out six and used a biting curveball to induce 14 groundouts.

Collins scored both runs for the Americans, coming home on a Parent sacrifice fly in the fourth and on a Stahl single in the eighth.

Hughes would not appear again in the series or ever again, for that matter, in a Boston uniform. In December the team traded him to New York for pitcher Jesse Tannehill. The tiny lefty would win 21 games for Boston in 1904 and 22 in 1905, while Hughes would go 7–11 in the first half of 1904 before being traded to Washington.

GAME 4: PIRATES 5, AMERICANS 4

	1	2	3	4	5	6	7	8	9	R	H	E
Boston	0	0	0	0	1	0	0	0	3	4	9	1
Pittsburgh	1	0	0	0	1	0	3	0	X	5	12	1

WP   Deacon Phillippe
LP   Bill Dinneen

Sunday and Monday were travel days as the two teams and more than 100 Royal Rooters rode the rails to the Smokey City, as industrial Pittsburgh was then called.

Exposition Park sat at the juncture of the Monongahala and Allegheny Rivers, and often flooded when the rivers breached their banks. But on October 6, 1903, the field was dry as Clarke sent Phillippe back to the mound for the second straight game and third time in four contests. Collins countered with Dinneen.

If the Americans hadn't seen enough of Charles Louis Phillippe, a.k.a. "The Deacon of the National League," already, they sure had by the end of Game Four. Phillippe shut down Boston again, although this time there was at least some reason for hope. The Americans nearly erased a 5–1 deficit, scoring three runs in the ninth.

After handling Pittsburgh so easily in Boston, Dinneen allowed the Pirates to score a first-inning run, as Clarke, who had reached on a fielder's choice, came home from second on a Bransfield single.

The Americans tied the game 1–1 in the fifth when Criger singled to drive home LaChance, who had singled and moved into scoring position on a groundout.

But the stalemate did not last long. The Pirates regained the lead in the bottom of the fifth, courtesy of a one-out Beaumont triple and a two-out single by Leach.

Dinneen allowed three more Pittsburgh runs in the seventh. Leach again had the key hit, a two-run triple that made the score 5–1.

In his only poor outing of the series, Dinneen allowed 12 hits and five earned runs in eight innings.

Phillippe allowed nine hits, just one less than he had surrendered in his first two starts combined, but he didn't walk anyone. Clearly, he was a tired pitcher in the ninth when he allowed five singles before getting pinch-hitter Jack O'Brien, who batted for Dinneen, to pop out to second base to strand the potential tying run at second and preserve a 5–4 win.

Through four games, Phillippe had earned three wins and Pittsburgh had a three-games-to-one lead.

Game 5: Americans 11, Pirates 2

	1	2	3	4	5	6	7	8	9	R	H	E
Boston	0	0	0	0	0	6	4	1	0	11	14	2
Pittsburgh	0	0	0	0	0	0	0	2	0	2	6	6

WP Cy Young
LP Brickyard Kennedy

With a two-game lead, and Phillippe having thrown 27 innings in six days, Pittsburgh captain Clarke sent Brickyard Kennedy to the mound against Young in the fifth game. Kennedy was no slouch, having notched 187 wins and four 20-win seasons in a 12-year career. At age 36, though, his fastball was not what it had once been. He had made just 15 starts for the Pirates in 1903, going 9–6, in what would be his final season.

For five innings, Kennedy was as good as his 36-year old counterpart, but in the sixth and seventh innings Boston took advantage of some shoddy Pittsburgh fielding and blasted five ground-rule triples into the crowd. Boston scored ten runs in the two frames, knocking Kennedy out of the game and into retirement.

The contest was still scoreless when Stahl reached on an error by Clarke in left field to start the sixth. Freeman followed with a single, then Parent squared to bunt and sent a nubber toward Leach at third. Leach fielded and threw to Wagner, covering the base at second. The ball popped out of the shortstop's glove, though, loading the bases for the Americans with none out. A rattled Kennedy walked LaChance to force home the first run, then induced Kennedy to hit a potential double play ball to Wagner. The future-hall-of-famer threw errantly to second, though, allowing Freeman and Parent to score and giving Boston a 3–0 lead. Later in the inning, Young tripled into the crowd in left, driving home two runs, then Dougherty tripled to the same part of the park, scoring Young for Boston's sixth run.

Young, who was working on a three-hit shutout, set down the Pirates in the order in the sixth. Then Boston reached Kennedy for four hits and four more runs in the seventh, opening a 10–0 lead. Dougherty once again got the big hit, a two-run triple into the crowd in center.

Facing relief pitcher Gus Thompson, Stahl led off the Boston eighth with the Americans' fifth ground-rule triple of the day, and came home on a LaChance single, making the score 11–0.

Young allowed just two unearned runs in the bottom of the eighth. The Cyclone finished with a complete-game, six-hitter, with no walks and four strikeouts.

Game Five was notable not only for turning the tide in the series, but also for the notoriety it brought the Royal Rooters, who arrived at the ballpark with a band they had hired for the occasion. Throughout much of the game, they sang the song "Tessie," a number from the popular contemporary theatrical production *The Silver Slipper*. The Rooters cleverly changed the lyrics, using the song to mock Kennedy and the Pirates.

Years later Leach would recall, "I think those Boston fans actually won that series for the Red Sox. We beat them three out of the first four games, and then they started singing that damn 'Tessie' song.... from then on you could hardly play ball they were singing 'Tessie' so loud."[4]

And years later still, the song would reemerge from the annals of Red Sox lore. In 2004 the Boston-based punk rock band *The Dropkick Murphy's* released a new version of "Tessie" that became the 2004 Red Sox' battle cry.

After the Americans' Game Five victory, Farrell, whose leg injury had healed enough to allow him to serve as back-up catcher to Criger, predicted that Boston had seized the momentum in the series. "The people of Boston can rest assured that Boston will win the series," the Marlboro native said. "We have Pittsburgh on the run. They have but one good pitcher."[5]

GAME 6: AMERICANS 6, PIRATES 3

	1	2	3	4	5	6	7	8	9	R	H	E
Boston	0	0	3	0	2	0	1	0	0	6	10	1
Pittsburgh	0	0	0	0	0	0	3	0	0	3	10	3

WP Bill Dinneen
LP   Sam Leever

Overcast skies prevailed in the Smokey City on Thursday, October 8, and Pirates' captain Fred Clarke lobbied to postpone the game. Whether Clarke feared the prospect of a rain shower or the prospect of sending anyone other than Phillippe to the mound remained unclear, but Jimmy Collins wanted no part of a rainout.

In dry conditions, the Americans scored the first six runs to beat Leever for the second time in the series and even the series at three wins apiece. Every Boston starter except Freeman had at least one hit. Dinneen, meanwhile, kept the Pirates at bay, save for a rocky seventh inning.

The Americans took a 3–0 lead in the third. Dinneen started the rally, singling after two were out. After Dougherty walked, Collins singled to center to drive home the Americans' pitcher with the first run. Dougherty came around to score on a Stahl single, then Collins scored on an error by Leach, who fired wildly to first after fielding a chopper by Freeman that should have been the inning's final out.

Boston added two runs in the fifth. Stahl led off with a ground-rule triple into the crowd and the next hitter, Freeman, drove him home with a sacrifice fly. Later in the inning, Parent, who had reached when he was hit by a Leever pitch, scored on a throwing error by Wagner.

The final Boston run scored in the seventh when Parent tripled and LaChance doubled.

Dinneen carried a shutout into the seventh when Pittsburgh rallied for three runs on four hits and two walks. The damage could have been worse, but Dinneen got Ritchey to ground out with the bases loaded for the third out. The lanky right-hander settled back into a groove and retired the Pirates with ease in the eighth and ninth.

After the game, *Boston Globe* editor Charles H. Taylor sent a telegram to Collins at the team's Pittsburgh hotel. It read, "*The Boston Globe*, believing that victory is within the grasp of you and your comrades, offers to present to each player of the Boston team of the American League, if it brings to Boston the world's championship, a valuable gold medal, which can be worn as a watch charm, and be treasured as a reminder of the most notable achievement upon the diamond."[6]

Dreyfuss, the Pittsburgh owner, countered by offering his players 100 percent of the team's World Series profits should they win the series.

Game 7: Americans 7, Pirates 3

	1	2	3	4	5	6	7	8	9	R	H	E
Boston	2	0	0	2	0	2	0	1	0	7	11	4
Pittsburgh	0	0	0	1	0	1	0	0	1	3	10	3

WP Cy Young
LP Deacon Phillippe

Lobbying for a rainout yet again, Clarke prevailed upon Collins to delay the seventh game from Friday until Saturday. It never rained, but it was chilly in Pittsburgh on Friday. The postponement not only allowed the Pirates to rest Phillippe, but in moving the game from a workday to a Saturday it ensured a larger crowd and more lucrative till for the teams to split. While the previous three games in Pittsburgh had averaged about 10,000 fans, more than 17,000 turned out to see Phillippe and Young pitch on Saturday.

By extension, the postponement, and larger crowd, put plenty of fans on the field, and hence, ground-rule triples were again plentiful. The two teams combined to hit seven automatic threebies in nine innings.

Boston scored twice in the first, aided thanks to triples by Collins and Stahl.

Leading 2–0, Young allowed the first two Pirates to reach in the bottom of the inning, on a hit and an error, but got Leach to hit into a double play. Then he fanned Wagner to end the threat.

The Americans doubled their lead in the fourth, again using a pair of triples as the crux of their rally. This time Freeman and Ferris notched three-baggers, while Criger added an RBI single.

After Young allowed a run in the fourth, Boston scored two unearned runs in the sixth thanks to a Phillippe error.

Trailing 6–1 to the great Cy Young, the Pittsburgh crowd, which in the first five innings had attempted to drown out the Rooters' rendition of "Tessie" with their own unique version of "Yankee Doodle," grew quiet.

The Americans won 7–3, taking a four-games-to-three lead in the series. Afterwards, Collins credited Boston's traveling fans. "The support given the team by the Royal Rooters will never be forgotten," the Boston captain said. "They backed us up as only Bostonians could, and no little portion of our success is due to this selfsame band of enthusiasts. Noise — why they astonished all Pittsburgh by their enthusiasm..."[7]

Meanwhile, back in Boston a roiling ticket controversy was developing. The box office on Huntington Avenue had never run out of tickets before. Team management would always take fans' money, even if it meant compromising the integrity of the game by littering the field with onlookers. But as the Americans defeated the Pirates in Pittsburgh on a Saturday afternoon and Boston fans readied for a potential championship clinching game on Tuesday, the well had mysteriously run dry. At the same time, South Boston speculators had handfuls of tickets for hock at as much as three dollars apiece, six times their face value.

Game 8: Americans 3, Pirates 0

	1	2	3	4	5	6	7	8	9	R	H	E
Pittsburgh	0	0	0	0	0	0	0	0	0	0	4	3
Boston	0	0	0	2	0	1	0	0	X	3	8	0

Fans pack the Huntington Avenue Grounds during a 1903 game. (Courtesy of the Boston Public Library, Print Department)

WP Bill Dinneen
LP Deacon Phillippe

After traveling on Sunday, the Pirates and Americans arrived in Boston amidst heavy rain. Monday's game was rained out, allowing both teams to pencil their hottest starting pitchers into the lineup for Tuesday.

Many Royal Rooters returned from Pittsburgh to find that they would have to purchase tickets from speculators if they wanted to watch Games Eight and Nine. Outraged, they led a boycott of Game Eight, resulting in the smallest crowd of the series being on hand for the clincher. Only 7,455 fans witnessed Dinneen's four-hit shutout that gave Boston the first modern world championship.

Boston snapped a scoreless tie in the fourth when Freeman led off with a triple, Parent reached on an error by the catcher, Ed Phelps, and Ferris singled to center to score both runners.

The Americans scored the game's only other run in the sixth when LaChance tripled and Ferris singled.

Dinneen allowed base hits in the fourth and fifth inning and two in the sixth, while walking two and striking out seven. The hurler struck out the Pirates' best player, Wagner, on three straight swings to end the game.

With victory in hand, the fans stormed the field and hoisted Dinneen and Collins and several other Boston players upon their shoulders.

Dinneen finished the series with a record of 3–1 and a 2.06 ERA. He would pitch six more major league seasons, before retiring with a career mark of 170–177 in 1909.

Young, who still had eight seasons and 132 wins left in his right arm, finished the only World Series he would appear in with a 2–1 record and a 1.85 ERA.

The Americans smacked a total of 16 triples in the series, including three each by Freeman, Parent and Stahl.

Pittsburgh's Sebring registered the highest batting average of any player in the series, hitting .367 (11-for-30), while Wagner finished with a disappointing .222 average (6-for-27) and six fielding errors. Wagner would redeem himself in the 1909 World Series, hitting .333 to lead Pittsburgh past the Detroit Tigers.

Shortly after the series, the Boston players got their medals from *The Boston Globe*. They also received 60 percent of Boston's World Series revenues, as agreed to before the series. Killilea cut each player a check for $1,182, then he sold the team to Taylor. Even though his team had lost, Dreyfuss, the generous Pittsburgh owner, rewarded his players with 100 percent of the Pirates' postseason profits. The losers received a bigger payout than the winners, getting $1,316 each.

The Americans would finish with the best record in the AL again in 1904, but no World Series would be played because John McGraw's New York Giants refused to play the AL champions. McGraw made it known in early September that he had no intention of lowering himself to play an AL team, stating, "When we clinch the National League pennant, we'll be champions of the only real major league."[8] When McGraw did consent to play the AL champion Philadelphia A's in a best-of-seven championship in 1905, his team backed up his arrogance, pitching four shutouts in a five-game series win. After resuming the World Series in 1905, the AL and NL continued the tradition of meeting in the postseason uninterrupted until 1994 when acting commissioner Bud Selig canceled the World Series due to a labor dispute between the owners and players.

CHAPTER 2

The Regular Season: 105–47

The 1912 baseball season is remembered for producing the first great World Series goat. Long before Johnny Pesky and Bill Buckner and the cast of other players who have been blamed rightly or wrongly for their teams' World Series failures, there was Fred Snodgrass. The New York Giants centerfielder dropped a routine fly ball in the tenth inning of the 1912 World Series' final game, helping the Red Sox overcome a one-run deficit. This was also the year that Fenway Park opened in Boston and the year that the New York Highlanders first wore pinstriped uniforms. And last, but not least, 1912 is remembered as the year the Red Sox posted the best record in franchise history.

The Fenway Park that stands today does not look so different from the new ballpark that awaited the Red Sox and their fans when the 1912 season began. The trademark 37-foot high left field wall did not exist in 1912, nor did the bullpens in right field home run territory, but the field's general contours were the same as they are currently. At the time of Fenway's opening the bullpens were located on either side of the outfield in foul territory, and the left field fence was a short edifice perched atop a grass embankment. Boston left fielder Duffy Lewis became an expect at running up the hill to make catches visiting outfielders wouldn't dare attempt, and so, the embankment became known as "Duffy's Cliff."

From 1910 to 1915 Lewis teamed with future hall-of-famers Tris Speaker and Harry Hooper to form what is still considered by many to be the best starting outfield ever. All three were superior fielders — especially Speaker, whose record 450 outfield assists has not been challenged in the eight decades since his retirement. And all three were excellent hitters from the left side of the plate. The trio combined for 7,498 career hits.

The pitching staff also boasted three aces. Twenty-two-year-old Smokey Joe Wood enjoyed what would be the most dominant season of his career in 1912, while a pair of rookies, 22-year-old Hugh Bedient, and 30-year-old Buck O'Brien, both won 20 games.

As the Red Sox completed the construction of their new ballpark, they also welcomed a new owner, James McAleer, who bought the team for $150,000 in December of 1912, and

The 1912 Red Sox. (Courtesy of the Boston Public Library, Print Department)

a new manager, Jake Stahl, who would also play first base for Boston. Stahl had failed in a previous stint as manager of the Washington team and had, in fact, retired in 1910 to take a job in banking.[1] But he was a business associate of McAleer and that led to his return in 1912 to replace Patsy Donovan, the manager who had guided the Red Sox to a 78–75 fifth-place finish in 1911.

After spending March in Hot Springs, Arkansas, the Red Sox headed north to start the season with five road games. Then they would head home to christen their new stadium, which had been constructed from concrete and steel instead of the wooden planks more common in ballpark construction at the time.

Although the infield grass from the Huntington Avenue Grounds had been transplanted to the Red Sox' new yard, Stahl wanted to give his team a chance to get better acquainted with the new ballpark before the season began. Toward that end, before heading to New York to play their first regular season game, the Red Sox welcomed Harvard University to Fenway Park for an exhibition game on April 10. The professionals beat the preppies 2–0.

The next day the Red Sox beat the Highlanders 5–3 at Hilltop Park in Manhattan as Wood pitched a seven-hitter and singled home two runs against Ray Caldwell in the ninth inning. A day later, O'Brien pitched a complete game in a 5–2 win, and the day after that, the Red Sox won again, 8–4. Next it was on to Philadelphia where the Red Sox lost for the first time, but rebounded the next day when Wood won his second start of the season.

The *Titanic* sank in the icy waters of the North Atlantic between the date of the Red Sox' exhibition game with Harvard and the scheduled date of the home opener, April 17, and the massive ship's demise overshadowed newspaper accounts and public anticipation of the ballpark's debut. Then a lingering rainstorm postponed the grand opening for two days.

Finally on April 20, O'Brien, a Brockton, Massachusetts native, threw the first regular season pitch at Fenway Park. The 27,000 fans on hand enjoyed a back-and-forth game that wasn't settled until the bottom of the eleventh when Speaker delivered a walk-off hit to give Boston a 7–6 win.

The Red Sox bounced between first and third place during the first two months. On May 18, Chicago's Joe Benz out-dueled Bedient 3–1 to drop the Red Sox a season-low 5½ games behind the first-place White Sox. But the next day Wood blanked Chicago, 2–0, to begin a five-game win streak.

The Red Sox moved into a first-place tie with Chicago on June 10 when they beat the Browns 3–2 at Sportsman's Park in St. Louis. Boston's record stood at 30–18 at the time, while Chicago's was 31–19. The Red Sox held onto first place for the remainder of the season, buoyed by a nine-game win streak from June 15 to June 24 that improved their record to 41–19 and gave them a 5½ game lead over Chicago. They went 21–8 during June, then 21–9 in July, and 20–7 in August, to run away with the pennant. Speaker carried the team during the middle months of the season, hitting safely in 74 of 78 games between May 27 and August 14. While hitting .424 during the hot stretch, the center fielder had two 20-game hit streaks and a 30-gamer.

By August 1, Boston's record was 60–37, seven games better than second-place Washington. By the end of the month, the lead had grown to 14 games.

Despite the anticlimactic pennant race, Boston fans were riveted to their Fenway Park seats, as Speaker pursued the batting title and Wood established himself as one of the game's elite hurlers. The big right-hander reached the 20-win plateau on July 23, when he improved to 20–4 with a 6–3 win against Cleveland. On September 2, he won his 30th game, beating the Highlanders 1–0 in the second game of a double-header. The win was Wood's eighth shutout of the year, and second in a row, and gave him 13 straight victories. Earlier in the day, Boston had beaten New York 2–1 behind Bedient. The pair of victories gave Boston a perfect 10–0 record at Hilltop Park in 1912. Including their home games, the Red Sox finished the campaign with a 19–2 record against their New York rivals.

In place of a September pennant race, Speaker, Ty Cobb, and Joe Jackson flirted with .400 batting averages, while Wood and Walter Johnson set their sights on Rube Marquard's record 19 consecutive victories. A member of the NL's New York Giants, Marquard had set the mark in July of 1912.

On September 6 the AL's two best pitchers faced one another in Boston. Wood sought his 14th straight win, while Johnson had lost two games in a row after extending his win streak to 16. The two aces did not disappoint the throng that turned out to watch them. The lone run scored on back-to-back doubles by Speaker and Lewis in the sixth inning, and even that was a tainted run. Due to the enormous crowd, fans were permitted to stand in the outfield behind rope barriers. Speaker's hit would have been an easy fly out under ordinary circumstances, but fell into the crowd for a ground-rule double. Wood made the 1–0 lead stand up with a nine-strikeout gem. Afterwards, Johnson paid him the ultimate compliment, saying, "There's no man alive who throws as hard as Smokey Joe Wood."[2]

With wins against the White Sox and Browns in his next two starts, Wood ran his streak to 16 wins in a row, before finally succumbing to the Tigers 6–4 on September 20, no thanks to two unearned runs scored against him.

The Red Sox caught a bad break on September 21 when third baseman Larry Gardner, who at age 26 was having a breakthrough year, broke a finger on his throwing hand. Gardner would miss the remainder of the regular season, but would return for the World Series.

The Red Sox won their 100th game on September 25, and appropriately Wood was on the mound to celebrate. He beat the Highlanders 6–0 to improve to 33–5. Smoky Joe won his 34th game on October 3, when Lewis homered and the Red Sox beat the A's 17–5. After a loss the next day, O'Brien shutout the A's 3–0 in the season finale to send Boston into the World Series on a high note.

With their record of 105–47, the Red Sox not only set an AL record for the most wins in a season, but they finished 14 games ahead of second-place Washington and 55 games ahead of last-place New York. The Red Sox led the league in home runs with 29, and in runs with 799. They finished second in the league with a .277 batting average. Speaker led the circuit with 10 home runs and 53 doubles, but came up short in the batting race, finishing third at .383. Cobb was the only player to crest .400, hitting .409. Speaker finished second in runs with 136, just one behind Eddie Collins and second in total bases with 329, just two behind Jackson. He also drove in 90 runs and stole 52 bases. For his efforts, the Boston centerfielder was awarded the Chalmers Award, a precursor to the Most Valuable Player Award that was sponsored by the Chalmers Motor Company. Lewis also had a standout season, batting .284 with 109 RBI — second only to Philadelphia's Frank "Home Run" Baker. Gardner hit .315 with 18 triples and 86 RBI. Stahl batted .301 with 60 RBI.

The Boston pitching staff placed second in the AL to Washington with a 2.76 ERA. Remarkably, Boston's five main starters accounted for 102 of the tam's 105 wins. Wood led the league in wins with a record of 34–5, and also led in complete games with 35, and in shutouts with 10. His 1.91 ERA and 258 strikeouts were bested only by Johnson. Boston's other four pitching stars were: O'Brien (20–13, 2.58 ERA), Bedient (20–9, 2.92 ERA), Charley Hall (15–8, 3.02 ERA) and Ray Collins (13–8, 2.53 ERA). The only other pitcher to appear in more than nine games for Boston was Larry Pape, who started twice and made 11 relief appearances.

The Postseason: 4–3–1

Ordinarily a 105-win season would make a team a heavy favorite to win the World Series. But that was not the case in 1912, when the New York Giants were just as dominant in the National League as the Red Sox were in the American League. The Giants were 103–48.

The number of star players on the two teams, combined with the friendly rivalry that already existed between Boston and New York made the series one of the most highly anticipated postseason matches yet. Due to their geographic proximity to one another the Red Sox and Giants would shuttle back and forth between New York and Boston after each of the first five games, before playing Games Six and Seven in Boston.

There was another factor that added to the series' intrigue. The Red Sox had a grudge to settle with Giants manager John McGraw. Or more aptly, the Boston fans did. Though none of the players from Boston's 1904 edition remained with the team, the Royal Rooters remembered McGraw's slight. After the Boston Americans and Giants had finished atop their respective leagues in 1904, McGraw had refused to play Boston in the World Series. In the years since, the long-time NL partisan had grudgingly accepted the AL as worthy of competing against his league's best team. McGraw's Giants had won the 1905 World Series against the Philadelphia A's, before losing to the A's in 1911. But as the 1912 series approached, Red Sox fans still remembered how McGraw had dodged the Boston Americans in 1904 and they believed the Giants manager had deprived them of a world championship that had been rightfully theirs.

New York led the NL with a .286 batting average, 47 home runs, and 823 runs. The Giants' lineup featured slugging catcher Chief Meyers, who finished second in the league with a .358 batting average, second baseman Larry Doyle, who hit .330 with 10 HR and 90 RBI, right fielder Red Murray, who hit .277 with 20 triples and 92 RBI, and first baseman Fred Merkle, who hit .309 with 11 HR and 84 RBI. Merkle was already something of a goat due to a base-running blunder late in the 1908 season that cost the Giants a game against the Cubs. When the season ended a week later, the Cubs had finished one game ahead of the Giants atop the NL.

In the pitcher's box the Giants featured the one-two punch of the left-handed Marquard (26–11, 2.57 ERA) and the right-handed Christy Mathewson (23–12, 2.12 ERA). Rookie Jeff Tesreau (17–7, 1.96 ERA), Doc Crandall (13–7, 3.61 ERA) and Red Ames (11–5, 2.46 ERA) also contributed to a staff that led the circuit with a 2.58 ERA.

1912 World Series: Red Sox 4, Giants 3

GAME 1: RED SOX 4, GIANTS 3

	1	2	3	4	5	6	7	8	9	R	H	E
Boston	0	0	0	0	0	1	3	0	0	4	6	1
New York	0	0	2	0	0	0	0	0	1	3	8	1

WP Joe Wood
LP Jeff Tesreau

The series began at the Polo Grounds in New York. After much of the facility had burned down in 1911, the infield grandstand was rebuilt before the 1912 season. The field dimensions were unusually short down the lines where the distance from home plate to the foul poles measured 256 feet in right and 277 feet in left.

Stahl sent Wood to the mound for the Red Sox, while McGraw opted to save aces Mathewson and Marquard to face lesser opponents, and gave the ball to Tesreau.

Wood pitched well, but he was not his usual dominant self. He allowed two runs in the third inning and one in the ninth, before squelching a New York rally to seal a 4–3 win.

The Giants took a 2–0 lead in the third when Murray knocked a two-out single to center field, driving home Josh Devore, who had walked, and Doyle, who had singled.

Tesrea carried a no-hitter into the sixth, but the Red Sox broke through for their first hit and first run in the inning when Speaker tripled with one-out and Lewis brought him home with a groundout. Speaker's hit narrowly eluded the outstretched hands of Snodgrass in left-center.

After Wood set down the Giants in the bottom of the sixth, the Red Sox took the lead in the seventh. Stahl grounded out to start the inning, but then Boston shortstop Heinie Wagner and catcher Hick Cady followed with back-to-back singles to center. After Wood tapped into a fielder's choice for the second out, Hooper delivered Wagner with a double down the right field line. Then Boston second baseman Steve Yerkes brought home Wood and Hooper with a single to left to put the Red Sox ahead 4–2.

Wood held the Giants hitless in the seventh and eighth, before getting roughed up a bit in the ninth. He retired Murray on a fly ball to start the final frame, then allowed three straight hits to Merkle, Buck Herzog, and Meyers. The barrage brought the Giants within one run of the lead, gave them runners at second and third with one out, and caused many of the 35,730 fans in attendance to litter the field with their hats and seat cushions. But Wood rose to the occasion and struck out Art Fletcher and then struck out the slugging pitcher Crandall, who went to the plate as a pinch hitter, to end the game. Wood got Crandall to chase a shoulder-high fastball for his 11th strikeout.

GAME 2: RED SOX 6, GIANTS 6

	1	2	3	4	5	6	7	8	9	10	11	R	H	E
New York	0	1	0	1	0	0	0	3	0	1	0	6	11	5
Boston	3	0	0	0	1	0	0	1	0	1	0	6	10	1

WP N/A
LP N/A

On Wednesday, October 6, the two teams took the field at Fenway after Boston mayor John "Honey Fitz" Fitzgerald, a Royal Rooter and the future grandfather of U.S. President John F. Kennedy, threw out the ceremonial first pitch. Three hours later, the series stood exactly where it had at the outset, with the Red Sox leading one game to none. Eleven exciting innings resulted in a 6–6 tie when the game was ruled a draw due to impending darkness. The game would have to be replayed in its entirety the next day.

While ominous storm clouds loomed overhead at the time of the ruling, some on hand felt the game could have continued for another inning or two, fueling speculation that the two owners had conspired to end the game prematurely to capitalize on another big turnout at the turnstiles the next day.

Mathewson pitched all 11 innings for the Giants and did not allow an earned run. The gentlemanly hurler was let down by five errors behind him, including one in the first inning that allowed the Red Sox to take a 3–0 lead. After Fletcher booted a groundball by Yerkes, Stahl got the big hit for Boston, a two-run single.

The Giants chipped away, scoring single runs against Collins in the second and fourth, before Boston upped the lead to 4–2 on a Yerkes triple in the fifth that brought Hooper home. Hooper should have been out stealing earlier in the inning, but Fletcher had dropped Meyers' throw for his second error. The Giants scored three runs on three hits and a Boston error in the eighth to take a 5–4 lead, but in the bottom of the inning the Red Sox came back, thanks to yet another Fletcher error. This time the second baseman muffed a two-out grounder by Gardner, allowing Lewis to score from second.

The game headed to extra innings tied 5–5.

Merkle tripled to lead off the tenth and scored on a sacrifice fly by pinch-hitter Moose McCormick to put New York ahead 6–5.

In the bottom of the tenth, Speaker came to the plate with one out and no one on base and blasted a drive off the center field wall in the deepest part of the ballpark. "The Grey

Eagle" streaked around the bases as Beals Becker chased the ball in center. As Speaker rounded third, he collided with Herzog, the Giants third baseman, but he regained his footing and stumbled toward home plate. Becker relayed the ball to Tillie Shafer, who had taken over for Fletcher at short, and Shafer fired to the plate. The ball beat Speaker home, but Art Wilson, the backup catcher who had replaced Meyers in the top of the inning, dropped the ball. Speaker was credited with a triple and Wilson was charged with an error. The score was tied again, at 6–6. After Stahl made the final out for the Red Sox, the Boston players headed to their positions in the field and the New York players headed for the first base bench. Speaker and Herzog met in foul territory and exchanged harsh words, then punches, still angry about their collision at third base.

Eventually order was restored and Bedient came on to pitch the eleventh for the Red Sox. The young righty allowed a hit batsman and a walk but both runners were gunned down trying to steal second base by Bill Carrigan.

The Red Sox went quietly against Mathewson in the bottom of the eleventh, and then home plate umpire Silk O'Loughlin declared the game a draw. It marked the second time a World Series game had been ruled a tie. Similar circumstances had resulted in a stalemate between the Tigers and Cubs in Game One of the 1907 championship.

GAME 3: GIANTS 2, RED SOX 1

	1	2	3	4	5	6	7	8	9	R	H	E
New York	0	1	0	0	1	0	0	0	0	2	7	1
Boston	0	0	0	0	0	0	0	0	1	1	7	0

WP Rube Marquard
LP Buck O'Brien

A day after the Red Sox and Giants tied, another 34,624 fans filed through the Fenway Park turnstiles to watch the second act. The game was another tightly played contest, but no extra innings were needed on this day. Marquard, repeating Joe Wood's heroics of the first game, extinguished a late Red Sox rally and the Giants evened the series.

The Giants scored single runs in the second and fifth innings against O'Brien. In the second, Murray doubled and scored on a sacrifice fly by Herzog. In the fifth, Herzog doubled and scored on a Fletcher single.

Meanwhile, Marquard did not allow a Red Sox runner to advance to second base until Stahl doubled with two outs in the seventh. Wagner followed with a fly out to right field though, to end the threat.

Marquard entered the ninth with a 2–0 lead, having allowed only five hits. For a moment it looked as though the Red Sox would go quietly, as Speaker popped out to start the inning, but then Lewis reached on a bunt single, and Gardner followed with a double to right that brought Lewis home. Trailing by just a run, the Red Sox had the potential tying run on second base with one out. A base running blunder by Gardner helped Marquard out of the jam, though, when Gardner broke for third on a chopper up the middle by Stahl. Marquard leapt and speared the ball, then threw to third to cut down Gardner. Olaf Henriksen came in to run for Stahl and advanced all the way to third when Merkle couldn't handle a throw from Fletcher at second on a Wagner grounder. Then Wagner stole second to put two men in scoring position. If Cady could deliver a hit, the Red Sox would tally a walk-off win. The crowd roared and the Red Sox stood in front of their bench. Marquard delivered a high fastball that Cady slashed into right-center field. When it left the

Game 4: Red Sox 3, Giants 1

	1	2	3	4	5	6	7	8	9	R	H	E
Boston	0	1	0	1	0	0	0	0	1	3	8	1
New York	0	0	0	0	0	0	1	0	0	1	9	1

WP Joe Wood
LP Jeff Tesreau

The series resumed in New York the next day and for the third time in three decisions, the visiting team escaped with a narrow victory. In a rematch of the first game, Wood again beat Tesreau. Smoky Joe scattered nine hits over nine innings, while striking out eight. He chipped in at the plate with two hits and an RBI.

The Red Sox staked Wood to a 1–0 lead in the second when Gardner led off with a triple to right and scored on a wild pitch. In the fourth, the Red Sox added another run when Cady singled home Stahl who had reached on a fielder's choice and stolen second.

The first two Giants to bat in the sixth reached base, as Tesreau and Devore singled, but Wood bore down and retired Doyle on a pop to third, then induced harmless grounders from Snodgrass and Murray. In their next at bat, the Giants finally put a run on the scoreboard, as Herzog singled with one out and came home on a two-out double by Fletcher.

The Red Sox clung to their 2–1 lead in the bottom of the eighth while a single and a Wagner error put runners on first and third for the Giants with two outs. Wood struck out Merkle, though, to end the inning.

In the ninth, Wood helped his own cause, shooting a two-out single to right field to bring home Gardner and give the Red Sox a 3–1 lead. In the bottom of the inning, the Boston pitcher retired the Giants in order, getting Fletcher on a pop to Stahl for the final out.

Game 5: Red Sox 2, Giants 1

	1	2	3	4	5	6	7	8	9	R	H	E
New York	0	0	0	0	0	0	1	0	0	1	3	1
Boston	0	0	2	0	0	0	0	0	X	2	5	1

WP Hugh Bedient
LP Christy Mathewson

Back in Boston the next day, McGraw gave the ball to Mathewson whose fine effort in Game Two had gone for naught when nature and perhaps other forces conspired to end the game prematurely. Mathewson pitched well, but his opponent, Bedient was even better. The two teams combined for just eight hits and the Red Sox prevailed 2–1 on a Saturday afternoon.

Hooper and Yerkes brought the 34,683 fans present to their feet in the bottom of the third when they started the inning with back-to-back triples into the crowd in center field. The next batter, Speaker, hit a sharp grounder to Doyle, and when the second baseman let the ball get past him Yerkes trotted home with the second Boston run.

Mathewson held the Red Sox hitless over the final six innings, but Bedient already had all the runs he needed. The Red Sox rookie allowed harmless singles in the third and fifth, then surrendered the Giants' third and final hit in the seventh, when New York scored an unearned run. Merkle led off with a double and crossed the plate two outs later on an error by Gardner. Bedient shook off the setback though, retiring the final seven batters to finish a three-hit, three-walk, masterpiece.

The Red Sox had a three-games-to-one lead and were one win from clinching their second championship. Better yet, the scheduled off day ahead, as the two teams traveled back to New York, would allow Wood to start Game Six.

GAME 6: GIANTS 5, RED SOX 2

	1	2	3	4	5	6	7	8	9	R	H	E
Boston	0	2	0	0	0	0	0	0	0	2	7	2
New York	5	0	0	0	0	0	0	0	X	5	11	2

WP Rube Marquard
LP Buck O'Brien

Just as the Red Sox' championship in 1903 was to some degree tainted by ownership's greed when a large quantity of tickets fell into the hands of scalpers resulting in an unusually small crowd at the Huntington Avenue Grounds on the day the Red Sox clinched the first modern World Series, the 1912 series was also not without its controversy. By the end of a World Series that should have represented a glorious time to be a Red Sox fan, many Royal Rooters had again turned their backs on the team. The calamity began when McAleer, the Red Sox owner, ordered Stahl not to start Wood in Game Six in New York.[3] McAleer told the manager to save Wood for a potential seventh game at Fenway Park. In fairness to McAleer, Wood would have been pitching on just two-days of rest and it may have made sense to save him to pitch in his usual spot in the rotation. But, then again, it was not so uncommon for pitchers to start after two days of rest in this era, and Wood clearly wanted the baseball. The Red Sox players were angry about the interference and wondered if McAleer secretly wanted the series to return to Boston where he might reap another hefty till at the gates.[4]

In any case, O'Brien took the mound for the Red Sox in Game Six and did not fare well. He allowed six hits and five runs in the first inning before departing for a pinch hitter in the second. Doyle started the New York rally with a one-out single then he stole second as Snodgrass struck out. The Red Sox were within one out of escaping the inning unharmed, but O'Brien quickly fell apart. Murray reached on an infield single to deep short, putting runners at first and third, then O'Brien balked home the game's first run. A Merkle double brought home another run, then Herzog doubled to plate Merkle. After Meyers followed with a single to put runners at first and third, the Giants pulled a double steal, with Meyers sliding into second base just ahead of Cady's throw, and Herzog racing to the plate ahead of the throw home by Yerkes. The fifth Giant run scored on a single by Fletcher, who was summarily picked off first base by O'Brien to mercifully end the inning.

The Red Sox got on the scoreboard in the second when an error by Marquard paved the way to two unearned runs. After the pitcher botched a grounder by Gardner and Stahl reached on a single, Clyde Engle hit for O'Brien and delivered a pinch-double to score both runners. But Marquard held the Red Sox to just four hits and no runs the rest of the way.

Collins, who relieved O'Brien, matched the Giants' lefty nearly pitch for pitch, tossing seven shutout innings himself to keep the game close, but it didn't matter. The Red Sox boarded their train for Boston still holding a three-games-to-two lead, hoping that their meddlesome owner wouldn't prevent Wood from pitching the next day.

Game 7: Giants 11, Red Sox 4

	1	2	3	4	5	6	7	8	9	R	H	E
New York	6	1	0	0	0	2	1	0	1	11	16	4
Boston	0	1	0	0	0	0	2	1	0	4	9	3

WP Jeff Tesreau
LP Joe Wood

The stage was set for a Royal Rooters victory party on Tuesday, October 15. Before the game the Rooters held their usual pep-rally outside the park, complete with a brass band, then twenty minutes before the first pitch they filed through the Fenway turnstiles and headed for their usual seats in the left field pavilion. Much to the dismay of the 500 Rooters, they discovered that their usual seats were occupied by paying ticket holders. The Red Sox had sold their seats. Apparently the confusion was caused by the extra game added as the result of the tie. The Rooters were told that they had no choice but to split up and sit in the smattering of general admission seats still unoccupied throughout the park. Finding that option unacceptable, Mayor Fitzgerald led the massive fan club out of the stands and onto the Fenway lawn. The Rooters headed for Duffy's Cliff and took up residence atop the left field hill. Boston police tried unsuccessfully to get the Rooters off the field, while Wood was prevented from completing his pre-game bullpen session in left field.

By the time mounted police arrived to drive the Rooters off the field, it was time for the game to begin. Wood took the mound with a cold arm and got shelled. Like O'Brien before him, Wood lasted just one inning. In that short time, the Boston ace allowed seven hits and six earned runs. Devore started the onslaught with an infield single, then Doyle rapped a single. Next, the Giants executed another double steal, with both runners moving up a bag. Then Snodgrass doubled home both runners. After a sacrifice bunt by Murray, Snodgrass scored on a Merkle single and Merkle moved up to second on the throw home. Merkle then committed a base-running blunder when he got caught in a rundown between second and third on Herzog's tapper to Wood, but he managed to stay in the pickle long enough to allow Herzog to reach second. And it was a good thing. Herzog scored when the next hitter, Meyers, singled to left. Then Fletcher singled, moving Meyers to third. The fifth Giant run scored when Meyers raced home on a bunt single by Tesreau. And the sixth Giants run scored when Tesreau broke for second and Cady threw down to second, just as he had in the first inning of the previous game. This time, the trail runner pulled up short before reaching second base and got caught in a rundown long enough to allow the lead runner to score.

After the Red Sox were retired quietly in the bottom of the first, Stahl sent Hall to the mound to start the second inning. Hall allowed five runs over the final eight innings, but had no problem solving Tesreau at the plate. The Boston reliever went 3-for-3 against the New York starter, but it didn't much matter because the game was never close. Tesreau limited the Red Sox to four runs, only two of which were earned, in a complete game effort.

The only bright spot for the Red Sox and their fans came in the form of a ninth-inning unassisted double play by Tris Speaker that still stands as the only such play turned in by an outfielder in World Series play. With Wilson leading off second base, Fletcher hit a line drive to center. Speaker, who was famous for playing shallow, got a good break on the ball and raced in to make a shoestring catch. Then he sprinted to second base to double off Wilson, who had taken a few too many steps toward third.

After the Red Sox went quietly in the last of the ninth, the Royal Rooters marched back into the ballpark, took their usual seats in left field, and lustily booed.

GAME 8: RED SOX 3, GIANTS 2

	1	2	3	4	5	6	7	8	9	10	R	H	E
New York	0	0	1	0	0	0	0	0	0	1	2	9	2
Boston	0	0	0	0	0	0	1	0	0	2	3	8	5

WP Joe Wood
LP Christy Mathewson

With the World Series tied at three wins apiece, the final game would take place at Fenway Park as had been determined by a coin-flip before the series. The home field was not quite the advantage it usually was for the Red Sox however. Incensed over management's treatment of them prior to the seventh game, the Royal Rooters led a boycott of the finale. Many other fans also stayed away, leaving the Fenway grandstands half empty. The first three games in Boston had all drawn more than 30,000 spectators, but on October 16 just 17,034 people turned out to watch the final game. The parallels between this unfortunate set of events and those that marred the final game of the 1903 World Series were too many to be overlooked. But just as had been the case in 1903, the Red Sox ignored whatever bad karma the empty seats might have given them, and emerged victorious. They did so thanks to two extra inning defensive lapses by the Giants.

Bedient and Mathewson started on the mound for their respective teams. Both were excellent.

The Giants took a 1–0 lead in the third when Devore led off with a walk, advanced to second and then third on a pair of groundouts, and scored on a double by Murray.

Neither team scored again until the bottom of the seventh when Stahl singled, Wagner walked, and Henriksen, batting in place of Bedient, cracked an RBI double to left field. While Stahl scored on the play, Wagner held at third where he was stranded when Hooper flied out to end the inning.

Wood came out of the Boston bullpen to replace Bedient and he held the Giants at bay in the eighth and ninth, as Mathewson did the same against the Red Sox.

In the top of the tenth, the Giants took a 2–1 lead when Murray lined a one-out double over Speaker's head in left-center and scored on a single by Merkle.

When the bottom of the inning began, the Giants were three outs from the world championship with the great Christy Mathewson on the mound.

Wood was due to hit first, and though he was a fine hitter, Stahl sent Engle to the plate instead. The pinch-hitter lifted a routine fly ball to center field. Snodgrass settled under the ball and had it in his glove before the ball came popping out. Engle stood safely at first base on the error.

Afterward, Snodgrass would recall, "It looked like an easy out. I yelled and waved [Murray] off, and then, well, I dropped the darned thing."[5]

Snodgrass got another chance when the next batter, Hooper, flied to center, and this time he made the play. Mathewson then walked Yerkes to put runners at first and second with one out for Speaker. It was then that the Giants made their second miscue of the inning. Speaker hit a foul pop between home and first that should have been caught for the second out, but Merkle, Meyers and Mathewson watched it fall between them. On the very next pitch, Speaker singled to right to score Engle and tie the game. On the belated throw home, Yerkes moved to third and Speaker took second. McGraw and Mathewson conferred and agreed to walk Lewis intentionally to load the bases and set up a possible double play. But Boston's next batter, Gardner, didn't comply. Instead he lifted a fly ball to right field. Devore made the catch and fired futilely toward home as Yerkes crossed the plate with the winning run. The Red Sox were champions of the baseball world for a second time.

The next day, the lead story in the *New York Times* began, "Write in the pages of world's series baseball history the name of Snodgrass. Write it large and black. Not as a hero, truly not. Put him rather with Merkle, who was in such a hurry that he gave away a National League championship. Snodgrass was in such a hurry that he gave away a world championship."[6]

Over the eight games, the Giants outscored the Red Sox (31 to 25), out-hit them (.270 batting average to .220), and out-pitched them (1.71 ERA to 2.55). But the Red Sox had the edge in the only category that mattered, wins. Speaker led Boston regulars with a .300 average, while Wood finished 3–1 with a 3.68 ERA and Bedient finished 1–0 with a 0.50 ERA in two starts and two relief appearances.

Chapter 3

The Regular Season: 101–50

Following Boston's victory in the 1912 World Series, baseball entered one of the most tumultuous periods in its history. Fans flocked to ballparks in record numbers, but the animosity between the owners and players, which had been festering since the game's infancy, suddenly intensified. The game was becoming a major U.S. industry and the players wanted a greater share of the profits. But their salaries were kept in check by the "reserve clause," which prevented players from ever becoming free agents and allowed the owners to pay them whatever they wanted. Players could either accept the salary offered by their current team or not play. Red Sox fans witnessed the friction between ownership and uniformed personnel locally when a dispute between Jake Stahl and owner James McAleer led to the installment of Bill Carrigan as the new Red Sox manager midway through the 1913 season. McAleer, himself, would step aside after the 1913 season, selling the team to Joseph Lannin, the team's fifth owner in 11 years. Fans witnessed the effects of management's stranglehold on baseball's revenues affecting the game across the country, as well. Some players, like Washington's Walter Johnson, spoke out publicly against the unfairness of the reserve clause in national publications. Others, like Hal Chase of the White Sox, began supplementing their income by fixing games for gamblers; it was so obvious that Boston fans would chant "What are the odds," whenever Chase took the field at Fenway Park.[1]

In 1914, the situation came to a head when the new Federal League declared war on the major leagues, building eight new ballparks across the country and luring many of the game's top stars away from the American and National Leagues. Billed as a third major league, the Federal League offered players more money, the right to free agency, and more home-run-friendly ballparks. In all, 81 players jumped to the new league, including such stars as Chief Bender, Joe Tinker, and Three Finger Brown. The Red Sox lost eight players, most notably, pitcher Hugh Bedient and second baseman Steve Yerkes. The formation of the Federal League also brought an unexpected windfall to the Red Sox. Feeling pressure from the new league's Baltimore Terrapins, midway through the 1914 season, Jack Dunn, owner of the International League's Baltimore Orioles, decided to move his team to Richmond, Virginia. To finance the relocation, Dunn needed to sell off some of his star players, and on July 9, 1914, he accepted $25,000 from the Red Sox for left-handed pitcher Babe Ruth, right-hander Ernie Shore, and veteran catcher Ben Egan. Ruth and Shore got their feet wet in the big leagues in the latter half of 1914, before becoming stars in 1915.

A number of other players also gained valuable experience with the Red Sox as the team compiled a 91–62 record on the way to a second-place finish in 1914. Dick Hoblitzel had a strong second half at first base after Boston claimed him off waivers from the Cincinnati Reds in July, while rookie Everett "Deacon" Scott claimed the starting spot at shortstop, and young pitchers Rube Foster and Dutch Leonard blossomed, winning 14 and 19 games respectively.

Although the Red Sox finished 8½ games behind the Philadelphia A's in 1914, Boston fans were still treated to a World Series at Fenway Park. The Boston Braves rose from last place in July to win the NL pennant, then swept the Philadelphia A's in the World Series, playing the final two games at Fenway because it could hold more fans than the South End Grounds.

The 1915 season began as federal judge Kenesaw Mountain Landis mulled a monopoly

Boston Mayor John "Honey Fitz" Fitzgerald (center) with Lord Aberdeen (far right), and Lady Aberdeen (with camera, next to Fitzgerald) and unidentified others. (Courtesy of the Boston Public Library, Print Department)

lawsuit the Federal League had brought against Organized Baseball. The frightened major league owners suddenly offered more money to their star players. In Boston, Tris Speaker's salary jumped from $9,000 to $18,000. Despite the uncertainty in the game, it was an exciting time to be a fan in Boston. The Braves were building a new 40,000-seat stadium on the former site of Allston Golf Course, while the Red Sox were the favorites to win the AL after a disgusted Connie Mack sold off the A's star players after they were embarrassed by the first four-game sweep in World Series history.

The depleted A's got the better of the Red Sox on Opening Day though, as Herb Pennock came within one out of pitching a no-hitter. An infield single by Harry Hooper was Boston's only hit in a 2–0 loss at Shibe Park. The Red Sox played unremarkably over the season's first two months, compiling a 17–15 record in April and May. The early season highlights included the 20-year-old Ruth's first major league home run on May 6. Batting ninth in the pitcher's spot in the lineup, Ruth knocked the first of his 714 long-balls off Yankee Jack Warhop at the Polo Grounds. Ruth had two other hits in the game, but earned the loss when he allowed an unearned run in the 13th inning of a 4–3 defeat. Ruth, who batted only on the days when he pitched, would go on to lead the 1915 Red Sox with four homers, despite batting only 92 times. He also finished second on the team with a .315 batting average.

The May 6 loss was also significant in that it marked the first of 29 consecutive road games for the Red Sox. While two-week road-trips were common in this era of rail travel, the sojourn was extra-long to allow the Braves to use Fenway Park while Boston's new National League stadium was under construction. A 22-game home stand for the Red Sox in September would help balance their schedule.

The Red Sox caught fire in June when they strung together the first of eight extended win streaks they would enjoy. The month began with the final two games of the long road-trip. On June 1, Smoky Joe Wood beat the Yankees' Ray Keating 4–3. The next day Ruth hit his second homer, a titanic shot that came in the second inning of a 7–1 win. The Yankees intentionally walked the young hurler in his next two at-bats, and Ruth responded by kicking the Red Sox bench in frustration. The Bambino kicked the bench too hard, though, and broke a toe. The injury kept him out of action for the next two weeks.

After losing 15–0 to Detroit on June 9, the Red Sox won their next eight games. The streak improved Boston's record to 29–18 and brought the team within 4½ games of first-place Chicago. Over the season's final three and a half months, Boston would compose seven seven-game win streaks.

On June 29, Speaker went 5-for-5 against the Yankees' Ray Caldwell at Fenway Park, and the Red Sox won 4–3 behind a complete-game ten-inning effort by Ruth. After a 19–8 June, the second-place Red Sox had a 36–23 record and trailed the White Sox by 5½ games.

The Red Sox moved into first place in July. They began the month with four straight double-headers, the first against Philadelphia, the final three against Washington, and they won seven of the eight games. The first of three twin-bill sweeps against Washington featured duel shutouts by Ruth and Foster on July 5. The Red Sox played 28 double-headers in all during the 1915 season.

Later in July, Boston overtook Chicago, winning four of five games at Comiskey Park from July 17–20. Both Leonard and Shore turned in shutouts during the series.

The AL race was close all season, as Chicago and Detroit challenged Boston, but the Red Sox never relinquished the lead. After winning 22 games in July, they won 21 in August and 20 in September.

Due to a scheduling quirk, the Tigers entered September having played five more games than the Red Sox and had more wins than the Red Sox throughout much of the month, even though the Red Sox remained in first place. Boston's record stood at 80–39, after Foster shut out the A's 6–0 on September 1, and Detroit's record was 81–43, leaving the Tigers a game and a half off the lead. By October 4, Detroit had played all of its games and its record stood at 100–54. The Red Sox, who had three games remaining, not counting three ties that would be re-played only if their outcome would have a bearing on the final standings, were 99–49. Needing two wins to clinch the pennant, the Red Sox delivered both victories with a double-header sweep at the Polo Grounds on October 6. In the opening game, Shore pitched a 2–0 shutout, the final of 19 blankings Red Sox pitchers would fire during the campaign. In the second game, Ruth went the distance to clinch the title with a 4–2 win. With the victory, Ruth improved his record to 17–3 since June 1.

The Red Sox lost their final game to finish 101–50, 2½ games ahead of the Tigers. Detroit's 100 wins represented the most ever by a second-place finisher in the American League. The defending champion A's finished last, with a record of 43–109.

In this season, which occurred during the height of the dead-ball era, the Red Sox hit the fewest homers in team history, finishing ahead of only Washington in the AL with 14 dingers. Boston's .260 batting average ranked second in the league though, and its 669 runs ranked third. Speaker finished fourth in the circuit with a .322 batting average and fourth in hits with 176, and led the team with 108 runs. Lewis had the second best average among Red Sox position players, batting .291 with 2 HR and 76 RBIs. Hooper (.235, 2 HR, 51 RBI) and Hoblitzel (.283, 2 HR, 61 RBI) were the only other Red Sox besides Ruth to hit more than one home run.

Boston's strength was its pitching staff, which featured all four of the top hurlers in the league as ranked by winning percentage. Five different Red Sox pitchers, all under age 27, won as many as 15 games. Despite appearing in only 25 games due to a nagging arm injury that would eventually force him to abandon pitching for a spot in the outfield instead, Wood went 15–5 and led the league with a 1.49 ERA. Shore (19–8, 1.64 ERA) and Foster (19–8, 2.11 ERA) tied for the team-lead in wins, while left-handers Ruth (18–8, 2.44 ERA) and Leonard (15–7, 2.36 ERA) also excelled. Saves would not be recognized as an official statistic for several decades, but if they had been, Boston's Carl Mays, a submarine-style rookie, would have led the league with seven. Mays also compiled a 6–5 record and 2.60 ERA in 131 innings. Despite their stellar staff, the Red Sox finished second to Washington with a 2.39 ERA.

The Postseason: 4–1

Just as Boston sent a team to the World Series for the second straight year, Philadelphia did too. While the powerhouse A's had appeared in five of the game's first 11 championships, in 1915 the Phillies qualified for their first after winning the National League with a 90–62 record. Manager Pat Moran's team boasted the best power hitter in the game, and arguably the best pitcher. Right fielder Gabby Cravath, who had made his major league debut with the Red Sox in 1908, set a twentieth century record in 1915, hitting 24 home runs. A short right field fence at Philadelphia's Baker Bowl aided the right-handed slugger, but most of his homers went to left field. As well as leading the NL in homers for the third straight year, Cravath also led in RBI (115), on base percentage (.393), slugging (.510) and strikeouts (86). Third baseman Beals Becker, a left-handed batter who clearly benefited from the 300-foot power alley in right field at Baker Bowl, finished fourth in the NL with 11 HR, despite hitting just .246 and driving in only 35 runs. First baseman Fred Luderus (.315, 7 HR, 62 RBI), another left-handed batter, and shortstop Dave Bancroft (.254, 7 HR, 30 RBI), a switch-hitter, also took advantage of the close quarters in right. The Phillies finished first in the NL with 58 HR, second with 589 runs, and fifth with a .247 average.

On the mound, the Phillies led all of baseball with a 2.17 ERA, buoyed by future-hall-of-famer Grover Cleveland Alexander. The 28-year old right-hander spun four one-hitters, while leading the NL in wins (31), ERA (1.22), complete games (36), shutouts (12), innings (376), strikeouts (241) and opponents' batting average (.191). The 1915 season was the second of four straight years in which Alexander led the NL in wins, complete games, and innings, and the first of three consecutive years in which he led in shutouts and ERA. Only World War II ended his string of dominance when he was called to battle in 1918. He returned the next year, shell-shocked, and descended quickly into alcoholism. But in 1915 Alexander was at the top of his game, and he was complimented by four other reliable starters: Erskine Mayer (21–15, 2.36 ERA), Al Demaree (14–11, 3.05 ERA), Eppa Rixey (11–12, 2.39 ERA) and George Chalmers (8–9, 2.42 ERA).

After the Braves used Fenway Park during the regular season while their stadium was being completed, they agreed to let the Red Sox use Braves Field in the World Series. The new ballpark, which opened on August 18, could hold 10,000 more fans than Fenway. The first two games of the best-of-seven series would be played at Baker Bowl, then the next two at Braves Field, then, if necessary, Games Five and Six would be played in Philadelphia, and Game Seven would be played in Boston. Aside from seating more fans than Fenway, Braves Field offered a larger playing field as well. The outfield fence stood 396 feet from home plate in left field, 550 feet away in center, and 375 feet away in right.

To no one's surprise, pitching dominated the series. Four of the five games were decided by one run and the other game was decided by two. The teams combined for just 22 runs. Boston used three pitchers in the series — Foster, Leonard, and Shore — who were a little bit better than Alexander, Mayer, and Chalmers.

1915 World Series: Red Sox 4, Phillies 1

Game 1: Phillies 3, Red Sox 1

	1	2	3	4	5	6	7	8	9	R	H	E
Boston	0	0	0	0	0	0	0	1	0	1	8	1
Philadelphia	0	0	0	1	0	0	0	2	X	3	5	1

WP Grover Cleveland Alexander
LP Ernie Shore

On October 8, nearly 20,000 fans — including Connie Mack who told reporters he was rooting for the Red Sox — turned out at Baker Bowl to watch Game One. More than 200 baseball writers were present, and no less than 50 telegraph operators who wired blow-by-blow accounts of the game to hotels and public gathering places across the country where electronic scoreboards kept fans abreast of the activities. In the Baker Bowl stands, roaming vendors sold smoked herring rolls, lemonade, and peanuts.

The Red Sox and Phillies rewarded baseball's adoring public with a tightly played game and Alexander was the star of the day. The Phillies ace allowed one hit in each of the first

The 1915 Red Sox. (Library of Congress)

eight innings, but never more than one, and his teammates scored twice in the last of the eighth to claim a 3–1 win.

All eight of the hits against Alexander were singles.

On the second pitch of the game, Hooper lined a base hit to center. Then he took second on a sacrifice bunt by Scott. But after Speaker walked, Hoblitzel hit into a fielder's choice, then Alexander picked Hoblitzel off first to end the inning.

In the second, Lewis led off with a single, and Larry Gardner sacrificed him to second. But Red Sox second baseman Jack Barry grounded into a fielder's choice, then catcher Hick Cady struck out.

The next time up for Boston, Scott singled with two outs, but Speaker flied to deep left to end the frame.

Every time the Red Sox put a man on base, Alexander's fastball seemed to zip a bit more quickly and his curveball seemed to break a bit more sharply.

Meanwhile, the Phillies also had problems solving Shore. The Boston right-hander allowed only one hit over the first three innings before Philadelphia reached him for two safeties and a run in the fourth. Phillies center fielder Dode Paskert led off with a single to right, then Cravath, the home run king, moved him to second with a sacrifice bunt. After Paskert took third on a groundout by Luderus, Bert Niehoff hit a chopper up the middle.

Barry fielded the ball behind second base, but he had no play to make as Niehoff reached first and Paskert crossed the plate with the first run.

The score stood at 1–0 until the top of the eighth when Speaker reached on a one-out walk, took second on a Hoblitzel groundout, and scored on a Lewis single. The Phillies quickly broke the tie in the bottom of the inning, though. Shore retired Alexander on a grounder to start the inning, but then he walked Milt Stock. The next hitter, Bancroft, hit a low liner past Shore that appeared ticketed for center field, but Barry made a great play to glove the ball behind second base. When Barry turned to flip the ball to Scott for the force out at second, though, the shortstop was nowhere to be seen. Apparently Scott had assumed Barry wouldn't be able to reach the ball and he didn't cover second. Shore compounded his problems when he walked the next batter, Paskert, to load the bases for Cravath. Philadelphia's clean-up hitter tapped a groundball to shortstop, and Scott's only play was at first, as Stock crossed the plate. With two outs and runners on first and third, Shore got Luderus to hit a slow grounder back to the mound but the pitcher fumbled the ball, allowing the third Philadelphia run to score.

In the ninth, Barry struck out to lead off, then pinch-hitter Olaf Henriksen reached on a Luderus error. With Shore due up, Carrigan looked to his bench and told Ruth to grab a bat. In his only appearance of the series, Ruth grounded out to first base. Then Hooper popped out to end the game.

Afterwards, Carrigan tipped his cap to the Phillies' pitcher. "Alexander won this game," the Boston manager said. "Give him full credit and don't let any one take it away from him. He pitched a splendid game, but so did Shore. I am satisfied with my team. They did the best they could against grand pitching."[2]

After changing out of their uniforms, Carrigan and his players retired to the Aldine Hotel to rest up for the next day's game.

Game 2: Red Sox 2, Phillies 1

	1	2	3	4	5	6	7	8	9	R	H	E
Boston	1	0	0	0	0	0	0	0	1	2	10	0
Philadelphia	0	0	0	0	1	0	0	0	0	1	3	0

WP Rube Foster
LP Erskine Mayer

As brightly as Alexander had shined in the first game, Boston's Foster shined even brighter in the second. The diminutive farmer's son from Arkansas limited the Phillies to three base runners all game, while matching his opponents' output with a 3-for-4 performance himself. Shore even got the game-winning hit in the ninth inning, as the Red Sox won 2–1.

The game was also historically significant, as President Woodrow Wilson became the first U.S. president to attend a World Series game. Upon arriving at Baker Bowl, President Wilson refused complimentary tickets, saying he preferred to pay for his seats like the other fans. Then he settled into a box seat beside the Red Sox bench. At 2:10 P.M., the president threw out the ceremonial first pitch, tossing a ball from the stands to Mayer, the Phillies starter. Then he sat back and taught his fiancée, Mrs. Norman Galt, how to keep score.[3]

The Red Sox took a 1–0 lead in the top of the first, thanks to a Phillies error. Hooper led off with a walk against Mayer, then took second on a sacrifice bunt by Scott. Speaker followed with a single to right that was struck too sharply to bring Hooper home. With runners at first and third and one out and their clean-up hitter, Hoblitzel, at the plate, Carrigan decided he didn't want to wait all game for a clutch hit, as had been Boston's fate in the first game. So, on the second pitch to Hoblitzel, the Red Sox attempted a double steal. It almost backfired. Catcher Ed Burns fired down to second to nab Speaker, and Niehoff's return throw to the plate arrived ahead of Hooper. But Burns dropped the ball as Hooper slid into him. Hooper, in fact, slid right past the plate without touching it, but he crawled back on all fours and slapped it with his left hand before Burns could retrieve the ball and tag him.

Foster retired the first 12 Phillies he faced before allowing back-to-back doubles to Cravath and Luderus in the fifth. The hits tied the score, 1–1, and put the go-ahead run in scoring position with no outs. But Foster escaped without allowing another run, getting Possum Whitted to ground to short, Niehoff to line to first, and Burns to strike out.

The game remained tied until the Red Sox batted in the top of the ninth. Larry Gardner led off with a single and advanced to second on a groundout. With two outs, Foster slashed a low line drive into center field. Paskert fielded the ball cleanly and fired toward the plate, but his throw was off the mark and Gardner scored standing up to put Boston ahead, 2–1.

Foster, who retired the final ten batters he faced, finished with eight strikeouts and no walks.

The series shifted to Boston tied at one win apiece.

Game 3: Red Sox 2, Phillies 1

	1	2	3	4	5	6	7	8	9	R	H	E
Philadelphia	0	0	1	0	0	0	0	0	0	1	3	0
Boston	0	0	0	1	0	0	0	0	1	2	6	1

WP Dutch Leonard
LP Grover Cleveland Alexander

The teams took a day off to travel and get situated in Boston before resuming play on October 11. By game-time, the wisdom of using Braves Field for the games in Boston had become apparent. More than 42,000 fans had filed through the turnstiles, the largest crowd in World Series history to date. The fans bathed in warm October sunshine on an unseasonably mild Monday afternoon.

For the second straight game, Boston's starter allowed just three hits and no walks. And for the third game in a row the outcome was not decided until the victor's final at bat. Lewis hit a walk-off single against Alexander with two outs in the bottom of the ninth to deliver Hooper with the winning run.

While Moran opted to start Alexander on two days' rest, Carrigan sent Leonard to the mound. The Red Sox lefty had not appeared in a game since his final regular season start on October 4 and had to shake off some rust in the first inning. He allowed a leadoff double to Stock to start the game, before retiring the next three hitters, including Cravath on three called strikes.

In the third, the Phillies got on the scoreboard. Burns started the inning with a single, then Alexander dropped a bunt down the third base line. Gardner fielded and fired to Hoblitzel, but the first baseman dropped the ball, giving the Phillies two runners with no outs. Stock bunted both runners along, as Gardner fielded again, and this time Hoblitzel held onto the throw, then Bancroft singled to center to score Burns. Speaker was playing shallow and fielded the ball quickly, holding Alexander at third. Cravath flied out to Lewis in deep left to end the inning.

The Red Sox knotted the game at 1–1 in the fourth when Speaker tripled with one out and Hoblitzel followed with a sacrifice fly to center.

The only hits for either team over the next four innings were a pair of singles by Boston in the seventh, but a double play grounder by Hoblitzel helped Alexander escape without allowing a run.

Leonard set down the Phillies in order in the top of the ninth, extending his string of consecutive batters retired to 19, then it was the Red Sox' turn to hit. Hooper led off with a single to right, then Scott stepped to the plate and squared to sacrifice. On his first two bunt attempts, Scott hit foul balls. But on his third attempt, he dropped the ball in fair territory, moving Hooper along. Alexander then elected to walk Speaker intentionally, hoping that Hoblitzel would hit into another double play. The big first baseman did hit the ball on the ground, to second base, but Niehoff's only play was at first. With runners at second and third and two outs, Lewis hit a screaming line drive over Bancroft's head at shortstop. Before Hooper had crossed the plate with the winning run, the Boston fans had already begun hopping out of the stands and onto the field. The Royal Rooters mobbed Hooper and Lewis and the rest of the Red Sox as they celebrated the win.

GAME 4: RED SOX 2, PHILLIES 1

	1	2	3	4	5	6	7	8	9	R	H	E
Philadelphia	0	0	0	0	0	0	0	1	0	1	7	0
Boston	0	0	1	0	0	1	0	0	X	2	8	1

WP Ernie Shore
LP George Chalmers

More than 60,000 fans showed up at Braves Field on Columbus Day, hoping to watch Game Four between the Red Sox and Phillies, but only 41,000 were allowed to enter Braves Field. Most of the rest milled around outside the stadium waiting for the roar of the crowd to tell them how the home team was faring, and receiving information from fans seated atop the bleachers who yelled down updates. Some fans climbed telegraph poles, coal elevators, or the face of the armory beside the stadium to steal a peak inside. For the third straight game, Boston won 2–1 behind a stellar effort from its starting pitcher and just enough timely hitting.

Both managers were obviously aware that the game would be another tightly played contest, and both instructed their players to run the bases aggressively in the early going. Stock started the game with a leadoff single against Shore, but was thrown out by Lewis trying to stretch the hit to a double. The next hitter, Bancroft, walked, and immediately attempted to steal second. Cady's throw beat him to the bag, but Barry dropped the ball, giving Philadelphia a runner in scoring position with one out. Shore struck out Paskert and Cravath, though, to end the inning.

In the bottom of the first, Chalmers struck out Hooper and Scott before allowing a walk to Speaker. The Grey Eagle took off for second base and was caught stealing by Burns.

The Phillies put runners on base against Shore in each of the next three innings, and twice bunted runners into scoring position, but they couldn't come through with a clutch hit. Their best chance came in the fourth when Cravath hit a two-out shot to left that Lewis caught with his back against the outfield wall.

The Red Sox scored a run in the third. After Barry walked, Cady dropped down a bunt.

Chalmers cut in front of Luderus to field the ball but stumbled and couldn't make the play. Shore then sacrificed both runners into scoring position, and Hooper brought home Barry with an infield hit to second. Niehoff charged the high chopper by Hooper and knocked it down with his glove but he had no play.

Boston put another run on the board in the sixth when Hoblitzel singled with one out and Lewis followed with a run-scoring double that rolled to the base of the fence in left.

Philadelphia finally got a big hit out of Cravath in the eighth. The slugger cracked a two-out triple to center and scored on single by Luderus. Oscar Dugey pinch-ran for Luderus and stole second, but Shore got Whitted to tap to the mound to end the inning.

In the ninth, Shore retired the Phillies in order to complete a seven-hit, four-walk, four-strikeout, complete-game win, and bring the Red Sox to the brink of their third world championship.

Game 5: Red Sox 5, Phillies 4

	1	2	3	4	5	6	7	8	9	R	H	E
Boston	0	1	1	0	0	0	0	2	1	5	10	1
Philadelphia	2	0	0	2	0	0	0	0	0	4	9	1

WP Eppa Rixey
LP Rube Foster

Compared to the first four games of the series, Game Five was a slugfest. The 20,306 fans at Baker Bowl on October 13th witnessed all four home runs hit in the series and the appearance of the series' only relief pitcher. They also saw a whopping nine runs cross the plate, five more than the number that had scored in the next highest scoring game. But one thing didn't change. For the fourth straight time the Red Sox posted a one-run victory. With their 5–4 win, the Red Sox became the second team to win three World Series.

The Phillies scored first and actually enjoyed two different two-run leads in the game. Boston played long-ball both times though to overcome the deficit and scored once in the ninth to account for the winning margin.

Mayer held the Red Sox scoreless in the first, as Speaker was caught stealing to end an opening frame for the second time in the series. Then two Philadelphia runs crossed the plate against Foster in the bottom of the inning. Luderus got the key hit, cracking a two-out double to plate Bancroft and Paskert, both of whom had singled.

Boston scored a run in its next at bat, thanks to a two-out triple to center by Gardner and a single by Barry. Then in the third, the Red Sox tied the score at 2–2 on a leadoff home run by Hooper. The high fly ball carried over the shallow fence in right field. One out later, Speaker ripped a single to right, and Moran decided he had seen enough of Mayer. The Phillies skipper summoned the left-handed Rixey to pitch to Hoblitzel. Carrigan countered with the right-handed hitting Del Gainer, but Gainer grounded into a double play to end the inning.

The Phillies regained a two-run lead in the fourth. The first run scored when Luderus hit a shot over the right field fence that touched down on Broad Street, where a newsboy picked it up.[4] Later in the inning, Niehoff singled with two outs, then Burns singled to right. Hooper fired toward third and his throw sailed into the stands, allowing Niehoff to trot home.

The score remained 4–2 in favor of Philadelphia until the top of the eighth when Gainer singled and Lewis followed with a home run over the right field fence.

With the score tied 4–4 in the last of the eighth, Foster allowed a two-out walk to Cravath, then hit Luderus with a pitch. But he got Whitted to ground to the mound to end the inning.

Foster struck out to begin the Red Sox' half of the ninth, bringing Hooper, who was already 2 for 3 in the game, to the plate. Hooper watched two straight strikes go by, then blasted Rixey's next pitch into the front row of bleacher seats in right-center for his second homer of the game. With his head down, Hooper jogged around the bases. As he crossed the plate, Speaker pounded him on the back and said, "Wake up, Harry, you just won the World Series."[5]

The Red Sox still had some work to do in the bottom of the ninth though, and Foster saw to it that it would not be too strenuous for his mates. He struck out Niehoff to start the inning, then got Burns on a grounder to first, then got pinch-hitter Bill Killefer on a grounder to shortstop to end the game.

"It was a hard fought series, and the better team won," Carrigan said afterwards. "I never saw a series so interesting and so hotly contested."[6]

Moran agreed that the Red Sox were the class of baseball. "When you are beaten four in a row there isn't any excuse to offer," he said. "Any team that wins four successive games in a World Series must get credit.... Our team was the best in the National League and the Sox' was the best American League club, and as they beat us they naturally should be regarded as the best ball club in the country."[7]

Indeed the statistics suggest Boston was the superior club. The Red Sox out-hit the Phillies (.264 to .182) and out-pitched them (1.84 ERA to 2.27) over the five games. Hooper batted .444 (8–18) with 5 RBI for Boston, while Luderus hit .438 (7–16) with 6 RBI for Philadelphia. Cravath hit just .125 (2–16) with one RBI.

After the series, Judge Landis continued to delay ruling on the Federal League's lawsuit against Organized Baseball. On December 22, the AL and NL settled with the FL, agreeing to pay $600,000 to the eight Federal League owners in exchange for their agreement to disband their league.

The major league owners then rolled back player salaries to their previous lows, and became more parsimonious than ever. In Boston, Lannin offered Speaker $9,000, compared to the $18,000 he had made in 1915.

Chapter 4

The Regular Season: 91–63

Despite trading Tris Speaker to Cleveland in a lopsided spring deal, and despite hitting just one home run at Fenway Park all season, the 1916 Red Sox successfully defended their championship. The team relied on strong pitching and defense to compensate for an offense that ranked sixth in the eight-team American League in runs. The star of Boston's talented pitching staff was Babe Ruth, who, after making a name for himself in 1915, blossomed into one of the league's elite pitchers in 1916.

As the Red Sox reported to spring training in Hot Springs, Arkansas, Speaker's contract situation was still unresolved. Team owner Joseph Lannin stood by his initial offer of $9,000, while the star center fielder wanted $15,000. Although he was unsigned, Speaker worked out with his teammates and played in the team's exhibition games, then accompanied the Red Sox north in anticipation of reaching a last-minute agreement with Lannin. But four days before Opening Day, Lannin traded Speaker to the Indians for a pair of 23-year-olds: right-handed pitcher Sam Jones and third baseman Fred Thomas. Jones had gone 4–9 as a rookie in 1915, while Thomas was a minor leaguer who would not appear in his first major league game until 1918.

When newspaper reporters informed Speaker on April 8 that he'd been traded, he said, "There is no need of my stating that this deal was a complete surprise to me. As I understood it, Mr. Lannin and I had practically agreed upon terms. I shall see Mr. Lannin tomorrow forenoon and look for an explanation."[1] Speaker met with the Red Sox owner and learned that in addition to receiving two players, the Red Sox were also getting $50,000 from the Indians in the exchange. He refused to sign with Cleveland unless he received some of the money changing hands and took his case to American League president Ban Johnson. Johnson awarded Speaker $10,000 of the sale price. Neither Jones nor Thomas would contribute to the 1916 Red Sox, though Jones would develop into one of the team's best starters in future years. Speaker, meanwhile, went on to lead the AL in hits, batting average, on base percentage, and slugging in 1916, and helped keep the Indians in first place for much of the season's first half. But the Indians faded in the heat of summer, as did the Yankees, who had also enjoyed a hot start. The AL wound up a three-team race between the Red Sox, White Sox, and Tigers. The Red Sox did not assume first place to stay until the third week of September, and did not clinch the pennant until just three days remained in the season.

The Red Sox replaced Speaker in center with Tilly Walker, whose contract they purchased from the St. Louis Browns just before the season began. Walker was a fifth-year player who covered a lot of ground in the outfield and could steal his share of bases, but he was not the feared hitter that Speaker was. With the exception of the change in center, the 1916 Red Sox were essentially the same team as the year before. Duffy Lewis and Harry Hooper flanked Walker in the outfield. Dick Hoblitzel played first, Jack Barry and Hal Janvrin split time at second, Larry Gardner played third, and Everett Scott played shortstop. Player-manager Bill Carrigan, Hick Cady, and Chester "Pinch" Thomas shared the catching duties. The pitching staff changed only slightly. With Joe Wood sidelined with a sore arm, Carl Mays moved into a starting role, behind returnees Ruth, Dutch Leonard, Ernie Shore, and Rube Foster.

On Opening Day, Shore drew the starting assignment from Carrigan but his arm refused to loosen in the Fenway Park bullpen, so Carrigan turned the ball over to Ruth instead. The Babe pitched eight innings in a 2–1 victory over Philadelphia, then went on to win his next four starts as well, including a 5–1 decision over Washington's Walter Johnson on April 17.

The Red Sox won nine of their first 15 games, then lost four of their next five. By the time Speaker visited Boston for the first time as an Indian on May 9, first-place Cleveland enjoyed a 4½ game lead over third-place Boston. The Indians entered the five-game-series riding an eight-game win streak, but Leonard held Speaker hitless in the first game and Boston prevailed 5–1. After one inning in the field, Speaker mistakenly ran to the Red Sox' dugout instead of the Indians', much to the amusement of the 15,000 fans in attendance.[2] The next night, Speaker found his batting stroke again and lashed two hits against Ruth and scored three runs in a 6–2 Indians win. The Red Sox dropped three of the five games against the Tribe, then rebounded to beat Chicago 3–2, as Leonard out-dueled Eddie Cicotte at Fenway Park on May 13th. After 26 games, the Red Sox were 13–13. Then came four straight days of rain. When play finally resumed in Boston on May 18, the Red Sox lost two games to St. Louis to fall a season-low seven games behind the Indians.

While Speaker and the Indians kept winning, the Red Sox spent the remainder of May and June bouncing between fourth and sixth place. After posting a 9–6 record in April, the Red Sox went 12–12 in May, and 13–12 in June. Over the season's first three months their opponents outscored them 209–205. But as June wound down, the team had shown signs of progress. On June 20, Walker hit what would be the Red Sox' lone homer of the season at Fenway Park when he drove a pitch from New York's Ray Keating over the left field wall in a 4–1 loss. The next day, Foster pitched the first no-hitter in Fenway history, blanking the Yankees 2–0 in a game that took only an hour and 31 minutes to play. Foster didn't allow a base runner until the sixth inning when Les Nunamaker drew the first of three Yankee walks in the game. Foster finished with a flourish, fanning pinch-hitter Slim Caldwell to end the game. To show his appreciation and to commemorate the event, Lannin awarded Foster a $100 bonus and a gold-handled pocketknife engraved with the date.[3] The next day, Ruth pitched a three-hitter, beating the Yankees 1–0 in a game that took only an hour and 18 minutes to complete. The next day, Shore blanked the A's 1–0. Then Leonard and Mays won their starts in a double-header sweep of the A's on June 24. The modest streak inched Boston within 2½ games of first place.

The Red Sox finally caught fire in July, winning 20 of 30 games. On July 11, Ruth started both ends of a double-header against the White Sox. The big lefty wasn't scheduled to pitch until the second game, but when Foster told Carrigan he needed a few more tosses in the bullpen before he could perform in Game One, Ruth volunteered for duty. He retired the first batter, then stomped around the mound stalling for a few minutes until Carrigan summoned Foster. The reliever pitched the remaining 8⅔ innings, earning a 5–3 win, then Ruth started and won the second game, 3–1. The next day, Boston swept another pair from Chicago as both Shore and Leonard turned in complete-game efforts despite the 100-degree temperatures in Boston. The four-game win streak moved Boston within two games of slumping Cleveland.

On July 30, the Red Sox got their first taste of the top seat in the AL since the opening week. By beating the Tigers 9–3 in Detroit, the Red Sox improved to 53–40, a half game better than Chicago, a game ahead of New York, 2½ ahead of Cleveland, and 3½ ahead of Detroit. The next day, Ruth shutout the Tigers 6–0, pitching a two-hitter and chipping in with two hits. The Red Sox held onto first place for two more days before the White Sox edged ahead of them in the first week of August. Then on August 9, the Red Sox moved back into first, a position they would hold for the next 40 days.

On August 15, Ruth outlasted Johnson, beating the Washington ace 1–0 in 13 innings. Barry led off the bottom of the 13th for the Red Sox with a chopper up the middle that struck Johnson's bare hand and went for a single. After Lewis struck out and Hoblitzel flied out, Walker singled to center, moving Barry to third. Then Gardner sent a single into center to score Barry with the winning run. The Red Sox had seven hits against Johnson in the game; the Nationals had eight against Ruth. Ruth finished with just two strikeouts, while Johnson had five.

The Red Sox won four games in a row against the Indians, August 19–23, dropping Cleveland 7½ games off the lead. Boston took the first game 2–1 behind the strong pitching of Ruth, then after Shore and Mays turned in shutouts in Games Two and Three, Ruth came back to earn a save in the fourth game, working two hitless innings in relief of Leonard. Despite the relief appearance, Ruth made his scheduled start the next day against Detroit and fired a three-hit shutout. The Tigers won the next two games though, to stay alive in the race.

As September began, the Red Sox held the top spot in the AL with a record of 71–52, followed by the Tigers, who were 3 games back at 70–57, and the White Sox, who were 3½ games back at 69–57.

By the time Ruth beat Washington's "Big Train" for the fourth straight time, firing a four-hitter in a 2–1 win at Griffith Stadium on September 9, Boston's lead had shrunk to a single game over Detroit and 1½ over Chicago.

On September 16, the Red Sox entered a crucial stretch of road games that would see them play three games in a row against the White Sox, who the day before had moved into a first place tie with the Red Sox, then three against the Tigers, who were only a game off the pace. Chicago won the first game, dropping Boston from first place all the way down to third, as Detroit won a double-header against Philadelphia to seize control of first, and Chicago moved a game ahead of the Red Sox. Ruth righted the ship the next day though, silencing a crowd of 40,000 fans with a 6–2 Boston win. The victory, Ruth's 20th, started the team's longest win streak of the season, a seven-gamer. Boston won the final game against

Chicago to regain sole possession of first place, then swept Detroit, then won the first two games of a series in Cleveland. The Red Sox clinched at least a tie for first place on September 30, when Leonard blanked the Yankees 1–0 in Boston. The game's only run scored on a sacrifice fly by Hooper in the bottom of the tenth inning.

The Red Sox and A's were rained out the next day, but the Indians defeated the White Sox, which clinched the pennant outright for the Red Sox. Carrigan rested most of his starters and the Red Sox lost both ends of a double-header against the hapless A's on the final day of the season, to finish 91–63, 2 games ahead of the White Sox and 4 ahead of the Tigers. The Indians, who had started so well, won just 18 of their final 50 games and finished sixth with a record of 77–77. Remarkably, seventh-place Washington finished just a game below the .500 mark at 76–77, highlighting the league's parity. The last-place A's were the circuit's only bad team, finishing 36–117.

Boston finished ahead of only Washington and Philadelphia in runs with 550, finished last in triples with 56 and ahead of only Washington with 14 home runs. The Red Sox hit .248 as a team, fourth best in the league. Gardner had the best batting average among Boston's regular position players, .308, while he also led the team with 62 RBI. Hooper had the next best average, .271, to go with his team-best 156 hits and team-best 75 runs. Walker hit .266 and tied for the team lead with 3 home runs. The man he replaced, Speaker, hit .386 in Cleveland. The 1916 Red Sox made 183 errors in the field, 22 fewer than the next best major league team.

Boston's pitchers finished second in the AL with a 2.48 ERA, first in shutouts with 24, and first in home runs allowed with 10. Ruth's 1.75 ERA led the league, as did his 9 shutouts, and .201 opponents' batting average. He finished with a 23–12 record and didn't allow a home run in 323 innings pitched. At the plate, he batted .272 with 3 home runs in 136 at bats. Leonard (18–12, 2.36 ERA) and Mays (18–13, 2.39 ERA) were the team's next best starters, followed by Shore (16–10, 2.63 ERA) and Foster (14–7, 3.06 ERA).

The Postseason: 4–1

The Brooklyn Robins won the National League, finishing 94–60, 2½ games ahead of the defending champion Philadelphia Phillies. The Brooklyn team name had been the "Superbas" at the turn of the century, then later the "Trolley-Dodgers," but by 1916 the team was most commonly known as the "Robins," in tribute to third-year Brooklyn manager Wilbert Robinson. The colorful Robinson was a former big league catcher whose original claim to fame was that he got seven hits in a nine-inning game for Baltimore in 1892. History has also linked his name to baseball's spring training lore, as Florida's "Grapefruit League" allegedly got its name when Robinson made a bet with Casey Stengel that he could catch a baseball dropped from an airplane at the team's camp at Daytona Beach in 1915. At the last minute Stengel substituted a grapefruit for the ball, though, and it splattered all over the confused Robinson, who thought the pink pulp was his own blood and began screaming hysterically. Word of the prank quickly spread and before long the game's players had coined a new name for Florida's exhibition circuit.[4]

Unlike Boston, an offensively challenged team that relied on stellar pitching to win games, Brooklyn was formidable on both sides of the ball. The Robins finished second in the NL in runs (585), and led the circuit in batting average (.261), on base percentage (.313), slugging (.345) and earned run average (2.12). The team's best hitter was future-hall-of-

Oppposing managers: Carrigan of the Red Sox and Robinson of the Brooklyn Robins. (Library of Congress)

famer Zack Wheat. The left-handed swinging left fielder batted .312 with 13 triples, 9 HR, and 73 RBI in 1916. Another lefty swinger, first baseman Jake Daubert, also batted over .300 for Brooklyn, finishing second in the league with a .316 average to go with 3 HR and 33 RBI. Chief Meyers, back in the NL after a stint in the Federal League, handled the catching duties and hit .247, while George Cutshaw (.260, 2 HR, 63 RBI) played second, Mike Mowrey (.244, 60 RBI) played third, and Ivy Olson (.254, 1 HR, 38 RBI) played shortstop. A trio of capable players shared time in the outfield with Wheat: Stengel (.279, 8 HR, 53 RBI), Jimmy Johnston (.252, 1 HR, 26 RBI), and Hy Myers (.262, 3 HR, 36 RBI).

Three Brooklyn pitchers allowed fewer than two earned runs per game in 1916: Rube Marquard (13–6, 1.58 ERA), Jeff Pfeffer (25–11, 1.92 ERA) and Larry Cheney (18–12, 1.92 ERA). Sherry Smith (14–10, 2.34 ERA) and Jack Coombs (13–8, 2.66 ERA) also pitched well. While 1916 represented Brooklyn's first World Series appearance, two of Robinson's pitchers had previous experience on the game's grandest stage. Marquard had pitched for the Giants in previous series, compiling a 2–2 record, while Coombs had compiled a 4–0 mark in previous series play with the A's.

The first two games were scheduled to take place at Braves Field in Boston, then the teams would move to Ebbets Field for Games Three and Four. The final three games, if necessary, would switch between the two ballparks.

The Red Sox claimed one-run victories in the first two games, then lost by a run in the third game, before posting more comfortable victories in Games Four and Five to win their second consecutive championship. The series is best remembered for its epic second game, a 14-inning duel between Ruth and Smith.

1916 World Series: Red Sox 4, Robins 1

Game 1: Red Sox 6, Robins 5

	1	2	3	4	5	6	7	8	9	R	H	E
Brooklyn	0	0	0	1	0	0	0	0	4	5	10	4
Boston	0	0	1	0	1	0	3	1	X	6	8	1

WP   Ernie Shore
LP   Rube Marquard
SV   Carl Mays

More than 36,000 fans filed through the turnstiles at Braves Field on Saturday, October 7, to watch the series opener. Meanwhile, 10,000 New Yorkers crowded into Times Square to follow the game on an electric scoreboard that had been provided courtesy of the *New York Times*. Although Ruth had emerged as Boston's best pitcher in 1916, he lacked World Series experience, so Carrigan decided to start Shore, one of Boston's heroes from the 1915 World Series, in the first game. Likewise, Robinson chose the battle-tested Marquard over his top winner, Pfeffer.

For the first six innings the game followed the expected script, that of a closely played pitcher's duel. But in the final three innings, both teams hung crooked numbers on the scoreboard. When the dust settled, the Red Sox were the team left standing. Boston survived a four-run top of the ninth inning, hanging on for a 6–5 win.

The Red Sox started the scoring in the third when Hoblitzel lashed a two-out triple to right and Lewis doubled him home.

The Robins answered immediately. Stengel led off the Robins' fourth with a single, and the next batter, Wheat, tripled him home. Shore then got some help from his defense. Cutshaw stroked a low liner to right field that looked sure to fall for a hit. But Hooper came running in and made a diving catch, then hopped to his feet and fired to the plate to cut down Wheat by ten feet.

Boston reclaimed the lead in the fifth when Hooper led off with a double, moved to third on a sacrifice by Janvrin, and scored on a Walker single.

The Red Sox led 2–1 entering the bottom of the seventh when they scored three runs on just one hit. Janvrin started the rally with a double, then Olson booted a Walker grounder, putting runners at the corners with no outs. Then Cutshaw bobbled a Hoblitzel grounder, allowing Janvrin to score. Lewis bunted both runners along, and they scored on a fielder's choice and a sacrifice fly.

In the bottom of the eighth, Pfeffer took over on the mound for Brooklyn after Robinson had elected to pinch-hit for Marquard in the top of the inning. Hooper reached on a one-out walk, then Janvrin singled to right and Stengel fielded the ball and threw toward third. The wild throw bounced into the stands and Hooper trotted home to put Boston ahead 6–1.

With a five run lead and Shore working on a six-hitter Boston seemed in control as the ninth inning began. Suddenly though, the Boston defense — perhaps inspired by Brooklyn's sloppy play — failed. And as Shore's pitch-count mounted, he dug a deeper and deeper hole for himself, until finally the outcome hung in the balance. Daubert led off with a walk, then Stengel followed with a single to right — the only ball the Robins would hit out of the infield in the inning that didn't hit the glove or body of a Red Sox fielder first. With two men aboard, Shore got Wheat to hit a hard groundball back to the mound. He spun and fired to Gardner at third to cut down the lead runner, but Gardner slipped as he came off the bag, preventing him from throwing across the diamond to complete the double play. The Red Sox had turned four double plays in the first eight innings, but when they needed one to finish off the Robins, they failed to execute. Shore got two quick strikes on the next hitter, Cutshaw, then hit him with a pitch to load the bases. The next batter, Mowrey, hit another tailor-made double-play ball, this one to Janvrin, but the second baseman let the ball bounce off his leg and into right field. Two runs scored, cutting Boston's lead to 6–3. The next hitter, Olson hit a slow roller to Gardner. The third baseman fielded on the run and threw to first, but Olson crossed the bag before the ball arrived in Hoblitzel's glove. The three potential tying runs were on base, and still there was only one out. While Mays warmed hurriedly in the Boston bullpen, Shore pitched to Meyers and got him to pop out to Hoblitzel in foul territory for the second out. But Shore walked the next batter, pinch-hitter Fred Merkle, to force home a run. Carrigan finally lifted his starter, calling upon Mays and his strange underhand delivery to get the final out. On the first pitch Mays threw, Myers hit a high chopper over the pitcher's head. Janvrin fielded between second base and the mound but had no play as another run crossed the plate. The Robins had cut the lead to 6–5 and had the bases loaded for Daubert. The hard-hitting first baseman sent a shot toward the hole at shortstop but Scott made a nice play to backhand the ball, then fired to first to end the game.

GAME 2: RED SOX 2, ROBINS 1

	1	2	3	4	5	6	7	8	9	10	11	12	13	14	R	H	E
Brooklyn	1	0	0	0	0	0	0	0	0	0	0	0	0	0	1	6	2
Boston	0	0	1	0	0	0	0	0	0	0	0	0	0	1	2	7	1

WP Babe Ruth
LP Sherry Smith

After his team lost the first game, Robinson told reporters that he would start either Cheney or Coombs in the second contest. But when Game Two began beneath foreboding skies in Boston the next day, the left-handed Smith took the mound for the Robins. In one of the most memorable games in early World Series history, Smith and Ruth dueled for more than three hours before game's outcome was determined in the 14th inning.

The game began ominously for the Red Sox when the Robins' third batter, Myers, hit an inside the park home run. On a 1–0 count Myers drove a Ruth curveball toward the gap in right-center. Walker and Hooper gave chase, but both fell down as the ball scooted past them and rolled to the fence. Myers could have scored standing up but chose instead to finish his race around the bases with a headfirst slide across the plate. The polite Boston crowd stood and cheered his effort, even though the Red Sox trailed 1–0.

Boston countered in the third, tying the game when Scott led off with a triple and Ruth brought him home with a groundout.

Neither team scored over the next ten innings, though both had their chances. Brooklyn's best opportunity came in the eighth when Mowrey led off with a single and moved to second on a sacrifice bunt. With one out, Brooklyn catcher Otto Miller singled to left-center. It appeared that Mowrey could have scored on the play, but he held up at third as Lewis fielded the ball then threw home. The next batter, Smith, hit a grounder to Scott at shortstop, and this time Mowrey started for the plate. But Scott fired home and Mowrey was eliminated in a rundown. Ruth got Johnston to ground out to the mound to end the inning.

In the Boston ninth, Janvrin led off with a shot to center that Wheat dropped. Although the ball had been in Wheat's glove, the official scorer ruled the play a double. The next hitter, Walker, squared to bunt and fouled Smith's first pitch to the backstop. Not wanting to take any chances with another misplaced bunt, Carrigan pulled Walker in the middle of his at-bat and sent Jimmy Walsh to the plate as a pinch-hitter. The move almost backfired when Walsh bunted the ball right back to Smith and the pitcher fired to third base ahead of Janvrin. Third base umpire Ernie Quigley originally ruled Janvrin out, but when he noticed the ball had popped out of Mowrey's glove he reversed his decision. The Red Sox had the winning run at third with no outs. Hoblitzel stepped to the plate and swung at the second pitch he saw, lofting a high fly ball to center field. The drive appeared deep enough to plate Janvrin with the game-winner, but Myers made the catch and fired a one-hop strike to the plate where Miller slapped the tag on Janvrin.

In the bottom of the tenth, another fine defensive play bailed Smith out of trouble. Scott led off with a single and took second on a sacrifice by Thomas. After Ruth swung and missed three times for the second out, Hooper hit a shot down the third base line. The ball appeared ticketed for left field, but Mowrey dove to his right and knocked it down. He retrieved the ball and pump-faked in the direction of first base before flipping the ball to Olson, the shortstop, who had slipped in behind Scott as he rounded third. Scott had taken too wide a turn and was tagged out diving back into the bag.

After Ruth retired the Robins without allowing a hit for the sixth straight time in the top of the 14th, the Red Sox took their turn at bat with a renewed sense of urgency. The dark clouds that had been hovering overhead all day grew more menacing by the minute and in all likelihood the game would be suspended after Boston batted. Hoblitzel began the inning by drawing his fourth walk of the day, then he moved to second on a Lewis sacrifice. Carrigan sent the speedy Mike McNally into the game as a pinch runner for Hoblitzel and sent Del Gainer — who specialized in hitting southpaws — to the plate instead of Gardner. In his only appearance of the series, Gainer delivered the game-winning hit. He sent a liner over Mowrey's head into left field. Wheat fielded the ball on one bounce and made a desperate heave to the plate, but the throw was off-line and McNally slid across the plate just ahead of the diving Miller's tag. The Red Sox were 2–1 winners of the longest World Series game played to date.

After the game, Ruth, still bitter at not drawing a start in the 1915 World Series, said to Carrigan, "I told you a year ago I could take care of those National League bums and you never gave me a chance."[5]

Game 3: Robins 4, Red Sox 3

	1	2	3	4	5	6	7	8	9	R	H	E
Boston	0	0	0	0	0	2	1	0	0	3	7	1
Brooklyn	0	0	1	1	2	0	0	0	X	4	10	0

WP   Jack Coombs
LP   Carl Mays
SV   Jeff Pfeffer

On Tuesday, October 10, Ebbets Field hosted its first World Series game. The ballpark had opened on the former site of the Pigtown garbage dump in 1913. Built for a record $750,000, the facility was the most elaborate ballpark the game had yet seen.[6] It featured a distinctive red brick façade, an Italian marble entrance rotunda, chandeliers that hung ornate crystal baseball bats from the ceiling, and gilded ticket windows. The outfield was spacious on the left side of the diamond, but in right field the fence stood just 300 feet from home plate. Brooklyn owner Charles Ebbets had built the park with his own money, selling a significant share of his interest in the team to finance its construction. The Brooklyn franchise had always struggled to attract fans, but Ebbets believed that if the team offered fans a top-notch stadium and a winning team, Brooklyn could survive as a major league city. Unfortunately, the fans never really rewarded Ebbets' faith in them. Even in these early days, there were signs that baseball would not last in Brooklyn. Game Three of the 1916 World Series was played before a great many empty seats. So many fewer fans than expected turned out, in fact, that ticket scalpers sold box seats with a face value of $3 for just $1. Among the 21,000 fans who did attend the game were several hundred Bostonians who assembled in the left field bleachers with a band that broke into "Tessie" at several points during the game.[7]

Coombs started on the mound for Brooklyn and the Robins staked him to a 4–0 lead against Mays. When Coombs eventually tired and the Red Sox cut the lead to 4–3 in the seventh inning, Pfeffer came out of the Brooklyn bullpen and preserved the lead.

Brooklyn scored first on consecutive singles by Daubert, Stengel and Cutshaw in the third inning. In the fourth, the Robins manufactured another run, thanks to a bunt single by Olson, a throwing error by Gardner, and an RBI single by Coombs. In the fifth, they scored two more as Wheat and Mowrey walked and Olson chased them both home with a triple to left.

The Red Sox fought back though, plating two runs in the top of the sixth. Olaf Henriksen pinch-hit for Mays and drew a one-out walk, then Hooper tripled him home. One out later, Hooper scored on a single to left by Chick Shorten who had started in center field in place of Walker.

Foster took over on the mound for Boston in the sixth and got some help from his defense when Daubert was thrown out trying to stretch a triple into an inside-the-park home run. Hooper retrieved the ball at the base of the left field wall, 410 feet from home plate, and relayed to Scott, who fired home to Thomas.

With one out in the top of the seventh, Gardner cut the lead to 4–3 when he drove a Coombs fastball over the right field fence and onto Bedford Avenue. With the lead down to a single run, Robinson lifted Coombs in favor of Pfeffer and the reliever retired the final eight Red Sox to end the game. After Stengel squeezed the last out, retiring Lewis on a fly ball to right field, several thousand happy fans stormed the field.

GAME 4: RED SOX 6, ROBINS 2

	1	2	3	4	5	6	7	8	9	R	H	E
Boston	0	3	0	1	1	0	1	0	0	6	10	1
Brooklyn	2	0	0	0	0	0	0	0	0	2	5	4

WP   Dutch Leonard
LP   Rube Marquard

Hoping to even the series at two games apiece, the Robins put their faith in Marquard, the winner of so many big games in the past, including two against the Red Sox in the 1912 World Series. Brooklyn scored two runs in the first inning, but Boston came right back to take the lead in its next at bat and by day's end had taken a commanding three games to one lead in the series. After scuffling in the first frame, Leonard pitched shutout ball the rest of the way to earn the win.

Marquard struck out two of the three batters he faced in the top of the first, then Johnston led off the Brooklyn half of the inning by slicing Leonard's first pitch into the gap in right-center for a triple. Leonard got two quick strikes on the next batter, Myers, then surrendered a run-scoring single to right. The flustered Leonard then walked Merkle — who was playing first in place of Daubert — on five pitches. Wheat came to bat with runners on first and second and grounded to Gardner at third. Gardner threw to second to force Merkle for the second out, but then Leonard bounced a pitch to Cutshaw that allowed Wheat to move up to second. Myers came home with Brooklyn's second run a moment later when Janvrin erred on a groundball by Cutshaw.

Trailing 2–0, the Red Sox struck quickly in the top of the second. Hoblitzel walked, then Lewis doubled off the right field fence to put two runners in scoring position for Gardner. The Boston third baseman worked the count full then sent a shot to the deepest part of the ballpark, the triangle just to the right of center field. Myers and Johnston gave chase, but by the time they could retrieve the ball and return it to the infield Gardner had crossed the plate. The home run put Boston ahead 3–2.

The Red Sox added single runs in the fourth, fifth and seventh, while Leonard took advantage of the second chance his teammates gave him. The Boston hurler allowed just three hits over the final eight frames — a double to Cutshaw in the fourth and singles to Merkle and Wheat in the fifth. He walked four and struck out three in a complete game win.

Four different Red Sox had two hits in the game, including Carrigan, who had inserted himself into the lineup in the eighth spot as Leonard's catcher.

GAME 5: RED SOX 4, ROBINS 1

	1	2	3	4	5	6	7	8	9	R	H	E
Brooklyn	0	1	0	0	0	0	0	0	0	1	3	3
Boston	0	1	2	0	1	0	0	0	X	4	7	2

WP   Ernie Shore
LP   Jeff Pfeffer

The Boston fans set a new World Series attendance record on October 12, 1916. Forty-two thousand, six hundred and twenty people crammed into Braves Field on Columbus Day, hoping to see the Red Sox clinch their third world championship in five years.

In this game, Shore, who had pitched well for eight innings in the first game before tiring, maintained his effectiveness over the full nine innings. He allowed just three hits and one unearned run, and coasted to his second victory of the series.

For the fourth time in five games, Brooklyn scored first, plating a run in the second inning. Cutshaw led off with a walk and moved around the bases on a sacrifice bunt, a groundout, and a passed ball by Cady.

The Red Sox answered against Pfeffer in the bottom of the second when Lewis tripled to left with one out and scored on a shallow fly out to left by Gardner as Wheat's throw to the plate was off line.

The score held at 1–1 until Boston's next at bat. Cady led off the Boston third with a single and Hooper reached on a one-out walk, then Olson muffed a grounder by Janvrin, allowing Cady to score and Hooper to take third. A two-out single by Shorten, who started in center, scored Hooper to give Boston a 3–1 lead.

The Red Sox added another run in the fifth when Hooper singled with two outs and Janvrin followed with a double.

Shore was dominant over the final seven innings, allowing just three singles — in the fifth, seventh and ninth. Stengel started the ninth with a single, but as the Boston crowd boisterously sang the lyrics to the popular contemporary song "This Is the End of a Perfect Day," Shore struck out Wheat.[8] Then Cutshaw grounded to Janvrin at second base for the second out, and Mowrey popped to Scott at shortstop to end the game.

The Boston fans hopped out of the stands and onto the field to celebrate with the team. The fans and players dragged Lannin out of the owner's box to lead them around the field in a parade formation as they sang "Glory, Glory, Hallelujah." In a wonderful display of sportsmanship, a gracious Charles Ebbets even joined Lannin at the front of the procession.[9]

Lewis hit for the highest average among Boston's regulars in the series, batting .353 (6–17) with two doubles and a triple, while Hooper hit .333 (7–21). Gardner batted just .176 (3–17) but led all players with two home runs and 6 RBI. Shore, who was 2–0, allowed just three earned runs in 17⅔ innings for a 1.53 ERA.

Less than three weeks later, Lannin sold the Red Sox to a group headed by New York theater magnate Harry Frazee for $675,000. A new era in Red Sox history was about to begin.

Chapter 5

The Regular Season: 75–51

In 1918 the Red Sox won their fifth world championship in fifteen years and their fourth in seven years, cementing their legacy as the most prolific dynasty of the century's first two decades. Over the course of the ensuing 86 years, all of which ended without another championship, the significance of the 1918 season would continue to grow in the minds of New Englanders. At the time, however, the 1918 Red Sox were widely acknowledged to be the least talented of Boston's early champions. And the 1918 season, like the anti-climactic World Series that followed, failed to capture the attention of baseball fans, nationally and locally, in the way that previous and subsequent baseball seasons did.

The 1918 season was played under a shroud of uncertainty due to the on-going First World War. The owners, players, and fans were all acutely aware that the season could end at any moment, pending U.S. Secretary of War Newton Baker's decision on whether baseball was an essential wartime industry. If Baker decided that it was, the players would be exempted from the draft. If he decided that it was a non-essential industry, all players aged 21–31 would have to either enter military service or find work in a defense industry. Many players didn't wait for Baker's ruling and enlisted — including Boston's player-manager Jack Barry, who had guided the team to a second-place, 90–62 finish in 1917, leftfielder Duffy Lewis, pitcher Ernie Shore, and ten other Red Sox. Other players in the league, such as Chicago White Sox slugger Joe Jackson, took preemptive measures to avoid the draft by taking jobs at shipyards where they could also play semi-pro baseball in leagues like the Delaware River Shipbuilding League. Consequently, the major league teams that took to the nation's fields as the 1918 season began bore only slight resemblances to their previous editions. And because many of the nation's male fans were overseas and those who weren't had their attention focused abroad, the game did not enjoy the following it had in previous years. Attendance in most cities, including Boston, declined by more than 50 percent, and newspaper headlines previously reserved for the heroics of men on baseball diamonds were replaced by accounts of U.S. soldiers' activities in France. In July, Secretary Baker ruled that baseball was a non-essential industry and gave the game one month to finish an abbreviated season. The last regular season games were played on Labor Day and the World Series began a month early. Then many of the players headed off to war.

The 1918 Red Sox had a completely different complexion from the team's recent championship incarnations, due to the war and three trades that Harry Frazee made in his first full off-season as Red Sox owner. On December 14, Frazee sent catcher Pinch Thomas, two minor leaguers, and $60,000 to the Philadelphia A's for catcher Wally Schang, outfielder Amos Strunk, and pitcher Joe Bush. Less than a month later, he sent third baseman Larry Gardner, centerfielder Tilly Walker, and catcher Hick Cady to the A's for star first baseman Stuffy McInnis. Having thus raided the A's, who had finished last in the American League for the third straight year in 1917, the Red Sox traded pitcher Rube Foster to the Cincinnati Reds for infielder Dave Shean. Shean filled the second base position left vacant by Barry's departure, while former International League president Edward Barrow was hired to replace Barry as manager.

The only returnees among Boston's starting position players were shortstop Everett Scott and right fielder Harry Hooper. The starting rotation featured returnees Babe Ruth, Carl Mays and Dutch Leonard, as well as Sam Jones, who had made just one start in 1917, and the newly acquired Bush.

In early April the Red Sox left their spring training camp in Hot Springs, Arkansas, and barnstormed across the deep south, playing a series of exhibition games against the Brooklyn Robins. Toward the end of the spring, Barrow experimented by putting McInnis in left field and inserting Ruth, who had previously played only pitcher, at first base. Ruth quickly showed that he could field the new position and hit several long home runs during the Red Sox' tour.

When Opening Day arrived, Ruth was back where he'd always been though, on the mound and batting ninth in the Red Sox order. For the third straight season, Ruth earned an Opening Day win, beating the A's 7–1 at Fenway Park.

The next day, Mays pitched a one-hitter and Scott singled to drive home McInnis in the last of the ninth as the Red Sox beat the A's 1–0.

In the third game, Schang hit a two-run single with the bases loaded in the last of the ninth to punctuate a 5–4 win.

The next day, Bush and Mays both earned wins in a double-header sweep of the Yankees while the Boston Marathon took place.

The Red Sox won their sixth straight game the next day, beating the Yankees 4–3, as Mays scattered 11 hits over nine innings, and Hooper broke a 3–3 tie with a double in the last of the eighth. At 6–0, the Red Sox were off to their best start ever.

Boston finally lost a game, falling to New York 11–4 on April 23. The next day, though, Ruth came off the bench as a pinch-hitter and delivered a key ninth inning hit as the Red Sox beat the Yankees 1–0 behind another stellar outing by Bush.

The Red Sox won 12 of their first 15 games, then lost six in a row. The sixth straight defeat, a 4–3 loss to Washington on May 9, dropped the Red Sox into second place for the first time. During the slump Barrow made what was considered at the time a bold decision when he penciled Ruth into the lineup at a position other than pitcher for the first time in regular season play. On May 6, the 23-year-old Ruth played first base, replacing Dick Hoblitzel, who had an injured finger, and McInnis who was struggling at the plate. The Babe responded with his second home run of the season, a long blast into the right field seats at the Polo Grounds, but Boston lost 10–3. The next day, Ruth played first again and tied a record by homering in his third straight game, but the Red Sox lost 7–2.

On May 14, Hoblitzel was appointed by the U.S. Senate to serve as a first lieutenant in the dental corps of the army. The loss further depleted the Red Sox' everyday lineup, making Ruth's bat an even more valuable commodity. Ruth continued to pitch every fourth day and play first base or left field when he wasn't pitching. He pitched and beat the Tigers 5–4 on May 15, to improve the team's record to 15–10 and vault the Red Sox back into first place. Then on May 19 he doubled home the go-ahead runs and the Red Sox beat the Tigers 3–1. Ruth's batting average stood at .407 (22–54), but the next day he was scratched from a start on the mound after collapsing in a Boston drugstore while waiting to have a prescription filled. He was diagnosed with tonsillitis and admitted to the Massachusetts Eye and Ear Infirmary where he would remain for a week.[1]

In Ruth's absence, "Sad Sam" Jones, one of the players acquired by the Red Sox in the 1916 trade that sent Tris Speaker to Cleveland, stepped into the starting rotation and pitched well. He lost to the Indians 1–0 on May 23, as Guy Morton pitched a one-hitter against the Red Sox, then he shutout the Senators and the Indians in his next two starts. When Ruth returned, Barrow told him to focus on his hitting. Ruth started on the mound against the Tigers on June 2 and lost 4–3, despite supporting his effort with a home run, then didn't make another pitching appearance for more than a month.

On June 4, Leonard pitched the second no-hitter of his career, blanking the Tigers 5–0 in Detroit. The lefty struck out Don Bush to end the game, and would have had a perfect game if not for a walk he issued to Bobby Veach in the first inning. In Leonard's gem, Ruth hit a long homer into the right field bleachers. The Babe then homered in each of the next three games, breaking the major league record he had tied earlier in the season.

Leonard pitched another shutout in his next start, beating the Indians 2–0 on June 9, then Bush blanked the White Sox 1–0 the next day. The Red Sox lost to the White Sox in the next game, then Mays shutout Chicago 7–0 on June 12th. On June 13th, the Red Sox registered their fourth shutout in five games as Leonard pitched his third shutout in a row, beating the White Sox 6–0 at Comiskey Park.

Boston finished June with a 39–28 record and a half-game lead over second-place New York. July would turn out to be the team's best month as the Red Sox won 20 of 29 games and added to their lead in the AL race. The month was not without its controversy though, as Ruth quit the team on July 2, only to return three days later. The trouble started when Barrow told Ruth to be more selective at the plate during a game in Washington. Ruth had made outs on Moxie Harper's first pitch to him in both of his first two at bats. After his chat with Barrow, he looked at three straight strikes in the sixth inning, then got in an argument with Barrow in the Red Sox dugout and threatened to punch the manager.[2] Barrow replaced Ruth in left field with Jack Stansbury, then, after the Red Sox lost 3–0, announced that he had fined Ruth $500 for insubordination. Ruth left the team in a huff and signed a contract the next day with the Bethlehem Steel Company to work in a shipyard in Chester, Pennsylvania, and play ball in the same semi-pro league as Joe Jackson. Frazee threatened legal action, issuing a statement that read, "Ruth has signed a contract with the Boston club and must play baseball with us until that contract expires. I shall notify both Ruth and Manager [Frank] Miller [of the shipyard club] of this, and if they try to use him I shall get out an injunction. After that, I will sue the Chester Shipbuilding Company for heavy damages and I believe I will win. Ruth can't get away with it. The courts will not stand for a deal like that."[3]

The Red Sox lost two of the three games they played in Ruth's absence, before he returned on July 5 to make his first start on the mound in five weeks. The Babe's sudden return to the pitcher's box fueled speculation that Barrow's unwillingness to pitch Ruth had led to the star's tantrum. In any case, Ruth pitched well in his first game back and scored the winning run on a McInnis triple in the tenth inning as the Red Sox beat the A's 4–3 at Shibe Park.

The Red Sox reclaimed first place the next day, as the Babe drove in three runs with a bases-clearing triple in the sixth inning to lead the Red Sox past the Indians 5–4 in the first of 17 straight games to be played at Fenway Park. With the win, Boston improved to 42–31 and moved half a game ahead of Cleveland. The Red Sox went on to win 14 of the 17 games on the home stand and by the end of July enjoyed a 4½ game lead over the second-place Indians. The baseball world was in turmoil though. On July 20 Secretary Baker ruled that baseball was a non-essential industry and that all draft eligible players had to either "work or fight." Some American League owners, like Cleveland's James C. Dunn, lobbied for the immediate cancellation of the baseball season, while others, like Frazee, said the game should continue for as long as possible.[4] The Boston owner went so far as to tell the *Boston Globe*, "If the proposition were put up to the fighting men themselves they would vote 1,000 to 1 to have the game kept going here at home."[5] Initially AL president Ban Johnson sided with the patriots, decreeing that the league would shut down after the completion of games on July 21, but when a majority of owners informed Johnson they preferred to continue playing, he relented. After Secretary Baker agreed to suspend enforcement of the work or fight order until September 1, Johnson announced the league would play its final regular season games on Labor Day, September 2.[6]

Harry Hooper hit .289 for the 1918 Red Sox. (Library of Congress)

Ruth won nine of his 11 pitching decisions after returning from his suspension and reclaiming his spot in the starting rotation, and he continued to swat home runs at a record pace. The Red Sox never relinquished their league lead over the final 53 games of the abbreviated season.

After beating the St. Louis Browns 3–1 at Fenway Park on

August 24, Ruth learned that his 45-year-old father had been beaten to death in Baltimore and that the assailant had been Ruth's own uncle.[7] The grieving star, who had already left the team twice during the season, left for a third time. But he returned on August 31 to post a 6–1 win against the A's and clinch Boston's sixth AL pennant since 1903.

Boston split a Labor Day double-header with New York to finish the season 75–51, 2½ games ahead of Cleveland and 4 games ahead of Washington.

Ruth finished eighth in the league with a .300 batting average, second with 26 doubles, tied for first with 11 home runs, and tied for third with 66 RBI, even though he appeared in only 95 games. The Red Sox finished fourth in the league in runs with 474, sixth with a .249 batting average, and third with 15 home runs. Besides Ruth, four other Boston players hit one long-ball apiece: Fred Thomas, Hooper, George Whiteman, and Jack Coffee. Hooper finished third in the league with 81 runs to go with a .289 batting average and 44 RBI, while McInnis (.272, 56 RBI), Shean (.264, 34 RBI) and Strunk (.257, 35 RBI) performed well in their debut seasons in Boston. Whiteman, a 35-year old career minor leaguer, appeared in 71 games as a left fielder and batted .266.

Ruth finished with a 13–7 record, one shutout, and a 2.22 ERA in 20 pitching appearances. He was one of five Red Sox starters to finish with a sub-3.00 ERA. Mays led the staff with a 21–13 record, 8 shutouts, and a 2.21 ERA, while the team also got solid seasons from Bush (15–15, 7 shutouts, 2.11 ERA), Jones (16–5, 5 shutouts, 2.25 ERA) and Leonard (8–6, 3 shutouts, 2.72 ERA). Boston's 2.31 ERA placed second in the league to Washington, while its 26 shutouts were seven more than any other team had.

The Postseason: 4–2

The Red Sox entered the World Series as underdogs against a Chicago Cubs team that had gone 84–45, while running away with the National League crown. Chicago's pitching was just as good as Boston's, if not better, while its balanced lineup had scored more runs than any other team in the league.

Although Boston's 1918 championship would later come to represent the end of a mythical era in Boston hardball history, to contemporaries the series was more notable for the disconnect it revealed between the heroes fighting for the U.S. in Europe and the supposed heroes of the baseball world. After the 1917 season, baseball's National Commission, which consisted of AL president Ban Johnson, NL president John Heydler, and Cincinnati Reds owner August Herrmann, proposed a change to the way World Series gate receipts were divided among the players. Instead of splitting the purse between the players of the two teams involved in the series, the Commission suggested awarding incrementally smaller shares to the first, second, third, and fourth place finishers in each league. The intention was to give players on all teams an incentive to finish in the upper division even when a run at the pennant became unrealistic. The game's owners approved the new plan in December of 1917, without consulting the players and without the foreknowledge that the war would severely diminish World Series attendance. The first four games of the 1918 World Series went on as planned. Due to the wartime travel restrictions, the first three games were played in Chicago, then the series shifted to Boston where the final four games would be played if necessary. The Red Sox and Cubs rode the same train east on September 7 and then played Game Four in Boston. After that, things got ugly. Instead of the sell-out crowds of 40,000 that the Red Sox typically attracted for the World Series, a third of the seats at Fenway Park were unoccupied for Game Four. Realizing that their World Series shares were going to be far smaller than the $3,600 and $2,600 that had been awarded to the champion White Sox and runner-up Giants in 1917, the players staged a strike on the morning of the fifth game. As wounded combat veterans and other fans waited for Game Five to begin, the Commission begged and pleaded with Harry Hooper, who had been chosen by his teammates to represent them, and Les Mann, who negotiated on behalf of the Cubs, to finish the series. Finally, after a delay of more than an hour, the players took the field amidst a chorus of boos. The next day, many angry fans stayed away, and so it was that the Red Sox won their fifth championship before the smallest World Series crowd in ten years and the smallest in Boston since 1903.

The Cubs pitching staff featured the three biggest winners in the NL in 1918, Hippo Vaughn, who went 22–10 and led the NL with a 1.74 ERA, Claude Hendrix, who went 20–7 with a 2.78 ERA, and Lefty Tyler, who went 19–8 with a 2.00 ERA. Fourth starter Phil Douglas was no slouch either, compiling a 10–9 record and a 2.13 ERA. While Chicago's 2.18 ERA was the best in either league, the Cubs offense led the NL with 538 runs and finished second with a .265 batting average. Shortstop Charlie Hollocher led the league with 161 hits and 202 total bases, and finished fourth with a .316 batting average, and fourth with 72 runs. Hollocher hit second in the batting order behind right-fielder Max Flack, who had a .257 average, 74 runs, 4 HR and 41 RBI. Mann (.288, 2 HR, 55 RBI) played left field and batted third, followed by center fielder Dode Paskert (.286, 3 HR, 59 RBI), and first baseman Fred Merkle (.297, 3 HR, 65 RBI). Seven different Cubs hit more than one home run during the 1918 season, while only Ruth accomplished the feat for the Red Sox. The long-ball did not come into play in the series though, and the teams combined to score just 19 runs — nine for the Red Sox, 10 for the Cubs. The Red Sox prevailed in six games, thanks to the pitching of Ruth and Mays.

1918 World Series: Red Sox 4, Cubs 2

Game 1: Red Sox 1, Cubs 0

	1	2	3	4	5	6	7	8	9	R	H	E
Boston	0	0	0	1	0	0	0	0	0	1	5	0
Chicago	0	0	0	0	0	0	0	0	0	0	6	0

WP   Babe Ruth
LP   Hippo Vaughn

For the first three games the Cubs borrowed Comiskey Park from the White Sox because it could hold twice as many fans as Wrigley Field, then known as "Cubs Park." During the 1917 World Series the White Sox had drawn more than 30,000 fans to each of their three home games, but just 19,274 people turned out on September 5, 1918 for the first game between the Red Sox and Cubs. Further reducing the gate revenue, the cost of box seats had been lowered from $5 to $3 due to the war's economic impact.

Those in attendance watched Ruth out-duel Vaughn 1–0, but more significantly they helped establish a new baseball tradition. During the traditional seventh inning stretch, a military band broke into "The Star Spangled Banner," and the fans sang along. The song, which would later become the National Anthem, has been played at every World Series game since.

After hurling 13 consecutive scoreless innings to finish his work in the 1916 World Series, Ruth nearly saw his scoreless streak end in the first inning of the 1918 series when he allowed two-out singles to Mann and Paskert, and then walked Merkle. Ruth escaped the bases-loaded jam though, getting Cubs second baseman Charlie Pick to fly out to Whiteman in left field.

Ruth pitched out more trouble in the third. Flack led off with a single and advanced to second on a bunt and to third on a groundout, but Paskert grounded to Scott for the third out.

Meanwhile, Vaughn, a 30-year-old southpaw who had earned his nickname due to his hulking physique, retired the Red Sox easily over the first three innings. But in the fourth, Shean led off with a walk, took second on a single to center by Whiteman, and scored on a McInnis single to left. Shean never hesitated rounding third and slid home just inches ahead of Mann's throw to the plate.

The Cubs made another run at Ruth in the sixth, but he rose to the challenge. After singles by Paskert and Merkle put two runners in scoring position, Ruth got Cubs third baseman Charlie Deal to fly to Whiteman to end the threat.

In the ninth, Ruth retired Merkle on a fly ball to left, got pinch-hitter Bob O'Farrell on a pop to third, gave up a bunt single to Deal, and then retired catcher Bill Killefer on a fly to Hooper. Ruth finished with one walk, four strikeouts, and a string of 22⅓ consecutive scoreless World Series innings pitched dating back to 1916. The Babe, who batted ninth, went 0–3 with two strikeouts against Vaughn.

"It was anybody's ball game all the way," Cubs manager Fred Mitchell said afterward. "They got their hits at the right time and we didn't. The base on balls to Shean at the start of the fourth beat us."[8]

GAME 2: CUBS 3, RED SOX 1

	1	2	3	4	5	6	7	8	9	R	H	E
Boston	0	0	0	0	0	0	0	0	1	1	6	1
Chicago	0	3	0	0	0	0	0	0	X	3	7	1

WP Lefty Tyler
LP Joe Bush

The second game featured another small crowd, a melee between two coaches, and some questionable managing by Barrow, who opted not to use Ruth as a pinch-hitter with the game on the line in the ninth inning. As the Red Sox' final rally fell short, the Cubs evened the series with a 3–1 win.

Bush started for the Red Sox, and struggled early. "Bullet Joe" allowed a leadoff single to Flack in the first, before escaping unharmed. He began the second by issuing a free pass to Merkle, and this time it cost him. The second hitter of the inning, Pick, chopped a swinging bunt down the third base line that went for a hit. Then, after Deal popped out, Killefer doubled home the Cubs' first run. Tyler followed with a single up the middle to put Chicago on top 3–0.

After the second inning, a fight broke out between the two teams. Red Sox third base coach Heinie Wagner had spent the first two innings heckling Tyler from the coaches' box. As Wagner took his position to start the third, Chicago coach Otto Knabe exchanged words with him and the two began grappling. As Knabe dragged Wagner toward the Chicago bench, the Red Sox players sprinted across the field to his rescue.

When the game resumed, Tyler continued to mesmerize the Boston hitters, holding them to one hit over the first five innings and to two hits over the first seven. Boston reached the left-hander for a pair of singles in the eighth, but Schang, who had led off with a single, was thrown out by Flack when he tried to take third on a one-out single by Hooper, and Boston failed to score.

The Red Sox bats made some louder noise in the ninth when Strunk and Whiteman began the inning with back-to-back triples. Then Scott walked with one-out. The Red Sox had the tying runs aboard with Fred Thomas due up. Barrow looked to his bench and summoned not the league's most feared home run hitter, Ruth, but Jean Dubuc, to pinch-hit. A pitcher, who had appeared in just five games in 1918 while collecting one hit in six at bats, Dubuc promptly struck out. Schang stepped to the plate next and popped out on Tyler's first pitch to end the game.

Barrow defended his decision not to use Ruth by pointing out that Ruth had struggled batting against the left-handed Vaughn the day before. And Mitchell admitted that he had left the left-handed Tyler in the game, despite his struggles, to keep Ruth on the bench.

Game 3: Red Sox 2, Cubs 1

	1	2	3	4	5	6	7	8	9	R	H	E
Boston	0	0	0	2	0	0	0	0	0	2	7	0
Chicago	0	0	0	0	1	0	0	0	0	1	7	1

WP   Carl Mays
LP   Hippo Vaughn

The third game was played Saturday, September 7, and it drew the largest crowd of the series. Although 27,054 fans filed through the turnstiles on Chicago's South Side, the crowd was still smaller than any gathering during the 1917 series. For the third straight game, those on hand saw a crisply played game that was completed in less than two hours. Vaughn started for Chicago on one day of rest, and though he was excellent, Mays, who made his first appearance of the series, was a little bit better. With the Red Sox leading 2–1 in the ninth inning, Pick was tagged out at the plate — as he attempted to score from second base on a passed ball — to end the game.

Hooper led off the game with a single, and Whiteman did the same in the second, but the Red Sox failed to score in each inning. In the fourth, Strunk struck out to start the Red Sox' turn, but his teammates rallied for two runs. Whiteman got things started when Vaughn hit him with a pitch. McInnis followed with a single to left, then Schang bounced a grounder up the middle to bring home Whiteman with the first run and move McInnis to third. When Scott hit a chopper back to the mound and Vaughn fumbled it, McInnis raced home with the second run. The next batter, Thomas singled to right and Flack fielded the ball and threw out Schang at the plate. Then Mays lined to center to end the inning.

The Cubs cut the lead in half in the fifth inning when Pick led off with a double and scored one out later on a Killefer single.

Mays allowed two hits in the sixth before striking out Merkle to end the inning, then he set down the Cubs without difficulty in the seventh and eighth. In the ninth, he quickly retired the first two batters, Paskert and Merkle, before allowing Pick to reach on a slow grounder to second base. Pick then stole second on Mays' first pitch to pinch-hitter Turner Barber. With a two balls and two strikes count on Barber, Mays threw an outside pitch that bounced off Schang's catcher's mitt and rolled a few feet away. The catcher pounced on the ball and fired to third, but his throw was too late to catch Pick who slid into the bag just ahead of Thomas' tag. When Pick noticed that the momentum of his slide had jarred the ball out of Thomas' glove and sent it rolling toward the Cubs dugout, he took off for home. But Thomas picked up the ball and threw to Schang who tagged Pick for the final out.

Having sent his team's best pitcher to the mound in two of the first three games and watched his team narrowly lose both contests, Mitchell said, "I thought Vaughn would beat them, but it seems we can't get any runs for him. Of course, we'll have to go some now to win the series, but it is not over by any means."[9]

Barrow, who still had his ace in the hole, sounded more confident. "We are in the lead, and intend to remain there," the Red Sox manager said. "I think we shall win the series, because I believe we have the better club. I am not ready to say who shall pitch [Game Four], but it is not unlikely that Ruth will be sent to the mound."[10]

GAME 4: RED SOX 3, CUBS 2

	1	2	3	4	5	6	7	8	9	R	H	E
Chicago	0	0	0	0	0	0	0	2	0	2	7	1
Boston	0	0	0	2	0	0	0	1	X	3	4	0

WP Babe Ruth
LP Phil Douglas
SV Joe Bush

As the Red Sox and Cubs shared an eastbound Michigan Central train on Sunday, Boston's championship aspirations were nearly dealt a serious blow. During the ride, Ruth hurt his pitching hand in a playful wrestling match with relief pitcher Walt Kinney. Ruth took a wild swing at Kinney just as the train lurched to one side and he accidentally struck the train's steel wall. Ruth's middle knuckle became quite swollen, but he insisted he would be able to pitch the next day.[11]

Ruth took the mound in Game Four with his middle finger painted with iodine. If the injury detracted from his effectiveness, the fact was lost upon the 22,183 Boston fans who watched the game. He held the Cubs scoreless over the first seven innings, setting a new record with $29\frac{2}{3}$ consecutive scoreless World Series innings. The record would stand until 1962 when White Ford stretched his streak to 33 innings. Ruth also tripled home the first two Boston runs. He tired in the late innings though, and needed an assist from Bush to finish a 3–2 Boston win.

The Red Sox won despite collecting just four hits and two walks against Tyler and Douglas. The Cubs reached Ruth for seven hits and six walks in eight-plus innings, before Bush pitched out of the trouble Ruth had left behind in the ninth.

Boston got on the scoreboard with two runs in the bottom of the fourth. After Tyler walked Shean to start the inning, then walked Whiteman with one-out, Ruth clocked a two-out triple off the right field fence, putting Boston ahead 2–0.

The score held until the eighth when the Cubs reached Ruth for a pair of runs. Killefer started the inning with a walk, then Hendrix pinch-hit for Tyler and delivered a single to left field. After Ruth threw a wild pitch, allowing both runners to advance, a groundout by Hollocher brought home Chicago's first run, and a single by Mann brought home the tying run.

Boston answered quickly against Douglas in the bottom of the eighth. Schang started the rally with a single to center and moved to second on a passed ball by Killefer. Hooper then laid down a bunt that appeared to be headed for foul territory, but Douglas picked it up and threw wildly to first base. The ball sailed over Merkle's head and into right field, allowing Schang to race home with the go-ahead run.

In the ninth, Ruth allowed a leadoff single to Merkle, then walked pinch-hitter Rollie Zeider. Barrow made his way to the mound and took the ball. He sent the Babe out to left field to replace Whiteman, and brought Bush in to pitch. The hard-throwing right-hander quickly squelched the Cubs rally, getting Chuck Wortman to bunt into a fielder's choice and Barber to hit into a six-four-three double play to end the game.

Afterwards, a cocky Barrow said, "We now have the big edge. The players came through as I have predicted, and when things looked bad they proved themselves a game bunch of men. Sam Jones will pitch the fifth game and I'll have Mays in reserve. We'll finish up the series with the next game."[12]

GAME 5: CUBS 3, RED SOX 0

	1	2	3	4	5	6	7	8	9	R	H	E
Chicago	0	0	1	0	0	0	0	2	0	3	7	0
Boston	0	0	0	0	0	0	0	0	0	0	5	0

WP   Hippo Vaughn
LP   Sam Jones

The fifth game was an hour late in starting due to a players strike. The players refused to dress then engaged the National Commission in a negotiating session beneath the Fenway Park grandstands. They asked the three commissioners to guarantee $2,000 to the players of the winning team and $1,400 to the players of the losing team. The drunken commissioners—who had spent the morning at the Copley Plaza Hotel bar—would offer no such promise.[13] The new system, which the owners had voted upon the previous December, was binding they said, and would be upheld.

As mounted police kept the nearly 25,000 angry fans from rioting, former Boston mayor John Fitzgerald implored the players to relent. Finally, Hooper was the voice of reason. "We will play," he said, "not because we think we are getting a fair deal, because we are not. But we'll play for the sake of the game, for the sake of the public, which has always given us its loyal support, and for the sake of the wounded soldiers and sailors who are in the grandstand waiting for us."[14]

When the players finally emerged from the dugouts, they were greeted by a mixture of cheers and boos, but mostly boos. Starting for the second time on short rest, Vaughn pitched his third excellent game of the series and finally earned a win. He scattered five hits over nine innings while striking out four. He faced just 30 batters, thanks to three double plays turned behind him, and the Cubs prevailed 3–0.

Chicago scored a run against Jones in the third inning when Hollocher walked with two outs, stole second, and scampered home on a double by Mann, and two runs in the eighth, when Flack walked, Hollocher singled, and Paskert doubled home both runners.

GAME 6: RED SOX 2, CUBS 1

	1	2	3	4	5	6	7	8	9	R	H	E
Chicago	0	0	0	1	0	0	0	0	0	1	3	2
Boston	0	0	2	0	0	0	0	0	X	2	5	0

Left to right: Mrs. E.D. Smith, Mrs. Harry Frazee, Harry Frazee Jr., Harry Frazee, and Thomas Barry. (Courtesy of the Boston Public Library, Print Department)

WP   Carl Mays
LP   Lefty Tyler

Nearly ten thousand fewer fans turned out to watch Game Six than had filed through the Fenway Park turnstiles the day before. The newspaper writers had drawn and quartered the players for thinking of their own personal fortunes when the nation was a war, and many fans had grown disenchanted. Thus, the Red Sox clinched the 1918 championship in front of just 15,238 fans. They won by a single run for the fourth time in the series.

Both Red Sox runs were unearned and both crossed the plate in the third inning. Mays led off with a walk against Tyler, then took second on a Hooper sacrifice. Tyler then walked Shean. Both runners advanced as Strunk grounded out to second base. Whiteman then lined a shot to right field. Flack came running straight in toward the infield to make the play and had the ball in his glove momentarily before it popped out, allowing both runners to score.

The Cubs scored their run in the fourth when Flack singled, took second on a groundout, stole third, and scored on a Merkle single. After allowing three hits over the first four innings, Mays held the Cubs hitless over the final five innings. The only Chicago base runner in the final five frames was Flack, who walked in the sixth.

In the ninth, Mays got Flack to pop to third, Hollocher to fly to left, and Mann to ground to Shean at second to end the game.

"It was a wonderful series," Barrow said. "The Red Sox played machine-like baseball and presented a defense the Cubs could not break down."[15]

The Cubs' skipper, Mitchell, said, "The pitching was the best in World Series games for years. It was a tough series to lose."[16]

Pick led all series regulars with a .389 batting average, while Whiteman and McInnis paced the Red Sox with .250 averages. Ruth, who drove in two runs with his lone series hit, was the only Boston player to collect more than one RBI in the series. The Babe finished with a 2–0 record and a 1.06 ERA, while Mays went 2–0 with a 1.00 ERA. Boston's team ERA was 1.70. For the Cubs, Vaughn was 1–2 with a 1.00 ERA, while Tyler was 1–1 with a 1.17 ERA, and Douglas was 0–1 with a 0.00 ERA. The Cubs' 1.04 ERA represents the lowest ever for a World Series loser.

Just as the players had feared, their shares were the smallest ever awarded: $1,103 for each Red Sox player, and $671 for each Cub. The players were also asked to donate 10 percent of their cut to the Red Cross. Adding further insult to injury, the National Commission decided not to award the players the customary commemorative pins (a precursor to today's rings) that had always been presented to the players of past World Series, as a penalty for the brief strike.[17]

After 1918, Boston's baseball fortunes took a dramatic turn for the worse. Frazee soon found himself in insurmountable debt and had to sell all of the Red Sox' star players to keep his theatrical interests and baseball team afloat. After the 1919 season, he sold Ruth to the Yankees for $100,000 and a $300,000 loan from Yankee owner Jake Ruppert. The Yankee Colonel held the mortgage to Fenway Park as collateral and over the next several years he purchased such Red Sox stars as Lewis, Shore, Mays, Leonard, Schang, Scott, Bush and Jones, from Frazee, who then turned around and returned the money as repayment on his loan. Even Barrow wound up in New York, becoming the Yankees' general manager in 1920. After purging the Red Sox of all of their valuable players, Frazee sold the team to a group headed by former St. Louis Browns business manager Robert Quinn in 1923.

Chapter 6

The Regular Season: 104–50

After beating the Cubs in the 1918 World Series, the Red Sox endured a 28-year drought before winning another American League pennant. Harry Frazee's ill-fated personnel decisions, which included selling Babe Ruth and several other players to the Yankees, led to 15 straight losing seasons between 1919 and 1933. Finally Tom Yawkey, bankrolled by his father's millions, bought the Red Sox from Robert Quinn in January of 1933, and the team's fortunes began to brighten. Joe Cronin took over as the Red Sox manager in 1935 and the team finished at .500 or better eight times over the next 11 seasons.

The Red Sox team that took the field to start the 1946 season was completely different from the squad that had finished seventh in the eight-team AL in 1945 with a record of 71–83. World War II was over and Ted Williams, Johnny Pesky, Bobby Doerr, Dom DiMaggio and several other prominent players rejoined the team after receiving their military discharges. Only one position player who started for the Red Sox in 1945 played a role on the 1946 team, Catfish Metkovich, who appeared in 86 games as an outfielder in 1946 after serving as the starting first baseman the year before. Metkovich was moved off first base to make room for Rudy York, whom the Red Sox acquired from Detroit in a January trade that sent shortstop Eddie Lake to the Tigers. Lake, had hit .280 with 12 homers and 74 RBI for the Red Sox in 1945, but became expendable when Pesky returned from the war. York was a nine-year veteran and five-time All-Star, but the Tigers needed to make room at first base for aging Hank Greenberg — who was no longer an effective defender in the outfield. Among pitchers, only Dave Ferris, who won 21 games for the 1945 Red Sox, made a contribution in 1946.

From the very start, the 1946 Red Sox were dominant. They won 21 of their first 24 games and 41 of their first 50, and held first place for all but two days of the season — April 24 and 25.

After missing three complete seasons while serving as a Navy pilot, Williams blasted a 400-foot homer on Opening Day to lead the Red Sox to a 6–3 win in Washington as President Harry Truman watched. The Red Sox won their first five games before the Philadelphia A's Bobo Newsom blanked them 3–0 at Fenway Park in the second game of a double-header on April 21.

Boston moved into first place to stay on April 26 when Ferris shut out the A's 7–0. The win was the second of what would be a 15-game win streak that still stands as the longest in team history. Memorable games during the streak included a May 2 game at Fenway in which Williams blasted a tenth-inning homer to give the Red Sox a 5–4 win over the Tigers. Then, two nights later, Williams drove in three runs with a homer and a double as the Red Sox beat Bob Feller and the Indians, 6–2. After a rainout, the Red Sox extended their streak to eleven wins in a row with a double-header sweep of the St. Louis Browns at Fenway Park on Monday, May 6. In the first game, Pesky grounded out in the eighth inning to end a streak of 11 straight plate appearances in which he had reached base safely, leaving him one safety shy of the record. It would not be long before Pesky got another chance to etch his name into the record books, though. Just two days later, he became the first American Leaguer to score six runs in a game in Boston's 14–10 win against Chicago. The Red Sox improved to 21–3 with a 5–4 win at Yankee Stadium on May 10 that put them 5½ games ahead of second-place New York. The win streak ended the next day, when "Tiny" Bonham, a right-hander who stood six-feet, two-inches tall and weighed more than 220 pounds, beat the Red Sox, 2–0

It was not long before the Red Sox found themselves in the midst of another prolonged win streak, though. They won 12 in a row from May 29 through June 11, outscoring their opponents 89 to 37 in the process, and improving to 41–9.

Fittingly, the All-Star Game was held at Fenway Park and no player shined more brightly than Williams. The "Splendid Splinter" had a walk, two singles, and two home runs in the game. He scored four runs and drove in five in the American League's 12–0 victory. The highlight of the day came in the eighth inning when Williams blasted a three-run homer into the right field bullpen against Rip Sewell's famous blooper pitch. The pitch, which the Pittsburgh pitcher called an "eephus ball," had an arc to it that rose twenty feet above the ground, and before Williams' clout no player had ever connected with it for a home run. Six other Red Sox joined Williams on the AL team, DiMaggio, Doerr, Pesky, catcher Hal Wagner, York, and pitchers Ferriss and Mickey Harris.

After finishing the first half of the season with a 54–23 record, the Red Sox won nine of their first ten games after the break.

On July 14, Cleveland's player-manager Lou Boudreau had a home run and four doubles in the first game of a double-header against the Red Sox at Fenway, setting a record for the most extra-base hits in a game. But Boudreau's Indians lost, 11–10, as Williams drove in eight runs, the last coming on his third homer of the day in the ninth inning. Boudreau decided he had had enough of Williams beating him, and in the second game the "Boudreau Shift" was born. In his autobiography, *My Turn at Bat*, Williams remembered the Indians' unusual defensive alignment against him that day:

> When I came up for the second time in the second game, the Indians started moving around, swinging to the right. The third baseman, Kenny Keltner, moved behind the bag at second; the shortstop, Boudreau, moved to the right of second base; the center fielder, Pat Seerey, moved into the right fielder's position; the right fielder moved to the line; the second baseman moved closer to first and back on the grass in short right; the first baseman moved to the line behind first. The only man remaining to cover the entire area left of second base was the left fielder, George Case, and he was about thirty feet behind the skin of the infield.[1]

Johnny Pesky, on furlough from the Navy, visits the Red Sox front offices at Fenway Park. (Courtesy of the Boston Public Library, Print Department)

Williams walked twice and grounded out in three plate appearances against the shift, as the Red Sox won 6–4. The unusual defensive approach would become a common strategy employed throughout the AL against Williams, who steadfastly refused to shorten his swing and hit to the left side.

On July 27 York had the best day of his career, hitting grand slams in both the second and fifth innings of a 13–6 win against St. Louis. The slugging first baseman also had a two-run double and collected 10 RBI.

Ted Williams accepts congratulations after a home run. (Courtesy of the Boston Public Library, Print Department)

After posting a 20–10 record in July, the Red Sox went 21–11 in August, and led the AL by as many as 16 games in early September. On the verge of clinching the pennant, the team began to struggle for the first time all season, losing six in a row between September 6 and 11. "The whole team lost its zip, one of those miserable, endless things," Williams remembered. "When you get off to the kind of start we did, you're not expected to have slumps."[2]

Finally, Williams and his teammates snapped out of their funk. On September 13, Tex Hughson shutout the Indians 1–0 at League Park and Williams drove home the lone run with an inside-the-park home run to left field against Boudreau's shift. Williams sliced the ball over the head of Seerey, who was stationed behind the shortstop's normal position, and the ball rolled into the deepest part of the ballpark, 460 feet from home plate. Of Williams' 521 career home runs, this was the only one that didn't leave the yard, but it was an important one. It clinched at least a tie for the AL title. Later that day, the Yankees defeated the Tigers to give the Red Sox the pennant. When word of Detroit's loss reached the Red Sox at the Statler Hotel, the players celebrated along with Yawkey, who had made the trip to Cleveland so that he could be with the team.[3]

The Red Sox had a 13–10 record in September, their worst month of the season, but still managed to win the AL by 12 games over second-place Detroit.

The Red Sox' 104 wins fell one short of the team record set in 1912. And their 61–16 record at Fenway Park reflected the most home wins ever by a Red Sox team. With such a fine team to watch and the soldiers returning home, the Red Sox set a new home attendance record in 1946, surpassing the one million mark for the first time ever. Some 1,416,944 spectators visited the fens, more than double the number that had turned out the year before.

The 28-year-old Williams was awarded his long-overdue first MVP Award after the season. He finished second in the league in batting with a .342 average, second in home runs with 38, and second in RBI with 123. He led the league in walks (156), runs (142), total bases (342), on base percentage (.497) and slugging (.667). Pesky led the league with 208 hits, while batting .335, while Doerr (.271, 18 HR, 116 RBI) and DiMaggio (.316, 7 HR, 73 RBI) reverted to pre-war form, and York (.276, 17 HR, 119 RBI) enjoyed a productive first season in Boston. As a team, the Red Sox scored a league-best 792 runs, while leading the AL with a .271 batting average. Their 109 home runs placed second in the league, 27 behind the Yankees.

Ferris finished with the third most wins in the AL, going 25–6 with a 3.25 ERA in what would be the finest of his four full big league seasons. Hughson finished fourth in the league in wins with a 20–11 record and 2.75 ERA, while the left-handed Harris (17–9, 3.64 ERA) and Joe Dobson (13–7, 3.24 ERA) rounded out the rotation. The Red Sox finished fourth in the league with a 3.38 ERA. The pitching staff was supported by a defense that committed a league-low 139 errors.

The Postseason: 3–4

While the Red Sox built an early lead and coasted to the AL pennant, their World Series opponents had to fight to the end, and then some, to win the National League title. The St. Louis Cardinals and Brooklyn Dodgers finished the 154-game schedule with identical 96–58 records, marking the first time two teams finished tied for first in either the NL or AL. After National League president Ford Frick decided the two teams would play a best-of-three game series to determine the champion, the Cardinals won the first two games to clinch the pennant at Ebbets Field in Brooklyn on October 3.

Meanwhile, Cronin was worried that his Red Sox would get rusty while they waited for the NL playoff to take place. The last game of the regular season had been September 29, and the World Series was not due to start until October 6. To keep the Red Sox sharp, a team of AL All-Stars was dispatched to Boston to play a three-game exhibition series against the Red Sox that would take place while the Cardinals and Dodgers battled for the NL crown. The series turned out to be a grave mistake. In the fifth inning of the first game, the 2,000 fans at chilly Fenway Park watched in horror as Washington southpaw Mickey Haefner drilled Williams with a pitch. Haefner threw a sidearm curveball that never broke and the ball hit Williams squarely in the right elbow. Within minutes the joint had swollen up like a balloon. As a result of the injury, Williams was unable to take batting practice in the days leading to the World Series.

Further casting a shadow on what should have been Williams' and the Red Sox' finest hour, on the eve of the series *Boston Daily Record* columnist Dave Egan, the dean of Boston sports writers at the time, published a story in which he claimed that as soon as the series ended, Williams would be traded to the Tigers for pitcher Hal Newhowser.[4]

Despite Williams' injury and the rumors of an impending trade, the Red Sox were heavy

In the Fenway Park dugout, left to right: Johnny Pesky, Bobby Doerr, Pinky Higgins, Rip Russell and Rudy York. (Courtesy of the Boston Public Library, Print Department)

favorites to beat the Cardinals. St. Louis was nonetheless a dangerous team that could hit, pitch, and field exceptionally well. A trio of future-hall-of-famers paced the Cardinals offensively: first baseman Stan Musial, second baseman Red Schoendienst, and right fielder Enos Slaughter. Musial led the league in a bevy of offensive categories in 1946, including runs (124), hits (228), doubles (50), triples (20), batting average (.365), slugging (.587), and total bases (366). He finished second in on base percentage (.434) and third in RBI (103). Slaughter, meanwhile, led the NL in RBI with 130, and finished second in runs (100) and total bases (283), and third in hits (183), home runs (18), and slugging (.465), while batting .300. Schoendienst hit .281 and led all NL second basemen with a .984 fielding percentage in his second big league season. Third baseman Whitey Kurowski also had a fine season, hitting 14 home runs and driving in 89 runs to go with a .301 average. St. Louis led the league in runs (712) and batting average (.265). As for the pitching staff, manager Eddie Dyer counted three talented left-handers among his top four starters: Howie Pollet (21–10, 2.10 ERA), Harry Brecheen (15–15, 2.49 ERA), and Al Brazle (11–10, 3.29 ERA). Right-handers Murry Dickson (15–6, 2.88 ERA), Johnny Beazley (7–5, 4.46 ERA), and Ken

Burkhart (6–3, 2.88 ERA) also contributed. The Cardinals led the NL with a 3.01 ERA, 75 complete games and 18 shutouts. Defensively, St. Louis was the class of the league, making just 124 errors.

The Cardinals matched up well against the Red Sox. Their left-handed pitchers neutralized Williams and Pesky. Brecheen, especially, shined in the series, posting a 3–0 record and a 0.45 ERA. The series was a seesaw affair. The Red Sox won the first game, then the Cardinals won, then the Red Sox won, then the Cardinals won, and so on, until the seventh game when the Cardinals snapped the pattern.

1946 World Series: Cardinals 4, Red Sox 3

Game 1: Red Sox 3, Cardinals 2

	1	2	3	4	5	6	7	8	9	10	R	H	E
Boston	0	1	0	0	0	0	0	0	1	1	3	9	2
St. Louis	0	0	0	0	0	1	0	1	0	0	2	7	0

WP Earl Johnson
LP Howie Pollet

The series opened on a sweltering Sunday afternoon in St. Louis. More than 36,000 fans crammed into Sportsman's Park to watch. The old stadium featured three tiers of seating around a field that measured 426 feet to center field, but just 354 feet in the power alleys.

Both starting pitchers were excellent — Hughson for Boston and Pollet for St. Louis — and the game was knotted 2–2 at the end of nine innings, setting the stage for a game-winning homer by York in the tenth.

The National Leaguers showed early on that they had studied the latest approaches to defending Williams, shifting seven defenders to the right side of the diamond whenever he came to bat. And it paid off. Williams reached Pollet for only a harmless sixth-inning single in three official trips to the plate.

The Red Sox scored first, pushing across a run in the second when a Pinky Higgins single scored York, who had reached base when he was hit by a pitch.

The Cardinals tied the game at 1–1 against Hughson in the sixth. Schoendienst reached on an infield single off the pitcher's glove and scored when Musial blasted a two-out double off the right field wall. Musial took third on the play on a throwing error by right-fielder Tom McBride. Then Slaughter was walked intentionally and Kurowski was hit by a pitch. But Hughson struck out 20-year-old catcher Joe Garagiola to strand the bases loaded.

The Cardinals took a 2–1 lead in the eighth when Kurowski singled with two outs and came around when Garagiola hit a high fly ball to center that DiMaggio lost in the sun. "The Little Professor" picked up the ball after it bounced and fired to Pesky, who relayed to third base to nab Garagiola. Nonetheless, the go-ahead run had crossed the plate before the inning's third out was recorded, at least according to home plate umpire Lee Ballanfant. Cronin argued fiercely to the contrary, but to no avail.

The Red Sox rallied in the ninth. Higgins and pinch-hitter Rip Russell singled with one out. Then Pollet struck out pinch-hitter Roy Partee and got two quick strikes on McBride to bring the Cardinals within one strike of victory. McBride swung at the next pitch and bounced it toward shortstop Marty Marion. It appeared the grounder would end the game, but at the last instant the ball took a funny hop and eluded Marion's glove. Higgins raced home on the single to tie the game.

After Boston lefthander Earl Johnson retired the Cardinals in order in the ninth, the game went into extra innings, marking the first time since 1924 that a World Series opener required extra frames. DiMaggio grounded out and Williams flied out to start the tenth, then York blasted a Pollet delivery into the left field bleachers to give Boston a 3–2 lead.

In the bottom of the tenth, an error by Pesky enabled the Cardinals to put a runner on third base with two outs, but Slaughter flied out to end the game.

Game 2: Cardinals 3, Red Sox 0

	1	2	3	4	5	6	7	8	9	R	H	E
Boston	0	0	0	0	0	0	0	0	0	0	4	1
St. Louis	0	0	1	0	2	0	0	0	X	3	6	0

WP   Harry Brecheen
LP   Mickey Harris

The second game belonged to Harry "The Cat" Brecheen. The southpaw scattered just four hits over nine innings to shutout Boston. And he helped himself at the plate, driving in a run and scoring a run. Boston's starter, Harris, allowed one earned run over seven innings to earn a tough-luck loss. The game lasted just an hour and 56 minutes.

The Cardinals scored the only run they would need in the third. Backup catcher Del Rice, starting in place of Garagiola because he enjoyed a strong rapport with Brecheen, led off with a double into the gap in left-center. Brecheen came to bat next and drove Rice home with a base hit into right field.

In the fifth, Rice again started a Cardinals rally, this time with a leadoff single. Brecheen followed with a grounder to third base and when Higgins tried to cut down the lead runner at second he threw the ball into right field. The error put runners at second and third with no outs. One out later, Terry Moore singled Rice home, then Musial plated Brecheen with a groundout, making the score 3–0.

The crafty Brecheen kept the Red Sox off balance all day, allowing harmless singles in the first, fourth, fifth and ninth, while walking three and striking out four. He held Williams 0-for-4, and struck him out in the fourth inning.

Game 3: Red Sox 4, Cardinals 0

	1	2	3	4	5	6	7	8	9	R	H	E
St. Louis	0	0	0	0	0	0	0	0	0	0	6	1
Boston	3	0	0	0	0	0	0	1	X	4	8	0

WP   Dave Ferriss
LP   Murry Dickson

After an off day, the series resumed in Boston on October 9. Ferris made sure the 34,500 fans who turned out at Fenway Park on a chilly autumn afternoon didn't go home disappointed. The Red Sox pitcher answered Brecheen's shutout with one of his own in a game that was even quicker than the previous one, just an hour and 54 minutes long.

Musial walked with two outs in the top of the first inning and stole second base, but Ferriss picked him off to end the inning.

Then it was Boston's turn to hit and the Red Sox quickly reached Dickson for three runs. Wally Moses, who started in right field in place of McBride since there was a right-handed pitcher on the mound, began the Boston half of the inning with a fly out to center. The second hitter, Pesky, singled, and took second on a groundout to first base by DiMaggio. That brought Williams to the plate with a man on second and two outs. Dyer instructed the pitcher to walk Williams intentionally, but the strategy backfired when Dickson served up a three-run homer to York. The shot sailed over Fenway's 37-foot high left field wall.

Unfortunately many Boston fans missed the decisive clout. In an attempt to limit confusion and overcrowding, Red Sox officials waited to sell 1,500 standing room tickets until all holders of reserved tickets had taken their seats. Thus many paying customers were not allowed to enter Fenway Park until the top of the second inning.

All were watching in the third inning though, when Williams stepped to the plate with two outs and no one on base and bunted to the left side for a hit. The crowd responded with a standing ovation.

Ferriss allowed just two singles over the first five innings, but Dickson led off the Cardinals' sixth with a double. The threat didn't last long. The next batter, Schoendienst, hit a fly out to center field and DiMaggio threw out Dickson at third as he attempted to advance.

The Red Sox tacked an unearned run onto their lead in the eighth. York started the rally with a one-out single, took third on a Doerr double, and scored on a two-out error by Schoendienst.

Ferriss nearly lost his shutout in the ninth when Musial tripled with two outs, but he struck out Slaughter to end the game and complete the 50th shutout in World Series history. The strikeout was just the second of the day for the Red Sox right-hander who allowed six hits and one walk.

After the game, the talk in the Red Sox clubhouse still swirled around the possibility of a Williams trade. Cronin tried his best to end the nonsense, barking at reporters, "Williams is not for sale."[5]

GAME 4: CARDINALS 12, RED SOX 3

	1	2	3	4	5	6	7	8	9	R	H	E
St. Louis	0	3	3	0	1	0	1	0	4	12	20	1
Boston	0	0	0	1	0	0	0	2	0	3	9	4

WP George Munger
LP Tex Hughson

The back-to-back shutouts were followed by the only blowout of the series, a 12–3 Cardinals win. Hughson, who had pitched so well in the opener, didn't survive the third inning in his second start. He allowed three runs in the second inning and three more in the third. By game's end, the Cardinals had tied a World Series record with 20 hits, including four apiece by Garagiola, Kurowski and Slaughter, and the Red Sox had tied a record by using six different pitchers in the game.

George "Red" Munger, a surprise starter for Dyer, held the Red Sox to just one earned run over nine innings. The 27-year-old right-hander had made just seven starts and pitched just 48 innings in the regular season, winning twice and losing twice. When asked after the game why he had given such an important start to such an unheralded player, Dyer responded, "You know, he's a good little worker, a good pitcher. I won't be surprised to see him win twenty games for me next season."[6] The manager wasn't far off; Munger went 16–5 in 1947.

The Cardinals took a 1–0 lead when Slaughter began the second inning with a home run. Kurowski followed with a double and scored one out later on a single by Harry Walker. Walker later scored on a squeeze bunt by Marion to put St. Louis ahead 3–0.

The Red Sox hit three shots off Munger in the bottom of the second, but the Cardinal defense rose to the challenge. After Williams led off with a walk, York blasted a drive to right-center that seemed sure to land in the triangle for a run-scoring triple. But Moore ran down the ball and caught it over his shoulder. Then Doerr and Higgins both smashed line drives to right field and Slaughter made running catches to rob them both.

The Cardinals stretched the lead to 6–0 in the top of the third, the runs scoring on a two-run double by Musial, and an RBI single by Garagiola. Jim Bagby was the first reliever to trot out of the bullpen for Cronin, coming on with two runs already in and no outs in the third. He was followed by Bill Zuber, Mace Brown, Mike Ryba, and Clem Dreisewerd. Dreisewerd, who recorded only one out, the final out in the Cardinals' ninth, was the only Boston pitcher not scored upon.

"I guess we showed 'em something today," Dyer said afterward. "It had to happen. I knew they couldn't go on stifling our hitters. It was just a question of when the explosion would let go and this was the day."[7]

Moses went 4 for 5 to account for Boston's lone bright spot, while Williams went 1 for 3 with a single and a walk. Afterwards, Williams said, "I'd rather lose that way, than by 3 to 2 in fifteen innings."[8]

GAME 5: RED SOX 6, CARDINALS 3

	1	2	3	4	5	6	7	8	9	R	H	E
St. Louis	0	1	0	0	0	0	0	0	2	3	4	1
Boston	1	1	0	0	0	1	3	0	X	6	11	3

WP Joe Dobson
LP Al Brazle

In the aftermath of the Game Four debacle, Cronin refused to say whether he would start Dobson or Harris in Game Five. In fact, he said he wasn't sure himself.[9] The Boston manager sang a different tune, however, after Dobson started the fifth game and delivered a four-hit complete game win, in which the only runs to score against him were unearned.

"Dobson pitched a great game," Cronin said, after the Red Sox won 6–3 to move within one win of the championship. "He was no surprise pick, either. I had him in mind as part of my pitching sequence right along. It was his turn and he came through marvelously."[10]

After Dobson set down the Cardinals in the top of the first, the Red Sox scored a run against Pollet in the bottom of the inning. Don Gutteridge, playing second base instead of Doerr who was out with an awful headache, led off with a single. Then Pesky followed with a single that put runners at first and second. Next up was DiMaggio, who tapped to third. Kurowski fielded the ball and stepped on third to eliminate Gutteridge, but there was no other play to make, so the Red Sox still had two men on when Williams stepped to the plate. Williams singled to right field to score Pesky and put Boston on top 1–0. And that was all for the St. Louis ace. Pollet had been pitching with a strained muscle in his side for more than a month and he couldn't bear the pain any longer. He signaled to Dyer that he was ailing, and the manager brought in Brazle.

Prize fighter Joe Louis signs autographs at Fenway during Game Four of the 1946 World Series. (Courtesy of the Boston Public Library, Print Department)

The Cardinals scored an unearned run in the second, thanks to a Pesky error, but the Red Sox came right back in the bottom of the inning and took a 2–1 lead on a one-out Gutteridge single that scored Partee.

The Red Sox added another run in the sixth when Leon Culberson, who had started in right field, led off with a home run. Then in the seventh the Red Sox broke the game open with three more runs as DiMaggio and Culberson had doubles in the inning.

Dobson carried a three-hitter and a 6–1 lead into the ninth. He allowed a leadoff walk to Musial, then struck out Erv Dusak for the first out. After Pesky booted a groundball that looked like it had a chance to be a game-ending double play, Garagiola grounded to Pesky for the second out, as both base runners moved up a base. After Walker singled to score both unearned runs, Marion popped to Pesky to end the game.

"I threw my atom ball at them," said Dobson, who had eight strikeouts and allowed just one walk. "Yep, that old atom ball destroyed 'em. Just wiped 'em out. A wonderful feeling too."[11]

After the game the Cardinals announced that Pollet would be unavailable to pitch again in the series. With a three game to two lead, and the opposition's ace sidelined, the Red Sox were in position to win their sixth World Series in six tries.

GAME 6: CARDINALS 4, RED SOX 1

	1	2	3	4	5	6	7	8	9	R	H	E
Boston	0	0	0	0	0	0	1	0	0	1	7	0
St. Louis	0	0	3	0	0	0	0	1	X	4	8	0

WP   Harry Brecheen
LP   Mickey Harris

While the Cardinals rode the rails home to the Gateway City, the Red Sox flew west to cut down their travel time and get an extra night of sleep in St. Louis before Game Six.

The game presented a rematch of the second contest, pairing Harris against Brecheen. As he had in the first game, Brecheen baffled the Red Sox for nine innings, and the result was another three-run Cardinals win.

The Red Sox had a chance to score in the first inning when Pesky singled, DiMaggio singled, and Williams walked, loading the bases with one out, but York grounded into an around-the-horn double play to end the rally.

In the second, the Red Sox had another good scoring opportunity, as Doerr singled to lead off, then Higgins followed with a single. But Dusak, the Cardinals leftfielder, threw Doerr out as he tried to take third on Higgins' hit, and the next two batters went quietly.

St. Louis scored three runs in the third. Rice, who again started at catcher for the Cardinals with Brecheen on the mound, began the rally with a single to left, then Brecheen tried to advance him with a bunt but Higgins came racing in from third and fired to Pesky covering second base to cut down the lead runner. With Brecheen on first, Schoendienst laced a double down the right field line to put men at second and third with one out. Moore followed with a fly ball to right field and Culberson conceded the run, throwing toward third to keep the trail runner, Schodendienst, from advancing. It didn't matter though. The next three hitters — Musial, Kurowski, and Slaughter — all singled, and by the time Cronin called on Hughson to take the ball from Harris, three runs had scored.

Hughson pitched 4⅓ scoreless innings, allowing just two hits. Brecheen was just as good, though, running his streak of shutout innings against the Red Sox to 15 before Boston finally broke through for a run in the seventh when York tripled and scored on a sacrifice fly by Doerr to make the score 3–1.

Johnson replaced Hughson to start the eighth and immediately got in trouble by issuing two walks. The Cardinals tacked on a run on a Marion double.

The Red Sox entered the ninth trailing 4–1. Williams knocked a one-out single into right field, but York followed with a grounder to Brecheen and the pitcher started a game-ending double play.

Brecheen finished with a seven-hit, two-walk, six-strikeout win. After going 0-for-4 against Brecheen in the second game, Williams went 1-for-3 with a walk in the sixth game. After the series, Garagiola, the young catcher who had watched from the Cardinals bench as Brecheen had his way with Williams, said Brecheen's ability to pitch inside to the Red Sox slugger made all the difference. "He had a screwball that broke in toward left-handed hitters. I thought, man, is he going to throw inside to Williams? I wouldn't want to be the first baseman," Garagiola said. "It was a gusty pitch because he was throwing it right into Williams' power, but if the ball broke, which it did, it would hit Williams' bat right on the handle."[12]

The good news for the Red Sox was that they would not have to face Brecheen again in the series ... or so they thought.

GAME 7: CARDINALS 4, RED SOX 3

	1	2	3	4	5	6	7	8	9	R	H	E
Boston	1	0	0	0	0	0	0	2	0	3	8	0
St. Louis	0	1	0	0	2	0	0	1	X	4	9	1

WP Harry Brecheen
LP Bob Klinger

The season had come down to one final game. Indeed, Game Seven of the 1946 World Series would be another turning point in Red Sox history. Before, the Red Sox had always managed to win the big game. Afterwards, the Red Sox would always seem to find a way to lose.

The Red Sox had the advantage of sending their ace, Ferriss, to the mound, while the Cardinals were forced to start Dickson, their third best pitcher.

The game was tied 3–3 entering the bottom of the eighth inning. By the inning's end, Pesky had earned his place in the Red Sox hall of shame, and the seeds were planted for generations of Red Sox fans to grow up believing their team was somehow cursed.

The Red Sox scored first, as Moses singled to lead off the game, then Pesky singled him to third and DiMaggio brought him home with a sacrifice fly.

The Cardinals tied the game at 1–1 in the second, when Kurowski doubled and came home on a sacrifice fly by Walker.

Dickson was brilliant, settling into a groove and retiring 18 of 19 batters from the second inning through the seventh, while allowing just a sixth inning walk to DiMaggio.

Ferriss, meanwhile, got knocked out of the game in the fifth inning when he allowed four hits and two runs. Dickson drove in one run with a double and scored the other run.

Dobson came in to pitch for Boston and managed to keep the deficit at 3–1, but as the innings wore on, the Red Sox were running out of time. Finally, in the eighth, the Boston bats made some noise against Dickson. Russell started the rally with a pinch-single, then Metkovich batted for Dobson and lined a double to left. After pitching nine innings the day before, Brecheen was summoned to replace Dickson on the mound. The lefty retired the first two batters he faced, before he allowed a double to DiMaggio that tied the game at 3–3. The Little Professor pulled a muscle in his leg though as he ran to second base and Culberson had to replace him as a pinch runner. Still, the Red Sox had the go-ahead run at second and Williams at the plate. In what would be the last World Series at bat of his career, Williams popped out to second base, leaving the potential go-ahead run in scoring position.

In the bottom of the eighth, Slaughter led off with a single that fell in front of Culberson in center field. Two outs later, Slaughter was still on first when Walker blooped a hit into the gap in left-center. Slaughter was running on the pitch and got a great jump off first. He rounded second as the ball landed softly in front of Culberson. Then he rounded third as Pesky, who was stationed about ten feet onto the outfield grass, received Culberson's throw. Pesky caught the ball and brought it down toward his waist as he turned toward the infield. He hesitated for a beat before realizing that Slaughter was trying to score and when he did throw to the plate, the throw had an arc to it. By the time Russell, the Boston catcher, caught the throw on a short hop, Slaughter had already slid across the plate amidst a cloud of dust. The play immediately entered Cardinals lore as Slaughter's "Mad Dash." It entered Red Sox lore as the play on which "Pesky held the ball." Although many Red Sox fans believe Slaughter scored from first on a single, the hit was, in fact, ruled a double. The grainy film of the game shows rather clearly, though, that Pesky hesitated.

Slaughter later recalled that before the inning his manager had told him to be aggressive on the base paths. "Dyer said, 'With two outs, if you think you have a chance to score, go ahead and gamble, and I'll be responsible,'" Slaughter said.[13]

He was aggressive and it paid off.

The Red Sox had a chance to tie the game in the ninth. York led off with a single, then Doerr singled, putting two aboard with no outs. But Higgins grounded into a fielder's choice, then Partee popped out, then McBride grounded into a fielder's choice on a close play that cut down Higgins at second. The game was over.

Years later, Pesky remembered the moments right after the game. "We sat with our heads down in the dugout and I looked down there ten feet away and there was Ted Williams and he actually wept," Pesky said.[14] Williams, who had five singles in 25 at bats and just one RBI in the seven games, gave his entire World Series check to clubhouse attendant Johnny Orlando.[15]

The players' shares were $3,748 for each Cardinal and $2,140 for each Red Sox player — the smallest since 1918. The gate receipts were just $1,052,900 because the series had been played in two of baseball's smallest ballparks. Also, the broadcast fees were funneled into a new pension fund for players.

In the visitors' clubhouse after the game, Pesky took responsibility for the loss, standing up and telling his teammates, "I'm the goat. It's my fault. I'm to blame. I had the ball in my hand. I hesitated and gave Slaughter six steps.... I couldn't hear anybody. There was too much yelling. It looked like an ordinary single."

His teammates told him to sit down, it wasn't his fault, and over the next several decades they would defend the likeable Pesky at their every opportunity. Doerr, for one, blamed the poor quality of the Sportsman's Park outfield grass and the untimely injury to DiMaggio. The Hall-of-Fame second baseman said, "The outfield was pieces of sod and pods and really rough. I'm sure Culberson played a little conservative on that particular ball, whereas had Dom been out there, he would have played it more aggressively. I really think that was a big factor."[17]

In time Pesky accepted less responsibility for the loss. In 1990, he said, "No one dreamed that Slaughter would try to score. I'm out in short left-center field. It was late in the afternoon and Christ, when I picked Slaughter up he was about twenty feet from home plate. I'd have needed a rifle to get him."[18]

CHAPTER 7

The Regular Season: 96–59

In 1948 Boston was the hub of the baseball universe. The American League Red Sox and National League Braves combined to win 187 regular season games, attracted more than three million fans to their respective ballparks, and for much of the season appeared headed for a meeting in the World Series. While the Braves did their part, handily winning the NL pennant, the Red Sox finished the season tied with the Cleveland Indians for first place, setting the stage for a one-game playoff to decide the AL title.

After losing to the Cardinals in the 1946 World Series, the Red Sox struggled through a transition year in 1947. The team set an attendance record for the second straight season, as night baseball debuted at Fenway Park, but starting pitchers Mickey Harris, Tex Hughson and Dave Ferriss all developed arm injuries. Before the season was out, first baseman Rudy York had been traded to the Chicago White Sox for rookie first sacker Jake Jones, and catcher Hal Wagner had been sent to Detroit for veteran backstop Birdie Tebbetts. The Red Sox finished third in the league, 14 games behind the Yankees.

Tom Yawkey vowed his Red Sox would return to championship form in 1948 and toward that end promoted longtime manager Joe Cronin to general manager and coerced former Yankee skipper Joe McCarthy out of retirement to pilot the Red Sox. The cigar-smoking McCarthy had won seven World Series in New York and arrived in Boston with a reputation as a stern disciplinarian.

Fueled by Yawkey's millions, Cronin made sure the team McCarthy inherited would be equipped to compete for the title. On November 18, 1947, Cronin sent ten players and $375,000 to the St. Louis Browns for all-star shortstop Vern Stephens and veteran right-handers Jack Kramer and Ellis Kinder. Stephens would hit 98 home runs and drive in 440 runs in his first three seasons in Boston, while teaming with Ted Williams to form the most dangerous tandem in the league. Kramer would win 18 games and lead the league in winning percentage in his first season with the Red Sox. Kinder would win 10 games in 1948, then 23 the next year. Meanwhile, none of the minor leaguers and journeyman Boston gave up in the deal would make an impact in St. Louis.

Ted Williams led the AL with a .369 batting average in 1948. (Courtesy of the Boston Public Library, Print Department)

As the Red Sox reported to spring training in Sarasota, Florida, there was speculation in the Boston press that McCarthy and Williams would butt heads. The 60-year-old McCarthy was an old fashioned manager who had been famous in New York for enforcing a rigorous dress code. Williams was a laid-back Californian who hated to wear neckties. McCarthy got off on the right foot with Williams when he showed up for the first day of spring training without a tie on himself, and he and Williams got along fine after that.

To make room for Stephens at shortstop, McCarthy moved Johnny Pesky to third base. Bobby Doerr held onto his second base position, while rookie Billy Goodman wrested the first base job away from Jones. Stan Spence joined Dom DiMaggio and Williams in the outfield. The pitching rotation consisted of Joe Dobson, Denny Galehouse, Ferriss and Harris at the outset, but by midseason Kramer, Kinder, and rookie Mel Parnell had replaced the latter three incumbents.

The Red Sox started the season slowly, losing the first three games to the Philadelphia A's, and by the end of May they were in seventh place with a record of 14–23, 11½ games off the lead. The early season's low points included a three-game sweep by the first place Indians at Fenway Park in early May, and a 13–4 loss in Cleveland on May 20, during which Harris and reliever Mickey McDermott combined to walk 18 batters.

The Red Sox turned things around in June, winning 18 of 24 games. On June 6, they beat the Tigers 6–4 at Fenway Park, as Williams, Spence, and Stephens hit consecutive home runs against Fred Hutchinson. On June 8, a bad call by an umpire cost the Red Sox a game when Parnell lost to Indians rookie Gene Bearden 2–0. The game would loom large later in the season when the two teams finished tied for the AL crown. On a foggy night at Fenway, the only runs scored when Cleveland's player-manager Lou Boudreau sliced a foul ball into the right field seats near the foul pole. First base umpire Charlie Berry ruled the drive a home run, even though the fan who had caught the ball was clearly seated short of the foul pole. Parnell argued the call and his manager did too, but to no avail.[1] The Red Sox bounced back when the teams met again two days later. They routed Bob Feller in a 15–7 win, moving within 9½ games of first.

On the Fourth of July, the Red Sox moved over the .500 mark to stay, beating the A's 19–5 at Fenway to improve to 33–32.

On July 10, Williams sat out the first of 15 games he would miss due to a rib cage injury suffered when he and back-up outfielder Sam Mele got into a skirmish during the train ride from Boston to Philadelphia the day before. The Red Sox won 4–0 though, as Kramer scattered nine hits to win his seventh game in a row. Stephens and Doerr hit back-to-back homers in the game, marking the sixth time they'd accomplished the feat in the season's first three months.

The Red Sox entered the all-star break in fourth place with a record of 39–35, 6½ games behind the first-place Indians. Williams sat out the Mid-Summer Classic due to his injury, but Dobson, Doerr, Stephens and Tebbetts made the trip to St. Louis, where the AL won 5–2.

Boston won 37 of its first 50 games after the break, including a string of 13 in a row between July 18 and 27. A pair of double-header sweeps against the White Sox and a double-header sweep against the Browns highlighted the streak. Williams returned to the lineup on July 23 and went 2 for 4 in a 13–1 win against the White Sox. The Red Sox moved into first place two days later when Dobson shutout Satchel Paige and the Indians 3–0. The date marked the first time since 1916 that both Boston teams held first place on the same day. Two nights later, the Red Sox posted another shutout win against a future-hall-of-famer, when Kinder beat Hal Newhouser 8–0 in Detroit.

A three-game losing streak at the beginning of August dropped the Red Sox out of first place, however, and they did not reclaim the top spot until August 24 when Dobson again faced Paige. This time the match-up resulted in a slugfest. Cleveland led 8–7 entering the ninth inning before Stephens blasted a two-run homer to give Boston a 9–8 win, and a half game lead over the Indians. Bob Lemon shut out the Red Sox, 9–0, the next night though, as the Indians routed Galehouse and regained first place. The Red Sox won the final game of the series on August 26 as Parnell beat Bearden, 8–4, in another match-up of the league's top rookie pitchers. The win started a nine-game win streak and the Red Sox held onto first place until September 26.

After losing to the Yankees on Friday, September 24, the Red Sox found themselves in a three-way tie for the AL lead. With seven games to play, Boston, Cleveland and New York all had 91–56 records. The next day, Kramer beat Allie Reynolds 7–2 at Yankee Stadium, dropping the Yankees a game off the lead and maintaining a first-place tie between the Red Sox and Indians. But the Yankees won the next day, giving the Indians a one-game lead over both teams with five to play.

The Red Sox won two of three games against the Senators and entered their final series of the year — a two-game set against the Yankees at Fenway Park — trailing the Indians by one game. The Yankees were also a game off the pace, meaning that whichever team lost the first game would be eliminated if Cleveland beat Detroit.

The Red Sox took an early lead, as Williams blasted a two-run first-inning homer against Tommy Byrne that sailed over the bullpens and into the right field bleachers. In the third, Williams added to the lead with an RBI double. Kramer took care of the rest, allowing the Yankees just five hits in a 5–1 win.

Meanwhile, Bearden, the Indians rookie, pitched his sixth shutout of the year in Cleveland, downing Detroit, 8–0. With one game to play, the Red Sox remained a game out of first, and the Yankees were eliminated.

Joe DiMaggio was spending the weekend at his brother Dom's house in Wellesley, as he always did when the Yankees visited the Red Sox. Joe sat in the passenger's seat of Dom's car as the two rode to Dom's suburban home. Joe vowed, "You knocked us out today, but we'll get back at you tomorrow — we'll knock you out. I'll take care of it personally."

Dom replied, "You're forgetting I may have something to do with that tomorrow. I'll be there too."[2]

And so, with both of their parents on hand to root for Dom's team, the DiMaggio brothers took the field for the season's 154th game on Sunday, October 3.

Trailing 2–0 in the bottom of the third inning, the Red Sox scored five times. After Dom DiMaggio led off with a single, Williams laced a one-out double down the left field line and DiMaggio came all the way around to score. Then Stephens reached on an infield hit and Doerr slashed a two-run double to right center. Two batters later, Goodman capped the rally with an RBI hit that made the score 5–2.

Although he was playing on two gimpy legs, Joe DiMaggio went 4-for-5 in the game. The Yankee Clipper smacked a double off the left field wall in the fifth to pull the Yankees within 5–4, but little brother Dom answered in the bottom of the sixth with a leadoff home run against Vic Raschi. Stephens also homered in the sixth, and by the time the inning was over the Red Sox had scored four times to take a 9–4 lead. In the ninth, with Boston leading 10–5, Joe DiMaggio singled off Ferriss. Yankee manager Bucky Harris sent Steve Souchock into the game as a pinch runner, and the Boston crowd responded with a thunderous ovation. "I turned and started for the dugout," DiMaggio later remembered. "I guess I was limping pretty bad. Anyway, that's what they told me later. I'll never forget that crowd. It was standing and roaring like one man. I tipped my cap but it didn't stop. I looked up at the stands at this ovation they were giving to a guy who had tried to beat them."[3]

Perhaps the Boston crowd would not have been so gracious if the Red Sox hadn't just pounded out 15 hits and if Bob Feller and the Indians weren't losing to the Tigers as the scoreboard in left field indicated. Boston won 10–5, and Detroit beat Cleveland 7–1.

After 154 games the Red Sox and Indians were tied with records of 96–58. In head-to-head play, they had split 22 games, 11 wins each, so it was fitting that they should meet for one final game. The playoff would take place the very next day, Monday, October 4, at 1:30 P.M. The site had been determined a week earlier by a coin-flip. The game would be played at Fenway Park where the Red Sox had a 55–22 record and where they had scored 479 of their league-leading 904 runs.

Boston's strength was clearly its offense. Stephens (.269, 29 HR, 137 RBI) and Williams (.369, 25 HR, 127 RBI) had finished second and third in the league in runs batted in, while Doerr (.285, 27 HR, 111 RBI) had also been potent. The Cleveland lineup featured a trio

Bobby Doerr, Ted Williams and Dom DiMaggio reach for the sky. (Courtesy of the Boston Public Library, Print Department)

of 100-RBI men as well: the league MVP, Boudreau (.355, 18 HR, 106 RBI), Ken Keltner (.297, 31 HR, 119 RBI), and Joe Gordon (.280, 32 HR, 124 RBI).

1948 One-Game Playoff

INDIANS 8, RED SOX 3

	1	2	3	4	5	6	7	8	9	R	H	E
Cleveland	1	0	0	4	1	0	0	1	1	8	13	1
Boston	1	0	0	0	0	2	0	0	0	3	5	1

WP Gene Bearden
LP Denny Galehouse

Monday's newspapers predicted that Boudreau would start 20-game winner Bob Lemon and that McCarthy would counter with Parnell, who had finished his rookie campaign with a 15–8 record and 3.14 ERA. Lemon was a converted infielder, who at age 28 was just beginning a hall-of-fame career during which he would win 207 games in 11 seasons. Parnell, though he was a lefty, had pitched exceptionally well at Fenway Park where southpaws often struggled, posting a 2.29 ERA, compared to his 4.13 ERA on the road. Both pitchers would be pitching on three days' rest ... that is, if they started. The truth was both managers refused to identify whom they intended to pitch.

The Indians rode the rails to Boston, sleeping on the train, and heading straight to the ballpark after arriving in the city at 10:00 AM. As the two teams took their turns warming up on the field before the game, it was still a mystery who would draw the starting nods on the mound. When the Red Sox took batting practice, Boudreau observed that Parnell was nowhere to be seen, while the rest of the Red Sox pitchers were shagging balls in the outfield. But then, midway through the Red Sox batting session, a batboy walked from the Red Sox dugout to left field. He found Denny Galehouse and the veteran right-hander followed him back to the Red Sox dugout. At 36, Galehouse was nearing the end of his career. He had gone 8–7 for Boston in 1948, earning most of his wins in relief after losing his spot in the rotation. But a short while later, Galehouse emerged from the dugout and reported to the bullpen where he began warming up. Boudreau figured it was a ploy. He thought McCarthy had Parnell, his real starter, warming up somewhere beneath the stands. But it was no trick.

Parnell remembered years later that McCarthy came to him, as he sat at his locker an hour before the game, and told him he would not be making the start. According to Parnell, the manager said, "Son, I've changed my mind. I'm going with the right-hander. The elements are against the left-hander going today because the wind is blowing out."[4]

McCarthy's decision to bypass the talented Parnell or one of his other starters in favor of Galehouse remains one of the great bafflers in Red Sox history.

Boudreau, for his part, had no qualms about sending a left-hander or a rookie to the mound. His surprise starter was Bearden. The 27-year old war veteran had gone 19–7 in his first season with the Indians, while pitching with aluminum plates in his head and left leg. He started the playoff game on one day of rest.

Galehouse struggled from the very beginning. In the first inning, Boudreau connected with a 2-0 fastball and sent it into the screen above the left field wall to put the Indians ahead 1–0.

The Red Sox tied the game at 1-1 in the bottom of the first when Pesky doubled to right-center and Stephens brought him home with a single.

In the bottom of the second, Bearden issued walks to Spence and Galehouse and a single to Tebbetts to load the bases. Feller and Lemon both began throwing in the Cleveland bullpen, but Bearden got DiMaggio to ground out to escape the inning unscathed.

The Indians knocked Galehouse from the game in the fourth, scoring four times. Boudreau started the rally with a line drive single to right, then Gordon singled to left, then Keltner cleared the bases with a home run that settled into the screen 400 feet away in left-center. Kinder replaced Galehouse and allowed a double to Larry Doby, and Doby came home a couple of batters later on a groundout by Jim Hegan.

Cleveland added a run against Kinder in the fifth to open a 6–1 lead.

After squandering their scoring chance in the second, the Red Sox did not get another hit against Bearden until the sixth inning when Doerr connected for a home run that also brought home Williams who had reached on an error. The clout cut the deficit to 6–3. But

Cleveland tacked on runs in the eighth and the ninth and Bearden held Boston to just one hit over the final three innings. On the rookie's 135th pitch, Tebbetts grounded to third base to end the game.

In the losing clubhouse, McCarthy issued only a terse statement, then refused to answer any questions about his choice of starters. "I've been licked before and I can be licked again," he said. "I'm sorry for the boys, that's all. And that's all I have to say, gentlemen."[5]

Several Red Sox players tipped their caps to Bearden. "He never gives you a fastball," DiMaggio explained. "Just keeps sending in those knucklers, sliders, and curves."[6]

While the Red Sox scattered after the game, heading to their homes across the country, the Indians stayed in Boston and celebrated at the Kenmore Hotel. Then, after an off day, the World Series began at Braves Field, and Johnny Sain beat Feller 1–0. The Indians bounced back though, and prevailed in six games. Bearden pitched another five-hitter, shutting out Vern Bickford 2–0, in Game Three of the World Series, then the rookie was on the mound in Boston when the Indians finished off the Braves, earning a save in relief of Lemon in Game Six.

It didn't take much longer for big league hitters to figure out how to hit Bearden's knuckleball though. He retired in 1953 with a record of 45–38. Galehouse, meanwhile, pitched just two innings for the Red Sox in 1949 before retiring. Parnell led both leagues in wins in 1949 with a record of 25–7 and averaged 19 wins over the next five seasons.

Years after his career ended, Parnell would still look back at the Red Sox' loss to the Indians in 1948 and lament that he didn't get a chance to compete. "I was the guy that should have pitched it," he said. "I had the most rest. I should have been the pitcher of that ball game, without a doubt."[7]

CHAPTER 8

The Regular Season: 92–70

Dubbed the season of the "Impossible Dream" by Red Sox radio announcer Ken Coleman, 1967 was the year that signified Boston's return to prominence in the baseball world. After Enos Slaughter's race around the bases in the 1946 World Series, the Red Sox spent most of the next two decades languishing in the American League's second division. After the Red Sox suffered through nine consecutive losing seasons, their pennant winning 1967 campaign started a streak of 14 winning seasons in a row.

At the season's outset there was little indication the 1967 Red Sox would be much better than the team that went 72–90 in 1966 to finish ninth in the ten-team AL, 26 games behind Baltimore. Although the Red Sox began the season with a new manager, Dick Williams, who was promoted over the winter from the team's Triple-A affiliate in Toronto, the odds-makers in Las Vegas listed the Red Sox as 100 to 1 long shots to win the AL.

When a crowd of just 8,234 fans showed up at chilly Fenway Park on Opening Day to watch Jim Lonborg beat Chicago, little notice was paid to the small crowd. In the years since Ted Williams' salad days, Boston fans had grown accustomed to ignoring the Red Sox, and the Red Sox had grown accustomed to being ignored. In 1966 the Red Sox had averaged only 10,014 fans per home date, and in 1965, when the team won just 62 games, there had actually been a September game played before just 461 spectators. All of that was about to change. The summer of 1967 rekindled Boston's love affair with the Red Sox and the embers of that passion have burned brightly ever since.

At the heart of the team's resurgence was 27-year-old left fielder Carl Yastrzemski. "Yaz" carried the team all season long and especially in September on the way to earning the Triple Crown for leading the league in batting average, home runs and runs batted in. He also won the league MVP Award. Lonborg also had a remarkable season. The lanky 25-year-old entered the season with a career record of 19–27, before leading the league in wins and ERA and for his efforts he was rewarded with the Cy Young Award. "Gentleman Jim" forever etched his name into the annals of Red Sox lore with several memorable performances in 1967, each bringing the Impossible Dream a bit closer to reality.

Mike Andrews (far left) and George Scott chase a foul ball. (Courtesy of the Boston Public Library, Print Department)

The 1967 pennant race captivated New Englanders not only because it had been so long since the Red Sox had competed for the AL flag, but because the race was so close all season long. The following season, 1968, would present the final ten-team race, before the expansion of 1969 ushered in the era of divisional play and made the races less competitive by reducing the number of teams competing for each playoff spot from ten to six. But in 1967 there were still ten teams battling for one berth, and up until the final weekend of the season four of the ten teams in the league had a legitimate shot to earn a trip to the World Series. As late as September 28, just 1½ games separated first place Minnesota from fourth place Chicago, while Boston and Detroit were both a game off the lead.

The Red Sox posted an 8–6 record in an April that included some of the most exciting baseball Boston fans had witnessed in a long time. On just the third day of the season a 21-year-old rookie named Billy Rohr made his major league debut for the Red Sox at Yankee Stadium. Rohr confounded the Yankees for 8⅔ innings before losing a no-hit bid when Elston Howard lined a single to right-center. The inning had opened with a remarkable catch by Yastrzemski on a ball hit by Tom Tresh that temporarily preserved the no-hitter and brought the Yankee Stadium crowd to its feet. Rohr finished with a one-hit, 3–0 win over Whitey Ford, which was still not a bad way to begin a career. "It would have been nice to have a no-hitter, but it's awfully nice to be 1–0 in the big leagues," he said.[1] The left-hander struggled in his subsequent starts though, before being demoted to the minors in May. Rohr would win just two more major league games, but for one night in April he had captivated the baseball world.

Two days later the Red Sox and Yankees played an 18-inning marathon on a Sunday afternoon that New York won 7–6. Red Sox hitters were 0-for-13 with runners in scoring position from the ninth inning on. The game was the first of several memorable extra-inning games for the 1967 Red Sox.

On Friday, April 28, Lonborg pitched his first gem of the year, striking out 13 Kansas City A's in a 3–0 win at Fenway Park.

The next day, Boston outlasted the A's 11–10 in 15 innings. The game entered the tenth knotted at 9–9 and stayed that way until the top of the 15th when Kansas City took a one-run lead. But in the bottom of the 15th the Red Sox loaded the bases with one out, setting the stage for a dramatic two-run single by pinch-hitter Jose Tartabull.

The Red Sox were 14–14 in May and 15–14 in June. In May, Williams benched a number of regulars, including Yastrzemski, due to their lackluster performances at the plate. Lonborg sparkled in the final week of the month, shutting out the Tigers and Denny McClain, 1–0, on May 24, and beating the Orioles 4–3 on May 28 to improve his record to 6–1. The Red Sox finished the month on a high note, sweeping a Memorial Day double-header from the Angels before a Fenway crowd of 32,012, the biggest in five years, and then beating the Angels 3–2 on May 31, behind Yastrzemski's ninth and tenth homers. The wins improved Boston to 22–20, 4½ games behind Detroit.

Red Sox executive vice president Dick O'Connell made pair of trades in early June, acquiring infielder Jerry Adair from the White Sox in exchange for pitcher Don McMahon and a minor leaguer, and then getting starting pitcher Gary Bell from the Indians for backup first baseman Tony Horton and reserve outfielder Don Demeter. Both new acquisitions turned out to be solid contributors over the final four months.

Bell made an immediate impact when he won his first Red Sox start, beating the White Sox 7–3 on June 8.

The Red Sox staged another dramatic comeback at Fenway when they beat first-place Chicago 2–1 in 11 innings on June 15. Rookie Gary Waslewski pitched a shutout over the first nine-innings, but the Red Sox didn't score either so the game went to extras tied at 0–0. In the top of the eleventh, the White Sox broke the deadlock, scoring a run against John Wyatt. The first two Red Sox went quietly against Chicago's John Buzhardt in the bottom of the eleventh, before third baseman Joe Foy kept the Red Sox alive with a single. Up to the plate stepped Tony Conigliaro, the 22-year-old right fielder who had hit 84 home runs in his first three big league seasons. "Tony C." worked the count full then blasted a curveball over the Green Monster for a game-winning homer.

On June 20, Foy smacked a grand slam to help Bell earn his third straight win at Yankee Stadium. The next night, Yankee starter Thad Tillotson drilled Foy in the helmet in the second inning. Foy trotted to first base, the helmet having done its job, but in the bottom of the inning Lonborg retaliated, hitting Tillotson in the shoulder. A brawl ensued. Red Sox shortstop Rico Petrocelli and Yankee outfielder Joe Pepitone exchanged punches, while Boston center fielder Reggie Smith tossed Tillotson to the ground. After a dozen New York City police officers pulled the teams apart, play resumed.[2] In the top of the third, Tillotson hit Lonborg with a pitch. Then in the bottom of the third, Lonborg hit Dick Howser. When things finally settled down, the Red Sox earned an 8–1 win behind a three-run homer by Conigliaro, a solo shot by first baseman George Scott, and three hits by Yastrzemski. With the win Lonborg improved to 9–2 and the Red Sox moved into third place, 6 games behind Chicago.

Conigliaro hit a 450-foot home run in Kansas City to lead the Red Sox to a 5–3 win over the A's on June 30, and after the game Orioles manager Hank Bauer announced his selections for the AL all-star team. Four Red Sox made the squad, Conigliaro and Yastrzemski as starters, Petrocelli and Lonborg as reserves. The game, played at Anaheim Stadium on July 11, turned out to be the longest Mid-Summer Classic ever. The NL prevailed 2–1 in 15 innings. Yastrzemski had three hits and two walks, Conigliaro went 0–6, Petrocelli went 0–1, and Lonborg didn't play.

The Red Sox entered the season's second half with a 41–39 record, 6 games behind the White Sox. After splitting a double-header against Baltimore to open the second half, Boston started a ten-game win streak that vaulted the team into the thick of the pennant race. The streak began with an 11–5 Lonborg win over the Orioles on a Friday night at Fenway, and continued through a double-header sweep of the Indians, as Lonborg and Bell earned wins in Cleveland. The streak galvanized Red Sox Nation. When the team landed at Logan Airport on Sunday, July 23, a delirious crowd of more than 15,000 fans welcomed home the second-place Red Sox, who were just half a game off the league lead. The Red Sox manager, like his players, was stunned by the groundswell of support. "They told us on the plane that there'd be fans at the airport," Williams said, "but I never expected anything like this."[3]

The streak ended two days later with a loss to the Angels, but the region's support of the Red Sox continued. Fenway crowds in excess of 30,000 were common over the remainder of the summer and all of New England was abuzz with talk of the 100 to 1 underdogs who had their sights set on the championship.

As July turned to August, the Red Sox were 56–44, 2 games behind Chicago. On August 3, O'Connell made another trade, picking up Howard, the Yankee catcher who had ended Rohr's no-hitter, in exchange for a minor leaguer. The batting averages of Boston catchers Mike Ryan and Russ Gibson had hovered around the .200 mark all season, and Howard gave Williams another option, although he was hitting just .196 himself at the time.

The season's worst moment and one of its best occurred just three days apart. On August 18 Conigliaro was hit in the face and nearly killed by a Jack Hamilton pitch in a 3–2 Red Sox win against the Angels at Fenway Park. The beaning occurred in the fourth inning. With two out Hamilton hit Conigliaro in the left cheekbone, shattering his eye socket. Tony C. lay motionless in the batters box for several minutes before teammates lifted his limp body onto a stretcher, then he was rushed to Sancta Maria Hospital in Cambridge. Initially, the medical reports said Conigliaro would miss three weeks, but, in fact, his season was over, and blurred vision would prevent him from ever again being the fearsome hitter he had been.

On August 20, the Red Sox swept a double-header from the Angels in the most improbable of fashions. After the Red Sox won the first game 12–2, they rallied from an 8–0 fourth-inning deficit to win the nightcap 9–8. Smith started the comeback with a solo homer in the fourth, and Adair capped it with a solo shot over the Green Monster in the eighth. The win was not only the Red Sox' biggest comeback since overcoming a 10–0 deficit against Bob Lemon and the Indians in 1950, but it brought them within 1½ games of the AL lead.

The Red Sox claimed first place on August 26 when they beat the White Sox 6–2 and the Twins lost to the Indians. The win moved Boston half a game ahead of Minnesota, and a game ahead of Chicago and Detroit, marking the latest in a season that Boston had been in first place in 18 years.

The next day the Red Sox split a twin-bill in Chicago, narrowly winning the first game when Tartabull threw out Ken Berry, the potential tying run, at the plate to end the game.

After a grueling 35-game August that saw the Red Sox go 20–15, the team began September with a record of 76–59, half a game behind the first-place Twins and a game ahead of the White Sox. Boston would alternate between first and second all month long, spending a total of 10 days at half a game off the lead, and four days at a game back.

Yastrzemski, who began the month with a .308 average, 23 percentage points behind league-leader Frank Robinson, took the lead in all three Triple Crown categories on September 18, going 3-for-4 with a homer and two runs batted in during a ten-inning 6–5 win against the Tigers. The game began a remarkable stretch for Yastrzemski during which he batted .523 (23 for 44) over the final 12 games, while mashing five home runs, scoring 14 runs, and driving in 16.

The Red Sox forged a first-place tie with the Twins the next night when they beat the Tigers 4–2. But by week's end, Boston had again fallen a game off the pace. Entering the final two days of the season, Minnesota was in first with a record of 91–69, Detroit (89–69) and Boston (90–70) were tied for second at a game back, and Chicago (89–70) was third at 1½ games back. To have a chance, the Red Sox had to sweep their final two games against the Twins and hope for the Angels to beat the Tigers and the Senators to beat the White Sox.

On September 30, Jose Santiago pitched seven solid innings and Yastrzemski hit a three-run homer to lead Boston passed Minnesota 6–4. The win pulled the Red Sox into a tie for first with the Twins. Meanwhile Detroit and California split a double-header, dropping the Tigers half a game back. Chicago was eliminated by virtue of a loss to Washington.

With one game to play, the Red Sox needed a win against the Twins to clinch at least a tie for first with the Tigers. Detroit needed to win both ends of another twin-bill against the Angels to stay alive. Although the Red Sox handed the ball to their ace, Lonborg, there was reason for skepticism. Gentleman Jim possessed a career record of 0–6 against the Twins, and his opponent, Dean Chance, had compiled a 4–0 record against the Red Sox in 1967. The Twins scored a run in the top of the first when Scott botched a relay to the plate that allowed Harmon Killebrew to score from first on a double to left field. Then Minnesota scored another run in the third. The Twins entered the sixth with a 2–0 lead. Leading off in the Boston half of the sixth, Lonborg got the winning rally started when he laid down a bunt single. Then Adair and Dalton Jones both singled to load the bases for Yastrzemski. Hollywood couldn't have written a better script, and Yaz gladly played the hero's role expected of him by the 35,770 fans at Fenway Park. He wrapped a game-tying single to center. Then Ken Harrelson, playing in place of Conigliaro, drove home the go-ahead run with an infield single. By the time the inning was through, the Red Sox had scored five times and were on their way to clinching at least a tie for the title. After Lonborg got Rich Rollins to pop to Petrocelli to end the game, bedlam broke out at Fenway. The fans stormed the field, surrounding Lonborg and his teammates. "It became a mania," Lonborg recalled later. "I was scared to death."[4] But Lonborg eventually made his way to the Red Sox clubhouse intact, though his uniform was in tatters. There, he and his teammates sipped beer with Red Sox owner Tom Yawkey and listened to the second game between the Tigers — who had won the first game to stay alive — and Angels to see if there would have to be a playoff to decide the AL pennant. When the Angels prevailed 8–5, the Red Sox celebrated again, as did all of New England. The Red Sox had won the AL title with a record of 92–70 and a .568 winning percentage — the lowest in history for an AL champ — and were going to the World Series for just the second time in 49 years.

Yastrzemski, who had ten hits in his final 13 at bats, finished the season with league leading totals in batting average (.326), on base percentage (.421), slugging (.622), hits (189), runs (112), home runs (44), runs batted in (121) and total bases (360). Scott finished fourth in the league in batting at .308, while hitting 19 homers and collecting 82 RBI. Despite playing in only 95 games, Conigliaro finished second on the team with 20 homers. Catching was clearly the team's weak spot, as Ryan batted .199, Gibson batted .203, and Howard batted .147. In an era dominated by pitching, the Red Sox led the AL in runs with 722, in homers with 158, and in batting average with a .255 mark. The pitching staff finished eighth in the league with a 3.36 ERA. Lonborg (22–9, 3.16 ERA) and Bell (12–8, 3.16 ERA) gave Boston a pair of aces, but after that, the rotation was suspect. Lee Stange tied Bell for the second most starts on the staff with 24, while going 8–10 with a 2.77 ERA. Spot-starter Santiago (12–4, 5 saves, 3.59 ERA) and reliever Wyatt (10–7, 20 saves, 2.60 ERA) were the only other pitchers to post double digit win totals on a staff that saw 12 pitchers make at least one start.

The Postseason: 3–4

While the Red Sox had won the AL with a record that would have placed third or fourth in most seasons, their World Series opponent, the St. Louis Cardinals, had proven thoroughly and convincingly that they were a championship-caliber team. The Cardinals finished with a record of 101–60, 10½ games ahead of the next best National League club. League MVP Orlando Cepeda (.325, 25 HR, 111 RBI) led an offense that finished first in batting at .263, and second in runs with 695. Leadoff man Lou Brock batted .299, while hitting 21 homers, driving in 76 runs, and swiping a circuit-best 52 bases, while Curt Flood finished fourth in the league with a .335 average, and the aging Roger Maris hit 9 homers and drove in 55 runs. Seven different St. Louis pitchers won at least nine games and the Cardinals placed second in the league with a 3.05 ERA. Dick Hughes led the staff with a 16–6 record and a 2.67 ERA, while 22-year-old Steve Carlton was 14–9 with a 2.98 ERA. Bob Gibson missed three months in the middle of the season with a broken leg but still finished with a 13–7 record and a 2.98 ERA. Nelson Briles went 14–5 with a 2.43 ERA while bouncing between the rotation and bullpen.

As had been the case when the same two teams met in the 1946 World Series, it took seven games to decide the champion. The Red Sox battled back valiantly from a three games to one deficit to force a final game that pitted Gibson against Lonborg at Fenway

Yastrzemski rips a hit on the final day of the 1967 season. (Courtesy of the Boston Public Library, Print Department)

Park. Gibson rose to the occasion, winning his third game of the series, while the overworked Lonborg wilted. But just the same, New Englanders were left with warm feelings for their Red Sox after a most improbable season.

1967 World Series: Cardinals 4, Red Sox 3

GAME 1: CARDINALS 2, RED SOX 1

	1	2	3	4	5	6	7	8	9	R	H	E
St. Louis	0	0	1	0	0	0	1	0	0	2	10	0
Boston	0	0	1	0	0	0	0	0	0	1	6	0

WP Bob Gibson
LP Jose Santiago

The Red Sox were forced to start Santiago in the opening game because Lonborg had pitched a complete game on the final day of the regular season. Meanwhile, Cardinals manager Red Schoendienst sent a well-rested Gibson to the mound. Santiago pitched well and helped his own cause with a third-inning home run, but his teammates struggled against Gibson and St. Louis prevailed 2–1.

Box seats to the 1967 World Series at Fenway Park cost $12. (Courtesy of the Boston Public Library, Print Department)

The Cardinals scored first when Brock singled to lead off the third inning, advanced to third base on a Flood double and scored on a Maris groundout. Santiago tied the game, 1–1, in the bottom of the inning when he connected with a hanging curve ball.

St. Louis nearly took the lead in the fourth, but Yastrzemski threw out Julian Javier at the plate as he tried to score from second on a single by Brock.

In the Boston half of the fourth, Scott doubled to left with two outs, but Petrocelli struck out to end the inning.

The Cardinals scored the go-ahead run in the seventh inning. Again it was Brock who crossed the plate. This time he led off with a single, stole second, took third on a ground-out, and scored on another Maris groundout.

Gibson allowed a two-out walk to Scott in the ninth, before getting Mike Andrews, who pinch-hit for Petrocelli, to fly out. Gibson finished with a six-hitter and 10 strikeouts. It was the first of three complete game wins he would toss in the series.

After the game, Yastrzemski, Petrocelli and Harrelson took the unorthodox measure of participating in a post-game batting practice session on the Fenway lawn. Just the same, Yastrzemski refused to compliment Gibson. "Nothing fooled me," Yastrzemski said, despite having gone 0-for-4. "I just got lousy at the plate. My son, even my little daughter, could've gotten me out. And my dog could've caught the balls I hit."[5]

GAME 2: RED SOX 5, CARDINALS 0

	1	2	3	4	5	6	7	8	9	R	H	E
St. Louis	0	0	0	0	0	0	0	0	0	0	1	1
Boston	0	0	0	1	0	1	3	0	X	5	9	0

WP   Jim Lonborg
LP   Dick Hughes

The Red Sox and their fans were not overly alarmed at having lost the first game. After all, they'd spent the entire season perfecting the art of coming from behind. And if ever there were a hotter pitcher heading into a World Series start, New Englanders hadn't seen his like. Lonborg stayed hot and the Red Sox won. The right-hander retired the Cardinals with ease on the way to completing one of the greatest World Series pitching performances ever. Gentleman Jim carried a perfect game into the seventh inning before Flood walked with two out. He lost his no-hitter with one out in the eighth when Javier lined a high slider into left field for a double. Lonborg responded by throwing his hands in front of his face in disappointment. But that was the extent of the Cardinals' offensive attack. Lonborg finished with a one-hitter, and faced just 29 batters in a 5–0 win.

After the game Lonborg said, "It was utter agony losing that no-hitter. I threw my arms up because I didn't want to look, as if seeing somebody in an automobile accident. I really wanted that no-hitter, but suddenly it was gone." He also admitted that he had flouted baseball superstition and talked about the prospects of pitching a no-hitter in the dugout throughout the game, encouraging his teammates to help him keep the no-no intact.[6]

As had been the case so many times during the regular season, Yastrzemski was the offensive star of the day, belting a leadoff homer against Hughes in the fourth, and a three-run homer against Ron Willis in the seventh. He also added a single in the eighth. The other Boston run crossed the plate in the sixth when Petrocelli knocked in Scott with a sacrifice fly.

Game 3: Cardinals 5, Red Sox 2

	1	2	3	4	5	6	7	8	9	R	H	E
Boston	0	0	0	0	0	1	1	0	0	2	7	1
St. Louis	1	2	0	0	0	1	0	1	X	5	10	0

WP Nelson Briles
LP Gary Bell

The series shifted to Busch Memorial Stadium, a big symmetrical ballpark that had opened the year before. In 1967 the field still featured natural grass. Bell drew the start for Boston but lasted just two innings before being lifted in the third for a pinch-hitter. By then the Red Sox trailed 3–0. Cardinals starter Briles, meanwhile, lasted the full nine innings, holding the Red Sox to seven hits and two runs.

Brock led off the bottom of the first with a triple and Flood followed with a single to put St. Louis ahead 1–0. In the second, Cardinals third baseman Mike Shannon hit a two-run homer on a breaking pitch that Bell left up in the zone. Bell finished the inning, but when his spot in the lineup was due to hit with one-out and a man on first base in the third, Williams called on George Thomas to pinch-hit. Unfortunately Thomas struck out.

Waslewski took over for Bell and kept the game close, pitching three perfect innings in relief, and the Red Sox cut the deficit to 3–1 in the sixth on a Dalton Jones single that scored Andrews. In the bottom of the inning St. Louis got the run back, though. Brock again ignited a rally, beating out a bunt single, then inducing a wild pick-off throw from Stange that allowed him to advance to third. He scored on a Maris single.

Reggie Smith homered in the seventh to pull the Red Sox within 4–2, but that was as close as the Red Sox got. Cepeda doubled home a run in the eighth and the Cardinals won 5–2.

Game 4: Cardinals 6, Red Sox 0

	1	2	3	4	5	6	7	8	9	R	H	E
Boston	0	0	0	0	0	0	0	0	0	0	5	0
St. Louis	4	0	2	0	0	0	0	0	X	6	9	0

WP Bob Gibson
LP Jose Santiago

The second of three games to be played in St. Louis offered a rematch of the series' opener, Santiago versus Gibson. Santiago struggled mightily, failing to escape the first inning, while Gibson was even more dominant than he'd been in the first game. The result was a 6–0 St. Louis win that pushed Boston to the brink of elimination.

Yastrzemski collected a two-out single against Gibson in the first but Scott followed with a strikeout to end the inning. Then Brock jumpstarted the Cardinals offense, beating out a grounder to Jones at third base to start the bottom of the first. Flood followed with a single, then Maris doubled to left to drive home both runners. Next up was Tim McCarver who singled to score Maris. Before the inning was through, Santiago had been replaced by Bell and four runs had crossed the plate.

The Cardinals added two more runs against Jerry Stephenson in the third.

Gibson knew what to do with a big lead. He came right after the Red Sox, holding them to five hits and one walk over nine innings, while striking out six.

When Yastrzemski doubled to lead off the ninth, he became the first Boston base runner to advance to second base. He took third on a fly out by Scott, but was stranded when Smith struck out and Adair grounded out to end the game.

GAME 5: RED SOX 3, CARDINALS 1

	1	2	3	4	5	6	7	8	9	R	H	E
Boston	0	0	1	0	0	0	0	0	2	3	6	1
St. Louis	0	0	0	0	0	0	0	0	1	1	3	2

WP   Jim Lonborg
LP   Steve Carlton

No one could have known in 1967 that Steve Carlton was beginning a Hall of Fame career that would see him win 329 games and strike out more batters than any other left-hander in history, or that Jim Lonborg had already enjoyed his finest moment in the game and would wind up practicing dentistry on Boston's south shore. For one day in October of 1967, though, Lonborg shined more brightly than the future legend.

Lonborg held the Cardinals to just one run on three hits and no walks over nine innings, while Carlton pitched six innings and allowed an unearned run on three hits and two walks. Lonborg came within one out of pitching his second straight shutout, but Maris homered in the ninth to account for the St. Louis run.

Boston scored against Carlton in the third. Foy got things started with a single to left then Andrews laid down a bunt that the third baseman Shannon bobbled. With runners at

Reggie Smith signs autographs at Fenway. (Courtesy of the Boston Public Library, Print Department)

first and second and no one out, Yastrzemski was called out on strikes, but the next hitter, Harrelson, singled to left to bring Foy home and give Boston a 1–0 lead.

In the top of the ninth, the Red Sox gave Lonborg two insurance runs — the importance of which would become apparent when Maris homered in the bottom of the inning. The Boston runs scored on a bloop single by Howard that brought home Scott, who had walked, and Smith, who had doubled.

Game 6: Red Sox 8, Cardinals 4

	1	2	3	4	5	6	7	8	9	R	H	E
St. Louis	0	0	2	0	0	0	2	0	0	4	8	0
Boston	0	1	0	3	0	0	4	0	X	8	12	1

WP John Wyatt
LP Jack Lamabe
SV Gary Bell

Williams raised some eyebrows when he tabbed Waslewski, who had pitched well in relief in Game Three, to be his Game Six starter instead of Bell or Stange. The rookie had made just eight regular season starts while compiling a 2–2 mark. He made his manager look smart, though, and the Boston bullpen pitched well in his wake. Meanwhile, the Boston batters had no problem solving Hughes.

Despite hitting four home runs in the first four innings, the Red Sox found themselves in a 4–4 deadlock entering the bottom of the seventh when they struck for four runs to ease the tension that gripped the 35,188 fans on hand at Fenway Park.

After Waslewski set down the Cardinals in order in their first two at bats, Petrocelli homered with two outs in the bottom of the second to give Boston a 1–0 lead.

The Cardinals responded with a pair of runs in the third to take a 2–1 lead, then the Red Sox played long-ball in the fourth. Yastrzemski, Smith, and Petrocelli all homered in the inning to put Boston ahead 4–2. Petrocelli's second homer of the day chased Hughes from the game.

Waslewski pitched 5⅓ innings, holding St. Louis to two runs on four hits. But the Cardinals tied the game at 4–4 when Brock stroked a two-run homer against Wyatt in the seventh. Boston answered in the bottom of the seventh. Facing reliever Jack Lamabe, Jones lined a one-out pinch-single to right and scored when Foy followed with a double off the wall in left. After Joe Hoerner replaced Lamabe, Andrews singled home Foy. Yastrzemski then singled, moving Andrews to third, and then Adair hit a sacrifice fly to score Andrews. After a single by Scott, Smith singled Yastrzemski home with the fourth Boston run of the inning.

Bell took over on the mound for the Red Sox to start the eighth and allowed the Cardinals to load the bases with two outs before getting pinch-hitter Dave Ricketts to fly to Yastrzemski to end the rally.

In the ninth, Bell allowed a deep fly ball to right by Brock to start the inning but Thomas leaned into the Red Sox bullpen to rob the Cardinals of a home run. With two outs, Maris singled, but Cepeda followed with a come-backer to Bell for the final out.

After the game, Red Sox first base coach and batting instructor Bobby Doerr, who had been the second baseman when Boston lost to St. Louis in the 1946 World Series, put the season, which had come down to one final game, in perspective. "I remember being in this position in 1946," he said. "But what's different this time is that we weren't supposed to get

Lonborg poses with Boston students. (Courtesy of the Boston Public Library, Print Department)

this far.... No matter what happens tomorrow, this team can be proud of itself. I know I'm so proud to be associated with these young men."[7]

When asked which pitcher he would pin his hopes on in the final game, Dick Williams didn't hesitate. "Lonborg and champagne," the manager said.[8]

GAME 7: CARDINALS 7, RED SOX 2

	1	2	3	4	5	6	7	8	9	R	H	E
St. Louis	0	0	2	0	2	3	0	0	0	7	10	1
Boston	0	0	0	0	1	0	0	1	0	2	3	1

WP Bob Gibson
LP Jim Lonborg

On the morning of Columbus Day, October 12, the *Boston Record and American* boldly predicted a Red Sox win with a headline that read "Lonborg and Champagne" in three-inch-high block letters. There was only one problem: Lonborg would be pitching on two days' rest, and he would be facing the fully rested Bob Gibson.

The match-up marked only the second time a Game Seven pitted two pitchers who both had 2–0 records in the series against one another. The game was not close. By the fifth inning the Cardinals had a 4–0 lead, by the sixth they led 7–1. Gibson allowed just three hits and two runs in his third complete game effort of the series, while striking out ten. He even helped his cause by belting a fifth-inning home run to the deepest part of the ballpark — the triangle in right-center.

Afterwards, McCarver said Gibson had been especially motivated by the headlines that touted Lonborg as Boston's savior in waiting. "He was determined and there's nothing more fearsome than a determined Bob Gibson," McCarver said. "I felt sorry for the Boston hitters in a sense."[9]

The Cardinals took a 2–0 lead in the third inning when their shortstop Dal Maxvill led off with a triple and scored two batters later on a Flood single. After Maris singled Flood to third, Lonborg threw a wild pitch that allowed Flood to cross the plate.

In the fifth, the Cardinals scored two more runs. After Gibson's homer, Brock singled, stole second and third, and scored on a sacrifice fly by Maris.

The Red Sox chipped away at the lead with a run in the fifth, as Scott led off with a triple and scored when Javier's throw skipped into the visitors' dugout.

But the Cardinals scored three more times against Lonborg in the sixth. McCarver doubled to right, then Shannon reached on an error by Foy, then Javier hit a three-run homer. Lonborg yielded to the bullpen corps after six innings, having allowed ten hits and seven runs.

The final Red Sox run of the season scored in the eighth inning when Petrocelli doubled and scored on an infield groundout.

Yastrzemski led off the Red Sox ninth with a single to right, but was erased on a double-play grounder by Harrelson. Gibson struck out Scott to end the game and stake his claim to the series' MVP award. He finished with three wins, 27 innings pitched, and a 1.00 ERA. The effort foreshadowed a mythical 1968 season in which Gibson would set a new record with a 1.12 ERA. Brock also stood out in the series, batting .414, scoring eight runs, and setting a record with seven steals. Yastrzemski batted .400 for Boston with three homers and five runs batted in.

Although Lonborg would never again enjoy the success he did in 1967, years later he would recall that Boston never looked at its baseball team or its boys of summer the same way after the season of the Impossible Dream. "I don't think any of us on that team fully realized what effect 1967 would have on our lives and on the lives of millions of baseball fans," he remembered. "It wasn't until the summers of years to come that the real feeling of that season became apparent to me personally. I could walk around Boston and walk into places and not feel like a stranger. It just became a warmer and warmer feeling as the years went along."[10]

Chapter 9

The Regular Season: 95–65

    The 1975 World Series is widely considered one of the most compelling October Classics in baseball history. And Carlton Fisk's dramatic home run to win Game Six is one of the game's most enduring images, even though the Reds beat the Red Sox the next day.

    The season that preceded Boston's showdown with Cincinnati's "Big Red Machine" offered Red Sox fans one exciting moment after another. The team reported to spring training in Winter Haven, Florida, trying to forget its dismal collapse the year before. The 1974 Red Sox had enjoyed a 7½ game lead in the American League's Eastern Division with five weeks remaining in the season, only to plummet 7 games behind the Baltimore Orioles and into third place by season's end.

    The most heart-warming story of spring training was that Tony Conigliaro — who had retired in 1971 at age 26 — was attempting a comeback. Meanwhile, leftfielder Carl Yastrzemski drew attention as he learned to play first base to make room for Jim Rice in left field. Rice had won the Double-A Triple Crown at Bristol in 1973, and the International League batting title at Triple-A Pawtucket in 1974. The slugger would be one of three youngsters patrolling the Boston outfield. Fred Lynn, just a year and a half removed from a stellar college career at USC won the center field job, and 23-year-old Dwight Evans entered his third season in right.

    Before the Grapefruit League season began, most prognosticators picked the Red Sox to finish third, behind the Yankees, who had added Catfish Hunter and Bobby Bonds, and the Orioles, who had added Lee May, Ken Singleton, and Mike Torrez. The Red Sox won just 11 of 32 Grapefruit League contests, though, and lost their starting catcher, Carlton Fisk, when he sustained a fractured elbow when he was hit by a pitch late in the spring. The Boston medical staff pronounced the backstop would miss the first half of the season. On the last day of spring training, Yastrzemski called a team meeting and berated his teammates. "If we play the season the way we did the spring, we'll end up in last place," he said. "We sat back all spring and waited to get beat. It was a disgrace."[1]

Thus challenged, the team responded with a 5–2 win over the Brewers on Opening Day, after a few inches of snow had been shoveled from the Fenway Park bleachers. Soon the Red Sox were struggling though. Four straight losses to close April dropped Boston into fifth place with a record of 7–9. The good news was that no one else in the division was doing very well either. Only Detroit (10–6) and Milwaukee (9–7) had winning records as May began.

The Red Sox won six of their first seven games in May, including three wins by lefty Bill Lee, but then they lost six of seven to give back the ground they had gained.

On Monday, May 19, Charlie O. Finley's three-time defending world champion Oakland A's arrived in Boston for a three game series. In the first game, Luis Tiant pitched a complete game 11-hitter, the Boston bats routed Blue Moon Odom, and Boston won 10–5. In the second, Bill Lee pitched a two-hit 78-pitch masterpiece and his teammates hit four home runs off Vida Blue in a 7–0 win. In the finale, third baseman Rico Petrocelli homered and Yastrzemski hit a grand slam in a 7–3 win.

Three days later the Red Sox moved half a game ahead of Milwaukee and into first place as Lee blanked the Angels 6–0 for his second straight shutout. California's Bob Allietta hit into a double play with the bases loaded to end the game and extend Lee's scoreless streak to 21 innings.

Red Sox executive vice president Dick O'Connell made a trade on June 14, acquiring California second baseman Denny Doyle, who had been buried on the Angels bench behind rookie Jerry Remy, in exchange for a minor leaguer. Doyle replaced the struggling Doug Griffin on the right side of the Red Sox infield and hit .310 over the final 89 games. To make room for the new second baseman, the Red Sox designated Conigliaro, who was hitting just .123 at the time, for minor league assignment. The effects of his eye injury too great to overcome, Tony C.'s comeback was over.

It was during early June that Lynn emerged as the most exciting young player in the game, excelling both at the plate and in center field. Lynn carried a 20-game hit streak into a series in Detroit. The streak ended, but Lynn bounced back a day later to knock three home runs, a triple and a single at Tiger Stadium on June 18. The rookie drove in 10 runs in the 15–1 win and his 16 total bases tied a record set by Ty Cobb in 1925. Rice was also having quite a rookie campaign, batting cleanup in place of the injured Fisk.

On June 23, Fisk returned to the lineup. The Red Sox lost 11–3 to the Indians though, and a day later they slipped into second place for the first time in a month, losing again to Cleveland, while the Yankees beat Baltimore to take the division lead. On June 26, the Yankees arrived in Boston for a four-game weekend series. Fisk hit his first homer of the season and Lynn drove in three runs in the opener, propelling Boston to a 6–1 win, behind Tiant who earned his eleventh win. The Red Sox reclaimed first place with a 9–1 victory the next day, but dropped back into second a day later with an 8–6 loss. On Sunday, June 29, Boston moved into first place to stay when Roger Moret out-dueled Hunter 3–2.

Milwaukee forged a first place tie with the Red Sox on July 4, but Boston responded with seven straight wins to finish the first half with a 4 game lead over New York and a 4½ game lead over Milwaukee. Five members of the Oakland A's represented the AL as all-star starters in Milwaukee, along with three Yankees, and Rod Carew of the Twins. Lynn and Yastrzemski were the only Red Sox to make the cut, both serving as reserves, despite the fact that a trio of Red Sox hurlers entered the break with at least ten wins—Tiant (12–8), Rick Wise (11–6) and Lee (10–6). Lynn singled in one at bat while Yastrzemski belted a three-run homer against Tom Seaver that temporarily tied the score in a 6–3 NL win.

The Red Sox continued their winning ways when the season restarted, winning 16 of their first 21 games to start the second half. In a 9–3 win over the Royals on July 18, Rice hit one of the longest home runs in Fenway Park history, a shot that sailed over the center field bleachers and onto Lansdowne Street. The clout marked just the sixth time a ball hit to the right of the center field flagpole left the yard. Tom Yawkey, owner of the Red Sox since 1933, called the blast the longest homer he'd ever seen at Fenway.[2]

No two wins during the Red Sox fabulous July were bigger than the back-to-back shutouts Lee and Moret pitched on July 26 and 27 in New York. The Red Sox and Yankees split the first two games of a four-game set played at Shea Stadium due to stadium renovations underway in the Bronx. In the third game, Lee and Hunter were both masterful and the game was scoreless entering the final inning. Lynn led off the Boston ninth with a walk, then stole second and scored on a single. In the bottom of the inning, the centerfielder made a tumbling catch in right-center to take extra-bases away from Graig Nettles and preserve the win. The next day Rice had four hits and Yastrzemski homered as Boston won 6–0 to open an eight-game division lead.

Boston's 16–12 August was notable for a family reunion that took place at Logan Airport. On August 21, Tiant embraced his parents for the first time in many years after they received special permission from Fidel Castro to visit their son in America. Pitching with a sore back five days later, Tiant lost 8–2 to the Angels to fall to 15–13 on the season.

Any thoughts of Earl Weaver's Baltimore club repeating its stunning 1974 comeback were squelched in early September when Boston swept a pair from the second-place Orioles. Wise out-lasted Jim Palmer in the first game, winning 3–2 thanks to designated hitter Cecil Cooper's tenth-inning homer off Palmer, then Dick Pole and Dick Drago combined to shut down the Orioles 3–1 the next day. The Red Sox had an 8 game lead with 25 to play.

Facing the Orioles again on September 16, Tiant pitched a five-hit shutout to beat Palmer 2–0 and give Boston a 5½ game lead with 12 to play. Fisk and Petrocelli homered for the Boston runs. Boston lost the next two games, though, allowing Baltimore to stay alive in the race.

The final week of the season presented a setback for the Red Sox. In the second inning of a game against Detroit on September 21, Rice was hit in the right hand by a Vern Ruhle pitch. The Red Sox won the game, 6–5, but Rice would miss the rest of the season, playoffs included, with a broken metacarpal bone. While the injury was far less serious than the one Conigliaro suffered in 1967, it reminded the Red Sox that they had entered that postseason, too, without their number-four hitter.

After Tiant and Reggie Cleveland pitched matching 4–0 shutouts in both ends of a double-header against the Indians on September 26, the Red Sox clinched the division title the next day when the Orioles dropped a pair to the Yankees.

Boston's 95 wins were its most since 1949 when the team finished in second place to the Yankees with a record of 96–58. While the pitching staff was solid, clearly the Red Sox' balanced offense set them apart from other AL East contenders. The Red Sox led the league in runs (796), batting average (.275), on base percentage (.343), and slugging (.417).

After the season, Lynn became the first player to ever win the MVP Award and the Rookie of the Year Award in the same season, and he also claimed a Gold Glove for good measure. He led the league in runs (103), doubles (47) and slugging (.566), and finished second to Carew in batting at .331. He also had 21 homers and 105 RBI. The other "Gold Dust Twin," Rice, finished third in the MVP balloting and second in the Rookie of the Year vote with a .309 average, 22 homers, and 102 RBI. Fellow youngsters Evans (.274, 13 HR, 56 RBI), Cooper (.311, 14 HR, 44 RBI), and shortstop Rick Burleson (.252, 6 HR, 62 RBI) chipped in too, while the 35-year-old captain, Yastrzemski, hit .269 with 14 homers and 60 RBI. After missing the first half of the season, Fisk hit .331 with 10 HR and 52 RBI in 79 games. Outfielder Bernie Carbo provided pop off the bench, hitting .257 with 15 HR and 50 RBI.

The pitching staff placed ninth in the 12-team AL with a 3.98 ERA. Thanks to the offensive support, five Boston pitchers won at least 13 games: Wise (19–12, 3.95 ERA), Tiant (18–14, 4.02 ERA), Lee (17–9, 3.95 ERA), Moret (14–3, 3.60 ERA), and Cleveland (13–9, 4.43 ERA).

The Postseason: 6–4

The world champion A's entered the ALCS as favorites against the upstart Red Sox. Although Oakland had lost Hunter the previous December when an arbitrator declared him a free agent due to a breach of contract on the part of Finley, the A's finished second in the league with a 3.27 ERA. And Oakland won more games than any other team in the AL, going 98–64. The A's rotation boasted three steady arms in Blue (22–11, 3.01 ERA), Ken Holtzman (18–14, 3.14 ERA) and Dick Bosman (11–4, 3.52 ERA), but the strength of the staff was the bullpen. Rollie Fingers, Paul Lindblad and Jim Todd all had ERA's below 3.00, while combining to pitch 371 innings, win 27 games, and save 43 games. Offensively, the A's finished second to the Red Sox with 758 runs. AL home run champ Reggie Jackson (.253, 36 HR, 104 RBI) led the way, along with Gene Tenace (.255, 29 HR, 87 RBI), Joe Rudi (.278, 21 HR, 75 RBI), Billy Williams (.244, 23 HR, 81 RBI), and the 20-year-old Claudell Washington (.308, 10 HR, 77 RBI). The A's featured a pair of future big league managers in Tenace and Phil Garner, a future general manager in Sal Bando, and a trio of future hall-of-famers in Jackson, Williams and Fingers. But Boston's pitchers held the A's to five earned runs, while its lineup scored 18 runs in a three-game sweep.

The Cincinnati team that Boston played in the World Series presented an even more formidable foe. The 1975 Reds won 108 games and clinched their division earlier than any previous team, wrapping up the NL West on September 7. The first four hitters in the lineup on most nights were Cooperstown inductees in waiting — Pete Rose (.317, 47 2B, 74 RBI), Joe Morgan (.327, 17 HR, 94 RBI, 68 stolen bases), Tony Perez (.282, 20 HR, 109 RBI), and Johnny Bench (.283, 28 HR, 110 RBI). Manager Sparky Anderson sometimes inserted Ken Griffey — a .305 hitter who was just beginning a career in which he would amass 2143 hits — between Rose and Morgan. George Foster (.300, 23 HR, 78 RBI) hit fifth or sixth on most nights. Foster was entering the prime of a career that would see him lead the NL in RBI for three straight seasons between 1976–1978 and finish with 348 home runs. Shortstop Dave Concepcion (.274, 5 HR, 49 RBI) was entering the sixth of 19 seasons he would play in a Reds uniform while collecting 2326 hits. The only weak link among Cincinnati's eight regulars was Cesar Geronimo, a center fielder who batted .257 in 1975.

Surprisingly, no Reds starter finished with more than 15 wins. Cincinnati finished third in the NL with a 3.37 ERA, thanks to a bullpen that led the majors with 50 saves. The relief corps featured a quartet of capable closers in Rawly Eastwick (22 saves), Will McEnaney (15 saves), Clay Carroll (7 saves) and Pedro Borbon (5 saves). All four appeared in at least 56 games and maintained an earned run average below 3.00. They combined for a 26–10 record. Starters Jack Billingham, Gary Nolan, and Don Gullett tied for the team lead with 15 wins, while Fred Norman won 12, Pat Darcy, 11, and Clay Kirby, 10.

On a historical note, the 1975 World Series was the last October Classic to be played without the use of the designated hitter — that innovation that had debuted in the AL on a trial basis in 1973. The AL owners voted to permanently adopt the DH in December of 1975, and all subsequent World Series have allowed teams to use designated hitters in games played in AL ballparks.

1975 American League Championship Series: Red Sox 3, A's 0

Game 1: Red Sox 7, A's 1

	1	2	3	4	5	6	7	8	9	R	H	E
Oakland	0	0	0	0	0	0	0	1	0	1	3	4
Boston	2	0	0	0	0	0	5	0	X	7	8	3

WP Luis Tiant
LP Ken Holtzman

After a six-day layoff between the end of the regular season and the start of the playoffs, the A's and Red Sox met at Fenway Park on a Saturday afternoon. Boston may have lacked postseason experience, which Oakland had in abundance, but it was the A's who made three first inning errors, leading to two Boston runs, and an eighth-inning error that resulted in three more unearned runs. Tiant took care of the rest, dazzling the A's with an assortment of breaking pitches delivered from all angles.

With Rice out, Yastrzemski started in left field and Juan Beniquez, a 25-year-old spare outfielder, moved into the Boston leadoff spot as the designated hitter. Fisk returned to his familiar clean-up spot. All three players contributed to the first Boston win.

Tiant struck out two of the three batters he faced in the first inning, then Yastrzemski singled to begin a two-out rally against Holtzman in the bottom of the first. A lefty, Holtzman drew the starting nod from manager Alvin Dark based on his 6–2 career record in the postseason. Fisk came to the plate after Yastrzemski and hit a hard groundball toward Bando at third, but the ball took a funny hop to elude the third baseman, and then Washington stumbled, allowing the ball to roll into the left field corner. Red Sox third base coach Don Zimmer waved home Yastrzemski as Washington overthrew both cutoff men. The official scorer credited Bando and Washington with errors. Lynn came to the plate next and pulled a groundball to Garner at second. After the ball bounced off the rookie's bare right hand, he inadvertently kicked it into right field, allowing Fisk to score.

The score remained 2–0 until the seventh when Boston erupted for five runs. Evans got things started with a double and scored one out later when Burleson ripped a double. Dark replaced Holtzman with Todd, and Beniquez greeted the reliever with an RBI single that opened a 4–0 lead. After Beniquez stole second and third, he scored when center fielder Billy North dropped a fly ball by Doyle. Running hard on the play, Doyle reached third, and scored one out later on a Fisk single. Lynn doubled home the final Boston run.

Tiant held Oakland to a pair of singles over the first seven innings — leadoff hits by Rudi in the fifth and Jackson in the seventh — and carried a two-hitter and 7–0 lead into the eighth. In the eighth, Oakland scored an unearned run when Burleson muffed a routine grounder at short, and Cooper botched a play at first. Unfazed, Tiant retired six of the seven final A's to cap a three-hit, eight-strikeout, 140-pitch performance.

Afterwards, Fisk told reporters that Tiant, as dominant as he'd been, hadn't even had his full repertoire of pitches working. "He didn't have more than three or four good pitches today," the Boston catcher said. "One thing he uses a lot and didn't throw is the knuckler."[3]

Game 2: Red Sox 6, A's 3

	1	2	3	4	5	6	7	8	9	R	H	E
Oakland	2	0	0	1	0	0	0	0	0	3	10	0
Boston	0	0	0	3	0	1	1	1	X	6	12	0

WP Roger Moret
LP Rollie Fingers
SV Dick Drago

Over the final two and a half months of the season, Yastrzemski had batted just .212. Thrust back into an outfield role and into the third spot in the batting order by Rice's injury, "Yaz" suddenly returned to form in the second game. After the Red Sox fell behind 3–0, he sparkled both at the plate and in the field, leading Boston to a 6–3 win.

Oakland scored twice against Cleveland in the first when Bando doubled with two out and Jackson cracked a home run over the right field bullpens.

Yastrzemski threw a runner out at third base in the third inning to help Cleveland out of a jam, but the A's extended the lead to 3–0 in the fourth on back-to-back doubles by Rudi and Washington.

Boston struck back with three runs in the bottom of the fourth. Doyle blooped a single over Garner's head, then Yastrzemski lined a Blue pitch into the left field screen for a two-run homer. Yastrzemski had not hit an opposite field homer all season. Fisk followed the home run with a double, then Lynn tied the game with a single.

After Cooper doubled to lead off the Boston fifth, Dark summoned his closer, Fingers. The handle-bar-mustached reliever had pitched exceptionally well against Boston in the regular season — posting three wins and a 1.03 ERA in 17⅔ innings — but he had not entered a game so early all season long. Fingers escaped the fifth unscathed when Cooper, trying to score on a Beniquez fly ball, was gunned down at the plate by Jackson. Boston took the lead in the sixth though, when Yastrzemski laced a one-out double to left and scored on a single by Fisk.

"Yaz brought them back," Jackson acknowledged after the game. "All their players hung in there, but Yaz brought them back."[4]

Petrocelli clanked a homer off one of the light towers above the left field wall in the seventh for Boston's fourth run, and in the eighth Lynn singled home Beniquez to make it 6–3.

The Boston bullpen allowed just three hits and a walk over the final four innings, as Moret, who was credited with the win, pitched a scoreless sixth, and Drago pitched the final three frames. As the Red Sox closed in on their second win, the Fenway faithful serenaded Finley, who sat behind the Oakland dugout, with chants of "Good-bye, Charlie."[5]

GAME 3: RED SOX 5, A'S 3

	1	2	3	4	5	6	7	8	9	R	H	E
Boston	0	0	0	1	3	0	0	1	0	5	11	1
Oakland	0	0	0	0	0	1	0	2	0	3	6	2

WP Rick Wise
LP Ken Holtzman
SV Dick Drago

As the series shifted to Oakland, the Red Sox sent a well-rested 19-game winner to the mound in the person of Rick Wise. Oakland, clearly in panic-mode, countered with Holtzman on two days' rest.

Boston jumped ahead 4–0 and held on for a 5–3 win. Yastrzemski again stood out defensively in left, and Drago delivered big outs when Boston needed them.

The Red Sox broke a scoreless tie in the fourth, thanks to another Oakland error. After Washington dropped a two-out fly ball by Lynn, Petrocelli singled Lynn home.

In the fifth, Boston scored three more runs to take a 4–0 lead. Burleson started the rally with a one-out double over the third base bag, then Doyle slapped a run-scoring double down the right field line, then Yastrzemski singled to put runners at the corners. With Holtzman tiring, Dark brought in Todd. Fisk greeted the reliever with a single that scored Doyle and move Yastrzemski to third, then Dark went to the mound again, and called for the left-handed Linblad to pitch to Lynn. Lindblad threw a wild pitch to score Yaz, then got Lynn to pop out.

The A's recouped a run in the sixth, and scored two more in the eighth, chasing Wise from the game. The damage in the eighth would have been worse, if not for the heroics of Yastrzemski and Drago. The A's had one run in and runners at first and second with one out for Jackson when the game was halted due to the unruliness of the Oakland fans. At first a few food wrappers and bottles were tossed toward Yastrzemski in left, then, suddenly, a number of firecrackers exploded in the outfield. After security got the crowd under control, Jackson laced what would be Wise's last pitch of the game toward the gap in left-center. As it left the bat, the liner had all the markings of a two-run double that would pull the A's within a run and put the tying run in scoring position with one out. But the aging Boston left fielder ran full bore, then laid out face first to trap the ball on one hop. Yastrzemski bounced to his feet and fired toward the infield to prevent the runner from first from scoring and hold Jackson to a single. Drago took over for Wise with the Red Sox clinging to a 5–3 lead and runners at the corners. He threw one pitch, a sinker that Rudi grounded to Burleson. The shortstop flipped to Doyle at second, and Doyle fired to Cooper at first for an inning-ending double play.

"I was intent on keeping [Jackson] on first where a double play could be made," Yastrzemski said after the game. "And Drago came in and threw it."[6]

In the Oakland ninth, Williams smashed a liner off Drago's shin to start the inning, but the ball bounced right to Cooper, who flipped to Drago covering first for the out. The next batter, Tenace, popped to shortstop. One out away from clinching the pennant, Drago threw seven straight balls, walking North and going to 3–0 on pinch-hitter Jim Holt. After a visit to the mound by Johnson, Drago regained his touch. He pumped in two called strikes, then Holt fouled off a pitch, then Holt sent a dribbler to Doyle for the final out.

"They just outplayed us," Dark said afterwards. "They out-fielded us, out-pitched us, out-hit us. We never really got to play any baseball against them."[7]

The Red Sox hit .316 in the series, to the A's .194. The Red Sox posted a 1.67 ERA, to the A's 4.32. Six Oakland errors led to six unearned Boston runs.

Yastrzemski batted .455 (5 for 11) in the series, while Burleson, Cooper, and Fisk also batted over .400.

When the Red Sox' team charter landed at Logan Airport the next morning, nearly 2000 fans were there waiting for them. "Bring on the Little Red Tinkertoy," pitcher Reggie Cleveland said, referring in jest to the Reds, who had swept the Pirates in the NLCS.[8]

1975 World Series: Reds 4, Red Sox 3

GAME 1: RED SOX 6, REDS 0

	1	2	3	4	5	6	7	8	9	R	H	E
Cincinnati	0	0	0	0	0	0	0	0	0	0	5	0
Boston	0	0	0	0	0	0	6	0	X	6	12	0

WP Luis Tiant
LP Don Gullett

After a three-day layoff, the World Series began on a rainy Saturday night in Boston. Both teams wasted chances to score early, before the Red Sox broke through for six runs in the seventh, and Tiant retired the Reds in order in the eighth and ninth to complete a five-hit shutout.

The Red Sox nearly scored against the left-handed Gullett in the first and sixth innings, but had runners thrown out at the plate to end both threats.

Meanwhile Tiant escaped jams in the fourth, sixth and seventh. In the fourth, the speedy Morgan singled and took second with one out when first base umpire Nick Colosi called a balk on Tiant. Tiant bore down though, and used an array of sliders, curves, change-ups and knuckleballs to retire Bench, who finally popped out after a 14-pitch battle. The next batter, Perez, watched a fastball sail over home plate for a called third strike.

In the sixth, Morgan again reached second with one out when he cracked a double. But Tiant got Bench to ground out to third, then struck out Perez, this time on three off-speed pitches.

In the seventh, Foster led off with a single, then Concepcion hit a blooper over Burleson's head that looked sure to fall for a hit. But Yastrzemski raced in and made a diving catch. With one out, Anderson gave Foster the steal sign, but Fisk gunned down the runner at second base. Griffey then doubled and Geronimo walked, before Tiant got Gullett to pop out to strand both runners.

The crowd was still chanting "Loo-ie, Loo-ie," when Tiant led off the Boston seventh. He promptly smacked a hanging change-up between third and short for a single. Evans came up next and laid down a bunt. Gullett fielded, and whirled to throw to second, but he lost his footing on the wet grass and his throw went into centerfield. The Red Sox had runners at first and second with no outs. Next up was Doyle. After getting the bunt sign before Gullett's first delivery and fouling it off, Doyle swung at the second pitch and shot a liner to left to load the bases. Yastrzemski delivered the first Boston run and knocked Gullett from the game with a single to right. Carroll took over for the Reds and walked Fisk to force home the second run. Anderson trotted to the mound again, and this time called upon

McEnaney, who struck out Lynn, but then allowed run-scoring singles to Petrocelli and Burleson and a sacrifice fly to Cooper.

Tiant struck out to end the inning, then took the mound amidst jubilation at Fenway. The crowd stood and cheered as "El Tiante" mowed down the final six Reds.

Afterwards, Rose, who had gone an uncharacteristic 0-for-4, lauded the Red Sox starter. "In the National League we don't face anyone who throws a spinning curve that takes two minutes to come down," he said.[9]

Anderson was less complimentary. "This was the weakest five-hitter I've ever seen," the brash manager said. "I don't know how many shots we hit right at people, shots that were caught or turned into outs."[10]

GAME 2: REDS 3, RED SOX 2

	1	2	3	4	5	6	7	8	9	R	H	E
Cincinnati	0	0	0	1	0	0	0	0	2	3	7	1
Boston	1	0	0	0	0	1	0	0	0	2	7	0

WP Rawly Eastwick
LP Dick Drago

A day after winning the opener, the Red Sox were within one out of taking a two-game lead in the series, before the Reds came back. Lee, who did not pitch in the ALCS after struggling over the final month, got the starting nod from Red Sox manager Darrell Johnson, while Anderson tabbed Billingham, who had also struggled late in the season.

On a rainy Sunday afternoon, Lee struck out Rose to start the game, then got Morgan to ground out and Bench to fly out. The Red Sox wasted no time in reaching Billingham in the bottom of the first, though they might have done more damage if not for some suspect base running. Cooper shot Billingham's first pitch over Foster's head in left for a double, then advanced to third on an infield hit by Doyle. With no outs, Yastrzemski hit a high chopper that Billingham snared on the back of the mound. The ball had bounced too high for the Reds to turn a double play, so Billingham looked Cooper back to third, then threw to second to force out Doyle. But when Billingham threw to second, Cooper broke for the plate. Concepcion fired home and Bench tagged out Cooper. Yastrzemski wisely took second on the play, and it was a good thing. He came home a moment later when Fisk singled to right.

Lee protected the 1–0 lead for two innings, but in the fourth the Reds pulled even on a Morgan walk, Bench single, and run-scoring fielder's choice by Perez.

Boston reclaimed the lead in the sixth, scoring an unearned run. Yastrzemski singled with one out, and Fisk reached on an error by the normally sure-handed Concepcion. After Lynn flied to right for the second out, Petrocelli singled to center to give the Red Sox a 2–1 lead.

Lee retired the Reds in the seventh, then led off the Boston half of the inning by striking out against McEnaney. Then the heavens opened. The rain halted play for half an hour. After the delay, Lee returned to retire the Reds in the eighth. He entered the ninth with a four-hitter and a 2–1 lead, but when Bench sliced his first pitch of the inning into right field for a double, Johnson brought in Drago.

In his autobiography, *The Wrong Stuff*, published nine years later, Lee faulted Johnson for sending him out to pitch in the ninth. Lee wrote, "When in the memory of organized baseball, has a left-hander who's already thrown eight innings come out to face a Hall of Fame right-handed batter after a rain delay like that?"[11]

Petrocelli in the Red Sox dugout during a rain delay. (Courtesy of the Boston Public Library, Print Department)

Drago retired the first two batters he faced — Perez on a groundout that advanced Bench to third, and Foster on a pop up to left. With the crowd cheering for the final out, Concepcion hit a chopper over Drago's head that went for an infield single and tied the game. Concepcion stole second on a close play, then Griffey lined an outside fastball into left-center to put the Reds ahead 3–2.

The shocked Red Sox went down in order in the bottom of the ninth.

Game 3: Reds 6, Red Sox 5

	1	2	3	4	5	6	7	8	9	10	R	H	E
Boston	0	1	0	0	0	1	1	0	2	0	5	10	2
Cincinnati	0	0	0	2	3	0	0	0	0	1	6	7	0

WP   Rawly Eastwick
LP   Jim Willoughby

The series shifted to Riverfront Stadium in Cincinnati where the Reds had posted a 64–17 record in 1975. Riverfront and Fenway could not have been more different. With symmetrical outfield dimensions and artificial turf, the field that sat on the banks of the Ohio River was the quintessential "cookie-cutter" stadium. The park played to the speedy Reds' advantage, providing a fast track for a team that swiped a league-best 168 bases in 1975.

On this night, Riverfront served as a launching pad, though, not a racetrack. The teams combined for six home runs in forging a 5–5 tie through nine innings. In the end, a controversial umpiring call, or non-call, that to this day makes Larry Barnett's name anathema in New England, helped the Reds score the winning run.

Fisk got the scoring started in the second when he blasted a Nolan pitch over the fence in left-center.

Wise, who had pitched a no-hitter against the Reds at Riverfront while playing for the Phillies in 1971, carried a no-hitter into the fourth. But Perez walked with two outs and then Bench made the Reds' first hit count, sending a shot over the fence in left field to put the National Leaguers ahead 2–1.

The Reds added three more in the fifth to open a 5–1 lead when Concepcion and Geronimo started the inning with back-to-back home runs, and Rose tripled and scored on a sacrifice fly.

Boston gamely battled back, adding single runs on a sacrifice fly by Lynn in the sixth and a pinch-hit homer by Carbo in the seventh. Evans tied the game in the ninth with a one-out, two-run homer against Eastwick.

Jim Willoughby retired the Reds in order in the bottom of the ninth to send the game into extra innings, and Doyle led off the Boston tenth with a single. Johnson chose not to sacrifice with Yastrzemski and Yaz flied out. Then Fisk hit into a double play.

In the bottom of the tenth, Geronimo led off with a single, and Anderson chose to advance the runner with a bunt. The decision for the Reds manager was easier to make than Johnson's decision had been, since Cincinnati's pitcher was due to hit next. Anderson sent utility man Ed Armbrister to the plate as a pinch-hitter and Armbrister bounced a bunt off the plate, took two quick steps, then stopped right in front of Fisk, who had pounced out of his crouch to field the ball. The catcher and runner were tangled for an instant, then Fisk gloved the ball and threw wildly toward second. The ball sailed past Burleson into center field, putting Reds runners at second and third with no outs. A livid Fisk argued that the runner had interfered with him, but Barnett, the home plate umpire, told him the play did not constitute interference since the runner had not intentionally obstructed his pursuit of the ball.[12]

Most in the baseball world agreed that Barnett should have ruled the batter out and sent Geronimo back to first. Rule 2.00 (a) stated then, as it does now, "Offensive interference is an act by the team at bat which interferes with, obstructs, impedes, hinders, or confuses any fielder attempting to make a play. If the umpire declares the batter, batter-runner, or a runner out for interference, all other runners shall return to the last base that was, in the judgment of the umpire, legally touched at the time of the interference."[13] The rule says nothing about intent. And clearly, Armbrister's collision with Fisk knocked the catcher off balance as he gloved the ball and threw toward second.

After arguing to no avail, Johnson called upon Moret to replace Willoughby. The lefty intentionally walked Rose to load the bases, and then struck out pinch-hitter Merv Rettenmund, who batted for Griffey. With one out, Morgan ended the game with a drive over Lynn's head in center.

Game 4: Red Sox 5, Reds 4

	1	2	3	4	5	6	7	8	9	R	H	E
Boston	0	0	0	5	0	0	0	0	0	5	11	1
Cincinnati	2	0	0	2	0	0	0	0	0	4	9	1

WP Luis Tiant
LP Fred Norman

Trailing two-games-to-one, the Red Sox sent Tiant back to the mound on three days' rest in Game Four, and he delivered, offering another complete game effort and chipping in at the plate on the way to a 5–4 win.

With the left-handed Norman starting on the mound for Cincinnati, Johnson shuffled the Red Sox lineup, replacing Cooper at first with Yastrzemski and inserting the right-handed Beniquez in left field. But it didn't matter who was playing first or left in the first inning. Tiant struggled with his control, and when he left the ball up in the strike zone, the Reds made solid contact. Rose led off with a single, then Griffey doubled him home. Fortunately for the Red Sox, Griffey was thrown out by Lynn when he tried to stretch his hit into a triple. But the Reds' bats weren't done. Morgan walked and later came around to score on a two-out double by Bench. After one inning the Reds led 2–0.

The Red Sox scored their only runs of the night in the fourth inning. Fisk and Lynn struck for back-to-back singles to start the frame, before Evans tripled them home with one out. Evans came home on a Burleson double to left-center, then Tiant singled to center to put runners at the corners. Burleson scored on a Beniquez tapper that Perez booted at third, and Tiant scored on a single by Yastrzemski. Boston led 5–2.

The Reds got two runs back in the bottom of the fourth though, thanks to a two-out single by Foster, a double by Concepcion, and a triple by Geronimo. With the potential tying run at third, Tiant fanned pinch-hitter Terry Crowley to end the inning. After four innings, the score was 5–4. It would remain that way.

Tiant allowed three hits and three walks over the final five innings, but Cincinnati stranded all six runners. The Reds had men on first and second in the last of the ninth with just one out, but Griffey lined out to Lynn — who snared the ball on a full sprint before crashing into the outfield fence — and Morgan popped to first on Tiant's 163rd pitch to end the game.

Game 5: Reds 6, Red Sox 2

	1	2	3	4	5	6	7	8	9	R	H	E
Boston	1	0	0	0	0	0	0	0	1	2	5	0
Cincinnati	0	0	0	1	1	3	0	1	X	6	8	0

WP Don Gullett
LP Reggie Cleveland
SV Rawley Eastwick

After playing three straight closely contested games, the Reds and Red Sox played a bit of a clunker in Game Five. The Reds did their part, performing well on both sides of the ball, but after a fast start the Red Sox bats struggled against Gullett. The result was a 6–2 Cincinnati win.

Doyle got things started for the Red Sox in the first when he sent a Gullett pitch into the right field corner for a triple and scored on a Yastrzemski sacrifice fly. Boston protected the 1–0 lead until the fourth when Perez snapped out of an 0–15 slump with a two-out solo homer off Cleveland.

In the fifth, Gullett helped his own cause, lashing a two-out single then scoring on a double by Rose to give the Reds a 2–1 advantage.

Cincinnati broke the game open, scoring three times in the sixth. Morgan got things started with a walk, and then Bench was credited with a single on a ball that Doyle probably could have fielded. Perez came to the plate next and blasted his second homer of the night, a three-run shot off the facing of the second deck in left-center.

Gullett, meanwhile, retired 16 straight Red Sox between the first and sixth innings, and carried a two-hitter into the ninth. But after retiring the first two Boston hitters, the lefty had trouble finishing. Yastrzemski, Fisk and Lynn cracked consecutive hits to bring in one Red Sox run and bring Anderson out of the Reds dugout for a new pitcher. Eastwick came in and struck out Petrocelli to end the game.

Game 6: Red Sox 7, Reds 6

	1	2	3	4	5	6	7	8	9	10	11	12	R	H	E
Cincinnati	0	0	0	0	3	0	2	1	0	0	0	0	6	14	0
Boston	3	0	0	0	0	0	0	3	0	0	0	1	7	10	1

WP Rick Wise
LP Pat Darcy

Lee was originally penciled into Johnson's lineup to start the sixth game for the Red Sox. When rain washed out any chance of playing on October 18, 19 and 20, though, the Red Sox manager decided to give the start to Tiant. Tiant, like Nolan, the Reds starter, would be long departed, however, by the conclusion of one of the most memorable World Series games ever.

The Red Sox shook the rust off their bats in the bottom of the first, tagging Nolan for three straight two-out hits, capped by a Lynn homer over the Boston bullpen that opened a 3–0 lead.

The Reds came up with three runs of their own in the fifth. After Armbrister drew a walk and Rose singled, Griffey tripled to left-center to bring both runners home. Lynn nearly made a leaping catch on Griffey's shot, before crashing headfirst into the left field wall. The center fielder lay motionless on the warning track for several minutes but when he regained consciousness, he refused to leave the game. Once play resumed, Bench singled off the left field wall to plate Griffey and tie the game, 3–3.

Cincinnati scored two runs in the seventh on a Foster double and one in the eighth on a Geronimo home run.

Down to their final six outs, the Red Sox trailed 6–3. But Lynn singled to lead off the Boston eighth, and Petrocelli followed with a walk. Anderson made his way to the mound and replaced Borbon with Eastwick, a move that paid immediate dividends when Eastwick whiffed Evans and got Burleson to line out. With Boston down to its final four outs, Moret, who had replaced Tiant in the eighth, was due to hit next. Johnson sent the left-handed hitting Carbo to the plate instead, expecting Anderson to counter with the southpaw McEnaney who was warming up in the Reds bullpen. Then Johnson figured, he would send the right-handed hitting Beniquez to the plate. But Anderson called Johnson's bluff and left Eastwick on the mound. Carbo ran the count to 2–2, then barely fouled back a slider. With his next pitch Eastwick threw a belt-high fastball and this time Carbo made solid contact, driving the ball high into the Boston night. The shot finally landed in the centerfield bleachers, tying the game, 6–6.

The Reds went down quickly against Drago in the top of the ninth, then Boston loaded the bases with no outs in the bottom of the inning. Doyle led off with a walk, then Yastrzemski singled to put runners at the corners, then Fisk was walked intentionally. It seemed certain the Red Sox were about to force a seventh game, but as quickly as the rally had materialized, it ended. Lynn lofted a fly ball to shallow left, and although Zimmer instructed Doyle to tag up and stay at third, Doyle had other ideas. He tagged, then broke for home. Foster's throw beat him easily. The next batter, Petrocelli, grounded out to end the inning.

Cincinnati had excellent chances to score in the eleventh and twelfth innings. Morgan came to the plate against Drago in the eleventh with Griffey on first and one out and slashed a deep drive to right. Evans, who had already established himself as one of the best right fielders in the game, raced toward the outfield seats located to the right of the visitors' bullpen, leapt, and came down with the ball. The shot would have left the park if not for the brilliant catch. Griffey, who had raced all the way to third, began hastily retracing his steps, as Evans threw toward first. The throw was off-line, drawing Yastrzemski into foul territory in front of the Red Sox dugout, but the heady veteran flipped the ball to Burleson covering first to double off Griffey.

After the Red Sox pinch-hit for Drago in a fruitless bottom of the eleventh, Wise took over on the mound for Boston in the twelfth. Perez and Foster singled with one out, but Wise retired the next two hitters to preserve the 6–6 deadlock.

With the stage thus set, Carlton Fisk seized the moment in the bottom of the twelfth. Leading off against the eighth Reds pitcher of the night, Pat Darcy, Fisk hit a home run that is rivaled to this day in terms of its significance only by Bill Mazeroski's walk-off shot in Game Seven of the 1960 World Series against the Yankees. While the act of hitting a home run at such a dramatic moment would have been reason enough to earn Fisk iconic status in Boston, the homer was more than just an ordinary homer. As the ball sailed into the dark night, it drifted perilously close to the left field foul pole mounted above Fenway Park's fabled Green Monster. Fisk demonstratively leapt off the ground, his body perpendicular to the first base line, waving with both arms as if to implore the ball to stay fair. According to Boston legend, the enduring image of Fisk leaping like a desperate child was captured on camera only because an NBC cameraman stationed inside the left field scoreboard froze with fear when a giant rat emerged from the bowels of the stadium to confront him. The cameraman ignored his director's orders to follow the ascent of the ball, and as a result America was treated to Fisk's jubilant reaction when the ball, as if heeding his command, clanked against the foul pole for a game-winning home run, then dropped harmlessly onto the left field grass.

Afterwards, Fisk recalled telling Lynn, who had stood beside him in the on-deck circle before the inning, that he had a feeling something special was about to happen. The reality of the moment turned out even better than Fisk's wildest dreams, though. "I said, 'Freddy, I feel something good here,'" the Boston catcher remembered. "I'm gonna hit one off the wall. Drive me in."[14]

Fisk didn't need Lynn to drive him in. But Lynn was waiting at the plate along with twenty-five other men, giddy as school kids, when Fisk leapt onto the plate and then into their arms.

GAME 7: REDS 4, RED SOX 3

	1	2	3	4	5	6	7	8	9	R	H	E
Cincinnati	0	0	0	0	0	2	1	0	1	4	9	0
Boston	0	0	3	0	0	0	0	0	0	3	5	2

WP Clay Carroll
LP Jim Burton
SV Will McEnaney

Less than 20 hours after Fisk's home run, the two teams took the field for the final game of the 1975 baseball season. The game seemed likely to prove anti-climactic after the high-drama of Game Six. And yet, Game Seven provided many memorable moments in its own right, although Red Sox fans might prefer to forget them.

At the outset, the fates of the two teams rested on a pair of left-handers: for the Reds, the hard-throwing Gullett, for the Red Sox, the soft-tossing Lee.

The Red Sox scored three runs in the third when Gullett struggled with his control. Carbo reached on a one-out walk, then Doyle singled him to third, and Yastrzemski singled him home. Gullett then walked three of the next four batters to force home two runs.

The score held until the sixth when Rose broke up a potential inning-ending double play with a hard slide into Doyle at second and then Perez swatted one of Lee's famous blooper pitches over the screen above the left field wall for a two-run homer.

Clinging to a 3–2 lead and pitching with a blister on his thumb, Lee walked Griffey on four straight pitches with one out in the seventh. Johnson lifted Lee in favor of Moret, and the reliever got the first man he faced, Geronimo, to pop to short. But after Griffey stole second and Armbrister walked, Rose lined a single to center to tie the game.

Carroll retired the Red Sox in order in the bottom of the seventh, then faced just three batters in the eighth as Burleson hit into a double play after Evans led off with a walk. Willoughby, meanwhile, held the Reds in check.

With the game knotted at 3–3 to start the ninth, rookie left-hander Jim Burton, who had faced just two batters previously in the series, came in to pitch for Boston. Burton walked Griffey to start the inning, then Geronimo followed with a sacrifice bunt to move Griffey to second. Griffey took third on a grounder to second by pinch-hitter Dan Driessen. The Red Sox were within one out of escaping the jam with the tie intact. After Burton walked Rose on four pitches, he jumped ahead of Morgan 0–2. Morgan broke his bat on Burton's next pitch, a slider down and away, but got enough wood on the ball to drop it into shallow center field for a run scoring single.

The Red Sox went down in order against McEnaney in the bottom of the ninth with Yastrzemski making the final out on a fly ball to Geronimo.

Rose, who reached base in 11 of his final 15 plate appearances in the series and in 15 of 32 plate appearances overall, was named series MVP. Yastrzemski finished with the best average among Red Sox players, hitting .310 (9-for-29).

The next spring, Lynn, Fisk and Burleson held out for larger contracts, and although all three eventually rejoined the team, Boston finished third, 15½ games behind the Yankees. Tom Yawkey died of leukemia in July, his beloved Red Sox having broken his heart for the final time.

CHAPTER 10

The Regular Season: 99-64

On October 2, 1978 the Red Sox and Yankees took the Fenway Park lawn for a one-game playoff to decide the American League East title. The second one-game playoff in AL history was preceded by one of the most remarkable division races the game has ever known. The Red Sox led the Yankees by as many as 14 games in July before wilting in the heat of summer. At the same time the Red Sox began to slump, the Yankees began a remarkable tear, catalyzed by the arrival of new manager Bob Lemon who replaced Billy Martin. By mid-September, Boston had fallen 2½ games behind New York, but the Red Sox won their final eight games to finish tied with the Yankees atop the division.

The season began amidst great promise in Boston, and for the first half of the campaign the Red Sox lived up to New England's lofty expectations. Despite winning 97 games in 1977, the Red Sox had finished 2½ games behind George Steinbrenner's World Series bound Yankees. Red Sox president Jean Yawkey responded by firing general manager Dick O'Connell and promoting assistant general manager Haywood Sullivan. Sullivan wasted little time before strengthening the Red Sox and weakening the Yankees, signing free agent Yankee pitcher Mike Torrez on November 23, 1977. The right-hander had won 14 games for New York the year before and had claimed a pair of victories against the Los Angeles Dodgers in the World Series. Sullivan then strengthened the Boston infield with a December trade that sent pitcher Don Aase to California for speedy second baseman Jerry Remy.

In their final major move of the off-season, the Red Sox acquired 23-year-old flamethrower Dennis Eckersley, an all-star the year before, in a six-player trade with Cleveland on March 30, 1978.

Meanwhile, things were relatively quiet in New York, where it was impossible for Steinbrenner to trump the headlines he had made the previous winter when he had reeled in free agent slugger Reggie Jackson. The Yankees' biggest move was the signing of free agent closer Rich Gossage.

The Red Sox stumbled out of the gates, but after returning from a 2–3 opening road-trip, they caught fire. They won their first seven games at Fenway Park on the way to winning 26 of their first 30 home games.

Boston assumed the division lead on May 14 when Eckersley beat the Twins 6–2. The Red Sox and Tigers then flip-flopped between first and second for the next week, before Boston moved into sole possession of first on May 24 behind Torrez's sixth win of the year against the Blue Jays. Boston would not relinquish the division lead until September.

The Red Sox racked up four different winning streaks of at least seven games over the season's first half en route to a 57–26 record at the break and a 9-game lead over second-place Milwaukee and an 11½-game lead over third-place New York. Eckersley and Torrez had 21 wins between them, but were not among a cast of seven Red Sox chosen to represent the AL in the All-Star Game. Heading to the Midsummer Classic in San Diego were second baseman Remy, shortstop Rick Burleson, right fielder Dwight Evans, center fielder Fred Lynn, outfielder Jim Rice, outfielder/first baseman Carl Yastrzemski, and catcher Carlton Fisk. Only first baseman George Scott and third baseman Butch Hobson, among Boston's regular position players, failed to make the AL squad.

Boston's four All-Star outfielders would combine for 109 HR and 365 RBI before the season's end, but clearly the 1978 Red Sox were Rice's team. By the season's midpoint he was already well on his way to winning the league MVP award and to leading the league in hits (213), triples (15), home runs (46), runs batted in (139), and slugging (.600). Rice also became first AL player since Joe DiMaggio in 1937 to amass as many as 400 total bases in a season, collecting 406.

By the All-Star break, legendary *New York Times* writer Red Smith had already conceded the AL East title to the Red Sox, while Jackson agreed, stating, "Even Affirmed couldn't catch the Red Sox now," referring to the horse that had just won racing's Triple Crown.[1] Lefty Ron Guidry was having a remarkable season on the mound, but not much else was going well for the Yankees. A running feud between Martin and Jackson — who had reported to spring training late and had bickered with Martin ever since — symbolized the disharmony of the Yankee team. The acrimony between the neurotic manager and brash slugger came to a head on July 17 when the Yankees lost to the Royals at Yankee Stadium to fall to 47–42, 14 games behind the Red Sox. The game was tied 7–7 when Thurman Munson led off the Yankee half of the tenth inning with a single against Al Hrabowsky. Martin instructed third base coach Dick Howser to give Jackson the bunt sign. The macho Jackson read the sign, then glared in at Martin in the Yankee dugout before making an unconvincing bunt attempt at Hrabowsky's first pitch. Furious, Martin removed the bunt sign, but Jackson refused to swing away. He squared to bunt and fouled back the next two pitches, striking out. After the Yankees lost 9–7 in 11 innings, Martin and Jackson sparred in the Yankee clubhouse, and the next day the Yankees suspended Jackson without pay. The suspension lasted five days and the Yankees went 5–0 in Jackson's absence. When Jackson returned, Martin still refused to play him in a game in Chicago. Then Martin made what would be for him a fatal mistake, but one that ultimately resurrected the Yankee season. After a few too many drinks, Martin sat next to *New York Times* writer Maury Allen on the Yankees' flight from Chicago to Kansas City and lambasted Steinbrenner and Jackson. "If he doesn't shut up," Martin said of Jackson, "he won't play. I don't care what George says. He can replace me right now." Martin went on to say that Jackson and Steinbrenner "deserved" one another since, "One's a born liar, the other's convicted."[2] The reference to Steinbrenner's conviction in the Watergate scandal, which appeared in the *Times* the next day, sent the Yankee Boss over the edge. Before the Yankees played another game, a teary Martin resigned at a press conference in Kansas City. After Howser served one game as interim manager, Bob Lemon, a Hall of Fame pitcher who had previously served as the Yankee pitching coach, took over the team. With the distraction of the Martin-Jackson saga behind them, the Yankees won 47 of their final 67 games to erase what had already been whittled down to a 9½-game deficit when Lemon took over. A four-month newspaper strike that halted all three major presses in New York City beginning August 9 also played a role in restoring tranquility to the Yankee clubhouse, leaving Steinbrenner without a forum to criticize and threaten his players.

Back in Boston, the Red Sox were not only suffering through their first losing month in July but had begun bickering amongst themselves. They lost nine of ten games between July 19 and 28, cutting their lead to just 4½ games over Milwaukee. Left-handed starter Bill Lee, who had started the season 10–3, was suddenly struggling, and when manager Don Zimmer demoted him to the bullpen he began a revolt, taking every opportunity to call the manager a "Gerbil," a jab at Zimmer's pronounced jowls. Lee was a personable USC graduate who was not afraid to speak his mind or stump for controversial political causes. The consummate "zany lefty," he had deserted the team in mid-June when the Red Sox sold his friend Bernie Carbo to the Indians, then returned a day later wearing a tee-shirt that read, "friendship first, competition second."[3] An old school general who believed players should be seen, not heard, Zimmer hated Lee and his smooth rapport with the Boston media.

Emboldened by Lee's continued criticism of the manager, Torrez started grumbling about Zimmer's short leash with his starting pitchers and then Burleson ripped the skipper's penchant for tinkering with the batting order. The team was coming apart at the seams.

The Red Sox temporarily righted the ship when they swept a pair of games in New York, August 2 and 3. Bob Stanley and Torrez earned the wins and the Red Sox went on to post a 19–10 record in August, compared to the Yankees' 19–8. With the scare of a horrendous mid-summer collapse averted, the Red Sox began September with a 6-game lead over the Yankees. Seven games still loomed between the two teams, but as long as Boston won two or three, their division lead would be safe.

The Red Sox lost 14 of their next 17 games, including six-of-seven against New York, while the Yankees won 13-of-16. Boston batted .192 during the skein, allowed 4.58 earned runs per game, and committed an eye-popping 31 errors. Hobson, playing third base with bone chips in his right elbow, was on his way to a 43-error season. Scott was suffering through a 0-for-36 slump at the plate. Torrez was in the midst of losing five games in a row.

The slumping Red Sox still had a 4-game lead when the Yankees arrived in Boston on Thursday, September 7, to start a four-game series. The ghoulish quartet of blowouts that followed is remembered as the "Boston Massacre." The Yankees outscored the Red Sox 42 to 9 over the four games and out-hit them 67 to 21, pulling even with the Red Sox at 86–56. In the first game, Torrez allowed five runs in two innings before departing, and the Yankees won 15–3. In the second game, Fisk made a throwing error in each of the first two innings, and the Yankees pounded rookie starter Jim Wright and reliever Tom Burgmeier on the way to a 13–2 win. In the third game, Guidry allowed a single to Burleson to start the Boston first, then held the Red Sox hitless the rest of the way. The 7–0 shutout was the first by a visiting left-hander at Fenway Park since 1974. Afterwards, Lynn tried to ease the tension in the Boston clubhouse, telling reporters, "These aren't the same Yankees we saw before. I really think George Steinbrenner used his clone money. I think those were Yankee clones that were being used out there from the great Yankee teams of the past."[4]

With the division lead down to one game, Zimmer planned to pitch 22-year-old rookie Bobby Sprowl, who had recently been recalled from Triple-A Pawtucket, in the series' finale. Sprowl had lost his major league debut to Jim Palmer in Baltimore four days earlier. After the third loss, Yastrzemski, the team captain, visited Zimmer in his office and pleaded with him to start Lee instead of Sprowl. Lee owned a 12–5 career record against the Yankees and was a three-time 17-game winner. Zimmer refused. Years later Yastrzemski recalled, "He opened his desk and he tossed all these clippings at me, clippings where Lee had called him a gerbil." When members of the press asked Zimmer why he was pitching Sprowl, he barked, "The kid's got ice water in his veins."[5] The "kid," who would never win a major league game, walked the first two batters, Mickey Rivers and Willie Randolph, then Munson hit into a double play, then Jackson singled, then Lou Piniella and Chris Chamblis walked. Zimmer went to the mound and summoned Stanley, who immediately surrendered a two-run hit to Graig Nettles. The Yankees won 7–4.

Boston regained sole possession of first place the next day, beating Baltimore 5–4 behind Rice's 39th and 40th homers of the season, to move a half game ahead of idle New York. But Torrez lost the next day to Baltimore, then the Red Sox dropped a pair of one-run decisions in Cleveland. The Red Sox were 1½ games behind the Yankees when they arrived in New York for a three-game weekend series. Guidry pitched a shutout in the Friday night affair, beating Luis Tiant 4–0, then the Yankees took the second game, 3–2, when they scored a run against Torrez in the bottom of the ninth.

With 14 games to play, Boston trailed New York by 3½ games. The Red Sox went 12–2 over the final two weeks, beginning with a 7–3 Eckersley win against New York, and ending with a 5–0 Tiant masterpiece against Toronto. Eckersley earned four of the team's final 12 wins to finish 20–8, while Tiant won three to finish his final season in Boston 13–8.

The Yankees went 9–5 over the same span, including a 9–2 loss to Cleveland on October 1 that left the two ancient rivals tied with identical records of 99–63, better than any other team in baseball. But only one team could represent the AL East in the playoffs. A coin-flip determined Fenway Park would be the site of a one-game playoff.

1978 One-Game Playoff

YANKEES 5, RED SOX 4

	1	2	3	4	5	6	7	8	9	R	H	E
New York	0	0	0	0	0	0	4	1	0	5	8	0
Boston	0	1	0	0	0	1	0	2	0	4	11	0

WP   Ron Guidry
LP   Mike Torrez
SV   Rich Gossage

On a gorgeous Monday afternoon in Boston with temperatures that approached 70 degrees, Lemon gave the ball to Guidry, a pitcher who had shutout the Red Sox twice in the preceding three weeks and who would be named the AL Cy Young Award winner after finishing the season 25–3 with a 1.74 ERA. But the diminutive lefty was working on three days' rest, providing the Red Sox and their fans reason for hope. Yankee defector Torrez got the start for Boston, delivering the game's first pitch at 2:30 p.m. before a national television audience.

The Red Sox took a 1–0 lead in the second inning when the 39-year-old Yastrzemski lined a Guidry fastball down the right field line just inside the foul pole for a home run.

In the sixth, Rice singled home Burleson, who had doubled, opening a 2–0 lead. The Red Sox nearly broke the game open later in the sixth when Lynn ripped a two-out shot to right field with two men aboard, but Piniella made a great catch to end the inning. Squinting into a brutal late-day sun, Piniella drifted toward the right field corner, reached out, and speared the ball. "I saw the ball leave the bat and then I lost it in the sun," Piniella said. "I went to the place where I thought the ball would land. I didn't catch it cleanly, but kind of in the top of my glove. It would have short-hopped the wall and stayed in play. Without any doubt, two runs would have scored."[7]

Torrez carried a two-hitter into the top of the seventh, but he allowed one-out singles to Chamblis and Roy White, bringing to the plate Bucky Dent. New York's number-nine hitter fouled Torrez's second pitch off his foot and the result was a four-minute delay as the Yankee shortstop hobbled over to the on-deck circle where Rivers stood. It was then that Rivers, supposedly noticing a crack in Dent's bat, offered Dent his own bat to use. Dent accepted. Nine years later when Rivers and Torrez met at an old-timers game, Rivers would concede that the bat he gave Dent had been illegally corked.

While Dent took his time shaking off his injury, Torrez stood behind the mound. He did not throw any practice pitches to stay loose. "I lost some of my concentration during the delay," Torrez later admitted. "It was about four minutes, but it felt like an hour."[8]

Finally the Yankee shortstop stepped into the batters box. Dent had hit .243 with just four homers in 124 games in 1978. Torrez threw an inside fastball that Dent lofted to left field. When the ball left the bat, Torrez thought it was an out. He walked toward the first base dugout as Yastrzemski tracked the ball, gliding toward the foul line. "The wind was blowing from right to left," Yastrzemski said, "and it just kept on carrying and carrying and the wind blew it a little more toward the line, and boom. It was just an empty feeling."[9]

The ball settled into the screen above the Green Monster for a three-run homer. Torrez walked the next batter, Rivers, then Stanley came in and allowed an RBI double to Munson, giving the Yankees a 4–2 lead.

Jackson opened the Yankee eighth with his 27th homer of the season to open a 5–2 lead, but the Red Sox fought back. Facing Gossage, Remy led off the bottom of the eighth with a double, and came around to score on a single by Yastrzemski. Then Fisk singled. Then Lynn singled. The Red Sox were within 5–4, with runners on first and second with one out. Hobson flied out to shallow right and Scott struck out to end the inning, though.

Boston rallied again against Gossage in the bottom of the ninth. Burleson walked with one out, then Remy sent a liner to right. Piniella waved his arms to indicate he'd lost the ball in the sun, but Burleson froze between first and second, and did not advance to third after Piniella suddenly lurched to his left, reached out, and snared the ball on one hop. "When Remy hit it, I saw it for a second and then lost it," Piniella said. "I knew it would bounce, so I moved back three steps to prevent it from bouncing over me to the wall."[10]

The Red Sox had the potential tying and winning runs on base for their number-three and number-four hitters, but Rice flied out to deep right-center, advancing Burleson to third, and then Yastrzemski popped to Nettles at third base to end the season.

The Yankees went on to beat the Royals in the ALCS and the Dodgers in the World Series.

CHAPTER 11

The Regular Season: 95–66

Nineteen eighty-six is remembered as the most heartbreaking season in Red Sox history. Prior to the team's World Series collapse, the Red Sox had presented New Englanders with one magical moment after another, convincing even the most ardent skeptics that 1986 really was the year that Boston's championship drought would end. The Red Sox came within one strike of victory in the World Series but couldn't close the deal.

Spring training played out in Winter Haven, Florida without much fanfare. Boston returned essentially the same cast of players who had finished fifth in the American League East with a record of 81–81 in manager John McNamara's first season in 1985. The only major off-season move for Boston was a November trade that sent left-handed starter Bobby Ojeda to the New York Mets for young pitchers Calvin Schiraldi and Wes Gardner. Just before the season started, Boston general manager Lou Gorman made another move, sending left-handed hitting designated hitter Mike Easler to the Yankees for right-handed hitting DH Don Baylor. The swap marked the first trade between the two rivals since 1972 when Boston handed Sparky Lyle to New York for Danny Cater. An aging power hitter, Baylor arrived with a .350 lifetime average in 82 games at Fenway Park, and a winning attitude. If spring training was notable for anything else, it was the pounding 23-year-old right-hander Roger Clemens took. Half a year removed from the rotator cuff surgery that had ended his 1985 season prematurely, Clemens struggled in Florida, allowing 19 runs in 19 innings over his first five starts. Finally, on the last day of the Grapefruit League season, Clemens resembled the phenom he had once been, blanking the Tigers on three hits over seven innings. Clemens began the season as the Red Sox' fourth starter behind lefty Bruce Hurst, the flamboyant Dennis "Oil Can" Boyd, and Al Nipper.

Opening Day in Detroit provided an omen of good things to come when leadoff hitter Dwight Evans lined Jack Morris' first pitch into the left field seats for a home run. The clout represented the first time that the first pitch of the first game of the Major League season had resulted in a home run. Despite hitting three more long balls against Morris, the

Red Sox lost 6–5, though, when Kirk Gibson hit a two-run shot against reliever Sammy Stewart in the eighth.

In the season's second game, Boyd, who had raised eyebrows by reporting to spring training weighing just 133 pounds due to a case of hepatitis, took the mound. The Can carried a 4–2 lead into the eighth, but the bullpen again imploded and the result was another 6–5 loss. Finally, in the third game, Boston earned its first win as Nipper threw 149 pitches in eight innings and Joe Sambito registered a save in a 4–2 victory. Clemens took the mound the next day in Chicago and came within one out of a complete game, beating the White Sox 7–2.

After a 3–3 road-trip, the Red Sox lost their home opener, 8–2, to the Royals on April 14. The game was tied at 2–2 in the eighth, but Boyd tired and allowed a pair of runs, then McNamara brought in Bob Stanley, a highly paid reliever whom the fans detested, and the game quickly got out of hand. Afterwards, Stanley toasted the Boston fans, saying, "When I'm standing out there and save the final game of the season ... and I'm waving in the air, I'll be waving to my wife and family. The rest of 'em can go to hell."[1] Ironically, Stanley would indeed be on the mound six months later with a chance to clinch the world championship. He would not do any victory waving though.

The Red Sox moved over the .500 mark on April 26 in Kansas City when Nipper beat the Royals 6–1, improving the team to 9–8.

Three nights later, Clemens served notice that he was fully recovered from his shoulder surgery, becoming the first pitcher to strike out 20 batters in a nine-inning game. The previous record of 19 had been shared by Steve Carlton, Nolan Ryan and Tom Seaver. Due to a rainout, Clemens took the mound on six days of rest to face the Seattle Mariners, a team on its way to setting an AL record with 1,148 strikeouts. Before a sparse Fenway Park crowd of 13,414, due to a cross-town NBA playoff game at Boston Garden, Clemens struck out six batters over the first three innings. He then fanned eight in a row over the fourth, fifth and sixth, giving him 14 K's through six innings. Gorman Thomas' home run in the top of the seventh gave Seattle a 1–0 lead, but the Red Sox struck for three runs in the bottom of the inning on an Evans homer. In the ninth, Clemens whiffed his former University of Texas teammate, Spike Owen, to tie the record, then he punched out Phil Bradley on a called third strike to become the first pitcher in 111 seasons to notch 20 K's in a nine-inning game. After Ken Phelps grounded out to end the game, Clemens rushed to the first base seats to hug his wife, Debbie. Remarkably, Clemens didn't allow a single walk in the game, while yielding just three hits. Afterwards, Red Sox catcher Rich Gedman was in awe. "Wherever I put the glove, he hit it," said Gedman. "He was hitting spots with his fastball, and he was hitting them with his curve. It was unbelievable. It was almost like cheating it was coming so easily."[2]

The Red Sox won 21 of 28 games in May, a month that offered many of the season's most memorable moments. The 21–12 Red Sox took the AL East lead for good on May 15 when Chicago beat New York on an off day for the Boston nine.

On Sunday, May 18, Nipper was lost to injury in a game against the Rangers at Fenway. Covering home plate after uncorking a wild pitch, Nipper tagged out Larry Parrish who was attempting to score from third. But Parrish's spikes tore open a gash in Nipper's knee. The Red Sox trailed 3–1 when Nipper left the field with his leg covered in blood in the sixth, but rallied to tie the game, then claim a 5–4 win, scoring twice in the bottom of the tenth on a throwing error by Rangers right fielder George Wright.

The next night Boston staged another dramatic come-back, tying the Twins 7–7 with two outs in the last of the ninth when Jim Rice walked with the bases loaded, and winning when pitcher Ron Davis hit Marc Sullivan with a pitch to force home a run.

On May 20, Boston erupted for 17 runs against the Twins and Clemens improved to 7–0. Five days later, Clemens carried a no-hitter into the eighth inning in Texas before Oddibe McDowell singled with two outs. The Red Sox won 7–1 though, improving to 28–14.

On May 27, a surreal scene played out in Cleveland when in the bottom of the sixth inning the game was canceled due to a dense fog that had rolled in from Lake Erie. The Red Sox led 2–0 at the time, but the Indians had the potential tying runs on base. "That's what you get when you build a ballpark by the ocean," Boyd quipped.[3]

The pitching staff, already missing Nipper and lacking a legitimate number-five starter, got more bad news on the final day of May. Hurst collapsed on the mound in Minnesota with a severe groin pull. Later in the game, Stewart went down with a forearm injury that landed him on the disabled list as well. The Red Sox managed to win the game though, 7–2.

The Red Sox kept rolling, posting a 17–10 record in June, as Clemens racked up six wins to improve to 14–0, and give him the fifth best string of wins to start a season in major league history.

In the absence of Nipper and Hurst, Gorman made a move to bolster the piecemeal starting rotation on June 29, sending utility man Steve Lyons to the White Sox for Seaver. "Tom Terrific" was nearing the end of a great career, but he wasted no time in showing that he still had a few wins in his right arm, beating Toronto in his Red Sox debut on July 1 to improve Boston's record to 50–25. The win vaulted Boston 8 games ahead of second-place New York.

The rest of July did not go well for the Red Sox, though. They won just 10 of 26 games, as a series of unpleasant incidents involving Boyd further depleted the starting rotation.

The day after Seaver's successful debut, Clemens saw his win streak end in a 4–2 loss to Toronto. "The Rocket" carried a one-hitter and a 2–1 lead into the eighth before allowing two runs. Still, with a 14–1 record it was a foregone conclusion that Clemens would start the All-Star Game, scheduled for July 15 in Houston. On July 10, Royals manager Dick Howser announced the pitchers and backup players for the AL squad. Jim Rice, Wade Boggs, and Gedman would be joining Clemens at the Astrodome, but Boyd, who ranked second in the league in wins with an 11–6 record, had been left off the AL team. He found out right before the Red Sox were to take the field at Fenway for a game against the Angels. Always prone to pouting, "Oil Can" went ballistic, cursing out several teammates and McNamara. He then peeled out of the players' parking lot in shortstop Rey Quinones' Monte Carlo. The Red Sox suspended Boyd, and he quickly spiraled further out of control. In the next three weeks he spent several nights at U-Mass Medical Center in Worcester undergoing psychiatric treatment and drug testing, he was arrested and charged with assaulting two undercover narcotics officers outside his condominium in Chelsea, and he was arrested in a separate incident for not paying an outstanding speeding ticket.

Clemens won the All-Star Game MVP Award with three perfect innings in a 3–2 AL win, then the Red Sox began a grueling stretch in which they would play 31 of 40 games on the road. Without Hurst, Nipper and Boyd, they won only five of their first 17 games and by August 5, when Boyd returned, the division lead was down to 2½ games over second-place Baltimore.

The lead never got smaller than that, though. Boyd and a healthy Hurst bolstered the rotation, while Schiraldi, who had been converted to a reliever at Triple-A Pawtucket, stabilized the bullpen. After arriving in Boston on July 18, the hulking right-hander allowed just one earned run in his first 21⅓ innings to claim the closer's role from Stanley.

On August 19, Gorman made his final move of the season, sending Quinones, pitcher Mike Brown, and two minor leaguers to Seattle for Owen and Dave Henderson. A superior glove-man, Owen moved into the starting shortstop position, while Henderson provided insurance for center fielder Tony Armas' sore hamstrings.

In just his second game with the Red Sox, Owen tied Johnny Pesky's 40-year old record, scoring six runs in a 24–5 rout of Cleveland. First baseman Bill Buckner collected five hits in the game, while Armas drove in six runs.

An eleven-game win streak from August 30 through September 10 cemented Boston's stronghold on the division, opening an 8½-game lead over Toronto.

Boyd went the distance on September 28, beating the Blue Jays 12–3 at Fenway, to clinch the division crown with seven games to play. Buckner caught the final out, a Kelly Gruber pop-up. During the post-game celebration Clemens mounted a police horse and rode a memorable victory lap around the field. Afterwards, as the players doused each other in champagne, several indicated that they were not satisfied with merely winning the division. "The champagne tasted sweet today," second baseman Marty Barrett said. "It will taste great October 24. You can take the individual statistics and everything else and throw it out the door. Winning [the World Series] is what it's all about."4

Evans added, "You're talking to a man who is not embarrassed to say he got on his knees and prayed. I've been praying since spring training. And it's not over yet. I'm very pleased. We put our hearts, our souls and our spirits into this thing. When you're together for eight months of the year, you become very close to one another. This is the closest group that I've ever been with. The whole season has just been a great time, thanks to a tremendous effort by everybody. But we're still a long way away from where we want to be. This team has a goal, and we're going to go for it all."5

Boston won just two of the final seven games and went into the postseason at less than full strength. In his final tune-up before the playoffs, Clemens was hit in the right elbow by a line drive off the bat of Baltimore's John Stefero. Although X-rays were negative, no one knew how effective Clemens would be in the ALCS. Additionally, a knee injury suffered in Toronto on September 19, had rendered Seaver unavailable for the playoffs, and Buckner, whose chronically sore ankles had hampered him all season, was in pain. Still, the Red Sox finished the season with 95 wins, the most in the AL and the third most in baseball.

Boggs finished with a .357 batting average to edge Don Mattingly by five-hundredths of a percentage point and claim his third batting crown, while Rice was second among Red Sox regulars with a .324 average to go with 20 homers and 110 RBI. Buckner (.267, 18 HR, 102 RBI) was the only other Boston player to surpass 100 RBI. Baylor led the team with 31 home runs, despite batting only .238. Evans hit .259 with 26 homers and 97 RBI. Boston finished second in the twelve-team league with a .271 batting average, and fifth with 794 runs. Boston's 3.93 ERA ranked third in the league. Clemens finished with a league-best 24–4 mark and a league-leading 2.48 ERA. Boyd (16–10, 3.78 ERA), Hurst (13–8, 2.99 ERA), Nipper (10–12, 5.38 ERA), and Seaver (5–7, 3.80 ERA) rounded out the rotation. Stanley finished with 16 saves, while Sambito had 12, and Schiraldi had 9. After the season, Clemens was named the AL Cy Young Award winner and MVP, while McNamara was named Manager of the Year.

The Postseason: 7–7

The Red Sox played two thrilling seven-game series in the 1986 postseason. In the ALCS, Boston defeated California after trailing three-games-to-one. The Red Sox were one strike from defeat in Game Five when lightning struck in the form of a Henderson home run. Against the Mets in the World Series, the Red Sox were one strike from victory in Game Six before the Mets rallied for three runs to stave off elimination and set the stage for a Game Seven win.

The California team that Boston faced was an aging club that featured such well-traveled veterans as Reggie Jackson, Don Sutton, Bob Boone, and Rick Burleson, and notable newcomer Wally Joyner, a first baseman who placed second in the AL Rookie of the Year balloting to Oakland's Jose Canseco. The AL West champs posted a record of 92–70. Their strength was their pitching staff which ranked second in the AL with a 3.84 ERA, while offensively they batted just .255 — ninth best in the league.

In what would be his final winning season, the 41-year old Sutton had gone 15–11 with a 3.74 ERA, though the mantle of staff-ace already belonged to Mike Witt, a 25-year-old right-hander, who went 18–10 with a 2.84 ERA. Kirk McCaskill (17–10, 3.36 ERA) and southpaw John Candelaria (10–2, 2.55 ERA) added depth to the rotation, and Donnie Moore saved 21 games. Joyner, whose fans renamed Anaheim Stadium "Wally World" midway through the season, led the team in batting with a .290 average, finished second on the team with 22 home runs, and led the Angels with 100 RBI. California's other offensive stars were third baseman Doug DeCinces (.256, 26 HR, 96 RBI) and outfielder Brian Downing (.267, 20 HR, 95 RBI). The declining Jackson spent most of his time at designated hitter, batting .241 with 18 homers and 58 RBI.

Adding intrigue to the series, McNamara was familiar with the Angels players, having guided California to an 81–81 record in 1984, before getting his walking papers after two seasons as the California skipper. His replacement, Gene Mauch, was a baseball lifer. Currently in his second stint at the Angels' helm, Mauch had spent 25 seasons as a big league manager, dating back to his 1960 debut with the Phillies.

While the Angels were a solid, but unspectacular bunch, the Mets presented the Red Sox with a greater challenge, having posted a 108–54 record to win the NL East by a record-setting 21½ games. New York led the NL with 783 runs and a .263 batting average. Twenty-four-year-old right fielder Darryl Strawberry was the team's most feared hitter, having batted .259 with 27 homers and 93 RBI, while catcher Gary Carter (.255, 24 HR, 105 RBI), first baseman Keith Hernandez (.310, 13 HR, 83 RBI), third baseman Ray Knight (.298 11 HR, 76 RBI) and second baseman Wally Backman (.320 average) were also cogs in the attack.

The Mets pitchers posted a league-best 3.11 ERA, thanks to six double-figure winners — all in their 20's. The oldest was the 28-year-old Ojeda, who blossomed after being traded from Boston. The lefty went 18–5 with a 2.57 ERA. The other four members of the starting rotation were 21-year-old Dwight Gooden (17–6, 2.84 ERA), 23-year-old southpaw Sid Fernandez (16–6, 3.52 ERA), 25-year-old Ron Darling (15–6, 2.81 ERA), and 24-year-old Rick Aguilera (10–7, 3.88 ERA). Reliever Roger McDowell saved 22 games to go with a 14–9 record and a 3.02 ERA, while left-handed co-closer Jesse Orosco saved 21 games while going 8–6 with a 2.33 ERA.

1986 American League Championship Series: Red Sox 4, Angels 3

GAME 1: ANGELS 8, RED SOX 1

	1	2	3	4	5	6	7	8	9	R	H	E
California	0	4	1	0	0	0	0	3	0	8	11	0
Boston	0	0	0	0	0	1	0	0	0	1	5	1

WP Mike Witt
LP Roger Clemens

The series opener pitted the two teams' best starters against one another, Witt for California against Clemens for Boston. The expected pitchers' duel never materialized. Witt did his part, carrying a no-hitter into the sixth inning and pitching a complete game five-hitter, but Clemens, who hadn't pitched in two weeks due to the injury he'd suffered in Baltimore, was hit hard. The Red Sox ace allowed eight runs in 7⅓ innings.

After striking out Ruppert Jones to start the game, Clemens showed a bit of rust when he allowed a Joyner double and a Jackson walk before escaping the inning unharmed. The Rocket appeared to be settling into a groove when he fanned Rob Wilfong and Dick Schofield to start the second, but then his control deserted him and by the time he had recorded the third out, the Angels had scored four runs. Boone and Gary Pettis walked to start the rally, then Jones, Joyner and Downing collected run-scoring hits, before Jackson struck out.

The Angels stretched the lead to 5–0 in the third, scoring an unearned run after an Owen error.

Witt, meanwhile, faced 15 batters through the first five innings, having allowed just a first-inning walk to Boggs, who was erased on a Barrett double play.

In the sixth, Owen walked, then Boggs broke up Witt's no-hitter with an infield single. Barrett followed with a base hit to right to make the score 5–1.

The Angels scored three more runs in the eighth, though, after Clemens allowed singles to three of the first four batters and Stanley allowed two inherited runners to score. After the lopsided loss, Boston fans and pundits wondered why McNamara had left Clemens on the mound to throw 134 pitches in what had seemed like an obvious loss after three innings.

GAME 2: RED SOX 9, ANGELS 2

	1	2	3	4	5	6	7	8	9	R	H	E
California	0	0	0	1	1	0	0	0	0	2	11	3
Boston	1	1	0	0	1	0	3	3	X	9	13	2

WP Bruce Hurst
LP Kirk McCaskill

The Red Sox won the second game behind a gritty complete game effort by Hurst. The game started at 3:30 p.m. and the low sun contributed to a number of Angels miscues in the field.

Boggs led off the bottom of the first with a drive off the center field fence. When the carom bounced over Pettis' head, Boggs raced all the way to third. Barrett followed with a double to drive home the first run.

In the second, Boston collected four singles—including an Owen grounder that hit a rock and hopped over Schofield's head and a Boggs chopper that McCaskill lost in the sun — to open a 2–0 lead. The Red Sox had seven hits through the first 1⅓ innings but the second inning ended when Buckner hit into a double play.

California tied the game at 2–2, scoring an unearned run courtesy of a Boggs error in the fourth, and an earned run on a Joyner homer in the fifth.

Boston reclaimed the lead, 3–2, in the bottom of the fifth on a two-out double by Evans that scored Buckner. The Evans hit should have been caught for an out, but Angels second baseman Bobby Grich lost the high fly in the sun and the ball fell safely behind second base.

The Red Sox scored three unearned runs in the seventh thanks to errors by Grich, DeCinces, and Schofield, then three earned runs in the eighth on a Buckner sacrifice fly and a two-run homer by Rice.

Hurst was not dominant, but he stifled the Angels when they had men on base and he got some help in the sixth when Grich was caught in a rundown between third and home. The Red Sox lefty allowed 11 hits and at least one base runner in seven of the nine innings, but surrendered just one earned run.

After the game, many California players acknowledged they had handed the game to Boston. Sutton summed it up best, saying, "The last time I saw a gem like this, our coach wouldn't take us to Tastee-Freeze for a milkshake afterward."[6]

GAME 3: ANGELS 5, RED SOX 3

	1	2	3	4	5	6	7	8	9	R	H	E
Boston	0	1	0	0	0	0	0	2	0	3	9	1
California	0	0	0	0	0	1	3	1	X	5	8	0

WP John Candelaria
LP   Dennis Boyd
SV Donnie Moore

After a travel day, the series resumed in Anaheim. Boyd pitched shutout ball for five innings and the game was tied 1–1 through six, but the Angels hit a pair of two-out homers in the seventh to take a lead they would not relinquish.

The station-to-station Red Sox scored in the second inning on a walk and three hits against Candelaria. Meanwhile, Boyd held the Angels hitless for the first three innings, then allowed three safeties in the fourth before escaping unscathed when third base umpire Richie Garcia overturned a safe call by home plate umpire Terry Cooney, taking a run off the scoreboard for the Angels. The controversial call precipitated a fierce argument by Mauch who was subsequently ejected. Joyner was on second and Downing was on first when DeCinces hit a two-out roller down the first base line. The gimpy-legged Buckner stayed back on the ball and watched it hit the first base bag, then bounce off Boyd who was running to cover first. As DeCinces reached first safely and Joyner rounded third, Buckner retrieved the ball and threw home. To Cooney, who had followed the grounder down the line, Gedman's tag on Joyner — who crossed the plate standing up — appeared late. But Joyner never touched the plate. He stepped on Gedman's foot. After consulting with Garcia, Cooney reversed the call.

The Red Sox failed to score after loading the bases with one out in the fifth, then Joyner scored an undisputed run on a Jackson single in the sixth to tie the game, 1–1.

Boyd retired the first two hitters in the Angels seventh, then Schofield hit a home run. Boone followed with a single, then Pettis homered, chasing Boyd from the game.

Moore replaced Candelaria in the eighth and the Red Sox scored a pair of runs, cutting the lead to 4–3. Barrett led off with a single, then Rice stroked a one-out double. A Moore balk brought Barrett home and a Gedman single scored Rice.

Facing Schiraldi in the bottom of the eighth, the Angels answered with an unearned run after a Boggs error.

Moore retired the first two batters in the ninth before Barrett singled with two outs. The next hitter, Buckner, flied out to end the game.

Game 4: Angels 4, Red Sox 3

	1	2	3	4	5	6	7	8	9	10	11	R	H	E
Boston	0	0	0	0	0	1	0	2	0	0	0	3	6	1
California	0	0	0	0	0	0	0	0	3	0	1	4	11	2

WP   Doug Corbett
LP   Calvin Schiraldi

McNamara sent Clemens to the mound on three days' rest to start the fourth game, while Mauch countered with Sutton. Clemens carried a five-hitter and 3–0 lead into the ninth inning, but California scored three runs to force extra innings, then won in the eleventh.

The Red Sox caught a break before the game when Joyner, who had reached base in seven of 13 plate appearances over the first three games, was scratched from the Angels lineup. The young slugger had a 102-degree fever that the Angels training staff speculated was the result of an insect bite. The mysterious ailment, ultimately diagnosed as a staph infection, kept Joyner on the bench for the remainder of the series.

From the outset, Clemens had better command than in Game One. He struck out the first two batters he faced, Jones and Grich, then retired Downing on a groundball to the mound, for an easy first inning. In the second, he whiffed Jackson and Schofield. In the third, he fanned Boone and Grich.

As the innings flew by, Sutton matched the Red Sox hurler pitch for pitch. He retired the first nine Boston batters, before allowing a Boggs double to start the fourth. The Red Sox couldn't capitalize on the double though, and the game remained scoreless entering the sixth. Armas led off the Boston sixth with a single and advanced to second on a sacrifice bunt by Owen. After Boggs grounded out and Barrett walked, Buckner doubled to right to put Boston ahead 1–0.

The Red Sox added two runs in the eighth, the first scoring on a Barrett single, the second on a Grich error.

Entering the ninth, Clemens had nine strikeouts and hadn't allowed a runner beyond second base. But DeCinces led off with a homer to center, then, after Clemens retired George Hendrick on a groundout, Schofield and Boone connected for solid singles. McNamara made his way to the mound and summoned Schiraldi. The young closer induced Pettis to loft a fly ball that appeared headed for Rice's glove, but the leftfielder lost the ball in the stadium lights and it fell behind him for a run-scoring double. With the Red Sox clinging to a 3–2 lead, Schiraldi intentionally walked Jones to load the bases, then struck out Grich to bring Boston within one out of evening the series. Schiraldi got ahead of Downing 0–2, then hit him with a pitch to force home the tying run.

The first batter to reach base in extra innings came around to score. Backup catcher Jerry Narron led off the Angels eleventh with a single to right, advanced to second on a Pettis sacrifice, and raced home on a Grich single to left.

After walking off the mound with his head down, the 24-year-old Schiraldi wept in the Red Sox dugout while ABC's television cameras broadcast the portrait of defeat into living rooms across America.

GAME 5: RED SOX 7, ANGELS 6

	1	2	3	4	5	6	7	8	9	10	11	R	H	E
Boston	0	2	0	0	0	0	0	0	4	0	1	7	12	0
California	0	0	1	0	0	2	2	0	1	0	0	6	13	0

WP Steve Crawford
LP Donnie Moore
SV Calvin Schiraldi

On the brink of elimination, the Red Sox played like a dead team for eight innings on a Sunday afternoon in Anaheim before coming to life and claiming a dramatic 11-inning victory.

Working on short rest like Clemens before him, Hurst allowed three runs over six innings, including two runs that scored when Henderson accidentally carried a Grich fly ball over the center field fence for a home run in the sixth. The freak play put the Angels ahead 3–2. Filling in for Armas, who had suffered an ankle injury in the second inning, Henderson tracked Grich's fly ball, felt for the fence with his right hand, and leapt. The ball hit the heel of his glove as his momentum brought it above the top of the wall. The ball fell on the other side of the fence. "I was going back, I got the ball in my glove, and then I crashed into the wall and my wrist hit the wall. If my wrist hadn't hit the top of the wall, I would have had it," Henderson explained later.[7]

Stanley replaced Hurst to start the seventh and allowed two quick runs. With a 5–2 lead and Witt on the mound, California was six outs away from the AL pennant.

Witt set down the Red Sox with ease in the eighth, then returned to the mound in hopes of pitching his second complete game of the series. He would have to retire the heart of the Red Sox order. Number-three hitter Buckner led off with a single to center. McNamara sent Dave Stapleton in to pinch-run. After Rice struck out, Stapleton trotted around the bases ahead of Baylor who blasted a 3–2 Witt curveball over the fence in left-center, pulling the Red Sox within a run. Witt got the next batter, Evans, to pop out, leaving the Red Sox down to their last out, trailing 5–4, with no one on base.

Witt stared in at the plate and took a deep breath as he prepared to face Gedman who had already connected for three hits in the game. Just then, Mauch burst out of the Angels dugout and signaled to the bullpen. He wanted a left-hander to face the left-handed hitting Gedman, and Gary Lucas, who had struck out Gedman the day before, got the call. With his first and only pitch, Lucas hit Gedman, marking the first plunked batter for the pitcher in 322 innings, dating back to 1982. Mauch made his way to the mound again, and this time signaled for Moore, a right-hander, to face the right-handed hitting Henderson. In his only previous at bat, Henderson had struck out in the seventh inning, stranding the potential tying run on base. He had contributed little to the Red Sox' regular season effort, batting .196 in 51 at-bats with one homer and three runs batted in. The Angels closer quickly brought Henderson and the Red Sox within one strike of defeat, but Henderson fouled off a 2–2 fastball to stay alive. Moore's next pitch was a forkball. Henderson leaned out over the plate and got the fat part of the bat on the ball. There was never any doubt the shot would touch down somewhere in the left field bleachers, and soon enough it did, putting the Red Sox ahead 6–5. Henderson circled the bases as if he were walking on air.

"It was a big hit," Henderson said. "It came at the right time. I don't get too many chances to do that. Right when I swung [I knew] I had hit the ball solid out of the park. When I hit it like that, I knew it was gone."[8]

Now it was Boston's turn to blow a lead. Stanley gave up a leadoff single to Boone to start the Angels ninth, then fielded a Pettis bunt that moved the runner to second. McNamara summoned Sambito to face the left-handed Wilfong, and for the second time in the inning, the left-left strategy failed. Wilfong singled to right to tie the game, 6–6. McNamara called upon the rarely used Steve Crawford to pitch to Schofield who promptly singled to put runners at the corners with one out. Crawford then intentionally walked Downing to load the bases. DeCinces stepped to the plate with a chance to win the pennant with a hit, walk, infield chopper, or deep fly ball. He swung at the first pitch and lofted a fly to right field that California third base coach Moose Stubing rightly decided was too shallow to test the arm of Evans. The next batter, Grich, hit a soft liner to Crawford to end the inning.

Neither team threatened in the tenth, then Baylor got things started for the Red Sox in the eleventh. The hulking DH held his ground and allowed a Moore pitch to hit him. Baylor was an expert at getting plunked, having just set the major league record by recording 35 hit by pitches in his first season in Boston. Evans singled to center, then Gedman reached on a bunt to third that was intended to be a sacrifice. The Red Sox had the bases loaded with no one out and Henderson at the plate. This time he didn't homer, but his sacrifice fly to center was enough to put the Red Sox ahead 7–6.

After his meltdown in the previous game, Schiraldi got a measure of revenge in the bottom of the eleventh. He struck out Wilfong and Schofield, then retired Downing on a pop to Stapleton at first. The one-two-three effort saved Crawford's first win of the year, and sent the series back to Boston.

GAME 6: RED SOX 10, ANGELS 4

	1	2	3	4	5	6	7	8	9	R	H	E
California	2	0	0	0	0	0	1	1	0	4	11	1
Boston	2	0	5	0	1	0	2	0	X	10	16	1

WP Dennis Boyd
LP Kirk McCaskill

After three straight nail-biters in Anaheim, the sixth game was a lopsided affair. Boston led 7–2 after three innings and never looked back.

The Angels scored a pair of runs in the first on three hits, a walk and a hit batter, but after stranding the bases loaded to avoid further damage, Boyd settled down. He allowed three runs on nine hits in seven innings, striking out five.

The Red Sox answered with two runs in the bottom of the first without the virtue of a hit. McCaskill walked Boggs and Barrett to start the game, then, after Buckner advanced both runners with a groundout, McCaskill uncorked a wild pitch to score Boggs. Barrett came home on a Rice groundout.

McCaskill retired the Red Sox in order in the second, but the first four Boston batters in the third — Owen, Boggs, Barrett and Buckner — connected for hits. Then after Rice hit into a fielder's choice, Baylor and Evans singled. By the time the inning was through, McCaskill had been replaced by Lucas (who this time struck out Gedman), and five Boston runs had scored.

The Red Sox tacked on a run in the fifth when Baylor, who had been hit by yet another pitch, scored on a Henderson fielder's choice, and two more in the seventh when Owen tripled home Gedman and Henderson.

Stanley allowed two hits and an unearned run over the final two innings, to seal the victory and force a seventh game.

GAME 7: RED SOX 8, ANGELS 1

	1	2	3	4	5	6	7	8	9	R	H	E
California	0	0	0	0	0	0	0	1	0	1	6	2
Boston	0	3	0	4	0	0	1	0	X	8	8	1

WP Roger Clemens
LP John Candelaria

As the Red Sox had returned to Boston on their team charter after Game Five, Clemens had implored Boyd to extend the series to a seventh game, and Boyd had delivered. "After the fifth game, I told Oil Can, 'You've got [Game Six]. Just give me the chance,'" Clemens said.[9] The confident Texan seized his opportunity and delivered, despite battling a bout of influenza that left him dizzy and weak.

The Red Sox scored three unearned runs in the second inning after Schofield erred on a groundball by Rice, then four more unearned runs in the fourth after Pettis made an error in center to give Boston an extra out, allowing Rice to smack a Candelaria pitch over the left field wall for a three-run homer. The error was California's eighth of the series, which tied an ALCS record.

Evans hit a solo homer off Sutton in the seventh to give Boston its eighth and only earned run.

Clemens carried a three-hitter and 8–0 lead into the eighth. After the Rocket allowed a leadoff single to Jones to start the eighth, he departed, having thrown an economical 93 pitches while striking out just three.

Schiraldi entered and, though he allowed the inherited runner to score, fanned five batters over the final two innings, including all three Angels in the ninth.

Barrett who hit .367 in the series, including seven-for-ten with men in scoring position, was named MVP. His double-play partner, Owen, the number-nine hitter in the Boston order, who had hit .183 for the Red Sox in the regular season, hit .429 in the series.

1986 World Series: Mets 4, Red Sox 3

GAME 1: RED SOX 1, METS 0

	1	2	3	4	5	6	7	8	9	R	H	E
Boston	0	0	0	0	0	0	1	0	0	1	5	0
New York	0	0	0	0	0	0	0	0	0	0	4	1

WP Bruce Hurst
LP Ron Darling
SV Calvin Schiraldi

The Red Sox entered their first World Series in eleven years as decided underdogs. The odds-makers had the Mets favored 2½ to 1. After all, the Mets had won their division by more games than any team in history, their pitchers had been dominant against the Astros in the NLCS, and they enjoyed home field advantage. The Red Sox would have to play four of the seven games at Shea Stadium where they would be without the benefit of a designated hitter, meaning Baylor's potent bat would be on the bench. And Buckner, another important hitter in the Red Sox lineup, was severely hobbled by his chronically sore ankles, leading to speculation that he might not play in the series. Buckner was in the lineup though, when the series began at 8:30 on a Saturday night in New York. And all of the odds and streaks and advantages became irrelevant when Hurst threw strike one to Mookie Wilson to start the bottom of the first. Hurst followed with strikes two and three, then fanned Lenny Dykstra, then got Hernandez to fly to center. The Boston left-hander was dominant, using an array of curveballs, forkballs and fastballs to make the Mets look clueless at the plate.

For six innings Darling matched Hurst, but in the top of the seventh the Mets defense failed the central Massachusetts native and gave the Red Sox the only run they would need. Rice led off with a walk and took second on a wild pitch. He scored when Gedman's one-out grounder skipped between second baseman Tim Teufel's legs and into right-center field. Darling departed for a pinch hitter in the bottom of the seventh after allowing just three hits and one unearned run, while striking out eight.

Hurst cruised through a one-two-three eighth and appeared poised to pitch Boston's first complete game 1–0 shutout to begin a World Series since Babe Ruth accomplished the feat in 1918. He had allowed only four hits and four walks through eight while throwing 124 pitches and striking out eight. But McNamara elected to pinch hit for Hurst in the top of the ninth, sending rookie Mike Greenwell to the plate with the bases loaded and two outs. After Greenwell lofted a harmless fly ball to Dykstra in center, McNamara put the game in Schiraldi's hands.

Schiraldi walked Strawberry to start the Mets ninth, but defensive replacement Stapleton, who came in for Buckner at first, made a nice play and cut down Strawberry at second on a sacrifice bunt attempt by Knight. Schiraldi then got Wally Backman to fly out and Danny Heep to strike out to end the game.

GAME 2: RED SOX 9, METS 3

	1	2	3	4	5	6	7	8	9	R	H	E
Boston	0	0	3	1	2	0	2	0	1	9	18	0
New York	0	0	2	0	1	0	0	0	0	3	8	1

WP Steve Crawford
LP Dwight Gooden
SV Bob Stanley

The second game featured two of the best young pitchers in baseball. Clemens had gone 24–4 in 1986 to vault into the pantheon of the game's elite, while Gooden had posted a 24–4 record in 1985 to claim his spot among baseball's best. Who could have predicted in 1986 that Gooden had already enjoyed his greatest season at age 21, while Clemens was on the way to a hall-of-fame career?

The second game of the World Series did little to showcase the talent of either pitcher. The Red Sox hitters had no trouble catching up to Gooden's fastball, racking eight hits and scoring six runs in five innings, while Clemens couldn't survive the fifth inning.

Both starters held the opposition hitless through the first two innings, but in the third the Red Sox struck for three runs and the Mets answered with two.

Owen began the Red Sox rally with a walk, then Clemens reached safely when Hernandez threw low to first base on his sacrifice bunt attempt. Boggs doubled home the first Boston run, then Barrett and Buckner knocked RBI singles.

The bottom of the inning began in remarkably similar fashion to the top of the frame. New York's number eight hitter, shortstop Rafael Santana, reached on a single, then Gooden wound up safe at first with a bunt single on a sacrifice attempt. Dykstra then bunted to move both runners into scoring position, and they later came around to score.

Henderson got a run back for Boston in the fourth, leading off with a homer to left, then in the fifth Evans deposited a two-run homer onto the roof of the auxiliary press tent beyond the left field fence.

Clemens began the fifth with a 6–2 lead, but when he allowed a one-out walk to Backman followed by a Hernandez hit, McNamara decided he had seen enough. His ace was pitching on three days' rest for the third straight game, was recovering from the flu, and had yielded five hits and four walks in 4⅓ innings. Crawford entered and allowed a single that scored Backman. Then the shaggy-haired right-hander retired the next five hitters he faced.

Mets manager Davy Johnson lifted Gooden after five, but the New York bullpen was equally ineffective, surrendering 10 hits and three runs over the final four innings.

Stanley followed Crawford to the mound for Boston and earned a save, allowing two hits over the final three innings.

Returning to Boston with a 2–0 lead, the Red Sox had distant, if not recent, history on their side. Only once in 82 previous World Series had a team won the first two games on the road, then lost the series. It had happened in 1985 when the St. Louis Cardinals won the first two games in Kansas City before bowing in seven games.

Game 3: Mets 7, Red Sox 1

	1	2	3	4	5	6	7	8	9	R	H	E
New York	4	0	0	0	0	0	2	1	0	7	13	0
Boston	0	0	1	0	0	0	0	0	0	1	5	0

WP   Bobby Ojeda
LP   Dennis Boyd

On the workout day at Fenway Park on October 20, Game Three starter Oil Can Boyd basked in the national media spotlight shone upon him and took the opportunity to taunt the somnolent Mets. "I feel I can master those guys," Boyd said.[10]

The next day Dykstra led off the game with a home run down the right field line and the next three Mets followed with hits. By the time the top of the first was over, New York had a 4–0 lead.

"I saw what Boyd said in the papers," Dykstra said after the game. "We didn't take too kindly to it. The only one that got mastered tonight was him."[11]

Boyd allowed six runs in seven innings, while Ojeda held the Red Sox to one run on five hits through seven.

Barrett drove in the lone Red Sox run when he plated Henderson with a single in the third. Dykstra went 4-for-5, while Carter also had a big day, driving in a run with a double in the first, and two runs with a single in the seventh.

Game 4: Mets 6, Red Sox 2

	1	2	3	4	5	6	7	8	9	R	H	E
New York	0	0	0	3	0	0	2	1	0	6	12	0
Boston	0	0	0	0	0	0	0	2	0	2	7	1

WP   Ron Darling
LP   Al Nipper
SV   Jesse Orosco

Fans across New England greeted McNamara's decision to start Al Nipper in the fourth game with skepticism. The gritty right-hander had been the number-five starter once Seaver joined the rotation, and had not pitched well in the regular season, compiling a 5.38 ERA. Now he was being sent to the mound against the most feared lineup in baseball after not pitching in 17 days. McNamara's logic was that the Red Sox only needed to win two more games and pitching Hurst and Clemens on their regular four days of rest gave the team the best chance. The Mets enjoyed no such luxury and so, Johnson, sent Darling back to the mound on short rest.

Nipper pitched as well as Boston fans could have hoped he would, but Darling was as spectacular as he'd been in the opener. The result: a series tying 6–2 Mets win.

The two pitchers hung zeroes on Fenway Park's scoreboard until the Mets broke through for three runs in the fourth. Backman got things started with a single, then Carter sent a

Rice takes his position in left field during Game Four of the 1986 World Series. (National Baseball Hall of Fame Library, Cooperstown, New York)

one-out home run into the net above the Green Monster. A Strawberry double, followed by a Knight single, accounted for the third run.

Crawford replaced Nipper in the seventh. With two outs and a runner on second, Dykstra lofted a high fly ball to right field. Evans tracked the ball, felt for the fence, leapt, and had the ball in his glove momentarily, but it popped free and fell into the visiting bullpen. Carter tacked on another run in the top of the eighth with his second homer of the night, making it 6–0.

Darling pitched seven innings of four-hit shutout ball. The Red Sox scored twice against McDowell in the eighth, but stranded two runners when Boggs grounded into a fielder's choice. In the ninth, Orosco set the Red Sox down in order, striking out Rice to end the game and even the series.

GAME 5: RED SOX 4, METS 2

	1	2	3	4	5	6	7	8	9	R	H	E
New York	0	0	0	0	0	0	0	1	1	2	10	1
Boston	0	1	1	0	2	0	0	0	X	4	12	0

WP Bruce Hurst
LP Dwight Gooden

Through four games the home team was 0–4. Boston sent a well-rested Hurst to the mound in Game Five hoping to break the trend, while New York countered with Gooden on short rest. After steady rain canceled batting practice, and Ted Williams tossed out the first pitch, the game began on time on a warm Thursday night in Boston. Hurst picked up where he'd left off in Game One, mowing down the Mets with relative ease. He carried a six-hit shutout into the eighth, before Teufel stroked a one-out homer. But the homer only pulled the Mets within 4–1. The Red Sox had scored single runs against Gooden in the second and third, and a pair in the fifth.

The Seattle connection came through for Boston in the second when Henderson tripled to the triangle in center and Owen hit a sacrifice fly to put the Red Sox on the scoreboard first. The Red Sox added an unearned run in the third when Buckner reached on an error and scored on an Evans single. Boston started the fifth with three straight hits—a Rice triple, Baylor single and Evans single—to chase Gooden from the game, then Henderson doubled against Fernandez to plate Baylor with Boston's fourth run.

Hurst allowed a pair of two-out hits in the ninth as the Mets cut the deficit to 4–2, but the lefty struck out Dykstra with his 130th pitch, bringing the Red Sox within one win of the world championship.

GAME 6: METS 6, RED SOX 5

	1	2	3	4	5	6	7	8	9	10	R	H	E
Boston	1	1	0	0	0	0	1	0	0	2	5	13	3
New York	0	0	0	0	2	0	0	1	0	3	6	8	2

WP Rick Aguilera
LP Calvin Schiraldi

Game Six of the 1986 World Series stands alone as the most crushing defeat in Red Sox history. Never before and never since has a team come so close to winning the World Series, only to see its chance evaporate. It was just after midnight and the Red Sox had a two-run lead heading to the bottom of the tenth inning. Schiraldi quickly retired the first two Mets. The bright lights on the Shea Stadium message board read, "Congratulations Boston Red Sox, 1986 World Champions." A telegram from President Ronald Reagan arrived at Shea Stadium for Red Sox president Jean Yawkey. NBC announcer Bob Costas waited in the visiting clubhouse, along with twenty cases of champagne and the World Series trophy. An announcement in the press box declared Hurst had been voted the series MVP. But it was not to be.

The game began with Clemens and Ojeda on the mound. Both pitched well, and the Red Sox had a 3–2 lead after seven innings. Boston scored single runs on RBI hits by Evans in the first and Barrett in the second, and on a groundout by Evans in the seventh.

The only two runs New York scored against Clemens crossed the plate in the fifth.

Boston had a one-run lead with six outs to go and the best pitcher in baseball on the mound. But in the eighth, McNamara pinch-hit for Clemens, sending Greenwell to the plate with a man on second base and one out. Greenwell struck out on three pitches in the dirt, then Buckner lined to center to end the inning.

At the time, Clemens had a four-hitter and had struck out eight, but he had thrown 135 pitches and had developed a blister on his middle finger that made it difficult for him to throw his curveball. To this day there is debate as to whether Clemens asked out of the game, McNamara made the decision unilaterally, or McNamara made the decision based on the advice of pitching coach Bill Fischer. On this topic, the three men have widely varying memories. In any case, Schiraldi took the mound in the bottom of the eighth, and four batters later the Mets had the bases loaded with one out. A Carter sacrifice fly tied the game, 3–3, then Strawberry flied out to end the inning.

Henderson led off the Boston tenth with a home run that silenced the Shea Stadium crowd, then Boston pushed across another run when Boggs laced a two-out double and Barrett followed with a single to put Boston ahead 5–3.

Given a second chance to close the game, Schiraldi induced a pair of harmless fly balls from Backman and Hernandez. The Red Sox were one out away. But Carter lined a 2-1 pitch into left-center, then pinch-hitter Kevin Mitchell dumped a single in front of Henderson in center to put runners at first and third. Schiraldi jumped ahead of Knight 0-2, but the Mets third baseman fought off an inside fastball, fisting it over Barrett's head into right field to pull the Mets within 5–4 and put runners at first and third.

McNamara went to the mound and called upon Stanley. The Steamer ran the count to 2-2 against Wilson, bringing the Red Sox again within one strike of victory. But Wilson fouled off two curveballs, then Stanley threw an inside forkball that ticked off Gedman's glove and went to the backstop, allowing Mitchell to race home with the tying run and Knight to take second. The errant throw was ruled a wild pitch, though Gedman would later admit he should have caught it.

Clinging to a 5–5 tie, Stanley could have picked off Knight at second base, as Barrett sneaked in behind the runner, but the pitcher delivered a pitch to Wilson instead. Wilson hit a chopper that bounced once on the hard dirt in front of the plate and then a second time on the soft dirt in front of first base. The second hop never came up for Buckner and the ball rolled between his legs and into right field allowing Knight to race home with the winning run.

"I don't remember ever touching the ground. It was like I floated to home plate," Knight would later recall of the sprint that ended with a leap into the arms of his teammates who had burst from the dugout to meet him at the plate.[12]

After the game, the Boston media wanted answers. Why had Clemens been lifted? Why was Buckner left in the game after McNamara had replaced him with Stapleton at first base in the late innings of all seven of Boston's previous postseason wins?

While McNamara bristled at his critics, Buckner took responsibility for his gaffe. "I saw it well," the first baseman said. "It bounced and bounced and then it didn't bounce, it just skipped. I can't remember the last time I missed a ball like that, but I'll remember that one."[13]

Game 7: Mets 8, Red Sox 5

	1	2	3	4	5	6	7	8	9	R	H	E
Boston	0	3	0	0	0	0	0	2	0	5	9	0
New York	0	0	0	0	0	3	3	2	X	8	10	0

WP Roger McDowell
LP Calvin Schiraldi
SV Jesse Orosco

The Red Sox appeared to catch a break when the final game was delayed a day due to rain. The postponement allowed Boston to send Hurst back to the mound on three days' rest instead of Boyd. New York countered with Darling.

Hurst carried a one-hitter and 3–0 lead into the sixth, thanks to second-inning homers by Evans and Gedman and an RBI single by Boggs. But pitching on short rest for just the second time all season, the Boston lefty tired and yielded three singles and a walk in the sixth. New York tied the game at 3–3 on a one-out fielder's choice by Carter.

Even though a distraught Schiraldi had told reporters that he didn't deserve another chance to pitch in the series after his effort in Game Six, McNamara gave him the ball to start the seventh. Schiraldi served up a lead-off homer to Knight, as the Mets took a 4–3 lead, then allowed a Dykstra single, threw a wild pitch, and allowed a Santana single to make it 5–3. And the nightmare continued. By the time Sambito and Stanley finished the inning the Mets had a three-run lead.

Boston mounted one last challenge, scoring twice against McDowell in the eighth. Buckner singled, then Rice singled, then Evans doubled to score both runners and pull the Red Sox within 6–5. But Orosco came in and got Gedman to line out, Henderson to strike out, and Baylor to ground out, to strand the tying run on second.

New York added two runs against Nipper in the bottom of the eighth, as Red Sox fans wondered why Nipper was on the mound instead of Boyd or Clemens who had won 40 games between them in the regular season. Orosco set down the Red Sox in order in the ninth. Ed Romero popped out, Boggs grounded out, and Barrett struck out on a high fastball to end the game. Orosco threw his glove high into the air and dropped to his knees as his teammates piled on top of him. Meanwhile, several Red Sox players wept in the Boston dugout, most notably Schiraldi and Boggs. On the eve of his Hall of Fame induction two decades later, Boggs recalled, "My most vivid memory is Jesse Orosco throwing his glove up in the air, and that was probably the culmination of everything that just sort of sent me over the edge."[14]

Knight, who hit .391 in the series, was named MVP. Barrett was the Red Sox' star in defeat, setting a series record by hitting .433 (13-for-30).

Chapter 12

The Regular Season: 89-73

A remarkable midseason winning steak catapulted the 1988 Red Sox to the American League East title. Throughout much of the first half of the season, it appeared that 1988 would be another lost year for the Red Sox, who trailed in the division race by as many as 10 games. But a managerial change during the all-star break sparked a 12-0 start to the second half, and after the streak ended, the Red Sox immediately started another one. Winning games in dramatic fashion, Boston won 19 of its first 20 games under new skipper Joe Morgan, to rejoin the division race. The three weeks of excellence in midsummer, remembered fondly by New Englanders as "Morgan Magic," compensated for the club's slow start and equally slow finish, and gave the Red Sox a one-game margin over the Detroit Tigers at season's end.

After a disappointing 1987 season in which the Red Sox lost more games than they won for just the second time since 1967, general manager Lou Gorman acquired Cubs closer Lee Smith in exchange for pitchers Calvin Schiraldi and Al Nipper. The move made the Red Sox, who had recorded a league-low 17 saves in 1987, the favorite to win the lackluster AL East.

The season began dubiously though, when Smith allowed a tenth-inning homer to Detroit's Alan Trammell on Opening Day to seal a 5-3 loss. The Red Sox bounced back to win 14 of their next 19 games, but a May swoon, combined with a series of clubhouse scuffles, soon had fans and Boston sports writers calling for manager John McNamara's job. The team won just 11 of 27 games in May, as a rift widened between the team's many veterans, who the manager allegedly favored, and its many young players. The outfield of the future consisted of Mike Greenwell, Ellis Burks and Brady Anderson. That meant longtime left fielder Jim Rice had to play designated hitter, while longtime right fielder Dwight Evans bounced between right field and first base where he shared playing time with newcomer Todd Benzinger. Meanwhile, Jody Reed was unseating Spike Owen at shortstop. The veterans were reluctant to yield their positions, and the result was a polarized team. The tension boiled over after a game in Anaheim when Evans publicly berated Benzinger, saying, "The man's always hurt. How's he going to play first base if he's always hurt? How can you put him in the lineup? What are you going to do, move everybody else to cater to him?"[1] While Benzinger refused to respond publicly, Greenwell insinuated that McNamara was too cozy with the team's veterans, telling reporters, "What we need is a new manager. Do you notice how Dewey [Evans] is in his office every day? He spends an hour in there and Mac believes everything he's telling him."[2]

While Evans backed up his me-first attitude with steady offensive production, the equally surly Rice entered June still seeking his first home run. When McNamara dropped him from the cleanup spot in the batting order, he began grumbling. When Wade Boggs was moved from the number-three spot in the lineup — from which he had driven in 16 runs in his first 174 at bats — back to leadoff, he too grew discontented. Meanwhile, the pitching rotation was in shambles after the top two starters, Roger Clemens and Bruce Hurst. Number-three starter "Oil Can" Boyd was experiencing numbness in his pitching arm, a condition that would later be traced to a potentially life-threatening blood clot, and Mike Smithson and Jeff Sellers were being hit hard.

An already volatile situation worsened on June 3, when Margo Adams, a 32-year-old mortgage broker from Costa Mesa, California, filed a $6 million palimony suit against Boggs. Adams alleged the third baseman had been paying her $2,000 per month to be his mistress and that she had accompanied him on 64 road-trips dating back to the 1984 season. The suit said that whenever the Red Sox were on the road, "Boggs and Adams would spend virtually all of their time together living in a husband and wife relationship."[3] Boggs, a married father of two, had allegedly broken off the arrangement with Adams, and she wanted compensation for her lost wages. Adams took her story to *Penthouse* magazine and *Donahue*, and, as she did, implicated several other Red Sox players in illicit affairs of their own. The team's problems grew. Boggs and Evans exchanged punches on a team bus after a game in Cleveland, then the fight spilled over into the lobby of the Hollenden Hotel. The incident was precipitated by Evans, Marty Barrett and Jeff Sellers receiving subpoenas to testify in the Adams case. Evans and catcher Rick Cerone also exchanged shoves and harsh words in the incident, while McNamara was nowhere to be seen. Boggs, who sat out the next game with an injured right biceps, would eventually settle the suit out of court in December of 1989, but not before many players were exposed for having been unfaithful to their wives.

On June 13, Rice finally broke into a home run trot after a drought of 199 at bats, smacking two dingers against the Yankees at Fenway Park, but the game represented a new low for the 1988 Red Sox. Roger Clemens was torched for 15 hits and nine earned runs, as McNamara refused to relieve his ace until the eighth inning, and Boston fell ten games behind first place New York with a record of 28–30.

Boston rebounded to win the final two games of the Yankee series, though, then showed further signs of life on a four-win, three-loss road-trip to Baltimore and Cleveland. The Red Sox reached .500 to stay on June 19, defeating the Orioles 15–7, while setting a Memorial Stadium record with 23 hits. The next night, the Red Sox beat Cleveland 14–7, and the next they reached double figures again in a 10–6 win.

Boston entered the all-star break with a 43–42 record, tied for fourth in the division, 9 games behind the Tigers. When the break began, Gorman assured the Boston media contingent that McNamara's job was safe, but at some point in the ensuing three days Jean Yawkey decided otherwise, ordering the manager's immediate dismissal. Hours before the second half began, bullpen coach Morgan was named interim manager. A 57-year-old baseball lifer from Walpole, Massachusetts, Morgan had managed in the minor leagues for 16 years and had been repeatedly passed over for the Red Sox' top job. For years, he had subsidized his baseball income by driving a snowplow in the off-season. Now, he was handed the Boston reins until Gorman could find a permanent replacement for McNamara.

The Red Sox won four straight against Kansas City to start the second half, then three in a row against Minnesota, then four straight against Chicago. Meanwhile, Detroit lost eight of eleven. By the time the Red Sox completed their 11-game home stand, they trailed first-place New York by just 1½ games, and the "interim" label had been removed from Morgan's title.

Not only were the Red Sox winning, but they were doing so in dramatic fashion. In the third win against Kansas City, Kevin Romine, who had hit just .154 since being recalled from Pawtucket in June, made his first big league home run memorable, hitting it in the ninth inning to give the Red Sox a 7–6 win. In the seventh win, Benzinger hit a three-run homer in the tenth to defeat the Twins 9–7. The Benzinger clout symbolized the changing of the guard in Boston, as earlier in the game Morgan and Rice had nearly come to blows in the Red Sox dugout when Morgan pinch-hit for Rice, sending Owen to the plate in an obvious bunt situation. After several players pried Rice and Morgan apart, Morgan emerged atop the dugout steps shouting, "I'm the manager, I'm the manager."[4] Rice was suspended for three games for his actions and Gorman backed up his manager the next day, stating, "You can't allow any player on the club to question the manager's judgment in any situation during the ballgame. You can't have players undermining their authority. The manager runs the ball club, and if someone challenges that authority, you've got to take some action."[5]

Not only did Morgan stand up to the team's veterans, but he also related well to the young players, most of whom had played for him in the minors. Suddenly, youngsters like Burks, Benzinger, Reed, and even Greenwell, who had just returned from his first All-Star Game appearance, played with new confidence, leading the resurgence.

Upon learning that he would manage the team for the remainder of the season, Morgan said, "I think the best explanation I got for never being named manager was that I was a bad salesman. I always figured people would look at me and say, 'he's a good manager,' so I never pursued anything or went out to sell myself. After 12 years at Triple-A, though, I figured, what are the odds?"[6]

Boston embraced Morgan's underdog story. After interviewing the miserable McNamara for three and a half seasons, local beat writers ate up the new skipper's folksy wit and delighted in quoting him when he uttered cryptic axioms like "Six-two-and-even," even though they had no idea what he meant.

The Red Sox won their first road game of the second half, downing the Rangers 2–0 on July 25, to extend their winning streak to twelve. They lost the next night, but then reeled off seven more wins in succession. The Red Sox did not lose their first home game of the second half until August 14, when the Tigers beat them 18–6. By then Boston had set a league record by winning 24 consecutive home games.

Gorman made one significant trade as the Red Sox pursued the division title, acquiring veteran right-hander Mike Boddicker from the Orioles in exchange for Anderson and minor league pitcher Curt Schilling on July 29. The curve-ball specialist went 7–3 with a 2.63 ERA in 15 starts for the Red Sox over the final two months, while Anderson went on to become one of the era's better leadoff hitters, and Schilling became a top starter a few years later in Philadelphia.

The Red Sox claimed sole possession of first place on September 5, when they downed Baltimore 4–1 to improve to 76–61, and move a game ahead of Detroit. Evans drove in three runs with a homer and single and Larry Parrish, who had been signed as a free agent on July 16 after the Rangers released him, hit a solo shot.

The Red Sox lost seven of their final nine games, but still managed to clinch the division title with two games to play. They lost to the Indians on September 30, but their victory in the division was assured later that night when Oakland beat Milwaukee. At the end of the 162-game schedule, the Red Sox had edged Detroit by 1 game, Toronto and Milwaukee by 2 games, and New York by 3½ games.

In an ordinary season, Boston's 46–31 second half performance wouldn't have been enough to overcome the team's sluggish first half, and in fact, the Blue Jays (45–29) enjoyed a better second half than the Red Sox. But Toronto had been 2½ games behind Boston at the break. The Red Sox were lucky that all three teams they had trailed at the season's midpoint — Detroit, New York and Cleveland — submitted below .500 records in the second half.

The final statistics indicated that Boston's strong suit was its offensive attack. What the team lacked in power (124 home runs, tenth best in the AL) it made up for in consistency, embodying the philosophy of hitting coach Walt Hriniak. The Red Sox led the AL in a multitude of categories, including batting average (.283), on base percentage (.355), walks (623), fewest strikeouts (728), hits (1569), doubles (310), and runs (813). Greenwell (.325, 22 HR, 119 RBI) led the team in home runs and runs batted in and finished second in the AL MVP ballot to Jose Canseco. Evans (.293, 21 HR, 111 RBI) was the next best run-producer, followed by Burks (.294, 18 HR, 92 RBI), while Boggs led the AL with a .366 average, a .480 on base percentage, and 128 runs. In his final productive season, Rice finished with a .264 average, 15 HR and 72 RBI. Second baseman Marty Barrett and shortstop Reed hit only one home run apiece, but both were steady in the field.

The pitching staff placed seventh in the 14-team league with a 3.97 ERA, led by Clemens (18–12, 2.93 ERA) and Hurst (18–6, 3.66 ERA), the only Red Sox pitchers to reach double figures in wins. Boyd (9–7, 5.34 ERA) and Mike Smithson (9–6, 5.97) tied for third on the team in wins. Smith had 29 saves, while Bob Stanley and Dennis Lamp were reliable set-up men.

The Postseason: 0–4

When the Red Sox took the field for the first game of the 1988 American League Championship Series, it marked the first time since 1918 that they had appeared in the postseason twice in a three-year period. Boston fans hoped this was a good omen. After all, the 1918 Red Sox had won the franchise's most recent championship.

Boston faced the AL West champion Oakland A's, who had posted the best record in baseball, going 104–58, while winning nine of 12 games against the Red Sox. Oakland finished second in the AL with 800 runs, and led the league with a 3.44 ERA. Muscle-bound sluggers Mark McGwire (.260, 32 HR, 99 RBI) and Canseco (.307, 42 HR, 124 RBI) paced the A's offense, while former Red Sox Dave Henderson (.304, 24 HR, 94 RBI), Carney Lansford (.279, 7 HR, 57 RBI), and Don Baylor (.220 7 HR, 34 RBI) also contributed. Dave Stewart (21–12, 3.23 ERA), Bob Welch (17–9, 3.64), and Storm Davis (16–7, 3.70 ERA) headed the rotation, while former Red Sox starter Dennis Eckersley, who Oakland manager

Tony LaRussa had converted to closer in 1987, had his first great season as a reliever, registering 45 saves.

The first two games were played in Boston, and the A's claimed a pair of one-run wins. Oakland finished the series sweep in Oakland. Canseco homered in three of the four games, while Eckersley saved all four. The sweep represented the first time the Red Sox failed to win at least three games in a postseason series. Unfortunately, they would replicate the feat in their next three playoff appearances.

1988 American League Championship Series: Athletics 4, Red Sox 0

Game 1: Athletics 2, Red Sox 1

	1	2	3	4	5	6	7	8	9	R	H	E
Oakland	0	0	0	1	0	0	0	1	0	2	6	0
Boston	0	0	0	0	0	0	1	0	0	1	6	0

WP Rick Honeycutt
LP Bruce Hurst
SV Dennis Eckersley

Hurst and Stewart squared off on a blustery Wednesday afternoon at Fenway Park in the opener. Both starters were exceptional, but the A's got key hits when they needed them, while the Red Sox couldn't capitalize on two late-inning scoring opportunities.

The game is remembered for Boggs' inability to deliver in three crucial at bats, and for the Fenway fans heckling Canseco due to his suspiciously large physique.

A week before the season had ended, *Washington Post* sportswriter Thomas Boswell had appeared on the CBS-TV program *Newswatch* and said that Canseco was "the most conspicuous example of a [baseball] player who has made himself great with steroids."[7] Despite the slugger's vehement protestations of innocence, the Fenway fans serenaded him with chants of "Ste-roids, ste-roids, ste-roids," whenever he took his place in right field or stepped to the plate. In the bottom of the first, Canseco laughed, then turned toward the right field stands and flexed his right biceps for the crowd. A short while later, he put the A's ahead 1–0, drilling a 3–2 forkball into the screen above the Green Monster to lead off the fourth inning.

By then, the Red Sox had already squandered one scoring opportunity. After Stewart retired the first two batters in the Boston second, Rice singled, Reed walked, and Rich Gedman singled to load the bases for Boggs. But the AL batting champ struck out for the first time since September 9 to end the threat.

Boggs got a small measure of revenge when he came to the plate with the bases loaded again in the seventh. With one out, LaRussa replaced Stewart with Rick Honeycutt. This time, Boggs lofted a sacrifice fly to left to score Romine and tie the game 1–1. But the next batter, Barrett, grounded out to strand two runners.

Oakland wasted no time in reclaiming the lead against Hurst in the eighth. Two former Red Sox did the damage. Lansford led off with a double to left, and the next batter, Henderson, singled him home. Hurst went on to pitch a complete game six-hitter in the losing effort.

Facing former teammate Eckersley in the bottom of the ninth, the Red Sox put a pair of men on base after two were out. Reed doubled and Gedman walked, bringing Boggs to the plate with a chance to tie the game with a single. After striking out just 34 times in 719 regular season at bats, Boggs fell behind 0–2, then fouled off a pitch, before waving weakly at strike three, for his second whiff of the day. "It was a terrible swing," Boggs admitted after the game. "A real bad swing."[8]

In the visiting clubhouse, Canseco laughed off the fans' taunts. "The crowd wants to be involved in the game," Canseco said. "I don't think they really want to hurt anyone. The fans aren't the ones who started this ridiculous rumor. So I had fun with it. I gave 'em a couple of flexes and they got a big kick out of that."[9]

LaRussa, meanwhile, was outraged. "I talked to Jose about it before leaving the clubhouse," LaRussa said. "I wanted to hit it hard, but he said he was having fun with it. But I still think it was brutal, a really cheap shot. I said yesterday that the fans here are great, but these weren't the Fenway fans that I know."[10] Throughout his many more years as manager to Canseco and McGwire, LaRussa would continue to portray his sluggers as innocent victims of an unscrupulous media smear campaign. Finally in 2005, Canseco's autobiography *Juiced* and investigative reports by the *New York Daily News*, *San Francisco Chronicle*, *Sixty Minutes*, and other news outlets produced irrefutable evidence that both Canseco and McGwire had used steroids, leaving LaRussa with nearly two decades worth of egg on his face.

Game 2: Athletics 4, Red Sox 3

	1	2	3	4	5	6	7	8	9	R	H	E
Oakland	0	0	0	0	0	0	3	0	1	4	10	1
Boston	0	0	0	0	0	2	1	0	0	3	4	1

WP Gene Nelson
LP Lee Smith
SV Dennis Eckersley

Game Two pitted Clemens against Davis. For a while it looked like Boston might even the series at one game apiece, as Clemens took the mound in the seventh protecting a 2–0 lead. But the A's scorched the "Rocket" for three runs in the seventh, then, after Boston tied the game, the A's scored the game-winner against Smith in the ninth.

The starting pitchers hung zeroes on the scoreboard until the Red Sox broke through for two unearned runs in the bottom of the sixth. After the first two batters made outs, Evans and Greenwell walked, then Rice reached on a line drive to center that popped out of Henderson's glove. Evans scored on the play and Greenwell took third. Burks followed with a single to right to plate Greenwell and move Rice to third. The Red Sox led 2–0, and had a chance to score another run when Davis uncorked a wild pitch to Benzinger. But the slow-footed Rice didn't attempt to score, as Oakland catcher Terry Steinbach chased the ball nearly to the backstop and Burks took second. Benzinger then struck out to end the inning.

Clemens carried a two-hit shutout into the seventh, but seemed suddenly out of rhythm pitching with a lead for the first time. Henderson led off with a single, and the next batter, Canseco, blasted his second homer of the series to knot the game, 2–2. Dave Parker followed Canseco's blast with a single, then Lansford reached on a fielder's choice. Lansford advanced to second when umpire Ken Kaiser called a balk on Clemens, then took third on a wild pitch and scored on a single by McGwire.

Gedman homered to right field against reliever Greg Cadaret in the bottom of the seventh to forge a 3–3 tie, then Stanley replaced Clemens to start the eighth. The "Steamer" allowed two batters to reach, then Morgan summoned Smith with one out. The lumbering closer got Canseco and Parker to fly out to end the threat.

In the ninth, Ron Hassey stroked a one-out single against Smith. McGwire lined to center for the second out, but then Tony Phillips singled to right, advancing Hassey to third. Weak-hitting shortstop Walt Weiss delivered the go-ahead single, making it 4–3.

Eckersley set down the Red Sox in order in the bottom of the inning to earn his second save.

In the somber home clubhouse, the Red Sox wondered if they would play at Fenway Park again in 1988. They had collected just ten hits and scored just two earned runs in the series' first two games. Making matters worse, their next stop was the Oakland-Alameda County Coliseum where they had struggled famously in recent seasons, losing 14 of their previous 15 games. Morgan did not sound optimistic in his post-game press conference. "What are the odds? I ask you," the manager pondered. "Hit me with a number. We're down 0–2, we've lost 14 of 15 games. You could get good odds on that one."[11]

GAME 3: OAKLAND 10, BOSTON 6

	1	2	3	4	5	6	7	8	9	R	H	E
Boston	3	2	0	0	0	0	1	0	0	6	12	0
Athletics	0	4	2	0	1	0	1	2	X	10	15	1

WP Gene Nelson
LP Mike Boddicker
SV Dennis Eckersley

In an effort to ignite the stagnant Red Sox offense, Morgan juggled the batting order before Game Three. He dropped Boggs from first to third, and installed Burks, who had hit sixth for most of the season, in the leadoff spot. Barrett remained in the second spot, while Greenwell and Rice maintained their usual spots, fourth and fifth, while Evans dropped from third to sixth. The players made the manager look smart, sending nine men to the plate and scoring three times in the first inning, then scored two more in the top of the second to take a 5–0 lead. But Oakland came back.

The first four Red Sox batters got hits against Welch, who threw 43 pitches in the first inning. Burks, Barrett and Boggs all singled, then Greenwell doubled and before an out had been recorded, Boston led 3–0. After Rice grounded weakly to short, Evans and Gedman both walked, reloading the bases with one out. But Reed popped out, and then Benzinger flied out.

Burks doubled to lead off the Boston second and scored on a two-out homer by Greenwell. Welch departed, having allowed five runs while recording five outs

It didn't take long for the A's to get back into the game, though. Oakland struck for four runs in the bottom of the second, with the big blows coming on homers by McGwire and Lansford, then tacked on two more in the third on a Hassey homer that gave Oakland a 6–5 lead. Boddicker departed after surrendering eight hits and six runs in 2⅔ innings. His replacement, Wes Gardner, held the A's to just three runs over the next 4⅓ innings, while striking out eight, but it was too late. The Red Sox never caught up.

Boston nearly tied the game in the fifth, but the second controversial call of the series by Kaiser took a run off the scoreboard and ended a Red Sox rally. Trailing 6–5, the Red

Sox had Evans on third and Gedman on first with one out when Reed hit a grounder to third. Lansford fielded and threw to Mike Gallego at second for the force out on Gedman. Gallego pivoted and threw to first, but Reed beat his throw as Evans crossed the plate. But Kaiser ruled that Gedman had come up out of his slide too soon, interfering with Gallego's ability to throw to first. He ruled Reed out due to the interference. To the Red Sox and their fans, the call was ludicrous. Runners slid hard into second base all the time trying to break up double play attempts. Gedman's slide looked no worse than similar slides that occurred, without penalty, on a nightly basis during every season. Morgan argued the call, but to no avail, and the usually reserved Hurst was ejected from the Red Sox bench for voicing his outrage.

"Let me tell you about Mr. Kaiser," Morgan said after the game. "He's been doing this for years — these kind of cheap calls. He showed grounds to get thrown out of the series. This call was ridiculous."[12]

But AL President Bobby Brown backed up the umpire, saying, "If anything, Kaiser showed a lot of guts. The easiest thing to do is turn your back and walk away. But he's got to make that call. He's got to take control of the game. That's why he's out there. I wasn't sure when I saw the play live. But when I saw the replay on television, it was clear to me that the runner sliding into second base had used his elbow and shoulder in taking out [Gallego]. Regardless of what else was happening, he had to call it."[13]

The A's tacked on single runs in the fifth and seventh and scored two more in the eighth, while the Red Sox managed only an unearned run in the seventh.

Eckersley entered the game in the eighth with one man on and pitched out of the jam. In the ninth, Boggs stepped into the batters box to lead off, and the Oakland crowd chanted "Mar-go, Mar-go," in reference to la affaire Adams. Eckersley induced Boggs to line out to left, then got Greenwell to groundout, then struck out Rice to end the game.

GAME 4: ATHLETICS 4, RED SOX 1

	1	2	3	4	5	6	7	8	9	R	H	E
Boston	0	0	0	0	0	1	0	0	0	1	4	0
Oakland	1	0	1	0	0	0	0	2	X	4	10	1

WP   Dave Stewart
LP   Bruce Hurst
SV   Dennis Eckersley

Over the first three games, the A's had clearly demonstrated they were the superior team in all facets of the game. They sent their ace, Stewart, to the mound in Game Four, in a ballpark where the Red Sox simply could not win. The resulting 4–1 A's win seemed to surprise no one, including the Red Sox.

Oakland took a first inning lead against Hurst on a Canseco homer, and added another run in the third on a Henderson double that scored Weiss.

The Red Sox scored their only run in the sixth on a Rice groundout that plated Barrett to pull Boston within 2–1.

Stewart departed after seven innings, having allowed four hits and one run. After Honeycutt pitched an easy eighth, the A's scored a pair against Smith in the bottom of the inning to take a 4–1 lead.

Eckersley recorded the last three outs to nail down the series MVP Award.

The Red Sox' comments after the game indicated they had been overmatched. "I felt a little relieved that it was over," Greenwell said. "I was disappointed that we lost, but at the same time, I was a little relieved. Relieved and disappointed. I was mentally drained. We really had to be hitting, to put hits together to have a chance against these guys, and we didn't do it. They had everything else, plus the big bats. That's the best club in baseball."[14]

Added Evans, "They were the best-prepared team I think I've ever seen against us. They defensed us, they pitched us, about as well as any team I've seen. All season, they did this. They do all the little things well."[15]

"We have nothing to be ashamed of," Stanley said. "They've got a good ball club. It would have taken our best to beat them, maybe more. You can't make excuses when they sweep you. I'd feel bad if they weren't a good team, but they're a good ball club."[16]

"We just got the crap beat out of us," added Benzinger. "They were hard-fought games, and there's consolation in that, but we only had a couple of good innings. If you're going to win a series, you've got to do better than two good innings."[17]

Indeed, the final statistics indicated the Red Sox had not put up much of a fight. Only two Boston players hit better than .250 in the series, Boggs (.385) and Gedman (.357), as the team hit .206. The A's, meanwhile, hit .299 and posted a 1.96 ERA, compared to the Red Sox' 5.29 ERA.

After looking so invincible while pitching six shutout innings against the Red Sox, Eckersley allowed a walk-off homer to the Dodgers' Kirk Gibson in the first game of the World Series. The A's never recovered, and Los Angeles won the series in five games.

CHAPTER 13

The Regular Season: 88–74

Early in the 1990 season, *Boston Globe* writer Dan Shaughnessy published a new book entitled *The Curse of the Bambino*. The book detailed seven decades of evidence to support a long-held New England theory that the Red Sox would never win another World Series because Harry Frazee had committed a sacrilege by selling Babe Ruth to the Yankees in 1919. Not only would the Red Sox always lose, but as Shaughnessy's book explained, they would lose in the most excruciating ways, subjecting themselves and their fans to one heart-break after another. The book pointed to the Red Sox' seven game losses in all four of their World Series appearances since dealing Ruth. It also examined the many late-season collapses in team history.

As the 1990 season played out, Shaughnessy's theory gained more and more attention nationally. Boston had a 6½ game lead in the American League East in early September and appeared poised to coast to the division title, but true to form the team plummeted eight games in the standings in less than three weeks, to fall 1½ games behind Toronto with six to play. Shaughnessy was suddenly a popular interview subject on sports radio and television programs from coast to coast, as baseball fans wondered whether life was imitating art, or art was imitating life. But a funny thing happened on the way to another historic collapse in Red Sox history. The 1990 Red Sox brushed aside the talk of a curse and showed they were the class of the AL East after all, even if it was the weakest of baseball's four divisions, and even if it took 162 games to clinch the title.

The year began with relatively low expectations. After an 83-win, third-place finish in 1989, general manager Lou Gorman's biggest off-season move was signing free agent closer Jeff Reardon. Reardon was a fine player who had saved 31 games the year before, but the Red Sox already had a closer in Lee Smith, who had saved 25 games in 1989. The Red Sox had more glaring needs in their starting rotation and in their lineup, especially after losing their best power hitter of a year ago, Nick Esasky, to the Braves as a free agent. The Reardon signing was one of several suspect moves Gorman would make during his last run at a pennant at the Boston helm. In the short term, the signing created a closer-controversy, in the long term it left the team no better than it was before, though quite a bit lighter in the wallet.

The Red Sox made one other notable acquisition in the off-season, signing free agent Tony Pena on November 27, 1989. The catcher would help galvanize the clubhouse with his happy-go-lucky attitude, and help guide a piece-meal rotation. The winter was more notable for departures than arrivals, as stalwarts Jim Rice, "Oil Can" Boyd, Bob Stanley, Mike Smithson, Rick Cerone, and Sam Horn were not offered contracts.

After an abbreviated spring training due to an owners' lockout, the Red Sox hosted the Tigers on April 9 in the season opener. Roger Clemens carried a no-hitter into the sixth, and lame duck closer Lee Smith struck out Alan Trammell with the bases loaded in the ninth to seal a 5–2 win. But the highlight of the afternoon occurred before the game when Bill Buckner was introduced to the crowd during the pre-game festivities and greeted with the loudest ovation of the day. The goat of the 1986 World Series, Buckner had departed Boston midway through the 1987 season. After hitting .216 in 79 games with Kansas City in 1989, the 40-year old first baseman approached the Red Sox during the off-season and requested a tryout. He played his way onto the team with a torrid spring training.

In the season's early months, Buckner split time at first base with Carlos Quintana and Billy Jo Robidoux, and hit an inside the park home run when Angels right fielder Claudell Washington tumbled into the first row of right field seats at Fenway Park on April 25. But Buckner batted just .186 in 22 games before being released in June. "Making the club at the end of the shortened spring training was one of my biggest thrills, and I really thought I could help this team," Buckner said in a somber farewell to the game he had played for 22 seasons.[1]

On May 4, Gorman finally solved the logjam at closer by peddling Smith to St. Louis for slugging right fielder Tom Brunansky. At the time of the swap, Boston trailed Milwaukee by 3 games in the division, with a record of 12–10. Brunansky added pop to the lineup, hitting .267 with 15 HR and 71 RBI over the final five months.

On June 3, in one of the season's galvanizing moments, Clemens drilled Cleveland Indians leadoff hitter Stanley Jefferson in the elbow with his first pitch of a Sunday afternoon game. The plunking was retaliation for Indians closer Doug Jones throwing a pitch at Pena's head in the ninth inning of an Indian victory the night before, after Pena had hit a clutch triple against Jones in a 4–3 Red Sox win on Friday night. After Clemens hit Jefferson, both benches emptied, and Pena and Cleveland's Chris James were ejected. When play resumed, Clemens struck out eleven hitters, on the way to an 8–2 win. After the game Red Sox manager Joe Morgan admitted the incident had been premeditated. "I loved it. We got even, didn't we?" Morgan said. "We voted as a team 34–0 that it would be such. I think they figured after last night, this was inevitable."[2] For his comments, Morgan earned a three-game suspension.

The Red Sox moved into first place a day after the brouhaha in Cleveland, beating the Yankees 5–3 to improve to 26–23.

On June 8, Clemens became baseball's first ten-game winner when he beat Cleveland again, this time 4–3, extending the team's six-game win streak and improving the Red Sox to 30–23.

On July 1, the Red Sox offered the Fenway fans some early fireworks, trouncing the Rangers and emerging star Kevin Brown, 15–4. Boston collected 17 hits, and Tom Bolton retired the first 18 batters he faced after entering in relief of Wes Gardner who allowed four runs before departing with two outs in the top of the first. A 28-year-old lefty, Bolton would permanently replace Gardner in the rotation a week later. With the win, the 44–31 Red Sox moved 3½ games ahead of the Blue Jays. But the month ahead would not be kind to the Old Towne Team. Due to an anemic offense, Boston struggled through a 12–17 July and by the month's final week they were in second place. Realizing the team still needed power, Gorman traded three minor leaguers to the Mets for first baseman/outfielder Mike Marshall on July 27. Marshall played only sparingly for the Red Sox over the final two months though, because the team already had productive players at the positions he played.

The Red Sox' fortunes turned around, nonetheless, as they won 19 of 28 games in August and strung together a 12-game winning streak from August 24 through September 2. The streak began with three straight shutouts in Toronto. The Red Sox won the final three games of the four-game series by scores of 2–0, 1–0, and 1–0. Dana Kiecker, Clemens and the tandem of Greg Harris and Jeff Gray became the first Red Sox pitchers to throw three consecutive shutouts since Gene Conley, Bill Monbouquette and Ike Deloc in 1962. The final three wins of the streak came in a sweep of the Yankees in Boston. The Red Sox won the middle game of the series, 15–1, highlighted by Greenwell's inside the park grand slam on a groundball that got by Yankee first baseman Kevin Maas and then evaded Jesse Barfield in the right field corner.

As the August 30 waiver deadline approached, Boston passed up the chance to claim both Harold Baines and Willie McGee off waivers. AL West powerhouse Oakland instead claimed both players. When Gorman was criticized for not snapping up the two former all-stars, he uttered the soon-to-be-famous line, "What would we do with Willie McGee?"[3] A switch-hitter with speed, McGee was leading the National League in hitting at the time with a .335 average, while Baines perennially hit .290 with at least 20 homers.

On the last day of August, the Red Sox instead made a seemingly inconsequential move, sending minor league third baseman Jeff Bagwell to the Astros for right-handed set-up man Larry Andersen. Bagwell had hit .333 with 4 home runs and 61 RBIs for Boston's Double-A affiliate in New Britain in 1990. Over the next decade he would become one of baseball's most feared power hitters in Houston. The 37-year-old Andersen would appear in just 15 regular season games for Boston and would pitch ineffectively in two playoff losses before heading to San Diego as a free agent. "We had depth at third base with Wade Boggs, Tim Naehring and Scott Cooper," Gorman explained. "It was one area where we could afford to lose a player in order to get a pitcher who could help us win the pennant. If we win the pennant with Andersen, the deal is worth it."

For a few days in early September, it seemed like there had never been a better time to be a Red Sox fan. Not only did Boston enjoy a 6½-game lead in the AL East, but the hated Yankees were in last place, on the way to a 67–95 season, and commissioner Fay Vincent had just announced Yankee owner George Steinbrenner was being placed on baseball's permanently ineligible list, stripping him of his position at the Yankee helm, due to the owner's smear campaign against Dave Winfield. Boston's feel-good season first showed signs of cracking on September 4 when Clemens complained of a sore right shoulder after losing to his Oakland nemesis Dave Stewart. The "Rocket" missed more than three weeks, during which time the Red Sox suffered through a 2–8 road-trip to Chicago, Baltimore and New York and fell 1½ games behind Toronto. As talk of "The Curse" filled the Boston sports pages and the team began hearing boos at Fenway, several players voiced their frustration with the Boston fans. "I've never been in a place so negative," Marshall said, speaking for the team. "No matter what we do, it's not enough. Win ten games in a row, and people still say we'll break their hearts in October."[5]

The Red Sox didn't fold in the final week. They won two out of three, while the Blue Jays dropped a pair, forging a tie atop the AL East through 156 games. Both teams had identical 84–72 records on the morning of September 28 as the Blue Jays arrived in Boston to open a weekend series. Boston built a 4–0 lead behind Boddicker in the first game, but the lead had shrunk to 4–3 by the start of the ninth. When Morgan sent Gray to the mound to close the game, many Red Sox fans and players wondered why Reardon wasn't on the mound. Their concerns proved justified when Junior Felix hit a two-run homer to give Toronto a 6–5 lead. Only after Gray had surrendered the lead did Morgan bring in his closer, who recorded the final three outs of the ninth. The Red Sox rallied for two runs of their own against Toronto closer Tom Henke in the bottom of the ninth though, capped by a walk-off single by Jeff Stone that plated Boggs with the winning run. Stone, a minor league call-up batting for the first time, collected the winning hit on a liner to right field. It was his only hit for the Red Sox all season, but it put them in first place to stay. "I'm on cloud 10," Stone said afterwards. "I've never been in a situation like that before. I looked back to see if [Morgan] was going to call me back, but he didn't. I thought he would go with [Danny] Heep or [Phil] Plantier."[6]

Morgan explained why he stayed with a career journeyman who had entered the game as a defensive replacement, instead of opting for a more experienced hitter with the season on the line. "I just had a feeling that he'd do something good," the skipper said.[7]

The next day, Clemens took the mound for the first time in 25 days and pitched six shutout innings, while Brunansky blasted three home runs in a 7–5 win that gave Boston a two-game lead with four to play.

Toronto rebounded to win the series finale, chasing Harris early and knocking out 19 hits in a 10–5 rout.

The Red Sox clinched at least a tie for the division title the next night, beating the White Sox, but lost the next day. With one game left, the Red Sox had a one-game lead. If they lost to the White Sox and the Blue Jays beat the Orioles, there would be a one-game playoff to decide the division. In any other scenario, the Red Sox would be the champs.

Seizing control of their own destiny, the Red Sox jumped out to a 3–0 lead against Chicago's Alex Fernandez with three runs in the second inning. Boddicker, meanwhile, held the White Sox to one run over seven innings. This time Morgan brought his closer into the game while the team still had a lead, and Reardon pitched a scoreless eighth, setting the stage for a dramatic season crescendo in the ninth. After recording the first two outs, Reardon allowed a single to Sammy Sosa then hit Scott Fletcher with a pitch, bringing up Ozzie Guillen. The pesky shortstop tomahawked a high fastball down the right field line that looked sure to fall for a game-tying double. But Brunansky streaked toward the right field foul pole and slid on the warning track to make a game-saving catch. The play transpired in a corner of the old ballpark that was obscured from sight to those watching from the Red Sox dugout, and those watching on television, as no cameras captured a shot of the catch. New England held its breath as first base umpire Tim McClelland hesitated before finally making the out call. Brunansky handed the ball to McClelland, retrieved his cap from where it had fallen on the warning track, then joined his teammates in celebration.

"When you're a kid, you learn about reacting quickly to things," Brunansky said. That's what I did. When I saw the ball I went right for it. There was no hesitation. No time to think about what I should do. I just had to do it."[8]

Although the final out of the Red Sox' 1990 season remains one of the most exciting division clinching plays ever, in the end it didn't much matter whether Brunansky caught the ball or not. While the Red Sox soaked each other with champagne in the home clubhouse, Toronto lost to Baltimore, 3–2, giving the Red Sox a two-game margin of victory in the AL East.

Even with the addition of Brunansky and Marshall, the Red Sox finished 11th out of 14 AL teams in homers with 106. They made up for their lack of power by leading the league in batting average at .272, and on-base percentage at .343, but still finished only seventh in the league in runs with 699. After Buckner retired, Quintana emerged as the every day first baseman, hitting .287 with 7 HR and 67 RBI, while Jody Reed (.289, 5 HR, 51 RBI) unseated Marty Barrett at second. Shortstop Luis Rivera (.225, 7 HR, 45 RBI) and third baseman Wade Boggs (.302, 6 HR, 63 RBI) handled the left side of an infield that combined to hit just 32 home runs, counting the production from Pena (.263, 7 HR, 56 RBI). Centerfielder Ellis Burks hit .296 while leading the team in home runs (21) and runs batted in (89), while leftfielder Mike Greenwell hit .297 with 14 HR and 73 RBI. In his final year with the Red Sox, Dwight Evans (.249, 13 HR, 63 RBI) moved from right field to designated hitter and played through persistent back pain.

Surprisingly, Boston's strong suit was its starting pitching. All five primary starters posted ERAs of 4.00 or lower. Clemens went 21–6 with a 1.93 ERA on the way to winning his third Cy Young Award, while Boddicker (17–8, 3.36 ERA), Harris (13–9, 4.00 ERA), Bolton (10–5, 3.38 ERA) and Kiecker (8–9, 3.97 ERA) were steady. Boston finished fourth in the AL with a 3.72 ERA.

The Postseason: 0–4

Boston's 88 wins represented the lowest total for an AL division winner since the Detroit Tigers edged Boston by half a game in the strike-shortened 1972 season with a record of 86–70. Meanwhile, the defending world champion A's were the class of baseball, having followed their 1989 World Series sweep of the Giants with a 103–59 season to win the AL West. The A's finished eight games ahead of the next best team in baseball, the NL East champion Pirates. The Oakland dynasty of the late 1980s and early 1990s is best remembered for its rough and tumble image, and its hulking "Bash Brothers"—personified by Mark McGwire and Jose Canseco. While it is true that the 1990 A's finished third in the league with 733 runs scored, the real strength of the club was its pitching. With four effective starters and a lights-out bullpen, the A's led the league in several pitching categories, including ERA (3.18), shutouts (16), and opponents' batting average (.238). Dave Stewart, arguably the best big-game pitcher of the era, posted a 22–11 mark with a 2.56 ERA. Number-two starter Bob Welch (27–6, 2.95 ERA) won more games than any pitcher since Steve Carlton won 27 with the Phillies in 1972, while Scott Sanderson (17–11, 3.88) and Mike Moore (13–15, 4.65) were solid number-three and number-four starters. Tony LaRussa's specialized bullpen was anchored by former Red Sox starter Dennis Eckersley, who had one of the most remarkable seasons ever for a reliever, saving 48 games with a 0.61 ERA. The 35-year-old allowed just 9 runs, 41 hits, and 4 walks in 73 innings, while striking out 73. All four of the A's set-up men — Rick Honeycutt, Gene Nelson, Todd Burns, and Joe Klink — posted ERAs lower than 3.00. The pitching staff was supported by the best defense in all of baseball, as the A's flashed the leather to the tune of a .986 fielding percentage. Offensively, McGwire (39 HR, 108 RBI) and Canseco (37 HR, 101 RBI) provided a devastating one-two punch in the heart of the batting order, while Rickey Henderson had one of the best seasons ever by a leadoff man, batting .325 with 28 home runs, 119 runs and 65 stolen bases.

The Red Sox were underdogs entering the series, but at least the saga of their 1990 season had been a feel good-story up until that point. By series' end, the Red Sox would do much to undo the warm feelings they had engendered throughout the summer. Their four-game sweep at the hands of the A's would be remembered for the clubhouse infighting it brought to light and for one of the most embarrassing postseason episodes ever, as Clemens was ejected from the final game after threatening to kill an umpire, and a belligerent Barrett littered the field with the contents of the Red Sox dugout before pushing a Boston coach down the dugout steps.

1990 American League Championship Series: Athletics 4, Red Sox 0

Game 1: Athletics 9, Red Sox 1

	1	2	3	4	5	6	7	8	9	R	H	E
Oakland	0	0	0	0	0	0	1	1	7	9	13	0
Boston	0	0	0	1	0	0	0	0	0	1	5	1

WP Dave Stewart
LP Larry Andersen

Before the series, Morgan announced that Clemens and Kiecker would start Games One and Two at Fenway Park, followed by Boddicker, Harris, and then Clemens again in Oakland. Bolton, the odd-man-out of the rotation, immediately made waves in the clubhouse, complaining to the Boston press about his demotion to the bullpen. And thus, before a pitch had been thrown in the series, the anti-Morgan grumbling had begun. It would only get worse.

The first game was tight for six innings, before the A's erupted for nine runs in the final three frames to claim a 9–1 win. Pitching for just the second time in five weeks, Clemens was not his usual dominant self, but he gamely held the A's scoreless through six innings in a four-hit, four-walk, effort.

The A's started Stewart who sought to extend his career record against Clemens to 7–0.

Boggs got the Red Sox on the scoreboard with a solo home run in the fourth and the run stood up through six innings. On Clemens' 97th and final pitch of the night, he induced Terry Steinbach to fly out to center, stranding two men on base in the top of the sixth. Clemens told Morgan that he could pitch one more inning, but the manager elected to start the seventh with Andersen on the mound. It did not go well. Andersen walked the first batter he faced, McGwire, then, after Walt Weiss grounded into a fielder's choice, pinch hitter Jamie Quirk singled Weiss to third. Dave Henderson lofted a fly ball to center that tied the game 1–1 as Weiss slid home safely when Burks' throw hit him.

Andersen, Bolton, Gray, Dennis Lamp and Rob Murphy combined to allow 9 runs on 9 hits and 5 walks over the final three innings, while Stewart continued to hold the Red Sox at bay. After the A's ace scattered 4 hits and a walk over eight innings, Eckersley pitched a scoreless ninth.

"A beautiful game turned into a horrible evening, didn't it?" Morgan quipped afterwards, defending his decision to lift Clemens. "He was dead. He would have probably never got out of the seventh if he went out there, so I decided to make the move. He said he felt excellent before, during and after. It was my decision, but he knew it was time."[9]

GAME 2: ATHLETICS 4, RED SOX 1

	1	2	3	4	5	6	7	8	9	R	H	E
Oakland	0	0	0	1	0	0	1	0	2	4	13	1
Boston	0	0	1	0	0	0	0	0	0	1	6	0

WP Bob Welch
LP Greg Harris
SV Dennis Eckersley

The second game was not so different from the first. It was another pitchers' duel in which the Red Sox scored first and stayed within striking distance until the A's roughed up the Boston bullpen. On paper, the game looked like a mismatch, pitting baseball's top winner, Welch, against Kiecker, who had submitted a sub-.500 record as a rookie, after spending the previous season driving a UPS truck back home in Sleepy Eye, Minnesota. The rookie was nearly as good as the veteran, but the Boston offense could only muster one run for the second straight night on the way to a 4–1 loss.

The Red Sox took a 1–0 lead in the third on a Rivera double, a Reed groundout, and a Quintana sacrifice fly. Oakland tied the game at 1–1 in the fourth when McGee doubled and scored on a single by Baines, prompting fans across New England to again lament Gorman's refusal to claim either player off the waiver wire in August.

Kiecker departed with two runners aboard and two outs in the sixth, and Harris came in to induce Weiss to ground into an inning-ending fielder's choice.

After the Red Sox left the bases loaded against Welch in the bottom of the sixth, Harris allowed singles to Mike Gallego and Rickey Henderson to start the seventh. Morgan brought in Andersen, who recorded an out, then walked Canseco to load the bases. Baines drove in the eventual winning run with a groundout to first.

Boggs and Burks reached Welch for singles in the home half of the eighth, but LaRussa brought in Eckersley, who struck out his old friend Evans to end the inning.

The A's tacked on two more runs against Reardon in the ninth, as Baines and McGee again played leading roles in an A's rally. McGee led off with a bunt single, then stole second. After Canseco walked, McGee scored on a Baines double to center. McGwire followed with a single that plated Canseco to make the score 4–1.

GAME 3: ATHLETICS 4, RED SOX 1

	1	2	3	4	5	6	7	8	9	R	H	E
Boston	0	1	0	0	0	0	0	0	0	1	8	3
Oakland	0	0	0	2	0	2	0	0	X	4	6	0

WP Mike Moore
LP Mike Boddicker
SV Dennis Eckersley

As the series shifted to Oakland, any semblance of harmony within the Red Sox clubhouse was rapidly disintegrating. It would come to light after Boston scored first for the third straight time, only to see the A's roar back to claim a relatively easy victory. Afterwards, several Red Sox players blamed their manager for the team's struggles, while others took jabs at teammates. Even some members of the A's saw fit to comment on the Red Sox' freefall.

Boddicker pitched a complete game in the loss, allowing four runs — just two of which were earned, on six hits, in eight innings. Boston's only run against Moore scored in the second inning when Brunansky plated Greenwell with a sacrifice fly.

The A's scored two earned runs in the fourth, and two unearned runs in the sixth. Canseco led off the fourth with a walk and advanced to second on a Baines single. On strike-three to McGwire, Canseco broke for third and Baines broke for second. Pena pumped toward third but held onto the ball because Boggs didn't cover third, and both players were safe. Canseco later scored on a sacrifice fly by Dave Henderson, and Baines scored on a Willie Randolph single. Oakland's runs in the sixth scored thanks to errors by Rivera and Pena.

After the game, Boggs blamed his failure to cover third base on the double steal on Pena, saying the catcher was supposed to throw to second to nab the slower trail runner on the play. Backup second baseman Barrett, meanwhile, pointed a finger at the Red Sox scouting department, saying, "When we hit the ball today, they seemed to be standing exactly where our guys were hitting it. They've got computers, printouts. Baseball's changed a lot and we're not into that stuff. Maybe we should be."[10] The comments were also interpreted as a jab at Morgan, who was known for playing hunches in the old-school baseball tradition.

Speaking on the condition of anonymity, another player told *Boston Globe* writer Steve Fainaru that Morgan was the problem. "When we won the division, he didn't even come in and congratulate us," the player said. "You'd think he would at least call a meeting and say, 'Good job, I'm proud of the way you guys hung in there.' Even today, you'd think he might get us together and say something like, 'We're down, 3–0, but it's been a great year. Let's hang in there and try to get back in this thing.' The truth is, everything we've done this year, we've done ourselves. We wouldn't even have been here if it hadn't been for the last week. Even that Friday game against Toronto, when we came back after he had screwed it up, we just decided, 'Screw it, we'll win it despite him.' He hasn't done a thing for this team, and everybody on this team feels that way. It's sickening."[11]

Several members of the bullpen corps, meanwhile, stated that the reason for their ineffectiveness was Morgan's tendency to warm them up too long and too often before bringing them to the mound. Morgan responded, "That's a lot of hogwash. How the hell are they going to be ready if I don't warm 'em up? That's hogwash, child's talk. Do you believe that?"[12]

Even Stewart made headlines on the topic of the Red Sox manager, bashing the decision to skip Harris and pitch Clemens on three days' rest in the fourth game, with the Red Sox facing elimination. "I think [Clemens] should pitch on the fifth day," Stewart said. "You've got a horse on your staff, and basically, he's broken down because he's been abused throwing so many pitches.... Regardless of what Joe Morgan said, that wasn't the same Roger Clemens out there [in Game One]. I just don't see the point in risking his playing career on one game."[13]

Clemens would indeed start Game Four, but he would not last long, and the start would affect his future availability to the Red Sox, though not in the way eventual Game Four winner, and Series MVP Stewart had suggested it might.

GAME 4: ATHLETICS 3, RED SOX 1

	1	2	3	4	5	6	7	8	9	R	H	E
Boston	0	0	0	0	0	0	0	0	1	1	4	1
Oakland	0	3	0	0	0	0	0	0	X	3	6	0

WP Dave Stewart
LP Roger Clemens
SV Rick Honeycutt

Game Four of the 1990 ALCS remains one of the most surreal games in baseball's storied postseason history. It was somber enough for the Red Sox and their fans to watch their season end in a four-game sweep, but the game took on a ghoulish hue when Clemens went berserk in the second inning of a 3–1 loss.

From the outset, Clemens seemed overly aggressive and fidgety. As he warmed up in the visiting bullpen wearing eye-black on his face, he fired a ball into the right-field bleachers at a fan who had been heckling him. After warming up, he sprinted to the Red Sox dugout, knocking over a photographer who got in his way, then angrily spiked his glove into the dugout. He retired the A's without incident in the first. Then he lost control in the second. Clemens retired Baines on a pop out to start the inning, then allowed back-to-back singles to Carney Lansford and Steinbach, putting runners at first and third with one out. McGwire bounced into a fielder's choice to score Lansford and give the A's a 1–0 lead. Then Clemens walked Willie Randolph and, displeased with the calls of home plate umpire Terry Cooney, shook his head. According to Clemens, he yelled, "What the fuck? You better umpire."[14] Cooney heard, "Fuck you, umpire," and abruptly threw Clemens out of the game. While teammates tried to restrain Clemens, he shoved umpire Jim Evans and threatened to find and kill Cooney during the off-season. Eventually, Clemens was ushered by security up the runway to the Red Sox clubhouse. Barrett responded by throwing a bucket full of Gatorade and another bucket full of sunflower seeds onto the field and then pushed coach Dick Berardino down the dugout steps when Berardino tried to restrain him.

"It was just unbelievable," Clemens said after the game. "I really can't believe it. I don't feel I warranted anything. I didn't verbally abuse him. I didn't curse at him or call him anything. It was more of an adjective about shaking my head. I wasn't showing him up. I was fired up for the game."[15]

Stewart, who watched his rival unravel from the A's dugout, had a very different impression of the incident. "[Clemens] was yelling, everybody could hear it," Stewart said. "And this is exactly what he said. He said, 'Nobody's talking to you. Put your fucking mask back on and get your fucking ass back behind the plate.' He said it twice. If he denies he said that, he's a liar."[16]

Bolton came in to pitch for the Red Sox and the first batter, Gallego, doubled to drive home both base runners and give the A's a 3–0 lead.

Stewart carried a two-hitter into the ninth before Burks doubled and Reed singled to end the shutout bid. Honeycutt came in to record the last three outs.

The A's went on to lose four straight games against the surprising Cincinnati Reds in the World Series.

Clemens was suspended for the first three games of the 1991 season for his behavior. He appealed to Commissioner Fay Vincent, but lost. After reviewing the video footage of the incident with a professional lip-reader provided by the Players Association, Vincent agreed that Clemens had not initiated the confrontation by cursing at Cooney from the mound, but said that Clemens still deserved the suspension for pushing Evans and threatening to kill Cooney during the off-season.[17]

CHAPTER 14

The Regular Season: 86–58

The 1995 baseball season got off to a dubious start, beginning nearly a month late due to the same players' strike that canceled the 1994 World Series. Until a ruling by the National Labor Relations Board on March 31, 1995, the owners were prepared to start the new season with replacement players. Each team had signed 30 veteran minor leaguers — who were told in many cases that they would be released if they did not cross the picket line — to major league contracts. The replacement players received $5,000 signing bonuses and appeared in a handful of spring training games, but on the last day of March, U.S. District Judge Sonia Sotomayor ruled that the owners could not unilaterally impose a new work agreement without the consent of the Players Association and ordered the owners to reinstate the conditions of the previous Basic Agreement. On the day of the judge's decision, the Players Association announced it was no longer on strike, and shortly thereafter, acting commissioner Bud Selig announced that a 144-game season would begin April 26 under the same terms that had been in place in 1994. To fans, the turn of events only underscored that absolutely nothing had been accomplished by the owners' and players' sacrifice of the 1994 World Series. The two sides were still unwilling to work together to secure the game's long-term future.

When the regular season finally began, fans were understandably hesitant to re-embrace the sport, although Boston welcomed a capacity crowd to Fenway Park on Opening Day to watch the Red Sox cruise to a 9–0 wins against Minnesota. Aaron Sele started in place of the injured Roger Clemens, who stayed in Fort Myers to nurse a muscle strain in his right shoulder. Sele allowed just one hit over five innings. The opener marked the debut of new Boston manager Kevin Kennedy, whom general manager Dan Duquette had hired in the off-season to replace Butch Hobson. The game also marked the first appearance in a Red Sox uniform by designated hitter Jose Canseco, who was acquired from Texas in exchange for Otis Nixon and Luis Ortiz on December 9, 1994. Other newcomers included catcher Mike MacFarlane, designated hitter Reggie Jefferson, second baseman Luis Alicea and outfielder Troy O'Leary, who were signed as free agents. Returnees such as first baseman Mo Vaughn, leftfielder Mike Greenwell, third baseman Tim Naehring, and shortstop John Valentin rounded out a lineup that was expected to produce an abundance of runs.

The pitching staff was far more suspect at the season's outset and was the reason not a single *Boston Globe* writer picked the Red Sox to finish any higher than third in the AL East.[1] Of the team-record 53 players who appeared in a Red Sox uniform during the season, 26 were pitchers. No Red Sox pitcher started as many as 30 games, and 13 different pitchers started at least one game, including such forgettable names as Tim Van Egmond, Brian Looney, Vaughn Eshelman, and Matt Murray. In the season's early months, Erik Hanson and Tim Wakefield, both of whom had been signed to cheap free agent contracts in April, emerged as reliable starters, Clemens returned from his injury, and Sele was lost for the season due to an injury.

Hanson made a sparkling debut on April 29, pitching the first five innings of an 8–0 shutout against the White Sox. The 30-year-old right-hander posted a 15–5 record with a 4.24 ERA in his only season with the Red Sox, before signing with Toronto as a free agent. While Hanson was steady, Wakefield was spectacular, submitting a four-month stretch of pitching as impressive as any in Red Sox history. A knuckleballer, Wakefield had burst onto the major league scene with the Pirates in 1992, going 8–1 down the stretch and 2–0 in the National League Championship Series against the Braves, to lead Pittsburgh to the brink of the NL pennant. He had fallen on hard times though, by the time Duquette inked him to a one-year, $175,000 contract on the first day of the 1995 season. After his 1992 heroics, the infielder-turned-pitcher had compiled a record of 14–31 between the big leagues and Triple-A. He spent the entire 1994 season in the minors, recording a 5–15 record.

Wakefield's first start for the Red Sox came May 27 against California and it was a 12–1 Boston win. Just three days later he started again, bailing out Kennedy's depleted pitching corps, and he out-dueled Oakland's Ron Darling, 1–0. Without breaking 75 miles per hour on any American League radar gun, Wakefield raced to a 14–1 record with a 1.65 ERA. A late-season swoon inflated his final numbers to 16–8 with a 2.95 ERA, but he still won the AL Comeback Player of the Year Award. Unlike Hanson, Wakefield would stick around for the long term, filling a multitude of roles on the Red Sox pitching staff for more than a decade.

Boston's victory in the AL East race was barely contested. The Red Sox assumed first place for good on May 13 when Eshelman won his third straight start to begin his career, beating the Yankees 6–4 to improve the team's record to 10–5.

May was also notable in that it saw the Red Sox recall the second replacement player to join a big league roster. Outfielder Ron Mahay was called up from Triple-A Pawtucket on May 10. Because replacement players had crossed the Players Association's picket line, union leadership took a hard line with them, decreeing that no replacement player would ever be allowed to join the union or receive union benefits and licensing money. Additionally, many major leaguers had stated publicly that they would go out of their way to make life miserable for any replacement players to surface in the majors. Mets pitcher John Franco and Yankees pitcher Scott Kaminiecki said they would throw at the heads of any batters who had crossed the line, while Mets player rep Bobby Bonilla said, "Anyone crossing the picket lines will end up in the East River."[2]

Mahay's brief stint in Boston appeared to play out without incident, although television cameras often captured him sitting alone at the far end of the Red Sox dugout. Boston beat Seattle on May 23 when Mahay drew a bases-loaded walk to cap a 5–4 win. In his last at-bat with Boston on May 26, Mahay homered to help the Red Sox to an 8–3 win against California. Years later, Mahay would recall, "No one on the team spoke to me the first two days. I knew it was going to happen."[3] But Greenwell, the team's clubhouse leader, called a team meeting in which he offered some friendly words to the newcomer and some of the veterans followed his lead. Nonetheless, Mahay was optioned to Double-A Trenton shortly thereafter. He would later return to the majors, after reinventing himself as a left-handed relief pitcher, making him one of more than two-dozen former replacement players — including such others as Brian Daubach, Brendan Donnelly, Cory Lidle, Lou Merloni, Kevin Millar, Damian Miller and Shane Spencer — to have lengthy major league careers, despite the continued animosity of many union members.

Other highlights for the Red Sox, on their way to a final record of 86–58 and a 7-game margin of victory over the Wild Card Yankees, included a three-homer game by Valentin in a 6–5 win against Seattle at Fenway Park on June 2, a ten-inning effort by Wakefield against the Mariners that the Red Sox won 2–1 on a walk-off homer by O'Leary, on June 4, the acquisition of veteran closer Rick Aguilera in a trade with Minnesota for reliever Frankie Rodriguez on July 6, and a twelve-game win streak in the midst of a 20–2 stretch in August that put the Red Sox a season-high 15½ games ahead of the Yankees on August 25.

After they completed August with a 23–7 record, it was a foregone conclusion that the Red Sox would make the playoffs. They clinched the AL East crown with a 3–2 victory against Milwaukee on September 20. Canseco's broken bat single in the seventh inning drove home the winning run. Aguilera struck out Dave Nilson to end the game and notch his 19th save in 20 opportunities with the Red Sox. During the post-game celebration, ancient bench coach Johnny Pesky and several Boston players mounted police horses and rode them on the Fenway lawn. Although the Red Sox lost 13 of their final 23 games, the final month allowed them to take a look at minor league call-up Dwayne Hosey who wrested the center field job away from Lee Tinsley.

The 1995 Red Sox placed fourth in the AL with 791 runs. Vaughn, who won the AL MVP Award, hit .300 with 39 HR and a league-leading 126 RBI, while his former college teammate from Seton Hall, Valentin, hit .298 with 27 HR and 102 RBI, while leading the team with 108 runs. Canseco missed 40 games due to various injuries but still wound up with a .306 average, 24 HR and 81 RBI. Boston finished third in the AL with a 4.39 ERA. Hanson, Wakefield and Clemens (10–5, 4.18 ERA) were the only reliable starters. The next biggest winner was lefty Zane Smith, who went 8–8 with a 5.61 ERA in 21 starts. Aguilera finished the season with 32 saves overall, 20 with the Red Sox, while submariner Stan Belinda had 10 saves and Ken Ryan had 7.

The Postseason: 0–3

Due to the strike in 1994, baseball had to wait an extra year to unveil its new playoff format, and when it did, it quickly became apparent that the system had some wrinkles in it that still needed to be ironed out. The AL East Champion Red Sox (86 wins) and AL Central Champion Indians (100 wins) had the two best records in the American League, yet they were pitted against each other in the first round of the playoffs, while the AL West Champion Mariners (79 wins) and Wild Card Yankees (79 wins) were playing each other. Pundits and fans pointed out that ideally, and in other sports, playoff brackets are set so that the two best teams have a chance to meet in the final round, never the opening round.

Baseball's answer to its critics was that the American League had decided before the season that the AL East Champion would play the AL Central Champion and the AL West Champion would play the Wild Card team in the first round. Furthermore, home field advantage in each five-game series had been predetermined, meaning that despite posting the best record in baseball, Cleveland would not only face the second best team in the league, but play the final three games of the ALDS against the Red Sox on the road. In the years ahead, baseball would fix these problems, matching the highest seed against the lowest in the first round, awarding home-field advantage to the highest seed in each series, and redefining home-field advantage to be two home games, two road games, and then one home game, rather than two road games and then three home games.

Cleveland was clearly the best team in baseball, having posted a record of 100–44. The Tribe's .694 winning percentage projected to a record of 112–50 had a full 162-game schedule been played. Despite the shortened season, the Indians won their division by a record 30 games over Kansas City. They led the league in runs (840), home runs (207), stolen bases (132), batting average (.291), on-base percentage (.364), slugging (.479), ERA (3.83), shutouts (10), saves (50) and just about every other major category.

Centerfielder Kenny Lofton hit first in the Indians order and led the league with 54 stolen bases, while batting .310. Second baseman Carlos Baerga hit .314 with 15 HR and 90 RBI, third baseman Jim Thome hit .314 with 25 HR and 73 RBI, designated hitter Eddie Murray hit .323 with 21 HR and 82 RBI, right fielder Manny Ramirez hit .308 with 31 HR and 107 RBI, and AL MVP runner-up Albert Belle hit .317 with a league-leading 50 HR and 126 RBI. The surly left fielder also had 52 doubles and one triple, making him the first player in major league history to surpass 100 extra base hits in a season.

The Cleveland rotation was led by veteran right-handers Dennis Martinez (12–5, 3.08 ERA) and Orel Hershiser (16–6, 3.87 ERA), while sinkerballer Chuck Nagy chipped in with a 16–6 record and a 4.55 ERA. In the bullpen, Julian Tavarez went 10–2 with a 2.44 ERA while serving as set-up man for Jose Mesa, who led the league with 46 saves and had a miniscule 1.12 ERA.

Following their recent trend, the Red Sox quickly bowed out of the playoffs, losing three straight. The first game was an extra-inning heartbreaker that ended on a walk-off home run by former Red Sox catcher Tony Pena.

1995 American League Division Series: Indians 3, Red Sox 0

Game 1: Indians 5, Red Sox 4

	1	2	3	4	5	6	7	8	9	10	11	12	13	R	H	E
Boston	0	0	2	0	0	0	0	1	0	0	1	0	0	4	11	2
Cleveland	0	0	0	0	0	3	0	0	0	0	1	0	1	5	10	2

WP Ken Hill
LP Zane Smith

The Indians made the first playoff game played in Cleveland in 41 years a memorable one for their fans, beating the Red Sox in an extra-inning thriller that featured two rain delays, 14 pitchers, three extra-inning home runs, and a controversy involving Belle's bat.

The game ended in dramatic fashion when Pena walloped a homer against Smith in the bottom of the 13th inning.

Red Sox fans received some bad news before the game began when they learned that O'Leary had been left off the postseason roster due to back spasms. Hosey took his place in right field, while Tinsley played center.

After a 39-minute rain delay, Clemens toed the rubber for Boston, making his first playoff appearance since being ejected in the second inning of the final game of the 1990 ALCS. This time the right-hander kept his cool and allowed three runs in seven innings. Martinez also pitched effectively, and after seven and a half innings the game was knotted 3–3.

The Indians scored their three runs off Clemens in the sixth, while the Red Sox scored on a two-run homer by Valentin in the third and a leadoff homer by Luis Alicea in the eighth. After the second-baseman's homer, the game was halted for a second time due to rain, this time for 23 minutes, and when play resumed neither team could break the tie.

The Red Sox, who won eight of ten extra-inning games during the regular season, were in position to win the series opener after Naehring hit a one-out homer off Jim Poole in the eleventh to put Boston ahead 4–3.

In the bottom of the eleventh, Kennedy called on Aguilera to finish off the Indians. The closer jumped ahead of the leadoff hitter Belle, but the slugger fouled off a couple of 2-2 pitches, then tied the game with a line-drive homer to left field. Before Belle had finished rounding the bases, Kennedy was on the field, heading for home plate umpire Tim Welke. The manager asked that Belle's bat be confiscated and checked for signs of doctoring. The previous season Belle had been suspended for seven games after he was caught using a corked bat, and Kennedy told Welke that he had it on good authority that Belle was cheating again.

"We had some suspicion," Kennedy explained afterwards. "We had some information given to us."[4]

Belle responded by flexing his right bicep in the Indians dugout and shouting profanities across the diamond at Kennedy.

Aguilera retired two of the next four hitters before leaving the game with a groin pull, an injury that would sideline him for the remainder of the series. Mike Maddux came in to end the Indians' threat and send the game into the 12th.

Alicea led off the Red Sox twelfth with a double, but did not score. Hosey and Vaughn struck out against Poole, and Canseco struck out against Ken Hill, making the trio 0–17 in the game.

Maddux hit Lofton with a pitch to begin the bottom of the twelfth, then Omar Vizquel reached on an error by Alicea that put runners at the corners with no outs. The next hitter, Baerga, popped to short, then Belle was walked intentionally, and the left-handed Smith was summoned to pitch to Murray. The future hall-of-famer grounded to Naehring and the third baseman threw home to nab Lofton at the plate. Then Thome grounded out to first to end the inning.

Mike Greenwell led off the top of the 13th with a single, but Hill retired the next three hitters, setting the stage for Pena's heroics in the bottom of the inning. The 38-year-old backstop, who had served as Boston's starting catcher from 1990–1993, had entered the game in the eleventh after Indians manager Mike Hargrove elected to pinch-run for starting catcher Sandy Alomar in the tenth.

With two-outs and no one on base, Smith fell behind Pena 3–0. Pena had hit just five home runs in 91 regular season games, and Smith certainly didn't want to walk him and bring Lofton to the plate with the winning run on base. Smith threw a batting-practice-speed fastball and Pena sent it high into the raindrops, depositing it in the left field bleachers to end the game at 2:08 a.m.

After the game, AL president Dr. Bobby Brown supervised as Belle's bat was sawed in half, revealing that Kennedy's information was incorrect. The bat was perfectly legal.

"It's just a desperate effort by them to throw a monkey wrench into our season," Belle said. "[Brown] knows what he can do with those two pieces."[5]

Game 2: Indians 4, Red Sox 0

	1	2	3	4	5	6	7	8	9	R	H	E
Boston	0	0	0	0	0	0	0	0	0	0	3	1
Cleveland	0	0	0	0	2	0	0	2	X	4	4	2

WP Orel Hershiser
LP Erik Hanson

The second game presented little of the drama the first game did and Cleveland coasted to a 4–0 win. The loss marked only the second game all season in which the Red Sox were shutout.

After the Red Sox struggled to come up with clutch hits with men in scoring position in the first game, Kennedy penciled veteran switch-hitter Willie McGee into the lineup in right field and moved Hosey to center, to start Game Two. McGee went 1 for 3 in the seventh spot in the Red Sox order, but the move didn't do enough to jump-start the Red Sox offense. MacFarlane accounted for Boston's only other hits, a pair of singles, as the Red Sox managed just three singles and two walks in the game.

Hanson pitched a complete game in the losing effort, allowing four runs in eight innings. Hershiser was better, though, pitching shutout baseball for 7⅓ innings, while setting an Indians postseason record with seven strikeouts. Tavarez, Paul Assenmacher and Mesa combined to record the final five outs without allowing a base runner.

Boston's best chances to score came in the first and second innings. In the first, Belle committed an error to start the game, dropping a Hosey liner to put a runner at second base. The next batter, Valentin, grounded to shortstop. Hosey broke for third base as soon as Vizquel threw to first, but first baseman Paul Sorrento came off the bag and fired across the diamond to cut down Hosey. Valentin was ruled safe at first and soon found himself in scoring position when Hershiser threw a wild pitch. Vaughn struck out and Canseco flied out to end the inning, though.

In the second, Boston loaded the bases on singles by McGee and Macfarlane and a walk to Alicea, but Hosey grounded weakly to second to end the threat.

The Indians took a 2–0 lead in the fifth when Sorrento and Lofton scored on a one-out double to center by Vizquel. The Tribe padded the lead in the eighth on a two-run homer by Murray.

Game 3: Indians 8, Red Sox 2

	1	2	3	4	5	6	7	8	9	R	H	E
Cleveland	0	2	1	0	0	5	0	0	0	8	11	2
Boston	0	0	0	1	0	0	0	1	0	2	7	1

WP Chuck Nagy
LP Tim Wakefield

As the series shifted to Fenway Park for a Friday night tilt, the Red Sox and their fans knew Boston's struggling offense needed to get going if the team was to have a chance. Vaughn and Canseco, especially, needed to get untracked. The third and fourth hitters in the Boston lineup entered the game a combined 0-for-20 in the series.

Kennedy moved Canseco from designated hitter to right field, making way for Jefferson to DH and hit sixth behind Canseco, but again the manager's tinkering had little effect. The lifeless Red Sox fell 8–2, losing their 13th straight postseason game and sending New Englanders into their 77th consecutive winter without a world championship.

On a cold and windy night Wakefield could not command his knuckleball. He repeatedly left pitches up in the strike zone, and Cleveland touched him up for seven runs on five hits and five walks in 5⅓ innings.

Meanwhile, Nagy, a Connecticut native who grew up rooting for the Red Sox, held the Red Sox to just one run on four hits and five walks in seven innings, on the way to securing Cleveland's first postseason win since Bob Lemon beat the Boston Braves 4–3 to clinch the 1948 World Series.

Cleveland scored a pair of runs in the second on a two-run homer by Thome, then added another in the third when Wakefield walked Thome with the bases loaded.

MacFarlane cut the deficit to 3–1 in the fourth with a sacrifice fly that scored Jefferson, but the Indians answered with five runs on five hits in the sixth to put the game out of reach. Sorrento and Alomar had RBI hits against Wakefield, then Vizquel and Baerga connected for run-scoring hits against Rheal Cormier.

The Red Sox scored a run against Tavarez in the eighth to pull within 8–2 before Assenmacher retired the side in order in the ninth. After Vaughn struck out to lead off the final frame, he was given a standing ovation by the fans behind the Boston dugout. Canseco popped to second base for the second out, and Greenwell flied to left to end the season.

Boston finished the series with a .184 batting average, and collected just two hits in 28 at-bats with runners in scoring position. Vaughn and Canseco combined to go hitless in 27 at-bats and stranded 17 base runners between them.

Cleveland beat Seattle in six games in the ALCS, then lost to Atlanta in six games in the World Series.

Chapter 15

The Regular Season: 92–70

The 1997 campaign was a transitional one for the Red Sox as the team replaced manager Kevin Kennedy with Jimy Williams, bid adieu to the greatest pitcher in franchise history, Roger Clemens, and handed the shortstop position to Nomar Garciaparra, who won the American League Rookie of the Year Award. While the offense held its own, without a bona fide stopper atop the rotation or a reliable closer at the back end of the bullpen, the pitching staff struggled and the team finished 78–84, 20 games behind the first place Yankees. As the season waned, the attention of most Boston fans focused on whether or not general manager Dan Duquette would preemptively sign star first baseman Mo Vaughn to a long-term contract or if he would wait to make a contract offer until after the 1998 season when Vaughn could become a free agent.

Instead of approaching Vaughn, Duquette concentrated on shoring up the holes in the team's pitching staff. Late in the 1997 season, he traded closer Heathcliff Slocumb to Seattle for a pair of young players—catcher Jason Varitek and pitcher Derek Lowe. The move gave Williams a young arm in the bullpen and a switch-hitting catcher to platoon with incumbent Scott Hatteberg. It also made room in the bullpen for Tom Gordon, who had been used previously as a starter for the Red Sox. Gordon responded with 11 saves in September, giving the Red Sox reason to believe they had found a viable closer for the 1998 season. Also in the final month of 1997, the Red Sox gave six starts to Bret Saberhagen, Duquette's latest reclamation project, who had missed the entire 1996 season and the first five months of 1997 following arm surgery. The right-hander struggled, averaging just four innings per start and a 6.58 ERA, but he showed enough to convince Duquette to resign him. Gordon, Saberhagen and Lowe would all pay huge dividends for the Red Sox in 1998.

Duquette further rebuilt the pitching staff when he orchestrated a trade between the Red Sox and his former employer, the Montreal Expos. On November 18, 1997, the Red Sox acquired Pedro Martinez for minor league pitchers Carl Pavano and Tony Armas, Jr., and then immediately signed Martinez to a long-term contract extension.

To bolster the bullpen, in December the Red Sox signed Dennis Eckersley and Jim Corsi, a pair of veteran relievers, who would help set up Gordon in 1998.

The 1998 campaign began ominously for the Red Sox. After a spring training marred by a drunk driving trial involving Vaughn (who was acquitted) and bickering in the press between Vaughn and Duquette, the Red Sox lost five of their first eight games, all on the road. The home opener on April 10 proved to be a turning point in the young season. Rookie Brian Rose drew the start for the Red Sox against Seattle's Randy Johnson. The Mariners' gargantuan lefthander was dominant, striking out 15 Red Sox in seven innings. Heading to the last of the ninth, the Red Sox trailed 7–2. Adding insult to injury for the Red Sox, their former teammate Slocumb came in to pitch the final inning. But all seven Red Sox to bat in the ninth reached base against Slocumb and three other Seattle pitchers and the game ended on a walk-off grand slam by Vaughn that gave Boston a dramatic 9–7 victory. After the game, John Valentin lobbied for the Red Sox to offer Vaughn a contract extension. "The price gets higher. They better do something," the third baseman said. "If that doesn't send a statement, I don't know what does. Right now, there is no one that can hit like that, in this league, in this ballpark."[1] The Fenway faithful echoed the sentiment, chanting "Sign Mo, now," as they spilled onto Yawkey Way.

The momentum from the home opener propelled the Red Sox to a 14–3 record over their next 17 games and they finished April 18–8, the team's most wins ever in the opening month.

The Red Sox posted a 13–14 record in May though, after Garciaparra separated his throwing shoulder May 8, diving for a groundball with an 11-run lead in the eighth inning of a game at Kansas City. The team won just seven of 16 games in Garciaparra's absence as Mike Benjamin filled in at short.

Boston had lost six in a row before Saberhagen snapped a six-game losing streak May 30 at Yankee Stadium. The start was a turning point for the veteran pitcher who had allowed 19 earned runs in his previous 10 innings, raising doubts about whether he'd be able to help the team. Facing the first-place Yankees, Saberhagen allowed just one run in $6\frac{2}{3}$ innings. The Red Sox won 3–2, and the team played with renewed energy and confidence in the weeks to follow, going 17–10 in June.

By the season's midpoint the Red Sox had emerged as one of the league's better teams, but the division race clearly belonged to the Yankees, who would finish the season with a remarkable 114–48 record, 22 games ahead of the second-place Red Sox.

Martinez, Gordon and Vaughn represented the Red Sox in the All-Star Game at Colorado, and Cleveland Manager Mike Hargrove drew criticism from the national press for choosing his own shortstop, Omar Vizquel, instead of Garciaparra.

In his first start following the break, Martinez pitched a three-hitter to out-duel Cleveland's Bartolo Colon at Fenway Park. The game's only run scored on a line-drive home run by Midre Cummings that sneaked inside the right field foul pole in the fifth inning.

As the July 31 trading deadline approached, the Boston media speculated that Duquette would trade Vaughn, as it seemed less and less likely the team would make a serious bid to resign him. Vaughn was on his way to hitting .337, second in the AL only to Bernie Williams, with 40 home runs and 115 RBI, but management feared that his weight represented an injury risk. And although Vaughn did a lot of charity work in the Boston community, his off-field activities, namely his unapologetic visits to area strip clubs, offended Duquette and John Harrington. He had also been an outspoken critic of management when Kennedy and Clemens left the team. In the end, the trading deadline passed without a deal involving

Vaughn, though. Boston made only one significant move, reacquiring first-baseman/designated hitter Mike Stanley in a trade with Toronto.

Martinez earned his 19th win in Baltimore on September 24, the day the Red Sox clinched the AL Wild Card. Garciaparra hit two home runs in the 9–6 victory, while Vaughn had three hits, giving him 200 for the season. After Eckersley tied Hoyt Wilhelm's record for the most career appearances by a pitcher (1,070), Gordon struck out the side on 15 pitches in the ninth to earn his 45th save, and 42nd in a row — a major league record at the time. As the Red Sox celebrated in the Camden Yards visiting clubhouse afterwards, Martinez said, "The first game in spring training I looked at the lineup card, and I knew we'd win if the starting rotation was okay."[2]

Indeed, as home run records fell throughout baseball in the wild summer of 1998, the Boston pitching staff had been the team's strength. The Red Sox finished second in the AL to the Yankees with a 4.19 ERA. The rotation featured a quartet of double-figure winners: Martinez (19-7, 2.89 ERA), Tim Wakefield (17–8, 4.58 ERA), Saberhagen (15–8, 3.96 ERA) and Steve Avery (10–7, 5.02 ERA). Meanwhile, Gordon anchored the bullpen, going 7–4 with a 2.72 ERA, while leading the league with 46 saves. Eckersley, Lowe, Corsi and Rich Garces were reliable set-up men.

Offensively, the team finished third in both batting average (.280) and runs scored (876), and fifth in home runs (205). Williams, who liked to keep all of his players involved, used left-right platoons at catcher (Hatteberg and Varitek), designated hitter (Reggie Jefferson and Stanley), and right field (Darren Bragg and Damon Buford). Vaughn was complimented in the middle of the order by Garciaparra, who moved from the leadoff position to third or fourth in the lineup, and responded by hitting .323 with 35 home runs and 122 RBI. Valentin and left fielder Troy O'Leary were also steady run-producers, hitting 23 home runs apiece.

The Postseason: 1–3

The Red Sox drew the defending AL Champion Indians in the first round of the playoffs, after the Indians finished first in the Central division with a 89–73 record. The balanced Cleveland lineup was led by right fielder Manny Ramirez (.294 average, 45 HR, 145 RBI), first baseman Jim Thome (.293 average, 30 HR, 85 RBI) and third baseman Travis Fryman (.287 average, 28 HR, 96 RBI). Colon (14–9, 3.71 ERA), Chuck Nagy (15–10, 5.22 ERA) and Dave Burba (15–10, 4.11 ERA) all contributed more than 200 innings, while Mike Jackson saved 40 games and registered a 1.55 ERA.

The Red Sox entered the series 0–13 in their previous 13 postseason contests and losers of five straight playoff series. Meanwhile, Cleveland had performed above expectations in recent postseasons, appearing in two of the three previous World Series. Nonetheless, Boston was favored after taking eight of eleven games against the Tribe in the regular season. The biggest difference between the two teams was the ace at the top of the Red Sox rotation. Martinez had dominated Cleveland in the regular season and was scheduled to pitch Games One and Five. That meant as long as the Red Sox could muster one win in the middle three games, two of which would be played at Fenway Park, they stood an excellent chance of winning the series.

Martinez did his part, pitching the Red Sox to an easy win in the opener to end the team's postseason losing streak, but he never got a chance to pitch again in the series. The Red Sox lost the next three, and Williams decided not to pitch Martinez on three days' rest, facing elimination, in the fourth game. Ironically, Gordon who had blown just one save opportunity all season long, earned a blown save and a loss in the final game when he allowed two eighth inning runs.

1998 American League Division Series: Indians 3, Red Sox 1

GAME 1: RED SOX 11, INDIANS 3

	1	2	3	4	5	6	7	8	9	R	H	E
Boston	3	0	0	0	3	2	0	3	0	11	12	0
Cleveland	0	0	0	0	0	2	1	0	0	3	7	0

WP   Pedro Martinez
LP   Jaret Wright

Led by their three brightest stars, the Red Sox put to rest any talk about their postseason losing streak, blowing out the Indians 11–3 at Jacobs Field in the first game. Martinez allowed three runs on six hits in seven innings while striking out eight, while Vaughn had two home runs and a double to drive in seven runs, and Garciaparra drove in the other four runs with a three-run homer and a sacrifice fly.

Boston scored three runs before Cleveland starter Jaret Wright had recorded an out. Darren Lewis led off the game with a single to left and Valentin reached on an infield hit, setting table for Vaughn, who worked the count full then lofted a high fly ball to left field that carried over the fence to give the Red Sox a 3–0 lead.

Wright knocked Lewis out of the game in the fifth when he drilled him in the helmet with a fastball. Valentin followed with a walk, and then, after Vaughn struck out, Garciaparra homered to double the Boston lead.

Vaughn put the Red Sox ahead 8–0 with a two-run homer off reliever Doug Jones in the sixth. The dinger made Vaughn the first Boston player to homer twice in a postseason game since Carl Yastrzemski and Rico Petrocelli both accomplished the feat during the 1967 World Series.

Indians leadoff hitter Kenny Lofton reached Martinez for a two-run homer in the bottom of the sixth, then Thome added a solo shot in the seventh, before the Red Sox scored three times in the eighth to account for the final score.

"Things look pretty good for this ball club," said Vaughn afterwards, "because we got Game One and we've got Pedro going again."[3]

GAME 2: INDIANS 9, RED SOX 5

	1	2	3	4	5	6	7	8	9	R	H	E
Boston	2	0	1	0	0	2	0	0	0	5	10	0
Cleveland	1	5	1	0	0	1	0	1	X	9	9	1

WP   Dave Burba
LP   Tim Wakefield
SV   Mike Jackson

The second game featured a pitching match-up of Wakefield versus Dwight Gooden. After the two starters combined to record just five outs between them, Cleveland's long-

Garciaparra prepares to bat at Fenway.

relievers were more effective than Boston's and the Indians evened the series at one win apiece.

The Red Sox offense picked up where it left off in the first game, as Lewis led off with a walk and stole second, then Valentin walked. After Vaughn struck out, Garciaparra laced a double off the left field fence. Lewis scored easily, while Valentin raced around the bases, and slid headfirst into home plate. Although it appeared Cleveland catcher Sandy Alomar tagged Valentin before he touched the plate, home plate umpire Joe Brinkman signaled called him safe. Gooden, who had been backing up the play, barked an expletive in

Brinkman's face, then returned to the mound, unaware that Brinkman had just ejected him from the game. When the pitcher finally realized he had been tossed, he charged at Brinkman and had to be physically restrained by teammates, then corralled toward the Cleveland dugout by Indians coach Jeff Newman. As a parting shot, Gooden threw his glove and hat at Brinkman before heading up the runway to the home clubhouse. Hargrove was also ejected by Brinkman before play resumed, for arguing the umpire's ball and strike calls on the pitches to Lewis and Valentin.

The Indians handed the ball over to Burba, who was granted as much time to warm up as he needed. The veteran right-hander would earn the win, allowing three runs in 5⅓ innings of emergency duty.

The first inning delay forced Wakefield to return to the Boston bullpen to warm up for a second time, before he finally took the mound with a 2–0 lead. The outing would turn out to be the shortest of the season for the knuckleballer who allowed five runs on three hits and two walks in just 1⅓ innings.

Cleveland cut the lead to 2–1 in the first, as Lofton led off with a walk, stole second, advanced to third on a groundout, and scored on a sacrifice fly by Dave Justice. Then Cleveland scored five times in the second inning. After Wakefield allowed three hits and a walk, reliever John Wasdin served up a three-run homer to Justice, who sent the first pitch he saw into the right field seats to give Cleveland a 6–2 lead.

Both teams scored single runs in the third, then the Red Sox plated a pair in the sixth to pull within 7–5, but Cleveland answered with a run on back-to-back doubles by Justice and Ramirez against Lowe in the sixth, and another run on a Gordon wild pitch in the eighth.

GAME 3: INDIANS 4, RED SOX 3

	1	2	3	4	5	6	7	8	9	R	H	E
Cleveland	0	0	0	0	1	1	1	0	1	4	5	0
Boston	0	0	0	1	0	0	0	0	2	3	6	0

WP Chuck Nagy
LP Bret Saberhagen
SV Mike Jackson

After an off day, the series resumed with a Friday afternoon tilt at Fenway Park. Saberhagen pitched well for the Red Sox, but his opponent, Nagy, was even better, and a Red Sox rally against Cleveland closer Mike Jackson came up short in the ninth. All four Cleveland runs scored on solo homers.

Boston took a 1–0 lead in the fourth when Lewis scored on a Garciaparra fielder's choice, but Cleveland responded with solo homers in the fifth, sixth and seventh, by Thome, Lofton, and Ramirez. Saberhagen departed after seven innings, having allowed three runs on four hits while striking out seven.

Ramirez led off the ninth with a line drive homer into the screen above the Green Monster against Eckersley. The pitch was inside and low, just where Hatteberg had set up, but Ramirez turned it around in a hurry, sending it over the fence just inside the foul pole. Eckersley could only say "wow," and shake his head in disbelief, before setting down the next three hitters in what would turn out to be the final inning of his career.

Nagy allowed only one run on four hits, while recording 12 groundball outs, and throwing just 88 pitches, before yielding to Jackson to start the ninth.

Valentin lined out to lead off the Boston ninth, then Vaughn singled to left and Garciaparra homered to cut the deficit to 4–3. The rally fizzled, though, when Stanley and O'Leary followed with groundouts to Vizquel.

Game 4: Indians 2, Red Sox 1

	1	2	3	4	5	6	7	8	9	R	H	E
Cleveland	0	0	0	0	0	0	0	2	0	2	5	0
Boston	0	0	0	1	0	0	0	0	0	1	6	0

WP   Rick Reed
LP   Tom Gordon
SV   Mike Jackson

Facing elimination, many fans and sportswriters expected the Red Sox to hand the ball to Martinez in Game Four. People throughout New England seemed to agree that it was the logical move, except for the one person whose opinion mattered, the Red Sox manager. Reasoning that his team needed to win two games either way, Williams decided he would rather pitch Martinez on his usual four days of rest in Game Five, than on short rest in Game Four.

After losing the third game, Williams announced he would start Pete Schourek, a southpaw whom the Red Sox had acquired from Houston in August, in the fourth game. In ten appearances with Boston, including eight starts, Schourek had posted a 1–3 record with a 4.30 ERA. Prior to joining the team, he had gone 7–6 with a 4.50 ERA in 15 starts with the Astros. The decision caused many Red Sox fans to recollect Joe McCarthy's ill-fated decision to start Denny Galehouse instead of Mel Parnell in the playoff against Cleveland in 1948.

Further maddening Red Sox fans, even though the Indians had a lead in the series, Hargrove announced he would send Colon to the mound on three days' rest.

Williams was vindicated when Schourek carried a one-hit shutout into the sixth inning and left the game with a 1–0 lead after 5⅓ innings. But the Red Sox bullpen couldn't protect the lead, and Cleveland ended the series with a 2–1 win.

The Red Sox scored their run on a lead off homer by Garciaparra in the fourth.

Schourek departed after allowing a one-out double to Justice in the sixth, yielding to Lowe who came in to retire Ramirez on a liner to right and Fryman on a grounder to first.

In the bottom of the sixth, Justice threw Valentin out at the plate. The runner got the green light from third base coach Wendell Kim and was cut down trying to score from second on a one-out single to left by Stanley. If Kim had held Valentin at third, the Red Sox would have had the bases loaded with one out. Instead, they had runners at the corners with two out, and O'Leary struck out to end the threat.

In the top of the seventh, Lowe protected the lead, sandwiching a groundout between a pair of strikeouts. Although Lowe had retired all five hitters he had faced, three via strike out, Williams opted to summon his closer to start the eighth. The Red Sox had won all 47 games Gordon had entered in save situations during the regular season, and Gordon had converted 43 straight save opportunities, but he had not been called upon to start the eighth inning a single time during the regular season. He had been used as a one-inning pitcher, amassing 79⅓ innings in 73 games. Thrust into a new role at the most crucial moment of the season, he faltered. After retiring Joey Cora on a fly ball to start the eighth, Gordon allowed a broken-bat single to Lofton and then a hard single to Vizquel. After a double steal advanced the runners to second and third, Justice laced a double into the right-center field triangle to put Cleveland ahead 2–1.

After the game, Williams defended the move to bring in Gordon, saying, "If I had it to do over again, I would do it again, because he's been special, he's been great.... In this magnitude of a game you go to your best guy, and he is our best guy."[4] The comment caused some pundits to wonder why the same logic hadn't applied in the manager's decision to hold Martinez out for a potential fifth game that never materialized.

The Red Sox had a chance to tie the game in the bottom of the eighth. Vaughn stroked a one-out double, in what would be his final at bat for the Red Sox, and Donnie Sadler replaced him at second base as a pinch runner. Facing Paul Shuey, Garciaparra grounded out, then, after Stanley walked, O'Leary flied to center to end the inning.

The Red Sox went down in order in the ninth, as Jackson earned his third save, inducing groundouts from Hatteberg and Cummings, and striking out Bragg to end the game.

Despite the outcome, Boston out-hit (.252 to .206) and outscored (20 to 18) Cleveland in the series. Unfortunately for the Red Sox, the bulk of their offense came from the top four hitters in the lineup, while the bottom five contributed very little. Lewis, Valentin, Vaughn and Garciaparra combined to hit .393 (24 for 61), while the rest of the team hit .135 (10–74).

As many onlookers had suspected, the series turned out to be the last in a Red Sox uniform for Vaughn, who signed a free agent contract with the Angels in November.

After defeating the Red Sox, the Indians lost to the Yankees in six games in the ALCS. The Yankees swept the Padres in the World Series.

Chapter 16

The Regular Season: 94–68

When the Red Sox claimed the American League Wild Card in 1999, it marked just the second time ever that the team had earned playoff berths in two consecutive years. Although the feat was more impressive in the days before expanded playoffs when the Red Sox appeared in the 1915 and 1916 World Series, the 1999 season represented a coup nonetheless for the Red Sox front office. Team president John Harrington and general manager Dan Duquette had suffered a public relations debacle before the season, as fan-favorite Mo Vaughn signed with Anaheim as a free agent and the Red Sox failed in a bid to sign Yankees free agent Bernie Williams. Making matters worse, Roger Clemens, who had left the Red Sox in 1997 as a free agent, was traded from the Blue Jays to the Yankees. Despite losing their best power hitter and watching their top rival acquire one of the best pitchers in their history, the Red Sox went out and won 94 games in 1999, two more than in the previous season. More importantly, the Red Sox finished just four games behind the Yankees in the AL East, compared to the 22 games back they had finished in 1998, and the 20 games back in 1997. Clearly the gap between the two teams was narrowing, and as it did, an already fierce rivalry grew fiercer. Clemens and Pedro Martinez served as the chief catalysts of the new grudge, just as catchers Thurman Munson and Carlton Fisk had in the 1970s.

After bowing out in the first round of the 1998 playoffs, the Red Sox declined to match the Angels' six-year, $80 million offer to Vaughn. While fans waited for the team to acquire a power hitter to replace the burly slugger's production in the middle of the order, or a front-line starter to complement Martinez, the Red Sox signed free agent second baseman Jose Offerman, who Duquette noted would replace Vaughn's "on base capability," and minor league free agent Brian Daubach to try out at first, then signed a cast of mediocre pitchers that included Pat Rapp, Mark Portugal, Rheal Cormier, and Ramon Martinez, who was nine months removed from rotator cuff surgery.

As pitchers and catchers reported to spring training, Red Sox fans and pundits decried Harrington's unwillingness to spend the type of money needed to net top free agents, and questioned Duquette's acumen as a talent evaluator and as the public face of the franchise.

Sure, the general manager had pulled the trigger on the trade that brought Martinez to town a year earlier, but he had also let Clemens and Vaughn leave in the primes of their careers, and both partings had been less than amicable.

Meanwhile, the reigning world champion Yankees made a trade that improved a pitching staff that had won a league-record 114 games in 1998. On February 18, 1999 New York sent David Wells, Homer Bush, and Graeme Lloyd to Toronto in exchange for Clemens, the reigning Cy Young Award winner two years running.

As the new season played out, however, Martinez emerged as the American League's top hurler. While his debut season in the AL had been impressive, his 1999 season was spectacular. Martinez led the league in wins, earned run average, batting average against, strikeouts per nine innings, and a bevy of other categories, going 23–4 with a 2.07 ERA, and 313 strikeouts in 213⅓ innings. The effort would earn him the Cy Young Award and more importantly, give the Red Sox reason to believe they could beat the Yankees in a playoff series.

Martinez's second season in Boston was not without its share of turmoil, though, as he endured an arm injury in July and a rift with manager Jimy Williams in August.

On April 5, Martinez began the season with a victory, striking out nine Royals in a 5–3 win at Kansas City. Offerman temporarily silenced Duquette's critics, going 4–5 with a double and triple against his former team.

On May 7, Vaughn's Angels came to Fenway and Martinez upstaged the returning slugger, fanning a career-high 15 batters, including Vaughn twice, in a 6–0 win that evened Boston's record at 14–14.

Three days later, Nomar Garciaparra hit two grand slams and drove in 10 runs in a 12–4 win against Seattle.

On May 18, Martinez led the Red Sox into sole possession of first place, beating David Cone and the Yankees 6–3 at Fenway in Joe Torre's return as New York's skipper after he missed the first 36 games recovering from prostate cancer. Martinez did not have his best stuff, but he bore down and retired the Yankees when he needed to, stranding 15 runners in 7 innings, while holding the Yankees 3-for-19 with runners in scoring position. Martinez struck out 11 batters, marking the seventh consecutive time he reached double figures in the category.

When the 70th All-Star Game took place at Fenway Park on July 13, Martinez seized the moment, starting for the AL and striking out five of the six batters he faced to earn MVP honors in a 4–1 AL win. Martinez became the first pitcher to strike out the first four batters in the Mid-Summer Classic, whiffing Barry Larkin, Larry Walker and Sammy Sosa in the first, then Mark McGwire to lead off the second. After Matt Williams reached on an error and was caught stealing, Martinez whiffed Jeff Bagwell.

The first All-Star Game to be played in Boston since 1961 represented a magical moment for the game for another reason as well. The affair marked the final appearance in the national spotlight for Ted Williams. Before the game, 33 candidates for an All-Century Team were announced, including such retired stars as Carl Yastrzemski, Carlton Fisk, Dennis Eckersley and Nolan Ryan. The living members of this elite group joined the current all-stars on the field, and then "Teddy Ballgame" was chauffeured to the center of the diamond on a golf cart to throw out the first pitch. In an unplanned twist, the legends of the game's past and present surrounded Williams like children in awe of a favorite player. They took turns shaking his hand, embracing him, and talking baseball with him, while fans across the country watched the touching moment unfold.

With a record of 49–39 at the break, the Red Sox trailed the Yankees by four games, but shortly after the break Boston's fortunes took a turn for the worse. After Martinez allowed 9 runs in 3⅔ innings in a 10–7 loss to Florida, it was announced on July 25 that he was being placed on the disabled list with a shoulder injury. The ailment ended the pitcher's streak of 172 consecutive starts, dating back to April 8, 1994. At the same time, the Red Sox learned that closer Tom Gordon's elbow injury was more serious than initially suspected and that he would likely miss the remainder of the season. Gordon would appear briefly in late September in an attempt to get in shape for the playoffs, and would pitch just three innings in the postseason. In Gordon's absence, first Tim Wakefield, then Derek Lowe stepped into the closer's role.

While the Red Sox struggled through an 11–15 July, the Yankees went 16–11 to seize a 6½ game lead in the division.

Martinez's stay on the disabled list lasted two weeks, and when he returned he quickly made waves in the Red Sox clubhouse by showing up at Fenway Park just 30 minutes before a scheduled start against the Mariners on August 14. Williams sent reliever Bryce Florie to the mound instead of his tardy ace, and then brought Martinez into the game in the fifth inning of a 13–2 Red Sox rout. The Boston media had a field day with the incident. Martinez said he preferred to get loose at home with his personal trainer rather than at the ballpark, while Williams issued no public comment, but made it clear through his actions that no player would get star treatment on his team, even if the player had a 17–3 record. Martinez appeared angry, hurt, and bewildered after the game. "I was on time to start," he said. "I excused myself with my teammates, but Jimy didn't let me do it . . . Jimy wanted to be stubborn. I told him that there's no reason to do that. It could have stayed in the clubhouse, but instead he had to make a statement. He didn't have any reason to embarrass me out there. If I'm a bad influence on the team, they'd better get me out of here." Lost in the public relations nightmare was a 5-for-6, 5 RBI performance by Daubach, who was quietly having a steady year at first base.

With the warm feelings of the All-Star Game having dissolved, the Red Sox began September 7½ games behind the Yankees. They played well over the final month to cut that deficit nearly in half and edge Oakland by 7 games in the Wild Card race. Martinez accounted for two more season highlights in September, pitching a one-hitter and striking out a career-high 17 batters in a 3–1 Red Sox win at Yankee Stadium on September 10. The only hit was a second-inning home run by Chili Davis. Later in the month, Martinez established a new Red Sox single season strikeout record, besting Clemens's 1988 mark of 291. Martinez broke the record in style, mowing down 12 Blue Jays in a complete game 3–0 win on September 21.

The injury bug bit Boston again on September 25, though, when Garciaparra was hit on the wrist by a pitch from the Orioles' Al Reyes in a 4–1 Red Sox win. The event initially seemed harmless enough as the shortstop shook off the injury and trotted to first base, but it had long lasting consequences for the Red Sox. In the short term, the injury forced Garciaparra to sit out the final week of the regular season and one game of the ensuing Division Series. In the long term, a split tendon that team doctor Bill Morgan attributed to the incident caused Garciaparra to miss all but 21 games of the 2001 season.

The Red Sox clinched the Wild Card with a 6–2 win in Chicago on September 29. Thanks to the Martinez effect, Boston led the AL with a 4.00 ERA, despite using 13 different starting pitchers in a season that occurred at the height of baseball's steroid era. Bret Saberhagen (10–6, 2.95 ERA) started 22 games after returning from an arm injury and finished second on the team in wins and ERA. For much of the season the rotation included the unimpressive trio of Portugal (7–12, 5.51 ERA), Rapp (6–7, 4.12 ERA) and rookie Brian Rose (7–6, 4.87 ERA), but none of the three would contribute to Boston's postseason effort.

Ramon Martinez slid into the third slot in the Red Sox rotation in October, despite having started only four games in the regular season, and Kent Mercker, a mid-season pick-up, slid into the fourth slot, after starting just five games for Boston in the regular season.

Offensively, the team struggled to replace Vaughn's pop in the lineup, finishing ninth in runs (836) and home runs (176). Garciaparra led the AL with a .357 batting average, while hitting 27 home runs and driving in 104 runs. Left fielder Troy O'Leary had 28 homers and 103 RBI. Daubach and catcher Jason Varitek hit 21 and 20 long-balls respectively.

The Postseason: 4–6

For the second straight year and third time in as many playoff appearances, the Red Sox faced the Indians in the opening round. This time the Red Sox met better results than in their first two tries against the Tribe, rebounding from a two-games-to-none deficit to advance to the American League Championship Series. The Cleveland team that Boston faced in the Division Series was one of the best offensive teams ever assembled. Led by Manny Ramirez (.333, 44 HR, 165 RBI), Richie Sexson (.255, 31 HR, 116 RBI), Jim Thome (.277, 33 HR, 108 RBI) and Roberto Alomar (.323, 24 HR, 120 RBI), the Indians scored 1009 runs on the way to a 97–65 record. The Indians were just the seventh team ever to surpass the 1000 run plateau and were the first to do so since the 1950 Red Sox. Cleveland's ERA was nearly a run higher than Boston's at 4.90, but the Cleveland rotation was more balanced. A trio of Tribe starters won at least 15 games: Bartolo Colon (18–5, 3.95 ERA), Chuck Nagy (17–11, 4.95 ERA) and Dave Burba (15–9, 4.25 ERA).

Although Cleveland was the offensive juggernaut in the regular season, Boston's hitters stole the headlines in the ALDS, scoring 44 runs over the final three games. In the fifth and final game, an ailing Martinez entered in relief and offered one of the most spectacular pitching performances in postseason history to clinch the series.

Facing the Yankees in the ALCS for the first time ever, the Red Sox fell behind two-games-to-none, losing a pair of one-run decisions. Martinez and Clemens squared off in a highly anticipated Game Three, but only Martinez lived up to expectations and the game turned out to be a Red Sox blowout. The eventual world champion Yankees rebounded to win a tumultuous Game Four and then Game Five at Fenway Park, though, closing the book on yet another chapter in the game's most heated rivalry. Although the Yankees were clearly the more balanced team, after the series the Red Sox and their fans couldn't help but feel like they had been playing against the Yankees *and* the umpires, as three controversial calls went against the Red Sox while the members of the umpiring crew steadfastly refused to consult with one another to ensure they got the calls right.

1999 American League Division Series:
Red Sox 3, Indians 2

GAME 1: INDIANS 3, RED SOX 2

	1	2	3	4	5	6	7	8	9	R	H	E
Boston	0	1	0	1	0	0	0	0	0	2	5	1
Cleveland	0	0	0	0	0	2	0	0	1	3	6	1

WP Paul Shuey
LP Derek Lowe

The Red Sox entered the series having lost 16 of their 17 previous postseason games dating to the 1986 World Series. But Red Sox fans took solace in the fact that Martinez was lined up to pitch the first game in Cleveland. The slender ace had earned Boston's sole playoff win in the previous decade on the same mound, beating the Indians in the first game of the 1998 ALDS, and was 5–0 in his career against Cleveland. His Dominican countryman, Colon, drew the start for manager Mike Hargrove's Indians.

For 4½ innings the game proceeded as planned for the Red Sox. Boston took a 2–0 lead, plating a second-inning run on a Garciaparra home run, and adding a run in the fourth on a Garciaparra double and a Mike Stanley single. Meanwhile, Martinez held the Indians in check.

As the Red Sox batted in the fifth however, Derek Lowe began warming up in the Red Sox bullpen, and Martinez was no where to be seen in the Jacobs Field visitors' dugout. After the game it would come to light that Martinez had strained a muscle in his back while striking out Thome on a 96-mile-per-hour fastball to lead off the Indians' fourth.

Thome, like all of the Indians, was relieved to see Lowe take the mound for the Red Sox in the fifth. "We were excited," Thome said. "Pedro was pitching a real good game. "To get him out of the game like that, it livened us up."[3] And his next time up, the Indians slugger showed the Red Sox just how excited he was. Lowe had retired the first five men he faced before Ramirez reached with two outs in the sixth when third baseman John Valentin bounced a throw to first base that Daubach couldn't handle. On the very next pitch, Thome launched a 434-foot homer over the fence in right-center field to tie the game, 2–2.

Lowe and Colon both pitched shutout ball in the seventh and eighth innings. Then, after Paul Shuey retired the Red Sox in the ninth, Cleveland scored in its final at bat to win the game.

Lowe started the final frame, coming out for a fifth inning for the first time all season, and hit the leadoff man, Ramirez, with a pitch. Cormier was summoned and retired Thome, then gave up a pinch-single to Wil Cordero, putting runners at first and second with one out. Williams called upon Rich Garces to face Sexson, whom the portly hurler walked on four pitches to load the bases. Travis Fryman came up next and lined an inside fastball into left field on a 1-2 count to plate Ramirez and end the game.

Afterwards, Williams and pitching coach Joe Kerrigan explained that Martinez had pulled a muscle in his back and would be evaluated the next day, leaving his availability for the remainder of the series in doubt.

GAME 2: INDIANS 11, RED SOX 1

	1	2	3	4	5	6	7	8	9	R	H	E
Boston	0	0	1	0	0	0	0	0	0	1	6	0
Cleveland	0	0	6	5	0	0	0	0	X	11	8	0

WP Chuck Nagy
LP Bret Saberhagen

In the second game, Saberhagen struggled with his control and the Red Sox quickly found themselves facing an insurmountable deficit. In losing 11–1, Boston extended its skein to 1–18 in postseason play since the bullpen's meltdown in Game Six of the 1986 World Series. Saberhagen had only walked 11 batters in 119 regular season innings, but he issued three walks to Cleveland in a six-run third inning. His replacement, John Wasdin, allowed five more Cleveland runs in the fourth, and the rout was on.

The ten-run margin of defeat represented the most lopsided loss in Red Sox playoff history at the time. The mark would be surpassed in 2004 when the Yankees beat the Red Sox 19–8 in Game Four of the ALCS.

Harold Baines got the big hit for the Indians and the one that knocked Saberhagen out of the game, blasting a two-out, three-run homer in the third to put Cleveland ahead 6–1. In the fourth, Wasdin walked the bases load and allowed a grand slam to Thome.

Nagy pitched seven innings, allowing five hits and one run to earn the win.

GAME 3: RED SOX 9, INDIANS 3

	1	2	3	4	5	6	7	8	9	R	H	E
Cleveland	0	0	0	1	0	1	1	0	0	3	9	1
Boston	0	0	0	0	2	1	6	0	X	9	11	2

WP Derek Lowe
LP Jaret Wright

Before the third game Pedro Martinez tried to play catch in the Fenway Park outfield with Kerrigan, but gave up after just a few tosses, and Garciaparra informed Williams that his wrist was too sore for him to play. When the game began, the Red Sox sent Ramon Martinez, who had pitched only 20⅔ innings during the regular season, to the mound. The scenario was bleak. But facing elimination the Red Sox combined good pitching with timely hitting to earn a 9–3 win before an enthusiastic Saturday afternoon crowd. The game was closer than the final score indicated, and was in fact tied at 3–3 entering the bottom of the seventh inning.

Martinez held the Indians to two runs over 5⅔ innings, then his replacement, Lowe, allowed an unearned run in the top of the seventh after another costly throwing error by Valentin. Burba held the Red Sox scoreless on one hit over the first four innings, before departing in the fifth with a sore arm. Against his replacement, Jaret Wright, Boston scored two runs in the fifth on an RBI single by Darren Lewis and a sacrifice fly by Trot Nixon, and a run in the sixth on a Valentin home run into the centerfield bleachers.

In the bottom of the seventh, the Red Sox capitalized on the wildness of the Indians relief corps and scored six runs. Garciaparra's replacement at short, Lou Merloni, led off with a walk against Wright. Wright then hit Varitek. Hargrove called upon Ricardo Rincon to replace Wright, and after a Lewis fielder's choice and a Nixon strikeout, Rincon walked Offerman to load the bases. Valentin's ground-rule double down the leftfield line scored two runs, then Daubach followed with a three-run homer. The final run of the inning scored when Merloni singled home Mike Stanley.

After the game, Kerrigan fielded questions about Pedro Martinez's availability for the remainder of the series. "You guys saw it," the pitching coach said of the pitcher's pre-game workout. "He couldn't even pick up the ball."[4]

Meanwhile, Garciaparra addressed his own injury situation. He described telling Williams that he was unavailable to play as "One of the hardest things [he'd] ever had to do,"[5] and left considerable doubt regarding his future availability in the series.

Game 4: Red Sox 23, Indians 7

	1	2	3	4	5	6	7	8	9	R	H	E
Cleveland	1	1	0	0	4	0	0	0	1	7	8	0
Boston	2	5	3	5	3	0	3	2	X	23	24	0

WP Rich Garces
LP Bartolo Colon

Sensing that the Red Sox might be seizing momentum in the series, Hargrove sent his ace, Colon, to the mound in Game Four, hoping to finish off the Red Sox. The start represented the first time in Colon's career that he was asked to pitch on less than four days' rest, and it did not go well. After the series, the Cleveland manager would be criticized for not saving Colon to pitch on full rest in the fifth game. The Red Sox countered with Mercker, who offered a lackluster outing, but it did not matter. By the end of the Sunday night affair, Boston had handed Cleveland the most lopsided loss in postseason history, while breaking or tying 11 other playoff records in a 23–7 win. The Red Sox outscored or tied 20 of the 26 NFL teams to play on the day. The previous record for the most runs scored in a postseason game had belonged to the Yankees, who beat the Giants 18–4 in Game Two of the 1936 World Series.

The Red Sox jumped on Colon early, scoring in the bottom of the first inning on a two-run homer by Valentin to take a 2–1 lead. After Cleveland tied the game in the top of the second, the first five Red Sox hitters recorded hits in the bottom of the second, accounting for five runs and knocking Colon from the game. Stanley led off with a single, then Varitek singled, Lewis singled, Nixon doubled, and Offerman homered, opening a 7–2 lead. Against the Indians bullpen, Boston scored in every remaining inning except the sixth. The Red Sox finished the game having scored two or more runs in seven of the eight innings in which they batted.

In the late innings of the blowout, Red Sox fans chanted, "We want Pedro. We want Pedro," looking ahead to Game Five.

Valentin finished the game 4-for-5 with two homers and seven RBI, Stanley finished 5-for-6 with a triple and a home run, and Varitek finished 4-for-5 with a home run and five runs scored. Garciaparra returned to the lineup and went 1-for-3 before being replaced by Merloni in the sixth. The postseason records broken by the Red Sox in the game dubbed "The Boston Tee Party" and "The Valentin's Day Massacre" in the Cleveland press included most runs in a game, widest margin of victory, most hits (24), most extra-base hits (12) and most total bases (45).

"Everything we threw up, they hit, and where it came down, we weren't standing," Hargrove said after the game.[6]

Game 5: Red Sox 12, Indians 8

	1	2	3	4	5	6	7	8	9	R	H	E
Boston	2	0	5	1	0	0	3	0	1	12	10	0
Cleveland	3	2	3	0	0	0	0	0	0	8	7	1

WP Pedro Martinez
LP Paul Shuey

As the two teams flew to Cleveland following Game Four, speculation abounded that Pedro Martinez would return to start, or at least attempt to start the finale. But when it came time for the starting pitchers to take their pre-game tosses, Saberhagen headed to the Jacobs Field bullpen for the Red Sox instead. His opponent would be Nagy, who, like Colon before him, would make his second start on three days' rest.

Both starters got routed, though, before Martinez staggered out of the bullpen in the fourth inning of an 8–8 tie and proceeded to dominate the Indians over the final six innings, even though his fastball registered just 90 miles per hour, as opposed to its usual 98. With his six-inning, no-hit, eight-strikeout effort, Martinez etched his name into the annals of baseball's most dramatic postseason performances.

Both teams put crooked numbers on the scoreboard early, and Cleveland led 8–7 through three innings. Saberhagen allowed five runs before departing with none out in the second, and was followed by Lowe who allowed three runs in the third. The Red Sox scored twice in the first on a Daubach single and a Garciaparra homer, and five times in the third, capped by an O'Leary grand slam.

Boston tied the game in the fourth, scoring an unearned run thanks to an error by Cleveland catcher Sandy Alomar. As Martinez warmed up in the Boston bullpen while his teammates batted, an eerie silence fell over Jacobs Field. Martinez entered in the bottom of the inning and allowed just one ball to leave the infield—a fly out to center by Fryman in the sixth—for the rest of the night. Lacking his usual velocity, Martinez relied on a baffling curveball and devastating changeup to stifle the vaunted Cleveland lineup.

The Red Sox scored three runs in the seventh on O'Leary's second homer and fifth, sixth and seventh RBIs of the night, then added a run in the ninth on a Garciaparra double.

In the bottom of the ninth, Martinez struck out Omar Vizquel to end the game, then threw his arms into the air in a gesture that seemed to express more relief than jubilation.

Afterwards, Williams explained why he had opted not to use Martinez as a starter. "We thought maybe a couple of innings, tops," the manager said of Martinez's availability. "But after what happened, I didn't know if he'd be able to go one inning, two innings. I don't think in his mind he knew."[7]

"I had doubts about my feelings out there," Martinez admitted. "The first time I tried to pick up a ball, I was in pain. Today after I came in at about four [o'clock] and threw a few balls, I felt pretty good. I didn't want to find out anything else. I just wanted to get the adrenaline going and get the mind going and hopefully that would drive me to just throw the ball over the plate and see what I could do."[8]

O'Leary, who hit both of his home runs following intentional walks to Garciaparra, had been just 2–16 in the series with 0 RBI previously. Stanley led the Red Sox with a .500 average in the series (10-for-20), followed by Garciaparra who hit .417 (5-for-12). Valentin batted .318 (7-for-22) with 3 HR and 12 RBI. As a team, the Red Sox batted .318 with 10 HR and 47 runs in the five games, including .388 while averaging nearly 15 runs per game over the final three games.

1999 American League Championship Series: Yankees 4, Red Sox 1

Game 1: Yankees 4, Red Sox 3

	1	2	3	4	5	6	7	8	9	10	R	H	E
Boston	2	1	0	0	0	0	0	0	0	0	3	8	3
New York	0	2	0	0	0	0	1	0	0	1	4	10	1

WP   Mariano Rivera
LP   Rod Beck

The Red Sox traveled from Cleveland directly to New York to meet a Yankees team that was coming off a first-round sweep of the AL West champion Texas Rangers. While the rested Yankees sent their hottest pitcher, Orlando Hernandez, to the mound in the first game, Boston countered with Mercker. Nonetheless, the game turned out to be a pitchers' duel, and the Red Sox carried a lead into the late innings. But the Yankees rallied to tie the game in the seventh and win it in the tenth.

After a controversial umpiring decision hurt the Red Sox in the top of the tenth, Bernie Williams ended the game with a home run to centerfield against Rod Beck in the bottom of the inning.

Boston scored all three of its runs in the first two innings before Hernandez settled into a groove. In the first, Offerman led off with a single to center, then Yankee shortstop Derek Jeter made an error that led to two unearned runs. On the play Valentin pulled a grounder into the hole and Jeter backhanded the ball on the run and leapt into the air, twirling to throw to second in an attempt to force Offerman. But the throw sailed past second baseman Chuck Knoblauch, and by the time right fielder Paul O'Neil could retrieve the ball, Offerman had crossed the plate and Valentin was standing on third. Daubach blooped Hernandez's next pitch into right field to give Boston a 2–0 lead.

The Red Sox made it 3–0 in the second inning when Lewis scored from third on Offerman's infield single. After a rocky start, Hernandez then retired 21 of the final 24 batters he faced, before handing the ball to Mariano Rivera in the ninth. By then the score was tied, the Yankees having scored twice against Mercker in the second on a home run by Scott Brosius and once against Lowe in the seventh on an RBI single by Jeter.

Facing Rivera in the tenth, Offerman led off with a single to right. The next batter, Valentin, pulled a groundball to third. Brosius threw to second in an attempt to nab Offerman, but the throw bounced out of Knoblauch's glove. The crowd of more than 57,000 groaned audibly and Knoblauch pounded his mitt in frustration. But second base umpire Rick Reed raised his right hand and called Offerman out. The umpire claimed Knoblauch had lost the ball while transferring it from his glove to his throwing hand. After watching video footage of the play after the game, however, Reed admitted he had made the wrong call. "As an umpire it's my job to get it right," said Reed. "I hope [Red Sox fans] don't decide to take 81 years of frustration out on one call at second base, even though it was important at the time."[9] Instead of having two on with none out, the Red Sox had a man on first with one out. The next batter, Daubach, hit into a double play to end the rally.

In the bottom of the tenth, Beck replaced Cormier and Williams crushed his second pitch, an 0–1 fastball that was supposed to be on the inside corner but tailed back over the plate, over the center field fence.

GAME 2: YANKEES 3, RED SOX 2

	1	2	3	4	5	6	7	8	9	R	H	E
Boston	0	0	0	0	2	0	0	0	0	2	10	0
New York	0	0	0	1	0	0	2	0	X	3	7	0

WP   David Cone
LP   Ramon Martinez
SV   Mariano Rivera

The Red Sox lost both games at Yankee Stadium in the 1999 ALCS.

For the second straight game Boston sent a starter to the mound — Ramon Martinez — who had started less than five games in the regular season, and New York countered with one of its aces — David Cone (12–9, 3.44 ERA) — but for the second straight game Boston carried a lead into the seventh inning. This time, the seventh proved to be the Red Sox' undoing.

The Red Sox scored both of their runs in the fifth on a home run by Garciaparra, while Martinez pitched valiantly over the first six innings, allowing just a solo homer to Tino Martinez in the fourth. In the seventh, the tiring Red Sox starter walked the leadoff hitter, Rickey Ledee, then allowed a two-out double to Knoblauch that tied the score, 2–2, and put the potential go-ahead-run on second. Gordon entered in relief and allowed Knoblauch to steal third, as he walked Jeter. Cormier was summoned to face the left-handed O'Neil, who promptly knocked a tie-breaking single to center.

The Red Sox put two men on base against Rivera in the ninth, but Damon Buford struck out to end the game.

Pitching on 11 days' rest, Cone held the Red Sox to two runs on seven hits, while striking out nine over seven innings to earn the win.

GAME 3: RED SOX 13, YANKEES 1

	1	2	3	4	5	6	7	8	9	R	H	E
New York	0	0	0	0	0	0	0	1	0	1	3	3
Boston	2	2	2	0	2	1	4	0	X	13	21	1

WP Pedro Martinez
LP Roger Clemens

The third game presented a tantalizing pitching match-up that paired the greatest current power pitcher, Martinez, against the greatest power pitcher in Red Sox history, Clemens. The bad blood between Clemens and Duquette, who had said the pitcher was in the "twilight of his career" when he departed the Red Sox in 1997, heightened the drama, as did Martinez's dominance of the Yankees during his one-hitter in September. On the day before the game, four box seats to watch it sold for $12,100 on eBay.[10] The expected pitchers' duel never materialized, though, as the Red Sox prevailed 13–1.

Despite lower than usual velocity, the injured Martinez was brilliant, allowing just two hits and striking out 12 in seven innings. Clemens, meanwhile, got rattled early by the derisive Boston crowd and allowed five runs on six hits in two innings.

The Red Sox scored twice against Clemens in the first when Offerman led off with a triple and Valentin followed with a home run to left. They padded the lead with two runs in the second, as Offerman singled with one out, Nixon doubled, Varitek walked, and Garciaparra doubled to left.

After Clemens gave up a single to Stanley to start the third, Torre called for Hideki Irabu. The Yankee reliever did no better than Clemens, though, allowing 13 hits and eight runs in 4⅔ innings.

The Fenway crowd chanted, "Where is Roger?" then rejoined, "In the shower," during the late innings of the blowout.

Valentin finished 3-for-6 with a homer and five runs batted in, while Garciaparra was 4-for-5 with a homer and three RBI. Offerman and Nixon also had three hits apiece.

Martinez allowed a single to Jeter in the first inning and a single to Tino Martinez in the fourth, before yielding to Gordon, who allowed a run in the eighth, and Rapp, who pitched a scoreless ninth.

After growing his legend still larger, Martinez admitted he was far from his usual self. "I'm hurting and I'm not lying," he said. "I don't feel like I have my fastball like I should. I strained my back muscle. I haven't had time to get rest. I'm hurting every pitch I throw. The first inning, I had exactly what I had the whole game. Nothing."[11]

Game 4: Yankees 9, Red Sox 2

	1	2	3	4	5	6	7	8	9	R	H	E
New York	0	1	0	2	0	0	0	0	6	9	11	0
Boston	0	1	1	0	0	0	0	0	0	2	10	4

WP Andy Pettitte
LP Bret Saberhagen
SV Mariano Rivera

Pettitte out-dueled Saberhagen in a fourth game that was much closer than the final score indicated. The Yankees scored six times against the Red Sox bullpen in the ninth to turn a tightly played game into a blowout. The contest was marred by two more umpiring mistakes that hurt the Red Sox and led to the ejection of Jimy Williams.

The Red Sox led 2–1 after three innings, having scored single runs in the second and third on hits by O'Leary and Offerman. But the Yankees took a 3–2 lead in the fourth when a Garciaparra error led to two runs.

In the Red Sox eighth, a scene eerily reminiscent of the umpiring blunder in the first game played out. Just as in the first game, Offerman and Valentin were the principal participants for the Red Sox, and Rivera was on the mound for the Yankees, and the call in question involved a play by Knoblauch at second base.

Rivera entered the game after Offerman led off with a single against Pettitte. Valentin hit a check-swing grounder to second base that Knoblauch fielded. The second baseman made a swipe for the passing Offerman with his glove, then threw to first to retire Valentin. Although Knoblauch did not tag Offerman on his way to second, and replays would show that he missed him by more than two feet, second base umpire Tim Tschida called Offerman out. Williams ran onto the field and asked Tschida to get help from one of the other umpires who might have had a clearer view of the play, but Tschida refused.

"Can you ask somebody?" the Red Sox manager begged. "Can you get some help? Somebody can help you if they saw it from a different angle. Timmy, I know he didn't touch him."[12] But the manager's pleas fell on deaf ears.

After seeing a replay after the game, Tschida, like crewmate Rick Reed before him, admitted he had made the wrong call. "I didn't make the right call," he said. "I got the best position I could. It's difficult to get the angle you want without getting in the way. I called the play on the reaction of the runner and the fielder. It appeared to me that he got him."[13]

After the Yankees erupted for six runs against Garces and Beck in the top of the ninth, the men in blue bungled yet another call when first base umpire Dale Scott ruled Garciaparra out at first after he beat a throw by Brosius across the diamond. This time Williams went ballistic, kicking dirt on Scott, and throwing his cap. Within moments he was ejected and the Fenway lawn was soon littered with plastic soda bottles and paper cups. Home plate umpire Al Clark pulled the Yankees off the field while the Red Sox grounds-crew filled several trash bags with debris during an eight-minute stoppage in play. Finally, when the game resumed, Rivera recorded the final two outs to end the game.

Interviewed by Fox TV immediately afterward, self-righteous Yankee owner George Steinbrenner lambasted Williams, blaming him for the fans' behavior. "Their manager was my candidate for manager of the year until tonight when he really invoked it," Steinbrenner said. "He incited [the crowd], I should say."[14]

Williams refused to participate in the mandatory post-game press conference, but rebutted the Yankee boss's comments a day later. "I don't like to go out on that field. I really don't," Williams said. "I don't know why Georgie-Porgie would say something like that. I never worry about Georgie-Porgie. He's never been in the trenches, Georgie-Porgie. Torre, I have ultimate respect for. When Georgie-Porgie speaks, I don't listen."[15]

GAME 5: YANKEES 6, RED SOX 1

	1	2	3	4	5	6	7	8	9	R	H	E
New York	2	0	0	0	0	0	2	0	2	6	11	1
Boston	0	0	0	0	0	0	0	1	0	1	5	2

WP Orlando Hernandez
LP Kent Mercker
SV Ramiro Mendoza

The 82-year-old daughter of Babe Ruth, Mrs. Julia Ruth Stevens, threw out the first pitch at Fenway Park before the fifth game, hoping to change Boston's karma. It didn't help.

Hernandez pitched seven stellar innings to lead New York to a 6–1 win and leave the Red Sox and their fans no option but to wait till next year, once again.

The Yankees scored twice against Mercker in the first inning before an out had been recorded. Knoblauch led with a single, then Jeter homered. The Yankees tacked on two runs in the seventh when Stanley and Offerman made errors, and two more in the ninth on a Jorge Posada home run.

Trailing 4–0, Varitek led off the bottom of the eighth with a home run, and Garciaparra followed with a double. Torre used four relievers to escape the inning without further damage. Lefty Mike Stanton replaced Hernandez and walked O'Leary, bringing the tying run to the plate for the Red Sox with no outs. After Jeff Nelson induced Stanley to lineout to second, Allen Watson walked Butch Huskey to load the bases. Torre then called upon Ramiro Mendoza, who struck out Scott Hatteberg and got Nixon to pop out.

Mendoza retired the Red Sox in order in the ninth to end the series.

Hernandez was named the series MVP for winning two games and allowing just three runs in 15 innings of work. In a statistical anomaly, the Red Sox led the Yankees in batting average (.293 to .239) and ERA (3.68 to 3.80) in the series. The Yankees went on to sweep the Braves in the World Series, and finish the postseason with an 11–1 record.

CHAPTER 17

The Regular Season: 95–67

Entering their first full season with the Red Sox, new team owner John W. Henry and general manager, Theo Epstein, were confident the Red Sox could reach the championship level in 2003. They were nearly right. After the new ownership group had taken over during the 2002 spring training season and named Grady Little the new field manager, the Red Sox had won 93 games to finish second to the Yankees in the AL East and second to the Angels in the AL Wild Card race. While construction workers added 294 seats atop Fenway Park's famous left field wall during the ensuing off-season, Epstein had spent the winter upgrading the team's infield and bullpen personnel.[1] On December 12th, the Red Sox sent a pair of minor leaguers to the Reds in exchange for Todd Walker, solidifying a second base position that had been manned by the light hitting Rey Sanchez in 2002. To replace free agent Brian Daubach, the Red Sox then acquired three first sackers who were known for their high on-base percentages, sending a minor league pitcher to Philadelphia for Jeremy Giambi, signing free agent David Ortiz, and convincing former Florida Marlin Kevin Millar to renege on a $6.2 million, two-year contract he had just signed with the Chunichi Dragons of the Japanese League and to join the Red Sox. The Red Sox hoped that out of this trio an every-day first baseman would emerge, as well as a player who could split time at designated hitter with Shea Hillenbrand. Free agent acquisition Bill Mueller was expected to claim the third base job from Hillenbrand. By season's end Mueller would do more than just win the position, he would also win the AL batting title, finishing at .326, one one-hundredth of a point ahead of teammate Manny Ramirez.

To shore up a bullpen that had lost Ugueth Urbina and his 40 saves in 2002 to free agency, Epstein signed a cast of middle relievers that included Chad Fox, Mike Timlin, Bobby Howry, Ramiro Mendoza and Brandon Lyon. Along with incumbent lefty Alan Embree, this sextet became known as Epstein's "Bullpen by Committee." In an affront to the meticulously scripted bullpen approach that Tony LaRussa had introduced in Oakland more than a decade earlier, and that had since become the norm in baseball, the Red Sox indicated as the season began that they did not intend to have a designated closer.[2] Whichever reliever

The Red Sox added seats atop the Green Monster in 2003.

was pitching the best at the time would get the ball in the late innings. Epstein and Little believed that all six of the team's top relievers were capable of closing games, and saw no reason to pigeon-hole one pitcher into the seventh inning, another into the eighth, and another into the ninth. It was a bold experiment, but one that failed. The game had changed too much in the years since LaRussa had begun setting up Dennis Eckersley with Gene Nelson, Jim Corsi and Rick Honeycutt in Oakland. The modern pitcher was accustomed to knowing exactly what his role was, and without that certainty the Red Sox relievers did not perform at the highest level.

On Opening Day in Tampa Bay, the Bullpen by Committee coughed up five runs in the bottom of the ninth to spoil a stellar outing by Pedro Martinez. The final blow came in the form of a three-run, walk-off homer by Carl Crawford that gave the Devil Rays a 6–4 win. Six and a half months later the Red Sox season would end just as it had begun with the bullpen serving up another walk-off dinger, but first there was plenty of baseball to be played.

The Red Sox showed the first signs of the resiliency for which they would be known all season long in the season's second game. With callers to Boston talk radio already referring to the bullpen experiment as the "Bullpen by Catastrophe," the Red Sox won Game Two in Tampa Bay in dramatic fashion when Millar stroked a 16th inning home run off Jorge Sosa to break an 8–8 tie. Millar would go on to hit 25 homers and drive in 96 runs, while batting .276. He would do more than provide a steady bat in the middle of the Red Sox lineup. By the time the dog days of August arrived, he had solidified his status as a cross between the team leader and team mascot. Midway through the season a home video of a younger and much thinner Millar playing air-guitar and singing the Bruce Springsteen song "Born in the U.S.A." surfaced in the Red Sox clubhouse.³ It was not long before the "Rally Karaoke Guy" was making regular late-inning appearances on the Fenway Jumbotron. And as the Red Sox closed in on a playoff berth, it was Millar who introduced the phrase that became the team's battle cry, invoking his teammates to "Cowboy Up."

The most important addition to the 2003 team, though, turned out to be Ortiz. Signed for the relatively meager sum of $1,250,000 when Minnesota declined to offer him a contract, Ortiz did not earn a starting job in Boston until mid-June and played in only 128 games, but still finished with 31 home runs and 101 RBI. He hit just one long ball in both April and May, and just two in June, before emerging as the every-day designated hitter and swatting 27 homers in the season's final three months.

Offensive stalwarts Ramirez (37 HR, 104 RBI) and Nomar Garciaparra (28 HR, 105 RBI) also did their parts to keep the offense clicking, as the Red Sox finished first in the American League with 961 runs, second with 238 homers, and first with a .289 batting average. Six Boston players hit at least 25 home runs, and all nine Red Sox regulars reached double figures in the category. The Red Sox also set a new big league record with their .491 slugging percentage, besting a mark held by the 1927 Yankees.

The offensive highlight came on June 27 when the Red Sox set a major league record against the Marlins by scoring ten runs in the bottom of the first inning before the Marlins could record an out. In all, Boston scored 14 runs on 13 hits and four walks in a first at-bat that lasted 50 minutes, on the way to a 25–8 win.⁴

Another peak came in Arlington on July 29 when Mueller became the first player in baseball history to hit two grand slams from opposite sides of the plate in the same game. After hitting a solo shot from the left side of the plate in the third inning, Mueller connected from the right side with the sacks full in the seventh, and from the left side with the sacks full in the eighth. Paced by the switch-hitter's three homers and nine RBI, the Red Sox beat the Rangers 14–1.

The pitching staff continued to evolve as the season progressed. When Ortiz and Mueller convinced management they could be solid contributors to the lineup, the team began exploring trade opportunities involving Hillenbrand. Epstein pulled the trigger on a deal with the Diamondbacks on May 29, acquiring a bona fide closer to spell an end to the beleaguered Bullpen by Committee. Byung-Hyun Kim arrived in Boston with a reputation for possessing a nasty submarine-style slider. Unfortunately he also had a reputation for struggling against the Yankees, against whom he had blown saves in Games Four and Five of the 2001 World Series. Still, he was a proven closer and his acquisition gave the rest of the bullpen pitchers a clearer conception of their respective roles. Kim finished the year 8–5, with 16 saves in 49 games for the Red Sox. Epstein further bolstered the pitching staff with a series of July trades that brought lefty Scott Sauerbeck and righties Scott Williamson and Jeff Suppan to Boston. All three struggled over the final two months, but Williamson emerged as a key contributor in the postseason when Kim was sidelined with a sore shoulder.

Martinez paced the Boston starters, going 14–4 while posting a league-best 2.22 ERA. No other Boston starter had an earned run average under 4.00, as Tim Wakefield (11–7, 4.09 ERA), Derek Lowe (17–7, 4.47 ERA) and John Burkett (12–9, 5.15 ERA), were the next best starters.

In most seasons, the Red Sox' 95 wins would have put them in position to win the division, but the 2003 race belonged to the Yankees, who finished 101–61, six games ahead of the Red Sox. After moving into first place on Memorial Day, the Yankees never looked back. The race was tight at the All-Star break, with the Yankees (57–36) holding a 2-game lead over the Red Sox (55–38), and it remained tight throughout the second half, but the Red Sox were never able to catch up.

The Postseason: 6–6

In the first round of the playoffs, the Red Sox faced an Oakland team that had won 96 games to earn the AL West crown. Buoyed by the "big three" of Tim Hudson (16–7, 2.70 ERA), Barry Zito (14–12, 3.30 ERA), and Mark Mulder (15–9, 3.13 ERA), the A's led the league with a 3.63 ERA. Unfortunately for Oakland, Mulder had sustained a stress fracture in his hip in August and was unavailable to pitch in October. Offensively, the A's finished just ninth in the league with 768 runs and twelfth with a .254 batting average. Their best hitters were shortstop Miguel Tejada (.278, 27 HR, 106 RBI) and third baseman Eric Chavez (.282, 29 HR, 101 RBI), while catcher Ramon Hernandez (.273, 21 HR, 78 RBI) and designated hitter Erubiel Durazo (.259, 21 HR, 77 RBI) also contributed. The Red Sox lost the first two games against the A's in Oakland, then won the final three games — two in Boston and one in Oakland — to win the series.

The Red Sox once again drew the Yankees in the ALCS. During the regular season the two teams had been evenly matched in head-to-head play, as New York won 10 of 19 meetings between the AL East rivals. The Yankees' biggest advantage was in the area of starting pitching. While the Red Sox starters were average after Martinez, the Yankees boasted four starters who could have been aces on other teams. Andy Pettitte went 21–8 with a 4.02 ERA, followed by Roger Clemens (17–9, 3.91 ERA), Mike Mussina (17–8, 3.40 ERA), and David Wells (15–7, 4.14 ERA). The Yankees finished third in the league with a 4.02 ERA and third in runs with 877. Offensively, they were led by first baseman Jason Giambi (.250, 41 HR, 107 RBI), second baseman Alfonso Soriano (.290, 38 HR, 91 RBI), shortstop Derek Jeter (.324, 10 HR, 52 RBI), left fielder Hideki Matsui (.287, 16 HR, 106 RBI) and catcher Jorge Posada (.281, 30 HR, 101 RBI).

The ALCS underscored how intense the rivalry between Boston and New York had become in recent years. Just as in the vitriolic 1970s, fans across the country were left with the distinct impression that these were two teams that genuinely disliked one another. The sentiment was never more obvious than in Game Three when 72-year-old former Red Sox manager and current Yankee bench coach Don Zimmer ran onto the field and attacked Martinez. Later a fight broke out between a member of the Red Sox grounds-crew and two Yankee players. The series culminated with yet another historic Boston collapse, as the Red Sox held a three-run eighth-inning lead in the seventh game with Martinez on the mound, but wound up losing on a walk-off home run by Aaron Boone in the eleventh inning.

2003 American League Division Series:
Red Sox 3, Athletics 2

Game 1: Athletics 5, Red Sox 4

	1	2	3	4	5	6	7	8	9	10	11	12	R	H	E
Boston	1	0	0	0	1	0	2	0	0	0	0	0	4	12	2
Oakland	0	0	3	0	0	0	0	0	1	0	0	1	5	8	0

WP   Rich Harden
LP   Derek Lowe

Boston's loss in the opening game of the 2003 playoffs was reminiscent of the team's opening loss to Cleveland in the 1995 ALDS. In both games, the Red Sox sent their ace to the mound, Roger Clemens in 1995, Martinez in 2003, then lost lengthy extra inning affairs on walk-off hits by the opposing catcher. Unlike 1995 when Cleveland backstop Tony Pena delivered the knockout punch with a 400-foot homer in the 13th inning, this time Oakland's game-winning hit traveled only about 40 feet. All the same, the Red Sox came out on the losing end of a 5–4 decision, and the Boston fans who stayed awake to watch the game's conclusion at 2:45 a.m. EST could only hope this heartbreaking extra inning defeat didn't foreshadow another first round sweep.

Boston jumped ahead 1–0 when Walker connected for a home run against Hudson in the first. Walker had batted second for the Red Sox all season, but hit third as Little played a hunch and flip-flopped him with Garciaparra.

In the third, Oakland reached Martinez for three hits and three runs, keyed by a two-run double to right by Durazo. The Red Sox cut the deficit in half on a Jason Varitek homer in the fifth, and took a 4–3 lead on Walker's second homer, a two-run eighth inning blast off lefthander Ricardo Rincon.

Martinez departed with a 4–3 lead after seven innings, having thrown a season-high 130 pitches. Timlin pitched a perfect eighth, then Kim came in for the ninth. Pitching in his first playoff series since his 2001 implosion against the Yankees, Kim walked pinch-hitter Billy McMillon with one out, then hit Chris Singleton with a slider. He rebounded to strike out righty Mark Ellis, but with the left-handed Durazo coming up, Little went to the bullpen. Embree entered, hoping for a one-out save. Instead he allowed a line drive single to left that tied the game, 4–4.

In extra innings the Red Sox stranded runners on first and second in the eleventh and twelfth. After Williamson kept the A's at bay in the tenth, Little turned the ball over to Lowe, the scheduled Game Three starter. The outing marked Lowe's first relief appearance since 2001 when he had led AL relievers with 10 losses. In the twelfth, Lowe loaded the bases on three walks. With two outs, the slow-footed Hernandez dropped a bunt down the third base line. The play surprised everyone, including Mueller, who was playing deep and had no play on the ball. Chavez raced home from third to end the game.

Game 2: Athletics 5, Red Sox 1

	1	2	3	4	5	6	7	8	9	R	H	E
Boston	0	0	1	0	0	0	0	0	0	1	6	1
Oakland	0	5	0	0	0	0	0	0	X	5	6	0

WP   Barry Zito
LP   Tim Wakefield

Just 13 hours after their first game marathon ended, the Red Sox and A's took the field for a matinee at the Oakland Coliseum. The game lacked the drama of the first contest, as Zito stymied the Red Sox over seven innings, and the A's took advantage of Wakefield's wildness to claim a two-game lead in the series.

The A's scored all five of their runs in the second inning, despite connecting for only two hits in the inning. One of the hits should have been an out, as Ramirez got his feet tangled up on an Eric Byrnes fly ball to left that fell for a double. Wakefield issued two walks and hit a batter in the inning, while Doug Mirabelli committed a passed ball, and Walker made an error that led to two unearned runs.

Zito struck out nine Red Sox hitters, using devastating curveballs made even more unhittable by the afternoon shadows between home plate and the mound. The only run he allowed scored in the third when Mirabelli and Johnny Damon hit back-to-back doubles.

As the series shifted to Boston, the Red Sox knew their season would end quickly unless their bats heated up. Through two games the team batting average was .228 and Ramirez and Ortiz were a combined 1-for-17.

GAME 3: RED SOX 3, ATHLETICS 1

	1	2	3	4	5	6	7	8	9	10	11	R	H	E
Oakland	0	0	0	0	0	1	0	0	0	0	0	1	6	4
Boston	0	1	0	0	0	0	0	0	0	0	2	3	7	2

WP   Scott Williamson
LP   Rich Harden

The Red Sox returned home to play in front of the largest Fenway Park gathering in 13 years. The standing-room-only crowd of 35,460 fans saw an error filled game that ended on Trot Nixon's pinch-hit homer in the bottom of the eleventh inning.

Nixon began the day on the bench against left-handed Oakland starter Ted Lilly, but was summoned to bat for Gabe Kapler with one out in the eleventh. With Mirabelli on first, Nixon drove a Rich Harden pitch into the second row of the center field bleachers, to score the first earned runs of the day and to give the Red Sox the win.

"I was hoping [centerfielder] Byrnes would run out of room," Nixon said, "and I asked the Lord to pick up the feet of Mirabelli, who's not exactly fleet of foot. When I saw it go out, emotions took over."[5]

Continuing a growing clubhouse trend, Nixon had shaved his head midway through the game, following the lead of Millar who had shaved his own locks — with a little help from bench player Andy Abad — upon returning home to Boston after Game Two.[6]

The A's made four errors in the first four innings, including three in the second, but Boston came away with only one run. Varitek scored in the second, after being caught in a rundown between third and home, then being awarded home on an interference call against Chavez.

Oakland could have won the game in regulation if not for two other fortuitous umpiring decisions in the sixth inning. First Byrnes was ruled out when Varitek tagged him as he walked back to the A's dugout, thinking he had just scored the tying run. On the play, Byrnes raced home from third on a groundball that was fielded by Lowe. Lowe threw wildly to the plate and the ball sailed past Varitek as Byrnes collided with the catcher's left shin guard. Byrnes came up limping, and angrily shoved Varitek. Then he hobbled toward the dugout. Varitek retrieved the ball and tagged him and umpire Paul Emmel ruled that Byrnes had never touched the plate.

Later in the inning, with A's runners on every base, Garciaparra booted a one-hopper by Hernandez, allowing one run to cross the plate to tie the game 1-1. As Miguel Tejada approached third base, representing the go-ahead run, he collided with Mueller, who was backing up to serve as the cut-off man on the play as Ramirez fielded the ball. Umpire Bill Welke pointed at Mueller to signify that he had obstructed the base runner as Tejada rounded third. Seeing the umpire's signal, Tejada stopped running, assuming he would be awarded home. The Red Sox tagged him and after a long discussion, the umpires decided that Tejada was entitled to "the next base," in this case third, due to the defensive interference, but not home plate. He was out.

Having escaped the sixth with a 1–1 tie, Lowe returned for the seventh, before yielding to Timlin and Williamson who combined for four perfect innings.

Game 4: Red Sox 5, Athletics 4

	1	2	3	4	5	6	7	8	9	R	H	E
Oakland	0	1	0	0	0	3	0	0	0	4	11	1
Boston	0	0	2	0	0	1	0	2	X	5	7	0

WP Scott Williamson
LP Keith Foulke

The Red Sox began Game Four hoping Ramirez and Ortiz would come to life. The sluggers were a combined 1-for-25 in the series. By the end of the Sunday afternoon affair both players had made up for their earlier struggles, delivering clutch hits against Foulke in a two-run eighth inning rally that propelled the Red Sox to victory.

Burkett started for the Red Sox and allowed four runs in 5⅓ innings. For Oakland Hudson took the mound on three days' rest, then left the game after one inning with a strained left oblique muscle. Hudson retired the Red Sox in order in the first then warmed up for the second before deciding he could not continue.

"I felt a little tweak on the last pitch to Walker to end the [first inning], but I didn't think about it,'" Hudson said. "Then on my warm-ups the next inning, I threw a couple nice and easy, and it grabbed a little. I tried to let one go, and I knew I wouldn't be able to do it."[7]

After the game it came to light that Hudson had been involved in a late night bar fight on Friday night at the Boston club, Q. According to a report in *The San Francisco Chronicle*, Hudson got in a fight with a Red Sox fan and threw several haymakers, including one that connected with a Q bartender.[8] Whether Hudson's injury stemmed from the incident, fans will never know, but the Red Sox gained an advantage when Ken Macha was forced to lift his ace in the second inning.

Knuckleballer Steve Sparks pitched four innings, allowing just two runs, and the A's led 4–2 when Rincon entered in the sixth. For the second time in the series, the left-handed hitting Walker connected for a home run against the lefty, cutting the lead to 4–3.

Macha gave the ball to Foulke to start the eighth, hoping the closer, who had led the AL with 43 saves, would deliver the clinching win. After Damon grounded out, Garciaparra doubled off the left field wall. Walker made the second out on a fly to center that was too shallow to advance the runner. Ramirez followed with a single between third and short, and for a moment it appeared Garciaparra would attempt to score, but at the last moment third base coach Mike Cubbage put up the stop sign. With the tying run on third and the go-ahead run on first, Ortiz stepped to the plate looking to snap a 0-for-16 drought. He fell behind 0–2 then lined a deep drive to right field that Jermaine Dye lost in the late-day sunshine. The ball one-hopped the wall of the visiting bullpen and on the heels of Garciaparra, Ramirez scampered all the way around to put the Red Sox ahead 5–4.

Williamson, who had set down the A's in order in the eighth, pitched a perfect ninth to cement the win.

GAME 5: RED SOX 4, ATHLETICS 3

	1	2	3	4	5	6	7	8	9	R	H	E
Boston	0	0	0	0	0	4	0	0	0	4	6	0
Oakland	0	0	0	1	0	1	0	1	0	3	7	0

WP Pedro Martinez
LP Barry Zito
SV Derek Lowe

The two teams flew back to Oakland on Sunday night in advance of Monday night's deciding game. The Red Sox would send Martinez to the mound against the A's Zito. Unlike Martinez, who was pitching on his usual day, Zito would work on three days' rest, just as Hudson had before him.

Zito carried a two-hit shutout into the sixth inning before tiring and allowing four runs, as the Red Sox seized the lead. Varitek led off the inning with a home run that tied the game, 1–1, then four batters later Ramirez crushed a mammoth three-run homer to left to put the Red Sox ahead 4–1. Just as Ortiz had ended a series of personal frustration with his key hit in Game Four, Ramirez's hit made up for a lackluster performance during the first four games during which he was 3-for-16 and held without an RBI.

Oakland plated a run against Martinez in the sixth, on doubles by Durazo and Tejada, to cut the deficit to 4–2, then a scary moment occurred in the seventh when Damon and Damian Jackson — who had entered the game as a defensive replacement for Walker — collided in shallow center field trying to catch a pop-fly by Dye. When both players lunged to make the catch, they hit heads. The ball dropped and a heads-up Garciaparra scooped it up and threw to Mueller covering second base to nab Dye, but Damon remained on the field unconscious and bleeding near his right eye. After he lay on the grass for five minutes, he was loaded into an ambulance and taken to a local hospital where he was treated for a concussion.

The A's cut the lead to 4–3 in the eighth when Singleton stroked a leadoff double and McMillon singled to right. With Martinez tiring, Little brought in Embree for two outs and then Timlin for one, to escape the inning without further damage.

Since Kim was sidelined with shoulder tightness, in the ninth Little called upon Williamson who promptly walked Scott Hatteberg and then Jose Guillen to put the tying run on second and the winning run on first with no outs. Little went to the bullpen again, this time summoning Lowe to pitch to Hernandez. For the second time in the series the A's catcher laid down a bunt against Lowe, sacrificing himself to advance Byrnes — who had come in to run for Hatteberg — and Guillen. With a base hit standing between the A's and a series win, Lowe struck out pinch-hitter Adam Melhuse on a called third strike, then intentionally walked Singleton to load the bases for Terrence Long. Lowe jumped ahead 1–2 in the count, then painted the inside corner with a sinker that tailed over the inside corner. Long jackknifed out of the way, only to hear Welke bark "strike three." The series was over.

The Red Sox pitching staff, supposedly the team's Achilles heel, combined for a 2.77 ERA in the series, while the offense batted just .211. Lowe finished the series having allowed just one run in 9⅔ innings, while Williamson pitched five innings without allowing a run and Timlin pitched 4⅓ innings without allowing a run.

While Damon remained in a Bay Area hospital for observation, the Red Sox flew from Oakland to New York for a second-round match-up that would go down as one of the most exciting Championship Series ever.

2003 American League Championship Series: Yankees 4, Red Sox 3

GAME 1: RED SOX 5, YANKEES 2

	1	2	3	4	5	6	7	8	9	R	H	E
Boston	0	0	0	2	2	0	1	0	0	5	13	0
New York	0	0	0	0	0	0	2	0	0	2	3	0

WP Tim Wakefield
LP Mike Mussina
SV Scott Williamson

After his Yankees defeated the Twins three games to one in the first round of the playoffs, Joe Torre sent Mussina to the mound in the opening game against the Red Sox. Little countered with Wakefield, and the result was a 5–2 Red Sox win. Boston's knuckleballer allowed just two hits in six innings before Embree, Timlin and Williamson held the Yankees to just one hit over the final three innings.

Walker batted lead-off for the Red Sox, and Kapler played center field, replacing Damon who was still groggy due to the aftereffects of the concussion that would keep him sidelined

Championship banners hang on the Fenway façade in 2003.

for the first two games. Picking up where they'd left off in Oakland, the Red Sox used the long-ball to account for the bulk of their scoring. Ortiz hit a two-run homer in the fourth to put the Red Sox ahead 2–0, and Walker and Ramirez added solo shots in the fifth to make it 4–0. Walker's homer was originally ruled a foul ball when a fan seated in the right field corner reached in front of the foul pole in an attempt to catch it. Home plate umpire Tim McClelland correctly overruled right field umpire Angel Hernandez, though. Boston stretched the lead to 5–0 in the seventh when a Millar single scored Ramirez.

Wakefield faltered in the seventh, walking Giambi and Bernie Williams to start the inning, and Little brought in Embree, who allowed the inherited runners to score but did not allow further damage. Timlin pitched a perfect eighth, and Williamson pitched a perfect ninth.

GAME 2: YANKEES 6, RED SOX 2

	1	2	3	4	5	6	7	8	9	R	H	E
Boston	0	1	0	0	0	0	0	0	0	2	10	1
New York	0	2	1	0	1	0	2	0	X	6	8	0

WP Andy Pettitte
LP Derek Lowe

The Yankees evened the series in the second game behind a fine effort from Pettitte. The lefty improved his lifetime record to 15–5 against Boston, allowing just two runs in 6⅔ innings. Meanwhile, Lowe allowed six Yankee runs.

The Red Sox had an early chance to break the game open when seven of their first nine hitters reached base via a hit or walk, but they could only plate one run.

In the first, the Red Sox notched three hits and a walk without scoring. Kapler singled to lead off, and was caught stealing as Mueller struck out. Then Garciaparra and Ramirez singled and Ortiz walked, before Millar popped out to leave the bases loaded. In the second, Boston took an early lead when Varitek scored on a single by Jackson.

The Yankees took the lead for good in the bottom of the second, though, on Nick Johnson's two-run homer, then added single runs in the third and fifth on RBI hits by Williams and Matsui. Boston cut the lead to 4–2 in the sixth on a Varitek homer, but after Lowe departed with two on and two outs in the bottom of the sixth, Sauerbeck allowed both inherited runners to score, giving the Yankees a 6–2 lead.

As Mariano Rivera retired the Red Sox in the ninth, Yankee Stadium reverberated with the echoes of 56,000 voices that taunted, "We Want Pedro," referring to Martinez, the Red Sox' Game Three starter. Martinez was already Public Enemy No. 1 in the Bronx, but after the series' next game, the animosity between the pitcher and the Yankees and their fans would intensify exponentially.

GAME 3: YANKEES 4, RED SOX 3

	1	2	3	4	5	6	7	8	9	R	H	E
New York	0	1	1	2	0	0	0	0	0	4	7	0
Boston	2	0	0	0	0	0	1	0	0	3	6	0

WP Roger Clemens
LP Pedro Martinez
SV Mariano Rivera

In a reprisal of their showdown in Game Three of the 1999 ALCS, Martinez and Clemens met on a Saturday afternoon in Boston, both hoping to put their team ahead two games to one. This time the former Red Sox ace prevailed, but not before one of the zaniest scenes ever witnessed at the old ballpark played out on the Fenway lawn.

The Red Sox reached Clemens for two runs in the bottom of the first when Damon singled in his first at-bat since returning from his concussion, Walker doubled, and Ramirez singled to score both runners.

The Yankees scored runs in the second and third to forge a 2–2 tie.

In the fourth, Posada walked to lead off, then Johnson singled, and Matsui doubled to put the Yankees ahead 3–2 with men on second and third and none out. Martinez's next pitch drilled Karim Garcia in the back. Garcia and Martinez shouted at one another as Garcia made his way to first base, then Posada and Clemens started berating Martinez from the top step of the Yankee dugout. With the bases loaded, Martinez induced a run-scoring double play off the bat of Soriano, then got Enrique Wilson to pop out. The fourth inning fireworks were just beginning.

Ramirez led off in the bottom half of the inning and Clemens' fourth pitch was a head-high fastball over the inside corner of the plate. Although the pitch did not come close to hitting Ramirez, he glowered at Clemens and barked a few expletives in the pitcher's direction while shaking his bat at him. Both benches emptied. As the players pushed and shoved each other, Martinez stood outside the fray in the middle of the infield. Suddenly Zimmer charged across the field at the Red Sox pitcher. Martinez back-pedaled, then reached out with both hands and grabbed the coach's head and threw him to the ground. Boston police and players from both teams huddled around the dazed Zimmer as he lay on the ground.

"He reached for my right arm," Martinez explained afterwards. "I thought, 'Is he going to pull it? Is he trying to hurt me?' I tossed him down."[9]

In the days to follow, New York's Mayor Bloomberg said Martinez would have been arrested and charged with assault had the game been played in New York, several Yankee players ridiculed Martinez for injuring a senior citizen, and Zimmer tearfully apologized for his role in the incident.[10] "I'm embarrassed of what happened yesterday," Zimmer said. "I'm embarrassed for the Yankees, the Red Sox, the fans, the umpires, and my family."[11]

After a 13-minute delay, the game resumed with Ramirez feebly swinging and missing at a Clemens fastball. Both Clemens and Martinez settled into grooves, before the Red Sox scored a run against the Yankee bullpen in the seventh, and the Yankees scored a run against Timlin in the ninth. While Rivera took his warm-up throws before the bottom of the ninth, a fight broke out in the Yankee bullpen between Paul Williams, a member of the Red Sox grounds-crew, and Yankee reliever Jeff Nelson when Nelson took exception to Williams cheering for the Red Sox from his station in the Yankee pen. Garcia hopped over the right field fence into the pen to get a few kicks and punches in on Williams who was later taken to a local hospital with head and neck injuries. Afterwards, two Boston police officers filed a report that said Nelson and Garcia had engaged in an "unprovoked attack" on Williams. The report read, "Nelson was observed pushing/grabbing the victim in the chest area, at which time both parties fell to the ground, where Jeff Nelson began punching and flaring his legs at the victim."[12] A year later Nelson and Garcia both accepted a plea bargain, agreeing to serve six months probation and perform 50 hours of community service for their involvement in the assault.[13]

After Garcia left the field with an injured hand, Rivera set down the Red Sox in order to end the game.

Game 4: Red Sox 3, Yankees 2

	1	2	3	4	5	6	7	8	9	R	H	E
New York	0	0	0	0	1	0	0	0	1	2	6	1
Boston	0	0	0	1	1	0	1	0	X	3	6	0

WP Tim Wakefield
LP Mike Mussina
SV Scott Williamson

Sunday night's Game Four was rained out, but MLB chief of discipline Bob Watson kept the series in the news when he announced several people had been fined for their involvement in the previous game's unpleasantness. Martinez was fined $50,000, Ramirez $25,000, Garcia $10,000, and Zimmer $5,000.

When the two teams took the field the next day, both managers opted to bypass their original Game Four starters, Burkett for the Red Sox, and Wells for the Yankees, to bring back their Game One hurlers.

For the second time, Wakefield out-pitched Mussina, evening the series at two games apiece. The knuckleballer allowed just one run on five hits in seven innings, while Mussina allowed three runs in six innings.

The Red Sox scored first when Walker homered in the fourth. After the Yankees tied the game, 1–1, in the fifth, Boston took the lead for good on a solo homer by Nixon in the bottom of the fifth. Boston added a run in the seventh on a Varitek fielder's choice, and Williamson made the lead stand up in the ninth after allowing a one-out homer to Ruben Sierra.

Through four games, Wakefield's record stood at 2–0 with just seven hits and three runs allowed in 13 innings. When asked after the game if he could envision himself pitching again in the series, he responded, "Right now I feel great, but I may be running on adrenaline. I always have my spikes on, so we'll see how I feel tomorrow when I come out for batting practice and play catch."[14]

Game 5: Yankees 4, Red Sox 2

	1	2	3	4	5	6	7	8	9	R	H	E
New York	0	3	0	0	0	0	0	1	0	4	7	1
Boston	0	0	0	1	0	0	0	1	0	2	6	1

WP David Wells
LP Derek Lowe
SV Mariano Rivera

Just as he had surrendered an early lead to the Yankees in Game Two, Lowe fell behind quickly in the fifth game and the Red Sox were not able to recover.

The Yankees scored all the runs they would need when they struck for three in the second inning. Garcia and Soriano both tallied RBI singles to center. Ramirez homered off Wells in the fourth to cut the lead to 3–1, and the two teams traded runs in the eighth, before Rivera recorded the last six outs to earn the save and give the Yankees a 3–2 series lead.

Game 6: Red Sox 9, Yankees 6

	1	2	3	4	5	6	7	8	9	R	H	E
Boston	0	0	4	0	0	0	3	0	2	9	16	1
New York	1	0	0	4	1	0	0	0	0	6	12	2

WP   Alan Embree
LP   Jose Contreras
SV   Scott Williamson

As the series returned to New York, the Red Sox put their faith in Burkett, hoping to stave off elimination. The start would be the last in the career of the 38-year old right-hander. The Yankees, meanwhile, countered with Pettitte, who would pitch one more time for the Yankees in the World Series, then depart to Houston as a free agent. Both pitchers were ineffective, especially Burkett (3⅔ innings, five runs), but the Red Sox overcame a 6-4 deficit to prevail 9-6 and force a seventh game.

After the Yankees scored a run in the bottom of the first, the Red Sox scored four times in the third. Varitek led off with a homer, then Damon singled and Walker walked. Garciaparra grounded into a fielder's choice, forcing Damon at third, then Ramirez walked to load the bases. Ortiz followed with a two-run single, then Millar drove in a run with a single, before Mueller grounded into a double play to end the inning.

The Yankees knocked Burkett out of the game with four runs in the fourth however, then tacked on a run against Bronson Arroyo in the fifth on a Posada homer, to take a 6-4 lead.

Jose Contreras struck out the side in the sixth, bringing the Red Sox within nine outs of elimination. The Cuban defector was already part of Red Sox–Yankees lore. Before the season he had worked out in front of Red Sox scouts, but he spurned a Red Sox offer to sign a four-year $28 million contract with the Yankees. The New York coup had prompted Red Sox president Larry Lucchino to refer to the Yankees as the "evil empire," and George Steinbrenner to shoot back with an attack on Lucchino's character, and commissioner Bud Selig to issue a gag order between the Red Sox and Yankees.

Facing Contreras in the seventh, Garciaparra led off with a triple, and raced home when Matsui's throw to the plate ended up in the stands. The run brought the Red Sox to within 6-5. Ramirez followed with a double, and after a Contreras wild pitch, Ortiz singled him home to tie the game. One out later, Mueller singled to move Ortiz to second and chase Contreras. Felix Heredia entered and immediately threw a wild pitch to put runners on second and third. After he struck out Nixon, Heredia intentionally walked Varitek to load the bases, then he walked Damon to force home the go-ahead run.

Nixon plated two insurance runs with a homer in the ninth, and Williamson set down the Yankees in order to end. And so, the Red Sox, a franchise that had endured so many previous heartbreaking Game Seven losses, advanced to play a seventh game against their age-old rival.

GAME 7: YANKEES 6, RED SOX 5

	1	2	3	4	5	6	7	8	9	10	11	R	H	E
Boston	0	3	0	1	0	0	0	1	0	0	0	5	11	0
New York	0	0	0	0	1	0	1	3	0	0	1	6	11	1

WP   Mariano Rivera
LP   Tim Wakefield

Martinez and Clemens, the two greatest Red Sox pitchers of the previous 100 years, faced each other for a final time in the series' deciding game. The younger pitcher would get the better of the elder, bringing the Red Sox to within five outs of victory. But by night's end Game Seven of the 2003 ALCS would assume a place of special infamy in the history of excruciating Red Sox losses.

The Yankees scored three runs against a wilting Martinez in the bottom of the eighth to erase a 5–2 deficit, and Boone lofted a Wakefield flutterer into the left field seats to give the Yankees a 6–5 win in the eleventh.

The Red Sox took a 3–0 lead in the second inning on a two-run blast by Nixon and a run-scoring error by Wilson at second base. Millar stretched the lead to 4–0 on a leadoff homer in the fourth, and, after allowing a walk to Nixon and a single to Mueller, Clemens departed with runners on first and third and no outs. Torre summoned Mussina to make his first relief appearance in more than 400 professional games. Not only did Mussina end the rally without allowing the Red Sox to pad the lead, but he held Boston scoreless in the fifth and sixth innings as well.

Giambi hit solo homers against Martinez in the fifth and seventh innings, cutting the lead to 4–2, but after an Ortiz homer in the eighth Boston's lead seemed secure at 5–2. Martinez was still throwing well and Timlin, Embree, and Williamson, against whom the Yankees were a combined 5-for-36 in the series, were ready for action in the bullpen.

Martinez had thrown exactly 100 pitches through seven innings. As he walked off the mound after striking out Soriano to end the seventh, he pointed to the sky thanking God, as was his custom at the end of each appearance. While the Red Sox batted in the eighth, the pitcher told Red Sox trainer Chris Correnti that he was tired, then accepted congratulations from several teammates and pitching coach Dave Wallace.

"[Correnti] and Wallace told me that was pretty much it. They were going to talk to Grady," Martinez recalled afterwards.[15]

The trainer and pitching coach reported to the manager that Martinez was fatigued and Martinez prepared to head for the clubhouse. But Little approached Martinez and asked him to continue pitching. "I need you for one more [inning]," Little said. "Can you give me one more?"[16]

Martinez retired Johnson on a pop up to start the Yankee eighth, bringing the Red Sox within five outs of victory. The next four batters recorded hits though, all on two-strike counts, while the Yankees scored three times to knot the score at 5–5. Jeter doubled to right on a ball that Nixon got a late break on, then Williams singled to center. Little visited the mound, but surprisingly left Martinez in the game.

"I was actually shocked I stayed out there that long," Martinez said later. "But I'm paid to do that. I belong to Boston. If they want to blow my arm out, it's their responsibility. I'm not going to go to the manager and say, 'Take me out.' I'm not going to blame Grady for leaving me out there."[17]

But fans across New England, the national baseball media, and the Red Sox front office did blame Little, after Matsui followed with a double to right field, and Posada blooped a game-tying hit to center.

When Little finally handed the ball over to the bullpen, Embree and Timlin each recorded an out to preserve the tie.

The two teams went to extra innings, having each scored 29 runs in the series.

The Red Sox' best chance to score in extra frames came when Ortiz doubled with two outs in the tenth, but Rivera got Millar to pop out to end the threat.

Wakefield pitched a perfect tenth, before Boone stepped into the right-handed batter's box to lead off the bottom of the eleventh. The third baseman had been a disappointment in New York after being acquired in a trade with Cincinnati in July, and was just 2-for-17 in the series. But Wakefield left his first pitch up in the strike zone and Boone made solid contact. Red Sox fans could only hope the ball would hook foul, but it sailed over the left field fence about 15 feet inside the foul pole.

As Boone circled the bases and the Yankee players sprinted onto the field to celebrate, many Red Sox players cried, most noticeably Wakefield, who had pitched valiantly in the series, only to serve up the series-losing homer.

Rivera, who pitched the final three innings to earn the win, was named series MVP.

Two days after the Yankees lost to the Florida Marlins in the World Series, the Red Sox announced that Little would not return as their manager in 2004.

Chapter 18

The Regular Season: 98–64

After enduring a heartbreaking extra-inning defeat in Game Seven of the 2003 American League Championship Series, the Red Sox bore the weight of an 86-year championship drought. Just two days after the 2003 World Series ended, the team announced Grady Little would not be offered a new contract to return as Red Sox manager. After a month-long search, the Red Sox named Terry Francona the new Boston skipper on December 8. Francona had previously served as a manager in Philadelphia and had spent the 2003 season as a coach in Oakland.

By the time of Francona's hiring, the Red Sox had already made some bold moves to upgrade the team. Two days after Little was dismissed, they placed Manny Ramirez on irrevocable waivers, meaning that any team could claim him, provided it assumed his $22.5 million per year contract.[1] But no team claimed Ramirez, precipitating rumors that the Red Sox sought to trade the slugger to any team that would pay a sizeable portion of his salary over the final four years of his contract. While Ramirez was one of the most productive hitters in baseball, his contract was a holdover from the John Harrington and Dan Duquette era. The John Henry ownership group thought it ill advised to spend such a large portion of the team's payroll on just one player.

While the Ramirez saga festered, the Red Sox turned their attention to the west where the Arizona Diamondbacks were entering a rebuilding phase and were accepting offers for staff ace Curt Schilling. After receiving special permission from the Diamondbacks to negotiate a contract extension with the 38-year old former Red Sox farmhand, Theo Epstein flew to Arizona to have Thanksgiving Dinner with the Schillings. Schilling agreed to waive his no-trade clause and sign a two-year contract extension with the Red Sox and on the day after Thanksgiving, Schilling was traded from Arizona to Boston for a package of players that included young pitchers Casey Fossum and Brandon Lyon. At a press conference in Arizona announcing the deal, Schilling said, "I like the thought of pitching in the biggest rivalry in sports in front of some incredible fans." Before he would arrive in Boston, Schilling appeared on televisions throughout New England in a Ford commercial in which he stated he was heading to Boston "to break an 86-year-curse."[2] The burly right-hander would fulfill his promise, posting a 21–6 regular season record, and coming up big in the playoffs against the Yankees and Cardinals despite a serious injury.

Next, the Red Sox signed the dominant reliever that the 2003 edition had lacked, inking free agent Keith Foulke to a four-year contract. Like Schilling, the new Red Sox closer already enjoyed a cozy relationship with Francona, from their time together in Oakland. With Foulke at the back end of the bullpen, the Red Sox would win 88 of 89 games when leading after eight innings in 2004.

With the pitching corps significantly upgraded, Epstein turned his attention back to revamping a starting lineup that had scored more runs than any team in the league in 2003. Just as the Red Sox were questioning the wisdom of retaining Ramirez's contract, the Texas Rangers were coming to a similar realization regarding their relationship with Alex Rodriguez, the only player in the game making more money than Ramirez. The Rangers made it known they were willing to trade the reigning MVP as long as the acquiring team provided them with a star player in return and assumed most of Rodriguez's contract liability. The Yankees and Red Sox emerged as the only suitors. After Henry received permission to renegotiate Rodriguez's contract, the Red Sox, Rangers, and Chicago White Sox agreed on a pair of trades, one that would send Ramirez to Texas for Rodriguez, and one that would send Boston icon Nomar Garciaparra to Chicago for outfielder Magglio Ordonez. The deals hit a last-minute snafu, however, when Players Association head Gene Orza complained that by agreeing to accept a large percentage of the money owed him in deferred compensation, Rodriguez was lessening the value of his contract. When both trades fell through, the Red Sox were left with a pair of discontented stars in Ramirez and Garciaparra. Adding insult to injury, the Rangers promptly traded Rodriguez to the Yankees. To facilitate the deal, A-Rod agreed to move from shortstop to third base, to appease Yankee captain Derek Jeter.

With the two best shortstops in baseball anchoring the left side of their infield, the Yankees began the 2004 season as heavy favorites to win the American League East. In the season's first month, though, the Red Sox sent a resounding message to their despised neighbors to the south that the race would be a contested one. Not only did Boston finish April 15–7, three games ahead of New York, but the Red Sox won six of seven games against their archrivals in the month, including a three-game sweep in the Bronx.

With Garciaparra and Trot Nixon opening the season on the disabled list, however, Boston's momentum began to fade. A string of five straight losses to begin May foreshadowed an extended period of mediocre play. Garciaparra returned in mid-June but was a surly presence in the clubhouse, his feelings still damaged by the team's off-season attempt to trade him. Boston posted just a 41–40 record over the months of May, June and July and as the team stagnated, New York resumed its winning ways. By July 1, the Red Sox were 8½ games behind the first-place Yankees. Two weekends in late July, however, breathed new life into the Boston team.

Still 8½ games ahead of the Red Sox, the Yankees visited Fenway Park for a three-game weekend series, July 23–25. Despite three Kevin Millar home runs, the Yankees won the first game on a ninth-inning RBI single by Rodriguez. After a torrential rainfall overnight, Red Sox management was prepared to cancel the next day's game until Johnny Damon and several other players approached team officials and insisted that the game be played. The team listened, and played the game after a delay. Pedro Martinez had plunked Gary Sheffield with a pitch the night before, and the lingering ill feelings between the teams came to a head in the series' second game. In the third inning of the Saturday tilt, with the Yankees leading 3–0, Red Sox starter Bronson Arroyo drilled Rodriguez in the back with a pitch. Rodriguez slowly made his way toward first base, jabbering at Arroyo all the way, as Red Sox catcher Jason Varitek followed him down the line. Midway to first, Rodriguez stopped and made a two-handed gesture to Varitek as if to ask, "Do you want hit me?" Varitek left no doubt in the minds of the national television audience that watched on FOX, that indeed he did. The fiery backstop slammed his catcher's mitt into Rodriguez's face, and a heated bench-clearing brawl ensued. Afterward, Varitek explained, "I told him in choice words to get to first base, then he and Bronson started yelling at each other and things got out of hand." The fight reenergized the Red Sox who rallied for three runs in the ninth inning against Yankees closer Mariano Rivera to post an 11–10 win. Bill Mueller's walk off two-run homer into the visitors' bullpen sealed the comeback. The next night the Red Sox took the rubber-game, tagging Yankee starter Jose Contreras for eight runs in a 9–6 win. "To me, that was the first inkling we had that things were different this year," Henry said of the emotional midsummer weekend.[4]

The next weekend, as the July 31 trade deadline approached, Epstein made one of the boldest trades in Red Sox history. The young general manager sent Garciaparra to the Chicago Cubs in a four-team trade that netted first baseman Doug Mientkiewicz, shortstop Orlando Cabrera, and outfielder Dave Roberts. While none of the new Red Sox could match Garciaparra's star power, each was a superior defensive player and by season's end each would play a role in the Red Sox' World Series run.

Cabrera and Mientkiewicz had an immediate impact on the infield defense, and for the first time all season Red Sox pitchers seemed to settle into a collective comfort zone. "A week or two after the deal was made, we found our identity and took off," said Schilling of the trade's effect on the pitching staff.[5] The outspoken ace also acknowledged that the clubhouse chemistry improved with the removal of the gifted but petulant Garciaparra. "Nomar had a lot of things going on and he's introverted," Schilling said. "He had the Achilles [injury]. He had the contract [negotiations]. And it was its own story. Every day with the trade, that changed the atmosphere immediately in here."[6]

As the team gained confidence, the Red Sox won 16-of-17 games from August 16 through September 3, and at one point won 28-of-36 games, including three-game sweeps of Wild Card contenders Anaheim and Oakland in early September. Buoyed by a record of 21–7 in August and 21–11 in September, the Red Sox finished 98–64, three games behind the Yankees in the division, but seven games ahead of the A's in the Wild Card race. Boston clinched a playoff berth on September 27 in Tampa Bay with a 7–3 win, and raised eyebrows across the league with a raucous post-game celebration that seemed more befitting of a team that had just won a World Series, than one that had just qualified for the postseason as the best second place team in the league.

But the loosey-goosey 2004 Red Sox had taken no pains to tailor a reserved and proper image during the season's first six months, and they didn't intend to do so as the playoffs approached. They were a fun-loving bunch known for their eccentric hairdos, hearty celebratory hugs, and secret dugout handshakes. The leader of the self proclaimed "Idiots" was Damon, who had reported to spring training with long brown locks and a thick beard. With the look, he bore a slight resemblance to Jesus, prompting "Damon Disciples" to turn out at Red Sox games in visiting stadiums across the country, wearing shaggy wigs and fake beards, and holding signs that asked "WWJDD?" or "What would Johnny Damon Do?" Many of Damon's teammates fell in line with unique looks all their own. Arroyo sported cornrows, Ramirez wore dreadlocks, Martinez wore Jheri-curls, Millar a goatee, Francona and back-up outfielder Gabe Kapler shaved off their hair. In short, the 2004 Red Sox did everything in their power to embody the anti-Yankee image. Yankee players were, of course, required to adhere to a strict personal appearance policy enforced by owner George Steinbrenner.

"Chemistry cannot be underestimated," team president Larry Lucchino said after the season. "I've never seen a situation where there was such compatibility, closeness and productivity."[7] Indeed, the Red Sox had not only been a close-knit bunch, but an exceptionally productive one. The offense batted .282 and scored 949 runs to lead the league in both categories, anchored by Ramirez (.308, 43 HR, 130 RBI), David Ortiz (.301, 41 HR, 139 RBI), and Damon (.304, 20 HR, 94 RBI). And the pitching staff, led by dual aces Schilling (21–6, 3.26 ERA) and Martinez (16–9, 3.90 ERA) placed third in the league with a 4.18 ERA. Number-three starter Derek Lowe (14–12, 5.42 ERA) struggled for much of the season before pitching better over the final month, while Tim Wakefield (12–10, 4.87 ERA) and Arroyo (10–9, 4.03) rounded out the rotation. Foulke finished with 32 saves and a 2.17 ERA.

The Postseason: 11–3

In many ways, the Red Sox' playoff season mirrored their regular season. The Red Sox were quick out of the gate, sweeping the Angels in the American League Division Series, then they struggled, losing the first three games of the ALCS against the Yankees, then they finished on a hot streak, closing with eight straight wins, four against the shell-shocked Yankees, and four against the Cardinals in the World Series. Along the way, the 2004 Red Sox became the first team in baseball history to rebound from a three games to none deficit to win a postseason series. Previously 25 teams had found themselves needing to win four straight games to stave off elimination, and all 25 had failed. In fact, in the combined history of Major League Baseball, the NBA, and the NHL, 230 teams had fallen behind 3–0 in best-of-seven series, and only the 1942 Toronto Maple Leafs and 1975 New York Islanders had rallied to win. After joining such elite company, and doing so by vanquishing their most hated rival, the Red Sox rolled over the Cardinals, another historic rival, in a World Series that seemed anticlimactic after the pressure-packed ALCS.

2004 American League Division Series:
Red Sox 3, Angels 0

GAME 1: RED SOX 9, ANGELS 3

	1	2	3	4	5	6	7	8	9	R	H	E
Boston	1	0	0	7	0	0	0	1	0	9	11	1
Anaheim	0	0	0	1	0	0	2	0	0	3	9	1

WP Curt Schilling
LP Jarrod Washburn

The Red Sox traveled to Anaheim to meet the Angels in the ALDS and won the first game easily behind Schilling.

Ramirez stroked a two out double against Angels starter Jarrod Washburn in the bottom of the first inning, and Ortiz singled him home to put the Red Sox ahead 1–0.

In the fourth inning Boston struck for seven runs, keyed by Millar's two-run homer and Ramirez's three-run blast.

Schilling held the Angels to three runs on nine hits over 6⅔ innings, but pulled up lame while covering first base on a Garret Anderson chopper to first base to lead off the Angels' sixth. Although Schilling stayed in the game for four more outs, he visited a local hospital for precautionary X-rays. Francona downplayed the injury in his post-game press conference, telling reporters, "I think our trainers and medical staff are really confident that he can make his next start, whenever that is, without problems."[8] Schilling had battled a deep bone bruise in his right ankle joint all season, but had suffered new structural damage to his ankle tendons on the Anderson groundout.

GAME 2: RED SOX 8, ANGELS 3

	1	2	3	4	5	6	7	8	9	R	H	E
Boston	0	1	0	0	0	2	1	0	4	8	12	0
Anaheim	0	1	0	0	2	0	0	0	0	3	7	0

WP Pedro Martinez
LP Francisco Rodriguez
SV Keith Foulke

Although the lopsided final score might indicate otherwise, the second game in Anaheim offered more drama than the first. Martinez squared off against fellow Dominican Bartolo Colon, and both starters were effective.

The game was tied, 3–3, heading into the seventh when the Angels sent Francisco Rodriguez to the mound to replace Colon. Damon reached on a fielder's choice, stole second, advanced to third on a Rodriguez wild pitch, and scored the go-ahead run on Ramirez's sacrifice fly to center.

After Martinez retired Anaheim in the seventh to finish his night having allowed three runs on six hits in seven innings, Mike Timlin, Mike Myers and Foulke combined to hold Anaheim scoreless in the eighth.

Boston scored four runs in the ninth to put the game out of reach. Cabrera's three-run double was the big blow.

Then Foulke set down the Angels in the bottom of the ninth.

GAME 3: RED SOX 8, ANGELS 6

	1	2	3	4	5	6	7	8	9	10	R	H	E
Anaheim	0	0	0	1	0	0	5	0	0	0	6	8	2
Boston	0	0	2	3	1	0	0	0	0	2	8	12	0

WP Derek Lowe
LP Francisco Rodriguez

With the series shifting to Boston, the Red Sox were eager to complete the sweep, which would allow them to reset their pitching rotation while they waited to see if they would play Minnesota or New York in the second round.

It appeared the Red Sox would cruise to an easy win after they built a 6–1 lead against Angels starter Kelvim Escobar. But the Angels came back to tie the game in the

Pedro Martinez and Doug Mirabelli warm up in the outfield.

seventh, setting the stage for a dramatic series clinching home run by Ortiz in the tenth inning.

In the third, Nixon plated Mark Bellhorn with a single and Millar followed with a groundout to second that scored Ortiz. After a Troy Glaus solo-shot cut the lead in half in the fourth, the Red Sox scored three runs in the bottom of the frame on a Ramirez sacrifice fly, an Ortiz double, and a David Eckstein error on a groundball hit by Millar. An RBI single by Ramirez in the sixth opened a 6–1 lead.

The Angels scored five runs in the seventh, though, four of which crossed the plate on a game-tying grand slam by Vladimir Guerrero. The slugging right fielder drove a Timlin fastball the opposite way, into the Red Sox bullpen.

Both teams failed to score in the eighth and ninth, sending the game into extra-innings. In the tenth, Ortiz provided the type of last-minute heroics Red Sox fans had come to expect from a team that had won 17 games in its last at bat during the regular season. With two outs and Damon on second, Angels manager Mike Scioscia summoned the only left-hander on his pitching staff to face the Red Sox' hulking designated hitter. Game One loser Washburn threw just one pitch, a slider over the heart of the plate that Ortiz deposited into the Green Monster seats, giving the Red Sox an 8–6 win and sending 35,547 fans into jubilation. "I looked at Kevin Millar and said, 'Can he hit one here?'" Francona recalled. "No sooner than the words were out of my mouth than it left the bat."[8]

Lowe, who had been the odd-man-out among the Red Sox starters as the postseason began, earned the win in relief, the first of three series clinching wins he would claim in the 2004 playoffs.

The Red Sox pitching staff finished the series with 28 strikeouts in 28 innings and a 3.54 ERA. Ortiz hit .545 (6-for-11) and Damon hit .467 (7-for-15).

2004 American League Championship Series: Red Sox 4, Yankees 3

GAME 1: YANKEES 10, RED SOX 7

	1	2	3	4	5	6	7	8	9	R	H	E
Boston	0	0	0	0	0	0	5	2	0	7	10	0
New York	2	0	4	0	0	2	0	2	X	10	14	0

WP Mike Mussina
LP Curt Schilling
SV Mariano Rivera

For the second straight year the Red Sox found themselves facing a potent Yankee team in the ALCS. The 2004 Yankees were the most expensive baseball club ever assembled, as Steinbrenner had shelled out nearly $185 million for a roster that had placed eight players on the 2004 all-star team and acquired a ninth, Esteban Loaiza, just before the trade deadline expired. The Red Sox were confident though, having taken 11-of-19 regular season games against the Yankees.

At a press conference the day before the series began, Schilling fueled the flames of the Yankee-Red Sox fire when he said, "The awesome thing about being a starting pitcher is that you have the ability to make fifty thousand people shut up when you're on the road.

I'm not sure I can think of any scenario more enjoyable than making fifty thousand people from New York shut up."[9]

Schilling's bravado didn't carry him deep into Game One however, as he allowed six runs in the first three innings and left the game favoring his right ankle. Afterwards, he admitted his season might be over. "If I can't go out there with something better than what I had today, I'm not going back out there," Schilling said. "This is not about me braving through something. This is about us and winning the world championship, and if I can't give them better than I had today, I won't take the ball again."[11]

Yankee starter Mike Mussina carried an 8–0 lead into the seventh, having retired the first 19 batters he faced, before Bellhorn broke up the perfect game with a double. The Red Sox offense came alive, knocking Mussina out of the game with four hits. By the time Tanyon Sturtze came on in relief, Boston had scored three runs. Sturtze served up a two-run homer to Varitek, which made the score 8–5, then struck out Cabrera to end the inning. After the Yankees were retired in the bottom of the inning, the Red Sox pulled within 8–7 against Tom Gordon in the eighth, on an Ortiz triple to deep left that ticked off Hideki Matsui's glove, scoring Mueller and Ramirez. With the game hanging in the balance, Yankee manager Joe Torre called upon Mariano Rivera, who had returned to the Yankee clubhouse midway through the game after attending a family funeral in Panama. The closer recorded the final out of the eighth, then held the Red Sox at bay in the ninth, after New York had added a pair of insurance runs when Ramirez allowed a fly ball off the bat of Bernie Williams to sail over his head for an RBI double in the bottom of the eighth.

GAME 2: YANKEES 3, RED SOX 1

	1	2	3	4	5	6	7	8	9	R	H	E
Boston	0	0	0	0	0	0	0	1	0	1	5	0
New York	1	0	0	0	0	2	0	0	0	3	7	0

WP John Lieber
LP Pedro Martinez
SV Mariano Rivera

After dropping a 6–4 decision to the Yankees at Fenway Park on September 24, a distraught Martinez had appeared before the Boston and New York media contingent and said, "What can I say? I just tip my hat and call the Yankees my Daddy." The concession stood in stark contrast to the cocky Martinez of three years earlier who had scoffed at the notion that Babe Ruth had cursed his former team. "Wake up the damn Bambino and have me face him," Martinez had said in 2001. "Maybe I'll drill him in the ass."[12] At the time, the Red Sox were 5–2 in games started by Martinez against New York. Since then, including the heartbreaking Game Seven loss in the 2003 ALCS, the Red Sox were just 6–15 in games started by their ace against the Yankees. Indeed, if the most dominant pitcher of the previous decade had a nemesis, it was the Yankees. Since his debut in 1992, Martinez had posted a record of 182 wins and 76 losses, good for a winning percentage of .705. But in 28 career starts against the Yankees, his record was a pedestrian 10–10, and the Red Sox' team record was 10–18.

As Martinez took the mound in the bottom of the first inning hoping to even the series, the 56,136 fans who had packed Yankee Stadium, taunted him with chants of "Who's your daddy?" Martinez smiled, then uncharacteristically walked Jeter to lead off the game. The

Yankee captain stole second and scored on a single to center by Sheffield. For the second night in a row, the Yankees had taken a first inning lead.

Martinez eventually settled into a groove, though, and the score remained 1-0 until John Olerud connected for a line-drive two-run homer into the right field lower box seats that put the Yankees ahead 3-0 in the sixth. Martinez departed after finishing the inning, having allowed three runs on four hits while striking out seven.

The story of the night, however, was the performance turned in by Yankee starter John Lieber, who allowed just two hits over the first seven innings, before being lifted when Nixon led off the eighth with a hit. Nixon came around to score on a Cabrera groundout against Gordon, but that was the extent of the Red Sox scoring.

After Rivera recorded the save, notching the final four outs for the second straight day, the Red Sox found themselves facing a two games to none deficit. *The Boston Globe* noted the next day that since the League Championship Series had switch from a best-of-five to a best-of-seven event in 1985, teams taking a two games to none lead had won 13-of-15 times, including 13 in a row.

GAME 3: YANKEES 19, RED SOX 8

	1	2	3	4	5	6	7	8	9	R	H	E
New York	3	0	3	5	2	0	4	0	2	19	22	1
Boston	0	4	2	0	0	0	2	0	0	8	15	0

WP Javier Vazquez
LP Ramiro Mendoza

After a scheduled off day, heavy rains on October 15 postponed Game Three. When the series resumed October 16, many Red Sox fans soon wished it hadn't. The Yankees set several postseason records on the way to clobbering the Red Sox 19-8.

For the third straight time, New York took a first inning lead, this time plating three runs against Arroyo in the opening frame, keyed by a two-run homer by Matsui. The Red Sox rebounded to take their first lead of the series, 4-3, with four runs against Yankee starter Kevin Brown in the bottom of the second, but the lead was short-lived. Arroyo served up a game-tying shot to Rodriguez to lead off the third, then walked Sheffield and allowed a Matsui double before Francona came to the mound to rescue him. Reliever Ramiro Mendoza did not fare much better against his former team, allowing an RBI single to Bernie Williams and then balking home a run.

Trailing 6-4 entering the bottom of the third, the Red Sox mounted one final comeback. Varitek led off with a single against Javier Vazquez, who had been called upon by Torre to replace Brown, then Millar doubled, and Mueller walked to load the bases. With the sacks full and no outs, Cabrera stroked a double to the triangle in right-center that scored Varitek and Millar. Mueller, representing the go-ahead run, was cut down at the plate however, when Williams relayed the ball to second baseman Miguel Cairo, who threw a strike to Jorge Posada.

The Yankees again answered immediately, scoring five runs in the top of the fourth against Mendoza, Curtis Leskanic and Wakefield, to build an 11-6 lead. Before the night was over the Yankees set League Championship Series records with their 19 runs, 22 hits, and eight doubles. The two-through-five batters in New York's lineup — Rodriguez, Sheffield, Matsui and Williams — went 16-for-22 with 14 runs and 15 RBI.

Making matters worse for the Red Sox, Wakefield, who had pitched 3⅓ innings in emergency duty, was no longer available to start Game Four. Lowe, who had been scheduled to start Game Five, in place of Schilling, would have to start instead. After the game, Francona praised Wakefield for volunteering to eat up innings in the blowout. The manager said, "Because Wake did what he did, we were able to stay away from Timlin and Foulke. They can go multiple innings tomorrow and give us a chance to win. Wake really, really picked us up. He's a professional. If we win tomorrow, we will have Wake to thank."[13]

GAME 4: RED SOX 6, YANKEES 4

	1	2	3	4	5	6	7	8	9	10	11	12	R	H	E
New York	0	0	2	0	0	2	0	0	0	0	0	0	4	12	1
Boston	0	0	0	0	3	0	0	0	1	0	0	2	6	8	0

WP Curtis Leskanic
LP Paul Quantrill

The Red Sox took the field for pre-game warm-ups the next day knowing that no team in baseball history had come back from a 3–0 postseason deficit. The chattering Millar rallied the team by flitting around the field during batting practice, visiting each teammate to offer words of encouragement and lighten the mood. "It hasn't happened in the history of baseball, but don't let us win today," Millar said. "Because then we'll give Pedro the ball tomorrow, then Schilling in Game Six. Then anything can happen in Game Seven."[14]

For the fourth consecutive game, New York scored first on a two-run third-inning blast over the Green Monster by Rodriguez. A moment after the ball had left the park, it came flying back over the wall, having been thrown back by someone on Lansdowne Street. Damon picked the ball up and threw it back over the wall, but a moment later it came flying back into the yard. This time, umpire Joe West put the ball in his pocket.

The Red Sox took a 3–2 lead in the fifth on three walks and RBI hits by Cabrera and Ortiz against Yankee starter Orlando Hernandez, but the Yankees responded with two runs in the top of the fourth to knock Lowe from the game and reclaim a 4–3 lead.

Rivera pitched a scoreless eighth, then took the mound in the ninth to finish off the Red Sox. When Millar led off with a walk, Francona summoned the rarely used Roberts to pinch-run. "As I took the field, Terry looked at me and gave me a wink, and I knew what that meant," the fleet-footed Roberts would later recall.[15] Roberts broke for second on Rivera's first move to the plate, and slid into the base headfirst, narrowly beating Posada's throw. One pitch later, Mueller sent a shot up the middle to tie the game, 4–4.

Neither team scored until the bottom of the 12th inning, when Ramirez led off with a single and Ortiz blasted a Gordon pitch over the right field fence into the alley between the visitors' bullpen and the right field boxes, giving the Red Sox a dramatic 6–4 win. Ortiz was greeted by a mob of teammates at the plate.

As important as Ortiz's homer was, the work of the Red Sox bullpen, which had been spared by Wakefield in Game Three, was just as important. Boston's relievers allowed just one run in 6⅔ innings. The five-hour, two-minute marathon, which didn't end until 1:22 A.M., was the longest game in ALCS history to date, but Game Five would be even lengthier.

GAME 5: RED SOX 5, YANKEES 4

	1	2	3	4	5	6	7	8	9	10	11	12	13	14	R	H	E
New York	0	1	0	0	0	3	0	0	0	0	0	0	0	0	4	12	1
Boston	2	0	0	0	0	0	0	2	0	0	0	0	0	1	5	13	1

WP Tim Wakefield
LP Esteban Loaiza

When the series began, Monday, October 18 had been scheduled as an off day, but due to the Game Three postponement, the teams instead met for a late-afternoon affair in the Fens, with the Red Sox hoping to stave off elimination and the Yankees hoping to clinch the series. The game would not be decided until 14 innings and five-hours and 49-minutes of play. The game ended with Ortiz again being mobbed by jubilant teammates.

This time Boston scored first, tallying twice in the first against Mussina, on an RBI single by Ramirez and a bases-loaded walk by Varitek. Williams cut the lead in half with a leadoff homer against Martinez in the top of the second, and the Yankees scored three more in the sixth to take a 4–2 lead.

This time the Red Sox didn't wait until the ninth to rally. Ortiz led off the Boston eighth with an opposite field homer against Gordon, then Roberts, who had again entered as a pinch-runner for Millar, scored on a sacrifice fly by Varitek against Rivera. The Red Sox would not trail again at any point in the 2004 postseason.

The two bullpens submitted matching zeroes until the bottom of the 14th, when Loaiza issued walks to Damon and Ramirez, bringing Ortiz to the plate with two outs and runners on first and second. After fouling off several pitches, Ortiz blooped a single to center, and Damon raced home to give the Red Sox a 5–4 victory. Ortiz had notched his third walk-off hit of the postseason.

"The Yankees really have to think about who's their Big Papi," an exultant Martinez said after the game, referencing Ortiz's nickname.[16]

Again, the Red Sox bullpen deserved credit, having contributed eight innings of shutout pitching. Wakefield, who allowed only one hit in the game's final three innings, earned the win.

GAME 6: RED SOX 4, YANKEES 2

	1	2	3	4	5	6	7	8	9	R	H	E
Boston	0	0	0	4	0	0	0	0	0	4	11	0
New York	0	0	0	0	0	0	1	1	0	2	6	0

WP Curt Schilling
LP John Lieber
SV Keith Foulke

On a cold raw night in New York, the two rivals squared off in a Game Six match-up that seemed to favor the Yankees. Lieber, who had befuddled the Red Sox in Game Two, got the ball for New York, while Schilling, who had been shelled in the opener, limped to the mound for Boston. What viewers across the country didn't know, as FOX TV cameras zoomed in on a large blood stain on Schilling's right sock as Schilling took his warm-up pitches, was that Red Sox team doctor Bill Morgan had performed an experimental surgery on the Red Sox ace just two hours before the game. Schilling was in pain because a tendon around his ankle was dislocated. It was an injury that under normal circumstances would have necessitated season-ending surgery. But Schilling wanted to pitch. He told Morgan to do whatever he could to give him the chance to "shut up" the 50,000 fans who had jeered him off the mound after three innings in Game One. Performing a procedure that was unheard of in sports medicine, Morgan sutured the skin between the dislocated tendon and a tendon that was in its proper spot, creating a temporary sheath of skin to hold the wayward tendon in place. The suture was a stopgap solution that would have to be removed immediately following the game.

Pitching with one good ankle and a lot of heart, Schilling was not dominant but he was effective, holding the Yankees to one run on four hits in seven innings. By the time he departed, the Red Sox had a 4–1 lead.

All four Boston runs scored in the fourth. After the first two Red Sox batters were retired, the team strung together four straight hits, capped by a three-run opposite field home run by the number-nine hitter, Bellhorn. The ball was initially ruled a double after it was caught by a fan sitting in the left field seats who dropped it back onto the outfield warning track. But after the umpires conferred, it was ruled a home run. This was the first of two umpiring decisions that helped seal the Red Sox win. In both cases, the umpires got the calls right, but they were the types of calls that traditionally went against the Red Sox in the playoffs.

Arroyo replaced Schilling to start the eighth and controversy ensued. Rodriguez, who had jostled with Arroyo on a Saturday afternoon in July, once again was at the center of the brouhaha. Arroyo allowed one-out hits to Cairo and Jeter, pulling the Yankees to within 4–2, with Jeter on first base. Rodriguez hit a weak grounder down the first base line that Arroyo fielded. Rather than throwing to first, Arroyo reached out to tag Rodriguez who slapped the ball out of his glove with his left hand as he ran past. The ball wound up in right field, Rodriguez wound up on second base, and Jeter crossed the plate, pulling the Yankees within 4–3 with still only one out. Francona complained that Rodriguez had intentionally interfered with the play, and the umpires huddled before reversing the initial call and ruling Rodriguez out. The decision sent Jeter back to first base and took a run off the scoreboard. The Bronx fans responded by littering the field with bottles, baseballs and trash, and the game was delayed while the Red Sox players left the field. The umpires conferred with the New York City Police Department and finally, a small army of police officers outfitted in riot gear emerged from the bowels of Yankee Stadium and lined the field on both sides of the diamond so that play could resume. Arroyo induced Sheffield to pop out to Varitek to end the inning and preserve the 4–2 lead.

Against Foulke in the ninth, the Yankees put two men on base on a pair of walks before Tony Clark struck out to end the game and make Boston the first team in baseball history to battle back from a 3–0 deficit to even a postseason series. The Red Sox still had work to do, though, and Foulke, like his teammates, was confident they would succeed. "I firmly believe the pressure is on them," the Red Sox closer said after the game. "They put us down, 3–0, they're supposed to put us away. We keep talking about making history. We want to be the first team in history to come back from three games down. No one expects us to win. There's no pressure on us. It's all on them."[17]

Game 7: Red Sox 10, Yankees 3

	1	2	3	4	5	6	7	8	9	R	H	E
Boston	2	4	0	2	0	0	0	1	1	10	13	0
New York	0	0	1	0	0	0	2	0	0	3	5	2

WP   Derek Lowe
LP   Kevin Brown

Inspired by Schilling's gutsy performance and a desire to rewrite history, the Red Sox made sure the outcome of this Game Seven — unlike the ALCS finale between the same two teams a year earlier — would not be in question as the late innings arrived.

Boston tagged Brown for two runs in the first inning on an Ortiz homer, then struck for four more on a Damon grand slam in the second to take a 6–0 lead. Two innings later, Damon launched another homer, a two-run shot that put the Red Sox ahead 8–1.

Meanwhile, Lowe had his sinkerball working to near perfection as he worked on three days' rest. He allowed just one run on one hit in six innings, while recording 11 groundball outs.

Martinez pitched the seventh, allowing two runs, but the Red Sox got a run back in the eighth when a Bellhorn fly ball struck the right field foul pole, giving Boston a 9–3 lead. A Cabrera sacrifice fly in the ninth opened a 10–3 lead.

Lefthander Alan Embree recorded the game's last out, inducing Ruben Sierra to ground to second baseman Pokey Reese. Mayhem followed, on the field and in the visitors' clubhouse, as the Red Sox celebrated the greatest comeback in baseball history. "Thank you, Lord. Thank you, Lord," Pedro Martinez, sobbed as he clutched the American League Championship trophy and teammates drenched him with champagne in the clubhouse.[18] Wakefield returned to the field and stood for a while on the Yankee Stadium mound, where his hopes had been crushed a year earlier.

Ortiz, to no one's surprise, was named the series MVP on the laurels of his .387 average, 12 hits, three homers, and 11 RBI.

There was a dark footnote to the Red Sox' finest hour, however. After the last out was recorded in New York, the streets of Boston's Back Bay overflowed with jubilant fans in the early hours of October 21. An estimated 80,000 people flooded the Fenway District, and tragically the celebration turned deadly when a mounted Boston police officer opened fire on a crowd of revelers. The officer shot a plastic ball filled with pepper spray using a supposedly "less than lethal" device similar to a paintball gun. The shot struck and killed Victoria Snelgrove, a 21-year-old journalism major from Emerson College, who had grown up in East Bridgewater.[19]

2004 World Series: Red Sox 4, Cardinals 0

GAME 1: RED SOX 11, CARDINALS 9

	1	2	3	4	5	6	7	8	9	R	H	E
St. Louis	0	1	1	3	0	2	0	2	0	9	11	1
Boston	4	0	3	0	0	0	2	2	X	11	13	4

WP Keith Foulke
LP Julian Tavarez

The 2004 World Series represented the first time since 1975 when the Reds and Red Sox met in the October Classic that the two teams that had scored the most runs during the regular season met in the World Series. Baseball's 100th World Series pitted the Red Sox against the same team that had dashed Boston's hopes in 1946 and 1967. Although St. Louis had posted the best regular season record in baseball in 2004 with a mark of 105–57, this meeting would turn out quite different from the two hard-fought seven-game series in the teams' collective history. The Red Sox scored first-inning runs in all four games, and never trailed in the series.

Because the AL had won the 2004 All-Star Game, thanks in part to home runs by Ortiz and Ramirez, the series opened in Boston. In Game One, the two teams set a record for the most runs scored in the first game of a World Series, as the Red Sox prevailed 11–9, despite committing four errors.

After Wakefield retired the Cardinals in the top of the first, Damon led off the Red Sox half of the inning with a double to left against St. Louis starter Woody Williams. Williams then hit Cabrera with a pitch to put two men on base for Ortiz. The Red Sox designated hitter crushed an inside fastball directly over the right field foul pole for a three-run homer. Millar later scored the fourth Boston run in the inning on an RBI single by Mueller.

After St. Louis chipped away at the lead with single runs in the second and third, the Red Sox struck for three more in the home half of the third — on RBI hits by Damon and Cabrera, and a fielder's choice by Ramirez — opening a 7–2 lead. Wakefield issued four walks in the fourth inning, though, and catcher Doug Mirabelli committed a passed ball, as St. Louis scored three runs on one hit to pull within 7–5. The Cardinals tied the game, 7–7, against Arroyo in the sixth, on run-scoring doubles by Edgar Renteria and Larry Walker.

Boston reclaimed the lead in the seventh, scoring single runs on a Ramirez single to center and an Ortiz single off the chest of second baseman Tony Womack. The Red Sox had a 9–7 lead with six outs to go, but Ramirez made a pair of fielding errors in the top of the eighth, leading to two Cardinals runs and knotting the game at 9–9. The Red Sox again reclaimed the lead in the bottom of the inning. With one out, Varitek reached base when his grounder to deep short popped out of Renteria's glove, and Bellhorn followed with a fly ball off Julian Tavarez that struck the right field foul pole for a two-run homer and an 11–9 Red Sox lead. The hit represented the third homer in as many games for the Red Sox second baseman, and the second to hit a foul pole.

Foulke protected the lead in the ninth, retiring the Cardinals on just one hit.

"Once [Tavarez] got two strikes on me, I just tried to put the ball in play and let my natural talent take over," said Bellhorn afterwards.[20]

GAME 2: RED SOX 6, CARDINALS 2

	1	2	3	4	5	6	7	8	9	R	H	E
St. Louis	0	0	0	1	0	0	0	1	0	2	5	0
Boston	2	0	0	2	0	2	0	0	X	6	8	4

WP Curt Schilling
LP Matt Morris

The Red Sox made four errors in Game Two, becoming the first team ever to make eight miscues in the first two games of a World Series, but again they prevailed, this time behind another courageous performance by Schilling.

When the day began, Schilling's availability was very much in doubt. "When I woke up at 7:00 A.M., I couldn't walk," Schilling would confess after holding the Cardinals to just one unearned run in six innings. "I couldn't move. I didn't know what had happened. But I knew when I woke up that there was a problem. I honest to God did not think I was going to take the ball."[21]

When Schilling arrived at Fenway Park, the team doctor again performed the revolutionary surgery that had allowed the right-hander to answer the bell for Game Six in New York. "It's not a non-invasive procedure," Dr. Morgan explained after the game. "But once we anesthetized the area, he felt better and being the gamer that he is, he said, 'I'm going to go out and do it.'"[22]

With a new suture in place and another blood splotch on his right sock, Schilling set down the Cardinals on one hit in the first, before Ortiz and Ramirez worked two-out walks against Matt Morris in the bottom of the frame. Varitek tripled home both runners with a shot into the center field triangle, 420-feet from home plate. The Red Sox carried the 2–0 lead into the fourth, when St. Louis struck for an unearned run on a ground ball that ate up Mueller at third. The Red Sox got the run back, and another to boot, in the bottom of the inning, opening a 4–1. After Millar was hit by a pitch, Mueller atoned for his error with a double to right, then both runners scored on a double off the centerfield fence by Bellhorn. Boston tacked on a pair of insurance runs in the sixth on a two-run single by Cabrera.

Schilling departed with a 6–1 lead, having allowed four hits and one walk in six innings. The Red Sox bullpen recorded the last nine outs, while only allowing an eighth-inning run. Foulke again retired the last three batters in the ninth.

With the win, Schilling became the first pitcher to win a World Series game for three different teams, having previously notched W's in Game Five of the 1993 World Series for Philadelphia, and in Game One of the 2004 World Series for Arizona.

GAME 3: RED SOX 4, CARDINALS 1

	1	2	3	4	5	6	7	8	9	R	H	E
Boston	1	0	0	1	2	0	0	0	0	4	9	0
St. Louis	0	0	0	0	0	0	0	0	1	1	4	0

WP Pedro Martinez
LP Jeff Suppan

The Cardinals hoped their luck would turn as the series resumed at Busch Stadium in St. Louis after an off-day, but for the second straight game the Red Sox combined stellar starting pitching and early offense to take a commanding three games to none lead.

In the top of the first Ramirez stroked a solo homer into the left field seats off former Red Sox starter Jeff Suppan. The Red Sox never relinquished the lead.

The Cardinals had two excellent scoring opportunities against Martinez in the early innings, but both times the Red Sox defense rose to the challenge to thwart the rallies. In the bottom of the first, the Cardinals loaded the bases with one out on walks to Walker and Scott Rolen, sandwiched between an Albert Pujols single. The next batter, Jim Edmonds, lofted a fly ball to medium depth left field. Ramirez made the catch then threw a perfect one-hop strike to Varitek to cut down Walker at the plate and end the inning. In the Cardinals' third, Suppan led off with an infield single, then advanced to third on a Renteria double. With two men in scoring position, Francona opted to play the infield back, conceding the run at third base in the event of a groundball. Martinez induced Walker to hit a hard grounder to Bellhorn at second, and Cardinal third base coach Jose Oquendo yelled, "Go, go," to Suppan, encouraging him to run home. But Suppan misheard, thinking his coach had yelled, "No, no."[23] He took five steps toward home plate, then froze. Bellhorn threw to Ortiz at first to retire Walker. Ortiz was playing his first game of the postseason in the field due to the game being played in the National League park where there was no designated hitter but he made a perfect throw across the diamond to Mueller, who tagged Suppan out as he attempted to dive back into third base. After the double play, Martinez got Pujols to ground out. Martinez did not allow another base runner. He retired the final 14 batters he faced to finish his seven-inning outing having allowed just three hits and two walks.

The Red Sox padded their lead with a run in the fourth on a Nixon single, and two runs in the fifth on RBI singles by Ramirez and Mueller.

Walker homered in the ninth off Foulke, but it was too little, too late, for the Cardinals, who found themselves on the short end of a 4–1 loss.

Game 4: Red Sox 3, Cardinals 0

	1	2	3	4	5	6	7	8	9	R	H	E
Boston	1	0	2	0	0	0	0	0	0	3	9	0
St. Louis	0	0	0	0	0	0	0	0	0	0	4	0

WP Derek Lowe
LP Jason Marquis
SV Keith Foulke

The Red Sox entered Game Four vying to set a record with their eighth straight postseason win, and become the 18th team to register a World Series sweep. A full lunar eclipse occurred during the game, before the Red Sox ended 86 years of frustration and earned their sixth world championship.

For the fifth straight game the Red Sox scored in the first inning, and for the third straight game their starting pitcher did not allow an earned run.

Damon led off the game by stroking Jason Marquis's fourth pitch into the Cardinal bullpen in right field.

Nixon plated Boston's other two runs, stroking a bases-loaded double off the right field fence on a 3–0 pitch in the third.

The rest of the night belonged to Lowe, who allowed just three hits and one walk in seven innings on the way to his third straight series clinching win.

After Arroyo and Embree combined to retired St. Louis in the eighth, Foulke took over in the ninth, hoping to record the final out in all four World Series games. Pujols led off with a groundball single into center field. Then Rolen flied out to Gabe Kapler in right, and Edmonds struck out on three straight pitches. Renteria tapped to Foulke for the final out. After fielding the chopper, the closer ran half way to first base before under-handing the ball to Mientkiewicz. The first baseman threw both hands in the air in celebration, while Foulke turned to face Varitek, who leapt into his arms. The Red Sox were world champions for the first time since 1918.

The players celebrated briefly on the field before retiring to the visiting clubhouse and then returning to the field with the World Series trophy in their arms. Several thousand Red Sox fans assembled in the stands above the third base dugout to cheer for the team. Back inside the clubhouse, the celebration continued with Schilling pouring a victory beer over the head of the aged Johnny Pesky and then proposing a champagne toast to "the greatest Red Sox team ever assembled."[24]

Ramirez, who registered at least one hit in all 14 postseason games, and who batted .412 over the final four games, was named World Series MVP. Mueller (.429), Nixon (.357), Ortiz (.308), and Bellhorn (.300) also shined in the series.

New England was jubilant in the days and weeks following the historic win. After a sleepless night of celebration in St. Louis, the Red Sox landed at Logan Airport shortly before 7:00 A.M. on October 28. Tens of thousands of fans lined the route the team bus took from the airport to Fenway Park.

Two days later the largest crowd ever to gather in Boston assembled along a three-mile

The Red Sox clinched the World Series at Busch Stadium.

parade route in Boston's Back Bay and along the banks of the Charles River for a championship parade dubbed the "Rolling Rally."[25] Hanging out of office windows, standing on rooftops, and lining the streets thirty people deep, an estimated 3.2 million people cheered for the world champions as they rolled past in a convoy of amphibious "duck boats" that began at Fenway Park and ended up floating on the Charles. "The parade was like being at a rock concert for three straight hours, but you're moving," Varitek said afterward. "I can't tell you how happy those people were."[26]

After 86 years of waiting the Red Sox were not finished celebrating yet. Lucchino and the Red Sox front office pledged that the 2004 World Series trophy would visit all 351 cities and towns in the Commonwealth of Massachusetts before the next season began, and the team made good on its promise, finally finishing the tour in Gosnold, the smallest town in Massachusetts, that, perhaps not-so-coincidentally, had an official 2004 population of 86.

Chapter 19

The Regular Season: 95–67

The Red Sox finished the 2005 season tied for first place in the American League's Eastern division with the Yankees, as both teams posted 95–67 records. Because both teams had already qualified for the playoffs, they did not play an extra game to decide the division champion. Instead, the Yankees were granted the AL East crown by virtue of their 10–9 record against the Red Sox in head-to-head competition, and the Red Sox were granted the AL Wild Card. Boston clinched its postseason berth on the season's final day when Wild Card contender Cleveland lost to Chicago an hour before Boston completed a 10–1 win over New York behind the superb pitching of Curt Schilling at Fenway Park. While the season finale was exciting, it did not leave the Red Sox well positioned for a lengthy postseason run. Because Schilling had started the 162nd regular season game, he was not slated to pitch in the American League Division Series until the fourth game, and he never got the chance as the White Sox beat the Red Sox in a three-game sweep.

After the 2004 World Series, a busy off-season saw the Red Sox lose free agent pitchers Pedro Martinez and Derek Lowe to the Mets and Dodgers respectively, and re-sign catcher Jason Varitek. Boston acquired free agents Matt Clement and David Wells to shore up the rotation, and Edgar Renteria to anchor the shortstop position left vacant when Orlando Cabrera signed with the Angels as a free agent.

Because Schilling opened the season on the disabled list, nursing a surgically repaired right ankle, the Red Sox sent Wells to the mound in New York on Opening Day. The big lefty's opponent was new Yankee ace Randy Johnson. The Red Sox lost 9–2, then dropped the next game when Derek Jeter hit a ninth-inning walk-off homer against Keith Foulke. The Red Sox rebounded to win the series finale, then lost two out of three games in Baltimore before heading to Boston for the home opener.

For many Red Sox fans, the highlight of the 2005 season was April 11, Opening Day at Fenway Park. That was the day that the 2004 championship banner was raised in Boston, and that members of the 2004 team received their World Series rings. Just as the Red Sox' championship parade in the autumn of 2004 forever raised the bar as far as championship celebrations are concerned, the Red Sox presented a more elaborate Opening Day ceremony than any the game had seen before.

The event took place on a sun-struck April afternoon with members of the archrival Yankees looking on from the top step of Fenway's visitors' dugout. The festivities began with members of the Boston Symphony Orchestra and Boston Pops playing as the team unfurled massive World Series championship banners from the top of the famous Green Monster in left field. A different bright red banner unfurled to commemorate each of the Red Sox' previous five World Series titles — 1903, 1912, 1915, 1916, and 1918 — the banners spanning from the top of the wall down to the dirt of the warning track. Finally, the biggest banner of all unfurled from the top of the wall, this one spanning the entire length of the Green Monster, and covering all of the others banners. It read "2004 World Champions."

Next, singer/songwriter James Taylor took the field and performed "America the Beautiful," while several soldiers who had been injured in combat in the ongoing Iraq conflict walked from left field to the infield carrying the World Series trophy and the World Series rings. The players and coaches of the 2004 team then followed a red carpet from the Red Sox dugout to first base where Red Sox owners John Henry and Tom Werner and team president Larry Lucchino presented them with their World Series rings. Even former Red Sox players Lowe and Dave Roberts were on hand, having received special permission from the Dodgers and Padres respectively to attend the event. Each player wore his old Red Sox jerseys as he accepted his ring amidst thunderous applause from the capacity crowd that had packed the old ballpark. But no ovation was louder than the one granted 85-year-old Johnny Pesky who accepted his ring in full uniform, wearing his old number 6. Just when the last of the Red Sox players, coaches and trainers had received their rings, and it appeared a splendid ceremony was drawing to an end, the event took another delightful turn. Suddenly, from behind the massive banner that spanned the Green Monster, there emerged dozens of former Red Sox — both stars and role players — wearing vintage uniforms from their respective eras. The current edition of the team walked from first base to center field to meet the old-timers. Among the faces from Red Sox teams past suddenly appearing on the field were those belonging to Luis Tiant, Rico Petrocelli, Rick Miller, Sam Horn, Dennis "Oil Can" Boyd, Dennis Eckersley, Dwight Evans, Jim Rice, Carl Yastrzemski, Carlton Fisk, Dominic DiMaggio, Butch Hobson and Joe Morgan. These honorary World Champions greeted the members of the 2004 team, then all looked on as Pesky and Yastrzemski raised the 2004 World Champions flag on the center field flagpole.

The players, past and present, then walked across the field and filed into the Red Sox dugout. After the members of the 2005 Yankees and 2005 Red Sox were introduced and after they'd shaken hands and lined the third and first base lines, the Red Sox offered one final surprise. From behind the banner that still spanned the left field wall, a quartet of Boston legends suddenly appeared: Celtics great Bill Russell, Bruins great Bobby Orr, and Richard Seymour and Teddy Bruschi of the three-time Super Bowl champion New England Patriots. The four men walked from left field to the pitcher's mound, where each delivered a ceremonial first pitch.

Finally it was time for the new season to begin at Fenway, and the Red Sox did not disappoint, earning an 8–1 victory behind the dancing knuckleball of Tim Wakefield. The Red Sox would post a league-best 54–27 home record in 2005, attract a team-record 2,847,888 fans to the Fens, and extend their home sell-out streak to 226 consecutive games. But the campaign would present far more obstacles than the previous season had, and in the end the 2005 Red Sox would be exposed as a less complete team than the 2004 edition.

The 2005 Red Sox could hit. Boston finished with a team batting average of .281 to lead the AL. And the Red Sox led the circuit in runs (910) for the third straight season, becoming the first team since the 1951–54 Brooklyn Dodgers to do so. David Ortiz and Manny Ramirez led the way, combining to hit 92 home runs and drive in 292 runs, while forming the most potent one-two punch in the big leagues. From the start, though, the team's Achilles heel was its pitching staff. Although Wells and Clement won 15 and 13 games respectively, in effect replacing Martinez and Lowe in the starting rotation, Schilling and Foulke performed below their 2004 levels. Foulke had his season cut short by knee surgery and finished with 15 saves and a 5.91 ERA, while Schilling pitched out of the bullpen for several weeks while building up strength in his ankle and finished 8–8 with a 5.69 ERA. With the ace and closer performing below expectations, the Red Sox finished 11th in the league with a 4.97 ERA, and last in the league with a 5.17 bullpen ERA.

The clubhouse harmony of 2004 was also lacking. When Foulke was placed on the disabled list in early July and Schilling volunteered to pitch out of the bullpen, for example, Johnny Damon publicly stated that a contingent of players were upset with the move. "You've got a lot of upset people in here," Damon said. "I don't think he's ready to be our closer. I think Bronson [Arroyo] or [Mike] Timlin are the choice as the closer."[1]

Later, in July, *Sports Illustrated* broke the news that Ramirez had requested a trade due to privacy concerns related to playing in Boston. Lucchino downplayed the request in the next day's newspapers, saying "Manny's made the request consistently all [the] years [we've] been here. It's not anything unusual. It's a rite of passage. It was the fourth time."[2] Nonetheless, as the July 31 trade deadline approached, Red Sox players and fans waited to see if the team's prize slugger would get his wish. Ramirez was a last-minute scratch from the lineup on July 30 as the Red Sox hosted the Twins. Likewise, he was not in the lineup when the Red Sox and Twins met the next day as the trade deadline loomed at 4:00 P.M. Rumors had Ramirez possibly heading to the Mets in a three-team swap that would net center fielder Mike Cameron from the Mets and first baseman Aubrey Huff from the Devil Rays. Forty-five minutes after the trade deadline had passed, though, Ramirez resurfaced in the Red Sox dugout and registered an eighth-inning pinch-hit single to propel the Red Sox past the Twins 4–3.

Buoyed by Ramirez's game-winning hit, the Red Sox began August with a 59–45 record, good for a 2½ game lead over the Yankees. By September 1, the Red Sox had stretched the lead to 3½ games. On Saturday September 10, Schilling pitched his best game of the year, winning 9–2 at Yankee Stadium, and increasing Boston's lead in the division to four games. But the Yankees finished with 16 wins in their final 21 games, while the Red Sox finished with 12 wins in 21 games. By virtue of the head-to-head tiebreaker, the Yankees had won their eighth straight division title. And the Red Sox had captured their third consecutive Wild Card berth.

The Postseason: 0–3

As the 2005 playoffs began, a third consecutive Red Sox versus Yankees showdown in the ALCS loomed as a distinct possibility. But another chapter in the teams' blood feud was

Ortiz pops out at Fenway.

not to be. Neither team escaped the first round of the playoffs. The Yankees fell to the Angels, and the Red Sox bowed to the White Sox. The Division Series between Boston and Chicago pitted two teams with very different organizational philosophies. The Red Sox won by out-slugging teams, while manager Ozzie Guillen's White Sox won by playing "small ball." The White Sox lacked the offensive firepower that the Red Sox had, but were more adept at manufacturing runs with heady base running, well-placed hits and sacrifice bunts. The White Sox' 61–34 record in games decided by two runs or less served as testament to the effectiveness of this approach.

The AL Central champs finished with the best record in the league, 99–63, despite finishing ninth in runs with 741 and 11th in batting average with a .262 mark. Chicago's league-best 3.61 ERA made up for its mediocre offense. Four White Sox starters won at least 14 games: Jon Garland (18–10, 3.50 ERA), Mark Buehrle (16–8, 3.12 ERA), Freddy Garcia (14–8, 3.87 ERA) and Jose Contreras (15–7, 3.61 ERA). The team's best hitter was first baseman Paul Konerko (.283, 40 HR, 100 RBI), while right fielder Jermaine Dye (.274, 31 HR, 86 RBI), designated hitter Carl Everett (.251, 23 HR, 87 RBI), and center fielder Scott Podsednik (.290, 59 stolen bases) also made major contributions to the lineup.

The eventual world champions outperformed the Red Sox in all facets of the game in the three-game sweep.

American League Division Series:
White Sox 3, Red Sox 0

GAME 1: WHITE SOX 14, RED SOX 2

	1	2	3	4	5	6	7	8	9	R	H	E
Boston	0	0	0	2	0	0	0	0	0	2	9	0
Chicago	5	0	1	2	0	4	0	2	X	14	11	1

WP   Jose Contreras
LP   Matt Clement

The series began with an afternoon tilt at Chicago's US Cellular Field. The White Sox had not won a home playoff game since 1959 and had not won a playoff series since winning the 1917 World Series. Before the day was out, the White Sox would end the first streak, and have a leg up on ending the second. As for the Red Sox, the 12-run margin of defeat represented the widest losing margin in their postseason history.

Because the Red Sox did not clinch a playoff spot until the final game of the regular season, manager Terry Francona was unable to align the pitching staff to his liking. His only option was to start the struggling Clement in Game One. After a sparkling Red Sox debut that saw him make the 2005 AL All-Star squad with a 10–2 first half record, Clement had struggled mightily in the second half. He never regained his winning form after being struck in the head by a line drive by Tampa Bay's Carl Crawford on July 26. Clement entered the playoffs having lost his final three starts of the season regular, while his counterpart, Contreras, entered the series riding an eight-game win streak.

After Contreras retired the Red Sox in the top of the first, Clement hit two of the first three batters he faced with pitches, Podsednik and Dye. After Konerko plated one run with a fielder's choice and Aaron Rowand drove home another with a single to center, Chicago catcher A.J. Pierzynski launched a three-run homer to right-center to put the White Sox ahead 5–0.

Konerko's homer in the bottom of the third extended the lead to 6–0, before the Red Sox plated a pair of runs in the fourth on a Contreras wild pitch and an RBI double by Kevin Millar. Clement allowed yet another home run in the bottom of the fourth, though, a two-run blast to Chicago's number-nine hitter, Juan Uribe, to make it 8–2. Finally, Francona made his way to the mound to take the ball from Clement. In 3⅓ innings, Clement yielded eight earned runs, the most ever by a Red Sox pitcher in a playoff game. The Red Sox bullpen did not fare much better, allowing another six runs.

GAME 2: WHITE SOX 5, RED SOX 4

	1	2	3	4	5	6	7	8	9	R	H	E
Boston	2	0	2	0	0	0	0	0	0	4	9	1
Chicago	0	0	0	0	5	0	0	0	X	5	9	0

WP   Mark Buehrle
LP   David Wells
SV   Bobby Jenks

The second game presented a match-up of two left-handed starters, Buehrle for the White Sox and Wells for the Red Sox. Boston's southpaw pitched the better game, but his defense failed him, and by day's end the Red Sox found themselves facing a two-game deficit.

The game's pivotal play occurred in the bottom of the fifth inning when an error by Red Sox second baseman Tony Graffanino opened the floodgates for three unearned runs that proved the difference in the game. The White Sox had already scored two runs to cut the Red Sox lead to 4–2, when Uribe came to the plate with one out and a runner on first base. After fouling off several pitches, he hit a tailor-made double play grounder to Graffanino. But the second baseman lifted his head at the last minute and the ball rolled through his legs and into right field, giving the White Sox runners at the corners with still only one out. After Wells induced Podsednik to pop up for the second out, second baseman Tadahito Iguchi stepped into the batters box for the White Sox. Wells threw ball one, then made Iguchi look bad on a sharp curveball. When Wells tried to sneak a second straight curve past Iguchi, though, the Japanese League import did not miss. He drove the ball into the left field bleachers for a three-run homer, to put the White Sox ahead 5–4.

"I just missed it," Graffanino said of the error that gave the White Sox two extra outs. "Any time you get a ground ball like that you try to get the double play and get out of the inning. I took my eye off of it and missed it. That's a ball you need to catch."[3]

Prior to the White Sox' five-run fifth inning, the Red Sox had scored two runs in the first inning and two in the fourth. After Damon led off the game with a single to left field and Renteria stroked a double to left-center, Ramirez plated both runners with a single. Boston padded the lead in the fourth on an RBI single by Varitek and a fielder's choice by Trot Nixon.

The Red Sox had a chance to tie the game in the ninth when Graffanino reached on a one-out double. But White Sox rookie closer Bobby Jenks retired Damon on a pop-up to the catcher, and Renteria on a groundout to shortstop, to end the game.

GAME 3: WHITE SOX 5, RED SOX 3

	1	2	3	4	5	6	7	8	9	R	H	E
Chicago	0	0	2	0	0	2	0	0	1	5	8	0
Boston	0	0	0	2	0	1	0	0	0	3	7	1

WP Freddy Garcia
LP Tim Wakefield
SV Bobby Jenks

With the series shifting to Boston, Red Sox fans hoped the home cooking that had helped the team overcome two-games-to-none deficits in the 1999 and 2003 Division Series would awaken the team's sleeping offense. The 35,496 fans who packed Fenway Park on a chilly Friday afternoon left disappointed though, as an old nemesis from the Red Sox-Yankees rivalry resurfaced to clinch the series for the White Sox.

Chicago scored a pair of runs in the third inning on RBI hits by Podsednik and Iguchi, but the Red Sox tied the game at 2–2 in the fourth on back-to-back homers by Ortiz and Ramirez.

After the White Sox scored two more on a Konerko homer in the sixth, the Red Sox got a run back when Ramirez led off the bottom of the inning with his second homer of the day. Boston was poised to do a lot more offensively in the sixth, as the three batters that followed Ramirez all reached base. With the White Sox clinging to a 4–3 lead, Guillen summoned the ageless Orlando "El Duque" Hernandez from the Chicago bullpen. Hernandez entered a bases-loaded, no-outs situation. First, he induced Varitek to pop out, then he retired Graffanino on a pop out on a 3–2 pitch, then he struck out Damon on a 3–2 slider in the dirt. Damon tried to check his swing, but to no avail.

Having squandered a terrific chance to tie the game and perhaps take the lead, the Red Sox batters went down quietly against Hernandez in the seventh and eighth innings.

The White Sox added a run in the top of the ninth on a squeeze bunt by Uribe that scored Pierzynski, then Jenks retired the Red Sox in order in the bottom of the ninth. Oddly, Boston's season ended just as its previous one had, on a Renteria groundout.

The White Sox went on to beat the Angels in five games in the ALCS, then they swept the Astros in the World Series.

Appendix I: Regular Season Results

Year	Record	Finish	Regular Season Title
1901	79–57	2	
1902	77–60	3	
1903	91–47	1	AL Champion
1904	95–59	1*	AL Champion
1905	78–74	4	
1906	49–105	8	
1907	59–90	7	
1908	75–79	5	
1909	88–63	3	
1910	81–72	4	
1911	78–75	5	
1912	105–47	1	AL Champion
1913	79–71	4	
1914	91–62	2	
1915	101–50	1	AL Champion
1916	91–63	1	AL Champion
1917	90–62	2	
1918	75–51	1	AL Champion
1919	66–71	5	
1920	72–81	5	
1921	75–79	5	
1922	61–93	8	

*The World Series was not played due to a dispute between the AL and NL.

Year	Record	Finish	Regular Season Title
1923	61–91	8	
1924	67–87	7	
1925	47–105	8	
1926	46–107	8	
1927	51–103	8	
1928	57–96	8	
1929	58–96	8	
1930	52–102	8	
1931	62–90	6	
1932	43–111	8	
1933	63–86	7	
1934	76–76	4	
1935	78–75	4	
1936	74–80	6	
1937	80–72	5	
1938	88–61	2	
1939	89–62	2	
1940	82–72	5	
1941	84–70	2	
1942	93–59	2	
1943	68–84	7	
1944	77–77	4	
1945	71–83	7	
1946	104–50	1	AL Champion
1947	83–71	3	
1948	96–59	2†	
1949	96–58	2	
1950	94–60	3	
1951	87–67	3	
1952	76–78	6	
1953	84–69	4	
1954	69–85	4	
1955	84–70	4	
1956	84–70	4	
1957	82–72	3	
1958	79–75	3	
1959	75–79	5	
1960	65–89	7	
1961	76–86	6	
1962	76–84	8	
1963	76–85	7	
1964	72–90	8	
1965	62–100	9	

Year	Record	Finish	Regular Season Title
1966	72–90	9	
1967	92–70	1	AL Champion
1968	86–76	4	
1969	87–75	3	
1970	87–75	3	
1971	85–77	3	
1972	85–70	2	
1973	89–73	2	
1974	84–78	3	
1975	95–65	1	AL East Champion
1976	83–79	3	
1977	97–64	3	
1978	99–64	2†	
1979	91–69	3	
1980	83–77	4	
1981	59–49	5	
1982	89–73	3	
1983	78–84	6	
1984	86–76	4	
1985	81–81	5	
1986	95–66	1	AL East Champion
1987	78–84	5	
1988	89–73	1	AL East Champion
1989	83–79	3	
1990	88–74	1	AL East Champion
1991	84–78	2	
1992	73–89	7	
1993	80–82	5	
1994	54–61	4	
1995	86–58	1	AL East Champion
1996	85–77	3	
1997	78–84	4	
1998	92–70	2	Wild Card
1999	94–68	2	Wild Card
2000	85–77	2	
2001	82–79	2	
2002	93–69	2	
2003	95–67	2	Wild Card
2004	98–64	2	Wild Card
2005	95–67	2	Wild Card

†*Finished tied for first place, prompting a one-game playoff*

Appendix II: Postseason Results

1903

WORLD SERIES

Game 1, October 1, at Boston: Pittsburgh Pirates 7; Boston Americans 3
Game 2, October 2, at Boston: Boston Americans 3; Pittsburgh Pirates 0
Game 3, October 3, at Boston: Pittsburgh Pirates 4; Boston Americans 2
Game 4, October 6, at Pittsburgh: Pittsburgh Pirates 5; Boston Americans 4
Game 5, October 7, at Pittsburgh: Boston Americans 11; Pittsburgh Pirates 2
Game 6, October 8, at Pittsburgh: Boston Americans 6; Pittsburgh Pirates 3
Game 7, October 10, at Pittsburgh: Boston Americans 7; Pittsburgh Pirates 3
Game 8, October 13, at Boston: Boston Americans 3; Pittsburgh Pirates 0

1912

WORLD SERIES

Game 1, October 8, at New York: Boston Red Sox 4; New York Giants 3
Game 2, October 9, at Boston: New York Giants 6; Boston Red Sox 6 (11 innings)
Game 3, October 10, at Boston: New York Giants 2; Boston Red Sox 1
Game 4, October 11, at New York: Boston Red Sox 3; New York Giants 1
Game 5, October 12, at Boston: Boston Red Sox 2; New York Giants 1
Game 6, October 14, at New York: New York Giants 5; Boston Red Sox 2
Game 7, October 15, at Boston: New York Giants 11; Boston Red Sox 4
Game 8, October 16, at Boston: Boston Red Sox 3; New York Giants 2 (10 innings)

1915

WORLD SERIES

Game 1, October 8, at Philadelphia: Philadelphia Phillies 3; Boston Red Sox 1
Game 2, October 9, at Philadelphia: Boston Red Sox 2; Philadelphia Phillies 1
Game 3, October 11, at Boston: Boston Red Sox 2; Philadelphia Phillies 1
Game 4, October 12, at Boston: Boston Red Sox 2; Philadelphia Phillies 1
Game 5, October 13, at Philadelphia: Boston Red Sox 5; Philadelphia Phillies 4

1916

WORLD SERIES

Game 1, October 7, at Boston: Boston Red Sox 6; Brooklyn Robins 5
Game 2, October 9, at Boston: Boston Red Sox 2; Brooklyn Robins 1 (14 innings)
Game 3, October 10, at Brooklyn: Brooklyn Robins 4; Boston Red Sox 3
Game 4, October 11, at Brooklyn: Boston Red Sox 6; Brooklyn Robins 2
Game 5, October 12, at Boston: Boston Red Sox 4; Brooklyn Robins 1

1918

WORLD SERIES

Game 1, September 5, at Chicago: Boston Red Sox 1; Chicago Cubs 0
Game 2, September 6, at Chicago: Chicago Cubs 3; Boston Red Sox 1
Game 3, September 7, at Chicago: Boston Red Sox 2; Chicago Cubs 1
Game 4, September 9, at Boston: Boston Red Sox 3; Chicago Cubs 2
Game 5, September 10, at Boston: Chicago Cubs 3; Boston Red Sox 0
Game 6, September 11, at Boston: Boston Red Sox 2; Chicago Cubs 1

1946

WORLD SERIES

Game 1, October 6, at St. Louis: Boston Red Sox 3; St. Louis Cardinals 2 (10 innings)
Game 2, October 7, at St. Louis: St. Louis Cardinals 3; Boston Red Sox 0
Game 3, October 9, at Boston: Boston Red Sox 4; St. Louis Cardinals 0
Game 4, October 10, at Boston: St. Louis Cardinals 12; Boston Red Sox 3
Game 5, October 11, at Boston: Boston Red Sox 6, St. Louis Cardinals 3
Game 6, October 13, at St. Louis: St. Louis Cardinals 4; Boston Red Sox 1
Game 7, October 15, at St. Louis: St. Louis Cardinals 4; Boston Red Sox 3

1948

ONE-GAME PLAYOFF

Game 1, October 4, at Boston: Cleveland Indians 8; Boston Red Sox 3

1967

WORLD SERIES

Game 1, October 4, at Boston: St. Louis Cardinals 2; Boston Red Sox 1
Game 2, October 5, at Boston: Boston Red Sox 5; St. Louis Cardinals 0
Game 3, October 7, at St. Louis: St. Louis Cardinals 5; Boston Red Sox 2
Game 4, October 8, at St. Louis: St. Louis Cardinals 6; Boston Red Sox 0
Game 5, October 9, at St. Louis: Boston Red Sox 3; St. Louis Cardinals 1
Game 6, October 11, at Boston: Boston Red Sox 8; St. Louis Cardinals 4
Game 7, October 12, at Boston: St. Louis Cardinals 7; Boston Red Sox 2

1975

AMERICAN LEAGUE CHAMPIONSHIP SERIES

Game 1, October 4, at Boston: Boston Red Sox 7; Oakland Athletics 1
Game 2, October 5, at Boston: Boston Red Sox 6; Oakland Athletics 3
Game 3, October 7, at Oakland: Boston Red Sox 5; Oakland Athletics 3

WORLD SERIES

Game 1, October 11, at Boston: Boston Red Sox 6; Cincinnati Reds 0
Game 2, October 12, at Boston: Cincinnati Reds 3; Boston Red Sox 2
Game 3, October 14, at Cincinnati: Cincinnati Reds 6; Boston Red Sox 5 (10 innings)
Game 4, October 15, at Cincinnati: Boston Red Sox 5; Cincinnati Reds 4
Game 5, October 16, at Cincinnati: Cincinnati Reds 6; Boston Red Sox 2
Game 6, October 21, at Boston: Boston Red Sox 7; Cincinnati Reds 6 (12 innings)
Game 7, October 22, at Boston: Cincinnati Reds 4; Boston Red Sox 3

1978

ONE-GAME PLAYOFF

Game 1, October 2, at Boston: New York Yankees 5; Boston Red Sox 4

1986

AMERICAN LEAGUE CHAMPIONSHIP SERIES

Game 1, October 7, at Boston: California Angels 8; Boston Red Sox 1
Game 2, October 8, at Boston: Boston Red Sox 9; California Angels 2
Game 3, October 10, at California: California Angels 5; Boston Red Sox 3
Game 4, October 11, at California: California Angels 4; Boston Red Sox 3 (11 innings)
Game 5, October 12, at California: Boston Red Sox 7; California Angels 6 (11 innings)
Game 6, October 14, at Boston: Boston Red Sox 10; California Angels 4
Game 7, October 15, at Boston: Boston Red Sox 8; California Angels 1

WORLD SERIES

Game 1, October 18, at New York: Boston Red Sox 1; New York Mets 0
Game 2, October 19, at New York: Boston Red Sox 9; New York Mets 3
Game 3, October 21, at Boston: New York Mets 7; Boston Red Sox 1
Game 4, October 22, at Boston: New York Mets 6; Boston Red Sox 2
Game 5, October 23, at Boston: Boston Red Sox 4; New York Mets 2
Game 6, October 25, at New York: New York Mets 6; Boston Red Sox 5 (10 innings)
Game 7, October 27, at New York: New York Mets 8; Boston Red Sox 5

1988

AMERICAN LEAGUE CHAMPIONSHIP SERIES

Game 1, October 5, at Boston: Oakland Athletics 2; Boston Red Sox 1
Game 2, October 6, at Boston: Oakland Athletics 4; Boston Red Sox 3
Game 3, October 8, at Oakland: Oakland Athletics 10; Boston Red Sox 6
Game 4, October 9, at Oakland: Oakland Athletics: 4; Boston Red Sox 1

1990

AMERICAN LEAGUE CHAMPIONSHIP SERIES

Game 1, October 6, at Boston: Oakland Athletics 9; Boston Red Sox 1
Game 2, October 7, at Boston: Oakland Athletics 4; Boston Red Sox 1
Game 3, October 9, at Oakland: Oakland Athletics 4; Boston Red Sox 1
Game 4, October 10, at Oakland: Oakland Athletics 3; Boston Red Sox 1

1995

AMERICAN LEAGUE DIVISION SERIES

Game 1, October 3, at Cleveland: Cleveland Indians 5; Boston Red Sox 4 (13 innings)
Game 2, October 4, at Cleveland: Cleveland Indians 4; Boston Red Sox 0
Game 3, October 6, at Cleveland: Cleveland Indians 8; Boston Red Sox 2

1998

AMERICAN LEAGUE DIVISION SERIES

Game 1, September 29, at Cleveland: Boston Red Sox 11; Cleveland Indians 3
Game 2, September 30, at Cleveland: Cleveland Indians 9; Boston Red Sox 5
Game 3, October 2, at Boston: Cleveland Indians 4; Boston Red Sox 3
Game 4, October 3, at Boston: Cleveland Indians 2; Boston Red Sox 1

1999

AMERICAN LEAGUE DIVISION SERIES

Game 1, October 6, at Cleveland: Cleveland Indians 3; Boston Red Sox 2
Game 2, October 7, at Cleveland: Cleveland Indians 11; Boston Red Sox 1
Game 3, October 9, at Boston: Boston Red Sox 9; Cleveland Indians 3
Game 4, October 10, at Boston: Boston Red Sox 23; Cleveland Indians 7
Game 5, October 11, at Cleveland: Boston Red Sox 12; Cleveland Indians 8

AMERICAN LEAGUE CHAMPIONSHIP SERIES

Game 1, October 13, at New York: New York Yankees 4; Boston Red Sox 3 (10 innings)
Game 2, October 14, at New York: New York Yankees 3; Boston Red Sox 2
Game 3, October 16, at Boston: Boston Red Sox 13; New York Yankees 1
Game 4, October 17, at Boston: New York Yankees 9; Boston Red Sox 2
Game 5, October 18, at Boston: New York Yankees 6; Boston Red Sox 1

2003

AMERICAN LEAGUE DIVISION SERIES

Game 1, October 1, at Oakland: Oakland Athletics 5; Boston Red Sox 4 (12 innings)
Game 2, October 2, at Oakland: Oakland Athletics 5; Boston Red Sox 1
Game 3, October 4, at Boston: Boston Red Sox 3; Oakland Athletics 1 (11 innings)
Game 4, October 5, at Boston: Boston Red Sox 5; Oakland Athletics 4
Game 5; October 6, at Oakland: Boston Red Sox 4; Oakland Athletics 3

AMERICAN LEAGUE CHAMPIONSHIP SERIES

Game 1, October 8, at New York: Boston Red Sox 5; New York Yankees 2
Game 2, October 9, at New York: New York Yankees 6; Boston Red Sox 2
Game 3, October 11, at Boston: New York Yankees 4; Boston Red Sox 3
Game 4, October 13, at Boston: Boston Red Sox 3; New York Yankees 2
Game 5, October 14, at Boston: New York Yankees 4; Boston Red Sox 2
Game 6, October 15, at New York: Boston Red Sox 9; New York Yankees 6
Game 7, October 16, at New York: New York Yankees 6; Boston Red Sox 5 (11 innings)

2004

AMERICAN LEAGUE DIVISION SERIES

Game 1, October 5, at Anaheim: Boston Red Sox 9; Anaheim Angels 3
Game 2, October 6, at Anaheim: Boston Red Sox 8; Anaheim Angels 3
Game 3, October 8, at Boston: Boston Red Sox 8; Anaheim Angels 6 (10 innings)

AMERICAN LEAGUE CHAMPIONSHIP SERIES

Game 1, October 12, at New York: New York Yankees 10; Boston Red Sox 7
Game 2, October 13, at New York: New York Yankees 3; Boston Red Sox 1
Game 3, October 16, at Boston: New York Yankees 19; Boston Red Sox 8
Game 4, October 17, at Boston: Boston Red Sox 6; New York Yankees 4 (12 innings)
Game 5, October 18, at Boston: Boston Red Sox 5; New York Yankees 4 (14 innings)
Game 6, October 19, at New York: Boston Red Sox 4; New York Yankees 2
Game 7, October 20, at New York: Boston Red Sox 10; New York Yankees 3

WORLD SERIES

Game 1, October 23, at Boston: Boston Red Sox 11; St. Louis Cardinals 9
Game 2, October 24, at Boston: Boston Red Sox 6; St. Louis Cardinals 2
Game 3, October 26, at St. Louis: Boston Red Sox 4; St. Louis Cardinals 1
Game 4, October 27, at St. Louis: Boston Red Sox 3; St. Louis Cardinals 0

2005

AMERICAN LEAGUE DIVISION SERIES

Game 1, October 4, at Chicago: Chicago White Sox 14; Boston Red Sox 2
Game 2, October 5, at Chicago: Chicago White Sox 5; Boston Red Sox 4
Game 3, October 7, at Boston: Chicago White Sox 5; Boston Red Sox 3

Appendix III: Postseason Statistics

1903 World Series: Boston vs. Pittsburgh

Boston Americans

	G	AB	R	H	2B	3B	HR	RBI	BB	SO	BA	OBP	SLG	SB
Jimmy Collins	8	36	5	9	1	2	0	1	1	1	.250	.270	.389	3
Lou Criger	8	26	1	6	0	0	0	4	2	3	.231	.286	.231	0
Bill Dineen	4	11	1	2	0	0	0	0	2	2	.182	.308	.182	0
Patsy Dougherty	8	34	3	8	0	2	2	5	2	6	.235	.297	.529	0
Duke Farrell	2	1	0	0	0	0	0	1	0	0	.000	.000	.000	0
Hobe Ferris	8	31	3	9	0	1	0	5	0	6	.290	.312	.355	0
Buck Freeman	8	31	6	9	0	3	0	4	2	2	.290	.324	.484	0
Tom Hughes	1	0	0	0	0	0	0	0	0	0				0
Candy LaChance	8	25	5	6	2	1	0	4	3	2	.240	.300	.400	0
Jack O'Brien	2	2	0	0	0	0	0	0	0	1	.000	.000	.000	0
Freddy Parent	8	31	8	9	0	3	0	4	1	1	.290	.324	.484	0
Chic Stahl	8	33	6	10	1	3	0	3	1	2	.303	.324	.515	2
Cy Young	4	15	1	1	0	1	0	3	0	3	.067	.067	.200	0
Total	8	276	39	69	4	16	2	34	14	29	.250	.289	.402	5

	G	ERA	W–L	SV	CG	IP	H	ER	BB	SO
Bill Dineen	4	2.06	3–1	0	4	35.0	29	8	8	28
Cy Young	4	1.85	2–1	0	3	34.0	31	7	4	17
Tom Hughes	1	9.00	0–1	0	0	2.0	4	2	2	0
Total	8	2.15	5–3	0	7	71.0	64	17	14	45

Pittsburgh Pirates

	G	AB	R	H	2B	3B	HR	RBI	BB	SO	BA	OBP	SLG	SB
Ginger Beaumont	8	34	6	9	0	1	0	1	2	4	.265	.306	.324	2
Kitty Bransfield	8	29	3	6	0	2	0	1	1	6	.207	.233	.345	1

(continued)	G	AB	R	H	2B	3B	HR	RBI	BB	SO	BA	OBP	SLG	SB
Fred Clarke	8	34	3	9	2	1	0	2	1	5	.265	.286	.382	1
Brickyard Kennedy	1	2	0	1	1	0	0	0	0	0	.500	.500	1.00	0
Tommy Leach	8	33	3	9	0	4	0	7	1	4	.273	.294	.515	1
Sam Leever	2	4	0	0	0	0	0	0	0	0	.000	.000	.000	0
Ed Phelps	8	26	1	6	2	0	0	1	1	6	.231	.259	.308	0
Deacon Phillippe	5	18	1	4	0	0	0	1	0	3	.222	.222	.222	0
Claude Ritchey	8	27	2	4	1	0	0	2	4	7	.148	.258	.185	1
Jimmy Sebring	8	30	3	10	0	1	1	4	1	4	.333	.355	.500	0
Harry Smith	1	3	0	0	0	0	0	0	0	0	.000	.000	.000	0
Gus Thompson	1	1	0	0	0	0	0	0	0	0	.000	.000	.000	0
Bucky Veil	1	2	0	0	0	0	0	0	0	2	.000	.000	.000	0
Honus Wagner	8	27	2	6	1	0	0	3	3	4	.222	.323	.259	3
TOTAL	8	270	24	64	7	9	1	22	14	45	.237	.277	.341	9

	G	ERA	W–L	SV	CG	IP	H	ER	BB	SO
Deacon Phillippe	5	3.07	3–2	0	5	44.0	38	15	3	22
Sam Leever	2	5.40	0–2	0	1	10.0	13	6	3	2
Brickyard Kennedy	1	5.14	0–1	0	0	7.0	10	4	3	3
Bucky Veil	1	1.29	0–0	0	0	7.0	5	1	5	1
Gus Thompson	1	4.50	0–0	0	0	2.0	3	1	0	1
TOTAL	8	3.47	3–5	0	6	70.0	69	27	14	29

1912 World Series: Boston vs. New York

BOSTON RED SOX

	G	AB	R	H	2B	3B	HR	RBI	BB	SO	BA	OBP	SLG	SB
Neal Ball	1	1	0	0	0	0	0	0	0	1	.000	.000	.000	0
Hugh Bedient	4	6	0	0	0	0	0	0	0	0	.000	.000	.000	0
Hick Cady	7	22	1	3	0	0	0	1	0	3	.136	.136	.136	0
Bill Carrigan	2	7	0	0	0	0	0	0	0	0	.000	.000	.000	0
Ray Collins	2	5	0	0	0	0	0	0	0	2	.000	.000	.000	0
Clyde Engle	3	3	1	1	1	0	0	2	0	0	.333	.333	.667	0
Larry Gardner	8	28	4	5	2	1	1	5	2	5	.179	.250	.429	0
Charley Hall	2	4	0	3	1	0	0	0	1	0	.750	.800	1.00	0
Olaf Henriksen	2	1	0	1	1	0	0	1	0	0	1.00	1.000	2.00	0
Harry Hooper	8	31	3	9	2	1	0	2	4	4	.290	.361	.419	1
Duffy Lewis	8	32	4	6	3	0	0	1	2	2	.188	.235	.281	0
Buck O'Brien	2	2	0	0	0	0	0	0	0	2	.000	.000	.000	0
Tris Speaker	8	30	4	9	1	2	0	2	4	2	.300	.382	.467	1
Jake Stahl	8	32	3	8	2	0	0	2	0	6	.250	.250	.312	2
Heinie Wagner	8	30	1	5	1	0	0	3	6	.167	.242	.200	1
Joe Wood	4	7	1	2	0	0	0	1	1	0	.286	.375	.286	0
Steve Yerkes	8	32	3	8	0	2	0	4	2	3	.250	.294	.375	0
TOTAL	8	273	25	60	14	6	1	21	19	36	.220	.271	.326	5

	G	ERA	W–L	SV	CG	IP	H	ER	BB	SO
Joe Wood	4	4.50	3–1	0	2	22.0	27	11	3	21
Hugh Bedient	4	0.50	1–0	0	1	18.0	10	1	7	7

(continued)	G	ERA	W–L	SV	CG	IP	H	ER	BB	SO
Ray Collins	2	1.88	0–0	0	0	14.3	14	3	0	6
Charley Hall	2	3.38	0–0	0	0	10.7	11	4	9	1
Buck O'Brien	2	5.00	0–2	0	0	9.0	12	5	3	4
TOTAL	7	2.92	4–3	0	3	74.0	74	24	22	39

NEW YORK GIANTS

	G	AB	R	H	2B	3B	HR	RBI	BB	SO	BA	OBP	SLG	SB
Red Ames	1	0	0	0	0	0	0	0	0	0				0
Beals Becker	2	4	1	0	0	0	0	0	2	0	.000	.333	.000	0
Doc Crandall	1	1	0	0	0	0	0	0	0	1	.000	.000	.000	0
Josh Devore	7	24	4	6	0	0	0	0	7	5	.250	.419	.250	4
Larry Doyle	8	33	5	8	0	0	1	2	3	2	.242	.306	.333	2
Art Fletcher	8	28	1	5	1	0	0	3	1	4	.179	.207	.214	1
Buck Herzog	8	30	6	12	4	1	0	5	1	3	.400	.412	.600	2
Rube Marquard	2	4	0	0	0	0	0	0	1	0	.000	.200	.000	0
Christy Mathewson	3	12	0	2	0	0	0	0	0	4	.167	.167	.167	0
Moose McCormick	5	4	0	1	0	0	0	1	0	0	.250	.200	.250	0
Fred Merkle	8	33	5	9	2	1	0	3	0	7	.273	.273	.394	0
Chief Meyers	8	28	2	10	0	1	0	3	2	3	.357	.419	.429	1
Red Murray	8	31	5	10	4	1	0	4	2	2	.323	.364	.516	0
Tillie Shafer	3	0	0	0	0	0	0	0	0	0				0
Fred Snodgrass	8	33	2	7	2	0	0	2	2	5	.212	.278	.273	0
Jeff Tesreau	3	8	0	3	0	0	0	2	1	3	.375	.444	.375	0
Art Wilson	2	1	0	1	0	0	0	0	0	0	1.00	1.000	1.00	0
TOTAL	8	274	31	74	13	4	1	25	22	39	.270	.328	.358	11

	G	ERA	W–L	SV	CG	IP	H	ER	BB	SO
Christy Mathewson	3	0.94	0–2	0	3	28.7	23	3	5	10
Jeff Tesreau	3	3.13	1–2	0	1	23.0	19	8	11	15
Rube Marquard	2	0.50	2–0	0	2	18.0	14	1	2	9
Red Ames	1	4.50	0–0	0	0	2.0	3	1	1	0
Doc Crandall	1	0.00	0–0	0	0	2.0	1	0	0	2
TOTAL	7	1.59	3–4	0	6	73.7	60	13	19	36

1915 World Series: Boston vs. Philadelphia

BOSTON

	G	AB	R	H	2B	3B	HR	RBI	BB	SO	BA	OBP	SLG	SB
Jack Barry	5	17	1	3	0	0	0	1	1	2	.176	.222	.176	0
Hick Cady	4	6	0	2	0	0	0	0	1	2	.333	.429	.333	0
Bill Carrigan	1	2	0	0	0	0	0	0	1	1	.000	.333	.000	0
Rube Foster	2	8	0	4	1	0	0	1	0	2	.500	.500	.625	0
Del Gainer	1	3	1	1	0	0	0	0	0	0	.333	.333	.333	0
Larry Gardner	5	17	2	4	0	1	0	0	1	0	.235	.278	.353	0
Olaf Henriksen	2	2	0	0	0	0	0	0	0	0	.000	.000	.000	0
Dick Hoblitzel	5	16	1	5	0	0	0	1	0	1	.312	.294	.312	1
Harry Hooper	5	20	4	7	0	0	2	3	2	4	.350	.435	.650	0
Hal Janvrin	1	1	0	0	0	0	0	0	0	0	.000	.000	.000	0

(continued)	G	AB	R	H	2B	3B	HR	RBI	BB	SO	BA	OBP	SLG	SB
Dutch Leonard	1	3	0	0	0	0	0	0	0	2	.000	.000	.000	0
Duffy Lewis	5	18	1	8	1	0	1	5	1	4	.444	.474	.667	0
Babe Ruth	1	1	0	0	0	0	0	0	0	0	.000	.000	.000	0
Everett Scott	5	18	0	1	0	0	0	0	0	3	.056	.056	.056	0
Ernie Shore	2	5	0	1	0	0	0	0	0	3	.200	.200	.200	0
Tris Speaker	5	17	2	5	0	1	0	0	4	1	.294	.429	.412	0
Pinch Thomas	2	5	0	1	0	0	0	0	0	0	.200	.200	.200	0
TOTAL	5	159	12	42	2	2	3	11	11	25	.264	.314	.358	1

	G	ERA	W–L	SV	CG	IP	H	ER	BB	SO
Rube Foster	2	2.00	2–0	0	2	18.0	12	4	2	13
Ernie Shore	2	2.12	1–1	0	2	17.0	12	4	8	6
Dutch Leonard	1	1.00	1–0	0	1	9.0	3	1	0	6
TOTAL	5	1.84	4–1	0	5	44.0	27	9	10	25

PHILADELPHIA PHILLIES

	G	AB	R	H	2B	3B	HR	RBI	BB	SO	BA	OBP	SLG	SB
Pete Alexander	2	5	0	1	0	0	0	0	0	1	.200	.200	.200	0
Dave Bancroft	5	17	2	5	0	0	0	1	2	2	.294	.368	.294	0
Beals Becker	2	0	0	0	0	0	0	0	0	0				0
Ed Burns	5	16	1	3	0	0	0	0	1	2	.188	.235	.188	0
Bobby Byrne	1	1	0	0	0	0	0	0	0	0	.000	.000	.000	0
George Chalmers	1	3	0	1	0	0	0	0	0	1	.333	.333	.333	0
Gavvy Cravath	5	16	2	2	1	1	0	1	2	6	.125	.222	.312	0
Oscar Dugey	2	0	0	0	0	0	0	0	0	0				1
Bill Killefer	1	1	0	0	0	0	0	0	0	0	.000	.000	.000	0
Fred Luderus	5	16	1	7	2	0	1	6	1	4	.438	.500	.750	0
Erskine Mayer	2	4	0	0	0	0	0	0	0	2	.000	.000	.000	0
Bert Niehoff	5	16	1	1	0	0	0	0	1	5	.062	.118	.062	0
Dode Paskert	5	19	2	3	0	0	0	0	1	2	.158	.200	.158	0
Eppa Rixey	1	2	0	1	0	0	0	0	0	0	.500	.500	.500	0
Milt Stock	5	17	1	2	1	0	0	0	1	0	.118	.211	.176	0
Possum Whitted	5	15	0	1	0	0	0	1	1	0	.067	.125	.067	1
TOTAL	5	148	10	27	4	1	1	9	10	25	.182	.244	.243	2

	G	ERA	W–L	SV	CG	IP	H	ER	BB	SO
Pete Alexander	2	1.53	1–1	0	2	17.7	14	3	4	10
Erskine Mayer	2	2.38	0–1	0	1	11.3	16	3	2	7
George Chalmers	1	2.25	0–1	0	1	8.0	8	2	3	6
Eppa Rixey	1	4.05	0–1	0	0	6.7	4	3	2	2
TOTAL	5	2.27	1–4	0	4	43.7	42	11	11	25

1916 World Series: Red Sox vs. Brooklyn

BOSTON RED SOX

	G	AB	R	H	2B	3B	HR	RBI	BB	SO	BA	OBP	SLG	SB
Hick Cady	2	4	1	1	0	0	0	0	3	0	.250	.571	.250	0
Bill Carrigan	1	3	0	2	0	0	0	1	0	1	.667	.667	.667	0

Appendix III

(continued)	G	AB	R	H	2B	3B	HR	RBI	BB	SO	BA	OBP	SLG	SB
Rube Foster	1	1	0	0	0	0	0	0	0	1	.000	.000	.000	0
Del Gainer	1	1	0	1	0	0	0	1	0	0	1.00	1.000	1.00	0
Larry Gardner	5	17	2	3	0	0	2	6	0	2	.176	.167	.529	0
Olaf Henriksen	1	0	1	0	0	0	0	0	1	0		1.000		0
Dick Hoblitzel	5	17	3	4	1	1	0	2	6	0	.235	.435	.412	0
Harry Hooper	5	21	6	7	1	1	0	1	3	1	.333	.417	.476	1
Hal Janvrin	5	23	2	5	3	0	0	1	0	6	.217	.217	.348	0
Dutch Leonard	1	3	0	0	0	0	0	0	1	3	.000	.250	.000	0
Duffy Lewis	5	17	3	6	2	1	0	1	2	1	.353	.421	.588	0
Carl Mays	2	1	0	0	0	0	0	0	0	1	.000	.000	.000	0
Mike McNally	1	0	1	0	0	0	0	0	0	0				0
Babe Ruth	1	5	0	0	0	0	0	1	0	2	.000	.000	.000	0
Everett Scott	5	16	1	2	0	1	0	1	1	1	.125	.167	.250	0
Ernie Shore	2	7	0	0	0	0	0	0	0	2	.000	.000	.000	0
Chick Shorten	2	7	0	4	0	0	0	2	0	1	.571	.571	.571	0
Pinch Thomas	2	7	0	1	0	1	0	0	0	1	.143	.143	.429	0
Tilly Walker	3	11	1	3	0	1	0	1	1	2	.273	.333	.455	0
Jimmy Walsh	1	3	0	0	0	0	0	0	0	0	.000	.000	.000	0
TOTAL	5	164	21	39	7	6	2	18	18	25	.238	.310	.390	1

	G	ERA	W–L	SV	CG	IP	H	ER	BB	SO
Ernie Shore	2	1.53	2–0	0	1	17.7	12	3	4	9
Babe Ruth	1	0.64	1–0	0	1	14.0	6	1	3	4
Dutch Leonard	1	1.00	1–0	0	1	9.0	5	1	4	3
Carl Mays	2	6.75	0–1	1	0	5.3	8	4	3	2
Rube Foster	1	0.00	0–0	0	0	3.0	3	0	0	1
TOTAL	5	1.65	4–1	1	3	49.0	34	9	14	19

Brooklyn Robbins

	G	AB	R	H	2B	3B	HR	RBI	BB	SO	BA	OBP	SLG	SB
Larry Cheney	1	0	0	0	0	0	0	0	0	0				0
Jack Coombs	1	3	0	1	0	0	0	1	0	0	.333	.333	.333	0
George Cutshaw	5	19	2	2	1	0	0	2	1	1	.105	.190	.158	0
Jake Daubert	4	17	1	3	0	1	0	0	2	3	.176	.263	.294	0
Wheezer Dell	1	0	0	0	0	0	0	0	0	0				0
Gus Getz	1	1	0	0	0	0	0	0	0	0	.000	.000	.000	0
Jimmy Johnston	3	10	1	3	0	1	0	0	1	0	.300	.364	.500	0
Rube Marquard	2	3	0	0	0	0	0	0	0	1	.000	.000	.000	0
Fred Merkle	3	4	0	1	0	0	0	1	2	0	.250	.500	.250	0
Chief Meyers	3	10	0	2	0	1	0	0	1	0	.200	.273	.400	0
Otto Miller	2	8	0	1	0	0	0	0	0	1	.125	.125	.125	0
Mike Mowrey	5	17	2	3	0	0	0	1	3	2	.176	.300	.176	0
Hy Myers	5	22	2	4	0	0	1	3	0	3	.182	.217	.318	0
Ollie O'Mara	1	1	0	0	0	0	0	0	0	1	.000	.000	.000	0
Ivy Olson	5	16	1	4	0	1	0	2	2	2	.250	.333	.375	0
Jeff Pfeffer	4	4	0	1	0	0	0	0	0	2	.250	.250	.250	0
Nap Rucker	1	0	0	0	0	0	0	0	0	0				0
Sherry Smith	1	5	0	1	1	0	0	0	0	0	.200	.200	.400	0
Casey Stengel	4	11	2	4	0	0	0	0	0	1	.364	.364	.364	0

	G	AB	R	H	2B	3B	HR	RBI	BB	SO	BA	OBP	SLG	SB
(continued)														
Zack Wheat	5	19	2	4	0	1	0	1	2	2	.211	.286	.316	1
TOTAL	5	170	13	34	2	5	1	11	14	19	.200	.269	.288	1

	G	ERA	W–L	SV	CG	IP	H	ER	BB	SO
Sherry Smith	1	1.35	0–1	0	1	13.3	7	2	6	2
Rube Marquard	2	5.73	0–2	0	0	11.0	12	7	6	9
Jeff Pfeffer	3	1.69	0–1	1	0	10.7	7	2	4	5
Jack Coombs	1	4.26	1–0	0	0	6.3	7	3	1	1
Larry Cheney	1	3.00	0–0	0	0	3.0	4	1	1	5
Nap Rucker	1	0.00	0–0	0	0	2.0	1	0	0	3
Wheezer Dell	1	0.00	0–0	0	0	1.0	1	0	0	0
TOTAL	5	2.85	1–4	1	1	47.3	39	15	18	25

1918 World Series: Boston vs. Chicago

BOSTON RED SOX

	G	AB	R	H	2B	3B	HR	RBI	BB	SO	BA	OBP	SLG	SB
Sam Agnew	4	9	0	0	0	0	0	0	0	0	.000	.000	.000	0
Joe Bush	2	2	0	0	0	0	0	0	1	0	.000	.333	.000	0
Jean Dubuc	1	1	0	0	0	0	0	0	0	1	.000	.000	.000	0
Harry Hooper	6	20	0	4	0	0	0	0	2	2	.200	.273	.200	0
Sam Jones	1	1	0	0	0	0	0	0	1	0	.000	.500	.000	0
Carl Mays	2	5	1	1	0	0	0	0	1	0	.200	.333	.200	0
Stuffy McInnis	6	20	2	5	0	0	0	1	1	1	.250	.286	.250	0
Hack Miller	1	1	0	0	0	0	0	0	0	0	.000	.000	.000	0
Babe Ruth	3	5	0	1	0	1	0	2	0	2	.200	.200	.600	0
Wally Schang	5	9	1	4	0	0	0	1	2	3	.444	.545	.444	1
Everett Scott	6	20	0	2	0	0	0	1	1	1	.100	.143	.100	0
Dave Shean	6	19	2	4	1	0	0	0	4	3	.211	.348	.263	1
Amos Strunk	6	23	1	4	1	1	0	0	0	5	.174	.174	.304	0
Fred Thomas	6	17	0	2	0	0	0	0	1	2	.118	.167	.118	0
George Whiteman	6	20	2	5	0	1	0	1	2	1	.250	.348	.350	1
TOTAL	6	172	9	32	2	3	0	6	16	21	.186	.259	.233	3

	G	ERA	W–L	SV	CG	IP	H	ER	BB	SO
Carl Mays	2	1.00	2–0	0	2	18.0	10	2	3	5
Babe Ruth	2	1.06	2–0	0	1	17.0	13	2	7	4
Sam Jones	1	3.00	0–1	0	1	9.0	7	3	5	5
Joe Bush	2	3.00	0–1	1	1	9.0	7	3	3	0
TOTAL	6	1.70	4–2	1	5	53.0	37	10	18	14

CHICAGO CUBS

	G	AB	R	H	2B	3B	HR	RBI	BB	SO	BA	OBP	SLG	SB
Turner Barber	3	2	0	0	0	0	0	0	0	0	.000	.000	.000	0
Charlie Deal	6	17	0	3	0	0	0	0	0	1	.176	.176	.176	0
Phil Douglas	1	0	0	0	0	0	0	0	0	0				0
Max Flack	6	19	2	5	0	0	0	0	4	1	.263	.417	.263	1
Claude Hendrix	2	1	0	1	0	0	0	0	0	0	1.00	1.000	1.00	0

	G	AB	R	H	2B	3B	HR	RBI	BB	SO	BA	OBP	SLG	SB
(continued)														
Charlie Hollocher	6	21	2	4	0	1	0	1	1	1	.190	.227	.286	1
Bill Killefer	6	17	2	2	1	0	0	2	2	0	.118	.211	.176	0
Les Mann	6	22	0	5	2	0	0	2	0	0	.227	.261	.318	0
Bill McCabe	3	1	1	0	0	0	0	0	0	0	.000	.000	.000	0
Fred Merkle	6	18	1	5	0	0	0	1	4	3	.278	.409	.278	0
Bob O'Farrell	3	3	0	0	0	0	0	0	0	0	.000	.000	.000	0
Dode Paskert	6	21	0	4	1	0	0	2	2	2	.190	.261	.238	0
Charlie Pick	6	18	2	7	1	0	0	0	1	1	.389	.421	.444	1
Lefty Tyler	3	5	0	1	0	0	0	2	2	0	.200	.429	.200	0
Hippo Vaughn	3	10	0	0	0	0	0	0	0	5	.000	.000	.000	0
Chuck Wortman	1	1	0	0	0	0	0	0	0	0	.000	.000	.000	0
Rollie Zeider	2	0	0	0	0	0	0	0	2	0		1.000		0
TOTAL	6	176	10	37	5	1	0	10	18	14	.210	.291	.250	3

	G	ERA	W–L	SV	CG	IP	H	ER	BB	SO
Hippo Vaughn	3	1.00	1–2	0	3	27.0	17	3	5	17
Lefty Tyler	3	1.17	1–1	0	1	23.0	14	3	11	4
Phil Douglas	1	0.00	0–1	0	0	1.0	1	0	0	0
Claude Hendrix	1	0.00	0–0	0	0	1.0	0	0	0	0
TOTAL	6	1.04	2–4	0	4	52.0	32	6	16	21

1946 World Series: Boston vs. St. Louis

BOSTON RED SOX

	G	AB	R	H	2B	3B	HR	RBI	BB	SO	BA	OBP	SLG	SB
Jim Bagby	1	1	0	0	0	0	0	0	0	0	.000	.000	.000	0
Mace Brown	1	0	0	0	0	0	0	0	0	0				0
Paul Campbell	1	0	0	0	0	0	0	0	0	0				0
Leon Culberson	5	9	1	2	0	0	1	1	1	2	.222	.300	.556	1
Dom DiMaggio	7	27	2	7	3	0	0	3	2	2	.259	.310	.370	0
Joe Dobson	3	3	0	0	0	0	0	0	0	2	.000	.000	.000	0
Bobby Doerr	6	22	1	9	1	0	1	3	2	2	.409	.458	.591	0
Clem Dreisewerd	1	0	0	0	0	0	0	0	0	0				0
Dave Ferriss	2	6	0	0	0	0	0	0	0	1	.000	.000	.000	0
Don Gutteridge	3	5	1	2	0	0	0	1	0	0	.400	.400	.400	0
Mickey Harris	2	3	0	1	0	0	0	0	0	1	.333	.333	.333	0
Pinky Higgins	7	24	1	5	1	0	0	2	2	0	.208	.269	.250	0
Tex Hughson	3	3	0	1	0	0	0	0	1	0	.333	.500	.333	0
Earl Johnson	3	1	0	0	0	0	0	0	0	0	.000	.000	.000	0
Bob Klinger	1	0	0	0	0	0	0	0	0	0				0
Tom McBride	5	12	0	2	0	0	0	1	0	1	.167	.167	.167	0
Catfish Metkovich	2	2	1	1	1	0	0	0	0	0	.500	.500	1.00	0
Wally Moses	4	12	1	5	0	0	0	0	1	2	.417	.462	.417	0
Roy Partee	5	10	1	1	0	0	0	1	1	2	.100	.182	.100	0
Johnny Pesky	7	30	2	7	0	0	0	0	1	3	.233	.258	.233	1
Rip Russell	2	2	1	2	0	0	0	0	0	0	1.00	1.000	1.00	0
Mike Ryba	1	0	0	0	0	0	0	0	0	0				0

(continued)	G	AB	R	H	2B	3B	HR	RBI	BB	SO	BA	OBP	SLG	SB
Hal Wagner	5	13	0	0	0	0	0	0	0	1	.000	.000	.000	0
Ted Williams	7	25	2	5	0	0	0	1	5	5	.200	.333	.200	0
Rudy York	7	23	6	6	1	1	2	5	6	4	.261	.433	.652	0
Bill Zuber	1	0	0	0	0	0	0	0	0	0				0
TOTAL	7	233	20	56	7	1	4	18	22	28	.240	.309	.330	2

	G	ERA	W–L	SV	CG	IP	H	ER	BB	SO
Tex Hughson	3	3.14	0–1	0	0	14.3	14	5	3	8
Dave Ferriss	2	2.02	1–0	0	1	13.3	13	3	2	4
Joe Dobson	3	0.00	1–0	0	1	12.7	4	0	3	10
Mickey Harris	2	3.72	0–2	0	0	9.7	11	4	4	5
Earl Johnson	3	2.70	1–0	0	0	3.3	1	1	2	1
Jim Bagby	1	3.00	0–0	0	0	3.0	6	1	1	1
Bill Zuber	1	4.50	0–0	0	0	2.0	3	1	1	1
Mace Brown	1	27.00	0–0	0	0	1.0	4	3	1	0
Bob Klinger	1	13.50	0–1	0	0	0.7	2	1	1	0
Mike Ryba	1	13.50	0–0	0	0	0.7	2	1	1	0
Clem Dreisewerd	1	0.00	0–0	0	0	0.3	0	0	0	0
TOTAL	7	2.95	3–4	0	2	61.0	60	20	19	30

ST. LOUIS CARDINALS

	G	AB	R	H	2B	3B	HR	RBI	BB	SO	BA	OBP	SLG	SB
Johnny Beazley	1	0	0	0	0	0	0	0	0	0				0
Al Brazle	1	2	0	0	0	0	0	0	0	0	.000	.000	.000	0
Harry Brecheen	3	8	2	1	0	0	0	1	0	1	.125	.125	.125	0
Murry Dickson	2	5	1	2	2	0	0	1	0	1	.400	.400	.800	0
Erv Dusak	4	4	0	1	1	0	0	0	2	2	.250	.500	.500	0
Joe Garagiola	5	19	2	6	2	0	0	4	0	3	.316	.316	.421	0
Nippy Jones	1	1	0	0	0	0	0	0	0	1	.000	.000	.000	0
Whitey Kurowski	7	27	5	8	3	0	0	2	0	3	.296	.321	.407	0
Marty Marion	7	24	1	6	2	0	0	4	1	1	.250	.280	.333	0
Terry Moore	7	27	1	4	0	0	0	2	2	6	.148	.207	.148	0
Red Munger	1	4	0	1	0	0	0	0	0	2	.250	.250	.250	0
Stan Musial	7	27	3	6	4	1	0	4	4	2	.222	.323	.444	1
Howie Pollet	2	4	0	0	0	0	0	0	0	1	.000	.000	.000	0
Del Rice	3	6	2	3	1	0	0	0	2	0	.500	.625	.667	0
Red Schoendienst	7	30	3	7	1	0	0	1	0	2	.233	.233	.267	1
Dick Sisler	2	2	0	0	0	0	0	0	0	0	.000	.000	.000	0
Enos Slaughter	7	25	5	8	1	1	1	2	4	3	.320	.433	.560	1
Harry Walker	7	17	3	7	2	0	0	6	4	2	.412	.524	.529	0
Ted Wilks	1	0	0	0	0	0	0	0	0	0				0
TOTAL	7	232	28	60	19	2	1	27	19	30	.259	.320	.371	3

	G	ERA	W–L	SV	CG	IP	H	ER	BB	SO
Harry Brecheen	3	0.45	3–0	0	2	20.0	14	1	5	11
Murry Dickson	2	3.86	0–1	0	0	14.0	11	6	4	7
Howie Pollet	2	3.48	0–1	0	1	10.3	12	4	4	3
Red Munger	1	1.00	1–0	0	1	9.0	9	1	3	2
Al Brazle	1	5.40	0–1	0	0	6.7	7	4	6	4

	G	ERA	W–L	SV	CG	IP	H	ER	BB	SO
(continued)										
Johnny Beazley	1	0.00	0–0	0	0	1.0	1	0	0	1
Ted Wilks	1	0.00	0–0	0	0	1.0	2	0	0	0
TOTAL		2.32	4–3	0	4	62.0	56	16	22	28

1967 World Series: Boston vs. St. Louis

BOSTON RED SOX

	G	AB	R	H	2B	3B	HR	RBI	BB	SO	BA	OBP	SLG	SB
Jerry Adair	5	16	0	2	0	0	0	1	0	3	.125	.118	.125	1
Mike Andrews	5	13	2	4	0	0	0	1	0	1	.308	.308	.308	0
Gary Bell	3	0	0	0	0	0	0	0	0	0				0
Ken Brett	2	0	0	0	0	0	0	0	0	0				0
Joe Foy	6	15	2	2	1	0	0	1	1	5	.133	.188	.200	0
Russ Gibson	2	2	0	0	0	0	0	0	0	2	.000	.000	.000	0
Ken Harrelson	4	13	0	1	0	0	0	1	1	3	.077	.143	.077	0
Elston Howard	7	18	0	2	0	0	0	1	1	2	.111	.158	.111	0
Dalton Jones	6	18	2	7	0	0	0	1	1	3	.389	.421	.389	0
Jim Lonborg	3	9	0	0	0	0	0	0	0	7	.000	.000	.000	0
Dave Morehead	2	0	0	0	0	0	0	0	0	0				0
Dan Osinski	2	0	0	0	0	0	0	0	0	0				0
Rico Petrocelli	7	20	3	4	1	0	2	3	3	8	.200	.292	.550	0
Mike Ryan	1	2	0	0	0	0	0	0	0	1	.000	.000	.000	0
Jose Santiago	3	2	1	1	0	0	1	1	0	1	.500	.500	2.00	0
George Scott	7	26	3	6	1	1	0	0	3	6	.231	.310	.346	0
Norm Siebern	3	3	0	1	0	0	0	1	0	0	.333	.333	.333	0
Reggie Smith	7	24	3	6	1	0	2	3	2	2	.250	.308	.542	0
Lee Stange	1	0	0	0	0	0	0	0	0	0				0
Jerry Stephenson	1	0	0	0	0	0	0	0	0	0				0
Jose Tartabull	7	13	1	2	0	0	0	0	1	2	.154	.214	.154	0
George Thomas	2	2	0	0	0	0	0	0	0	1	.000	.000	.000	0
Gary Waslewski	2	1	0	0	0	0	0	0	0	1	.000	.500	.000	0
John Wyatt	2	0	0	0	0	0	0	0	0	0				0
Carl Yastrzemski	7	25	4	10	2	0	3	5	4	1	.400	.500	.840	0
TOTAL	7	222	21	48	6	1	8	19	17	49	.216	.276	.360	1

	G	ERA	W–L	SV	CG	IP	H	ER	BB	SO
Jim Lonborg	3	2.62	2–1	0	2	24.0	14	7	2	11
Jose Santiago	3	5.59	0–2	0	0	9.7	16	6	3	6
Gary Waslewski	2	2.16	0–0	0	0	8.3	4	2	2	7
Gary Bell	3	5.06	0–1	1	0	5.3	8	3	1	1
John Wyatt	2	4.91	1–0	0	0	3.7	1	2	3	1
Dave Morehead	2	0.00	0–0	0	0	3.3	0	0	4	3
Lee Stange	1	0.00	0–0	0	0	2.0	3	0	0	0
Jerry Stephenson	1	9.00	0–0	0	0	2.0	3	2	1	0
Ken Brett	2	0.00	0–0	0	0	1.3	0	0	1	1
Dan Osinski	2	6.75	0–0	0	0	1.3	2	1	0	0
TOTAL	7	3.39	3–4	1	2	61.0	51	23	17	30

St. Louis Cardinals

	G	AB	R	H	2B	3B	HR	RBI	BB	SO	BA	OBP	SLG	SB
Eddie Bressoud	2	0	0	0	0	0	0	0	0	0				0
Nelson Briles	2	3	0	0	0	0	0	0	0	0	.000	.000	.000	0
Lou Brock	7	29	8	12	2	1	1	3	2	3	.414	.452	.655	7
Steve Carlton	1	1	0	0	0	0	0	0	0	0	.000	.000	.000	0
Orlando Cepeda	7	29	1	3	2	0	0	1	0	4	.103	.103	.172	0
Curt Flood	7	28	2	5	1	0	0	3	3	3	.179	.258	.214	0
Phil Gagliano	1	1	0	0	0	0	0	0	0	0	.000	.000	.000	0
Bob Gibson	3	11	1	1	0	0	1	1	1	2	.091	.167	.364	0
Joe Hoerner	2	0	0	0	0	0	0	0	0	0				0
Dick Hughes	2	3	0	0	0	0	0	0	0	3	.000	.000	.000	0
Larry Jaster	1	0	0	0	0	0	0	0	0	0				0
Julian Javier	7	25	2	9	3	0	1	4	0	6	.360	.360	.600	0
Jack Lamabe	3	0	0	0	0	0	0	0	0	0				0
Roger Maris	7	26	3	10	1	0	1	7	3	1	.385	.433	.538	0
Dal Maxvill	7	19	1	3	0	1	0	1	4	1	.158	.304	.263	0
Tim McCarver	7	24	3	3	1	0	0	2	2	2	.125	.185	.167	0
Dave Ricketts	3	3	0	0	0	0	0	0	0	0	.000	.000	.000	0
Mike Shannon	7	24	3	5	1	0	1	2	1	4	.208	.240	.375	0
Ed Spiezio	1	1	0	0	0	0	0	0	0	0	.000	.000	.000	0
Bobby Tolan	3	2	1	0	0	0	0	0	1	1	.000	.333	.000	0
Ray Washburn	2	0	0	0	0	0	0	0	0	0				0
Ron Willis	3	0	0	0	0	0	0	0	0	0				0
Hal Woodeshick	1	0	0	0	0	0	0	0	0	0				0
TOTAL	7	229	25	51	11	2	5	24	17	30	.223	.274	.354	7

	G	ERA	W–L	SV	CG	IP	H	ER	BB	SO
Bob Gibson	3	1.00	3–0	0	3	27.0	14	3	5	26
Nelson Briles	2	1.64	1–0	0	1	11.0	7	2	1	4
Dick Hughes	2	5.00	0–1	0	0	9.0	9	5	3	7
Steve Carlton	1	0.00	0–1	0	0	6.0	3	0	2	5
Jack Lamabe	3	6.75	0–1	0	0	2.7	5	2	0	4
Ray Washburn	2	0.00	0–0	0	0	2.3	1	0	1	2
Hal Woodeshick	1	0.00	0–0	0	0	1.0	1	0	0	0
Ron Willis	3	27.00	0–0	0	0	1.0	2	3	4	1
Joe Hoerner	2	40.50	0–0	0	0	0.7	4	3	1	0
Larry Jaster	1	0.00	0–0	0	0	0.3	2	0	0	0
TOTAL	7	2.66	4–3	0	4	61.0	48	18	17	49

1975 American League Championship: Boston vs. Oakland

Boston Red Sox

	G	AB	R	H	2B	3B	HR	RBI	BB	SO	BA	OBP	SLG	SB
Juan Beniquez	3	12	2	3	1	0	0	1	0	1	.250	.250	.333	2
Rick Burleson	3	9	2	4	2	0	0	1	1	0	.444	.500	.667	0
Reggie Cleveland	1	0	0	0	0	0	0	0	0	0				0
Cecil Cooper	3	11	0	4	2	0	0	1	0	2	.364	.364	.545	0

(continued)	G	AB	R	H	2B	3B	HR	RBI	BB	SO	BA	OBP	SLG	SB
Denny Doyle	3	11	3	3	0	0	0	2	0	1	.273	.250	.273	0
Dick Drago	2	0	0	0	0	0	0	0	0	0				0
Dwight Evans	3	10	1	1	1	0	0	0	1	2	.100	.182	.200	0
Carlton Fisk	3	12	4	5	1	0	0	3	0	2	.417	.417	.500	1
Fred Lynn	3	11	1	4	1	0	0	2	0	0	.364	.364	.455	0
Roger Moret	1	0	0	0	0	0	0	0	0	0				0
Rico Petrocelli	3	12	1	2	0	0	1	2	0	3	.167	.167	.417	0
Luis Tiant	1	0	0	0	0	0	0	0	0	0				0
Rick Wise	1	0	0	0	0	0	0	0	0	0				0
Carl Yastrzemski	3	11	4	5	1	0	1	2	1	1	.455	.500	.818	0
TOTAL	3	99	18	31	9	0	2	14	3	12	.313	.330	.465	3

	G	ERA	W–L	SV	CG	IP	H	ER	BB	SO
Luis Tiant	1	0.00	1–0	0	1	9.0	3	0	3	8
Rick Wise	1	2.45	1–0	0	0	7.3	6	2	3	2
Reggie Cleveland	1	5.40	0–0	0	0	5.0	7	3	1	2
Dick Drago	2	0.00	0–0	2	0	4.7	2	0	1	2
Roger Moret	1	0.00	1–0	0	0	1.0	1	0	1	0
TOTAL	3	1.67	3–0	2	1	27.0	19	5	9	14

OAKLAND ATHLETICS

	G	AB	R	H	2B	3B	HR	RBI	BB	SO	BA	OBP	SLG	SB
Glenn Abbott	1	0	0	0	0	0	0	0	0	0				0
Sal Bando	3	12	1	6	2	0	0	2	0	3	.500	.500	.667	0
Vida Blue	1	0	0	0	0	0	0	0	0	0				0
Dick Bosman	1	0	0	0	0	0	0	0	0	0				0
Bert Campaneris	3	11	1	0	0	0	0	0	1	1	.000	.083	.000	0
Rollie Fingers	1	0	0	0	0	0	0	0	0	0				0
Ray Fosse	1	2	0	0	0	0	0	0	0	1	.000	.000	.000	0
Phil Garner	3	5	0	0	0	0	0	0	0	1	.000	.000	.000	0
Tommy Harper	1	0	0	0	0	0	0	0	1	0		1.000		0
Jim Holt	3	3	0	1	1	0	0	0	0	0	.333	.333	.667	0
Ken Holtzman	2	0	0	0	0	0	0	0	0	0				0
Don Hopkins	1	1	0	0	0	0	0	0	0	0	.000	.000	.000	0
Reggie Jackson	3	12	1	5	0	0	1	3	0	2	.417	.417	.667	0
Paul Lindblad	2	0	0	0	0	0	0	0	0	0				0
Ted Martinez	3	0	0	0	0	0	0	0	0	0				0
Billy North	3	10	0	0	0	0	0	1	2	0	.000	.167	.000	0
Joe Rudi	3	12	1	3	2	0	0	0	0	1	.250	.250	.417	0
Gene Tenace	3	9	0	0	0	0	0	0	3	2	.000	.250	.000	0
Jim Todd	3	0	0	0	0	0	0	0	0	0				0
Cesar Tovar	2	2	2	1	0	0	0	0	1	0	.500	.667	.500	0
Claudell Washington	3	12	1	3	1	0	0	1	0	2	.250	.250	.333	0
Billy Williams	3	7	0	0	0	0	0	0	1	1	.000	.125	.000	0
TOTAL	3	98	7	19	6	0	1	7	9	14	.194	.262	.286	0

	G	ERA	W–L	SV	CG	IP	H	ER	BB	SO
Ken Holtzman	2	4.09	0–2	0	0	11.0	12	5	1	7
Paul Lindblad	2	1.93	0–0	0	0	4.7	5	1	1	0

(continued)	G	ERA	W–L	SV	CG	IP	H	ER	BB	SO
Rollie Fingers	1	6.75	0–1	0	0	4.0	5	3	1	3
Vida Blue	1	9.00	0–0	0	0	3.0	6	3	0	2
Glenn Abbott	1	0.00	0–0	0	0	1.0	0	0	0	0
Jim Todd	3	0.00	0–0	0	0	1.0	3	0	0	0
Dick Bosman	1	0.00	0–0	0	0	0.3	0	0	0	0
TOTAL	3	4.32	0–3	0	0	25.0	31	12	3	12

1975 World Series: Boston vs. Cincinnati

BOSTON RED SOX

	G	AB	R	H	2B	3B	HR	RBI	BB	SO	BA	OBP	SLG	SB
Juan Beniquez	3	8	0	1	0	0	0	1	1	1	.125	.222	.125	0
Rick Burleson	7	24	1	7	1	0	0	2	4	2	.292	.393	.333	0
Jim Burton	2	0	0	0	0	0	0	0	0	0				0
Bernie Carbo	4	7	3	3	1	0	2	4	1	1	.429	.500	1.42	0
Reggie Cleveland	3	2	0	0	0	0	0	0	0	2	.000	.000	.000	0
Cecil Cooper	5	19	0	1	1	0	0	1	0	3	.053	.050	.105	0
Denny Doyle	7	30	3	8	1	1	0	0	2	1	.267	.312	.367	0
Dick Drago	2	0	0	0	0	0	0	0	0	0				0
Dwight Evans	7	24	3	7	1	1	1	5	3	4	.292	.393	.542	0
Carlton Fisk	7	25	5	6	0	0	2	4	7	7	.240	.406	.480	0
Doug Griffin	1	1	0	0	0	0	0	0	0	0	.000	.000	.000	0
Bill Lee	2	6	0	1	0	0	0	0	0	3	.167	.167	.167	0
Fred Lynn	7	25	3	7	1	0	1	5	3	5	.280	.345	.440	0
Rick Miller	3	2	0	0	0	0	0	0	0	0	.000	.000	.000	0
Bob Montgomery	1	1	0	0	0	0	0	0	0	0	.000	.000	.000	0
Roger Moret	3	0	0	0	0	0	0	0	0	0				0
Rico Petrocelli	7	26	3	8	1	0	0	4	3	6	.308	.379	.346	0
Dick Pole	1	0	0	0	0	0	0	0	0	0				0
Diego Segui	1	0	0	0	0	0	0	0	0	0				0
Luis Tiant	3	8	2	2	0	0	0	0	2	4	.250	.400	.250	0
Jim Willoughby	3	0	0	0	0	0	0	0	0	0				0
Rick Wise	2	2	0	0	0	0	0	0	0	0	.000	.000	.000	0
Carl Yastrzemski	7	29	7	9	0	0	0	4	4	1	.310	.382	.310	0
TOTAL	7	239	30	60	7	2	6	30	30	40	.251	.333	.372	0

	G	ERA	W–L	SV	CG	IP	H	ER	BB	SO
Luis Tiant	3	3.60	2–0	0	2	25.0	25	10	8	12
Bill Lee	2	3.14	0–0	0	0	14.3	12	5	3	7
Reggie Cleveland	3	6.75	0–1	0	0	6.7	7	5	3	5
Jim Willoughby	3	0.00	0–1	0	0	6.3	3	0	0	2
Rick Wise	2	8.44	1–0	0	0	5.3	6	5	2	2
Dick Drago	2	2.25	0–1	0	0	4.0	3	1	1	1
Roger Moret	3	0.00	0–0	0	0	1.7	2	0	3	1
Diego Segui	1	0.00	0–0	0	0	1.0	0	0	0	0
Jim Burton	2	9.00	0–1	0	0	1.0	1	1	3	0
Dick Pole	1	—	0–0	0	0	0.0	0	1	2	0
TOTAL	7	3.86	3–4	0	2	65.3	59	28	25	30

Cincinnati Reds

	G	AB	R	H	2B	3B	HR	RBI	BB	SO	BA	OBP	SLG	SB
Ed Armbrister	4	1	1	0	0	0	0	0	2	0	.000	.667	.000	0
Johnny Bench	7	29	5	6	2	0	1	4	2	4	.207	.258	.379	0
Jack Billingham	3	2	0	0	0	0	0	0	0	0	.000	.000	.000	0
Pedro Borbon	3	1	0	0	0	0	0	0	0	0	.000	.000	.000	0
Clay Carroll	5	0	0	0	0	0	0	0	0	0				0
Darrel Chaney	2	2	0	0	0	0	0	0	0	1	.000	.000	.000	0
Dave Concepcion	7	28	3	5	1	0	1	4	0	1	.179	.200	.321	3
Terry Crowley	2	2	0	1	0	0	0	0	0	1	.500	.500	.500	0
Pat Darcy	2	1	0	0	0	0	0	0	0	1	.000	.000	.000	0
Dan Driessen	2	2	0	0	0	0	0	0	0	0	.000	.000	.000	0
Rawly Eastwick	5	1	0	0	0	0	0	0	0	0	.000	.000	.000	0
George Foster	7	29	1	8	1	0	0	2	1	1	.276	.300	.310	1
Cesar Geronimo	7	25	3	7	0	1	2	3	3	5	.280	.357	.600	0
Ken Griffey	7	26	4	7	3	1	0	4	4	2	.269	.367	.462	2
Don Gullett	3	7	1	2	0	0	0	0	0	2	.286	.286	.286	0
Will McEnaney	5	1	0	1	0	0	0	0	0	0	1.00	1.000	1.00	0
Joe Morgan	7	27	4	7	1	0	0	3	5	1	.259	.364	.296	2
Gary Nolan	2	1	0	0	0	0	0	0	0	0	.000	.000	.000	0
Fred Norman	2	1	0	0	0	0	0	0	0	0	.000	.000	.000	0
Tony Perez	7	28	4	5	0	0	3	7	3	9	.179	.258	.500	1
Merv Rettenmund	3	3	0	0	0	0	0	0	0	1	.000	.000	.000	0
Pete Rose	7	27	3	10	1	1	0	2	5	1	.370	.485	.481	0
TOTAL	7	244	29	59	9	3	7	29	25	30	.242	.315	.389	9

	G	ERA	W–L	SV	CG	IP	H	ER	BB	SO
Don Gullett	3	4.34	1–1	0	0	18.7	19	9	10	15
Jack Billingham	3	1.00	0–0	0	0	9.0	8	1	5	7
Rawly Eastwick	5	2.25	2–0	1	0	8.0	6	2	3	4
Will McEnaney	5	2.70	0–0	1	0	6.7	3	2	2	5
Gary Nolan	2	6.00	0–0	0	0	6.0	6	4	1	2
Clay Carroll	5	3.18	1–0	0	0	5.7	4	2	2	3
Pat Darcy	2	4.50	0–1	0	0	4.0	3	2	2	1
Fred Norman	2	9.00	0–1	0	0	4.0	8	4	3	2
Pedro Borbon	3	6.00	0–0	0	0	3.0	3	2	2	1
TOTAL	7	3.88	4–3	2	0	65.0	60	28	30	40

1986 American League Championship: Boston vs. California

Boston Red Sox

	G	AB	R	H	2B	3B	HR	RBI	BB	SO	BA	OBP	SLG	SB
Tony Armas	5	16	1	2	1	0	0	0	0	2	.125	.125	.188	0
Marty Barrett	7	30	4	11	2	0	0	5	2	2	.367	.406	.433	0
Don Baylor	7	26	6	9	3	0	1	2	4	5	.346	.469	.577	0
Wade Boggs	7	30	3	7	1	1	0	2	4	1	.233	.324	.333	0
Bill Buckner	7	28	3	6	1	0	0	3	0	2	.214	.207	.250	0
Dwight Evans	7	28	2	6	1	0	1	4	3	3	.214	.290	.357	0

Postseason Statistics

(continued)	G	AB	R	H	2B	3B	HR	RBI	BB	SO	BA	OBP	SLG	SB
Rich Gedman	7	28	4	10	1	0	1	6	0	4	.357	.379	.500	0
Mike Greenwell	2	2	0	1	0	0	0	0	0	0	.500	.500	.500	0
Dave Henderson	5	9	3	1	0	0	1	4	2	2	.111	.250	.444	0
Spike Owen	7	21	5	9	0	1	0	3	2	2	.429	.478	.524	1
Jim Rice	7	31	8	5	1	0	2	6	1	8	.161	.188	.387	0
Ed Romero	1	2	0	0	0	0	0	0	0	0	.000	.000	.000	0
Dave Stapleton	4	3	2	2	0	0	0	0	1	0	.667	.750	.667	0
TOTAL	7	254	41	69	11	2	6	35	19	31	.272	.327	.402	1

	G	ERA	W–L	SV	CG	IP	H	ER	BB	SO
Roger Clemens	3	4.37	1–1	0	0	22.7	22	11	7	17
Bruce Hurst	2	2.40	1–0	0	1	15.0	18	4	1	8
Oil Can Boyd	2	4.61	1–1	0	0	13.7	17	7	3	8
Calvin Schiraldi	4	1.50	0–1	1	0	6.0	5	1	3	9
Bob Stanley	3	4.76	0–0	0	0	5.7	7	3	3	1
Steve Crawford	1	0.00	1–0	0	0	1.7	1	0	2	1
Joe Sambito	3	0.00	0–0	0	0	0.7	1	0	1	0
TOTAL	7	3.58	4–3	1	1	65.3	71	26	20	44

CALIFORNIA ANGELS

	G	AB	R	H	2B	3B	HR	RBI	BB	SO	BA	OBP	SLG	SB
Bob Boone	7	22	4	10	0	0	1	2	1	3	.455	.500	.591	0
Rick Burleson	4	11	0	3	0	0	0	0	0	0	.273	.273	.273	0
Doug DeCinces	7	32	2	9	3	0	1	3	0	2	.281	.281	.469	0
Brian Downing	7	27	2	6	0	0	1	7	4	5	.222	.333	.333	0
Bobby Grich	6	24	1	5	0	0	1	3	0	8	.208	.269	.333	0
George Hendrick	3	12	0	1	0	0	0	0	0	2	.083	.083	.083	0
Jack Howell	2	1	0	0	0	0	0	0	1	1	.000	.500	.000	0
Reggie Jackson	6	26	2	5	2	0	0	2	2	7	.192	.250	.269	0
Ruppert Jones	6	17	4	3	1	0	0	2	5	2	.176	.348	.235	0
Wally Joyner	3	11	3	5	2	0	1	2	2	0	.455	.538	.909	0
Jerry Narron	4	2	1	1	0	0	0	0	1	1	.500	.667	.500	0
Gary Pettis	7	26	4	9	1	0	1	4	3	5	.346	.414	.500	0
Dick Schofield	7	30	4	9	1	0	1	2	1	5	.300	.323	.433	1
Devon White	4	2	2	1	0	0	0	0	0	1	.500	.500	.500	0
Rob Wilfong	4	13	1	4	1	0	0	2	0	2	.308	.308	.385	0
TOTAL	7	256	30	71	11	0	7	29	20	44	.277	.337	.402	1

	G	ERA	W–L	SV	CG	IP	H	ER	BB	SO
Mike Witt	2	2.55	1–0	0	1	17.7	13	5	2	8
John Candelaria	2	0.84	1–1	0	0	10.7	11	1	6	7
Don Sutton	2	1.86	0–0	0	0	9.7	6	2	1	4
Kirk McCaskill	2	7.71	0–2	0	0	9.3	16	8	5	7
Doug Corbett	3	5.40	1–0	0	0	6.7	9	4	2	2
Donnie Moore	3	7.20	0–1	1	0	5.0	8	4	2	0
Gary Lucas	4	11.57	0–0	0	0	2.3	3	3	1	2
Chuck Finley	3	0.00	0–0	0	0	2.0	1	0	0	1
Vern Ruhle	1	13.50	0–0	0	0	0.7	2	1	0	0
TOTAL	7	3.94	3–4	1	1	64.0	69	28	19	31

1986 World Series: Boston vs. New York

BOSTON RED SOX

	G	AB	R	H	2B	3B	HR	RBI	BB	SO	BA	OBP	SLG	SB
Tony Armas	1	1	0	0	0	0	0	0	0	1	.000	.000	.000	0
Marty Barrett	7	30	1	13	2	0	0	4	5	2	.433	.514	.500	0
Don Baylor	4	11	1	2	1	0	0	1	1	3	.182	.308	.273	0
Wade Boggs	7	31	3	9	3	0	0	3	4	2	.290	.371	.387	0
Oil Can Boyd	1	0	0	0	0	0	0	0	0	0				0
Bill Buckner	7	32	2	6	0	0	0	1	0	3	.188	.212	.188	0
Roger Clemens	2	4	1	0	0	0	0	0	0	1	.000	.000	.000	0
Steve Crawford	3	1	0	0	0	0	0	0	0	0	.000	.000	.000	0
Dwight Evans	7	26	4	8	2	0	2	9	4	3	.308	.400	.615	0
Rich Gedman	7	30	1	6	1	0	1	1	0	10	.200	.200	.333	0
Mike Greenwell	4	3	0	0	0	0	0	0	1	2	.000	.250	.000	0
Dave Henderson	7	25	6	10	1	1	2	5	2	6	.400	.448	.760	0
Bruce Hurst	3	3	0	0	0	0	0	0	0	3	.000	.000	.000	0
Al Nipper	2	0	0	0	0	0	0	0	0	0				0
Spike Owen	7	20	2	6	0	0	0	2	5	6	.300	.423	.300	0
Jim Rice	7	27	6	9	1	1	0	0	6	9	.333	.455	.444	0
Ed Romero	3	1	0	0	0	0	0	0	0	0	.000	.000	.000	0
Joe Sambito	2	0	0	0	0	0	0	0	0	0				0
Calvin Schiraldi	3	1	0	0	0	0	0	0	0	1	.000	.000	.000	0
Bob Stanley	5	1	0	0	0	0	0	0	0	1	.000	.000	.000	0
Dave Stapleton	3	1	0	0	0	0	0	0	0	0	.000	.000	.000	0
TOTAL	7	248	27	69	11	2	5	26	28	53	.278	.356	.399	0

	G	ERA	W–L	SV	CG	IP	H	ER	BB	SO
Bruce Hurst	3	1.96	2–0	0	1	23.0	18	5	6	17
Roger Clemens	2	3.18	0–0	0	0	11.3	9	4	6	11
Oil Can Boyd	1	7.71	0–1	0	0	7.0	9	6	1	3
Al Nipper	2	7.11	0–1	0	0	6.3	10	5	2	2
Bob Stanley	5	0.00	0–0	1	0	6.3	5	0	1	4
Steve Crawford	3	6.23	1–0	0	0	4.3	5	3	0	4
Calvin Schiraldi	3	13.50	0–2	1	0	4.0	7	6	3	2
Joe Sambito	2	27.00	0–0	0	0	0.3	2	1	2	0
TOTAL	7	4.31	3–4	2	1	62.7	65	30	21	43

NEW YORK METS

	G	AB	R	H	2B	3B	HR	RBI	BB	SO	BA	OBP	SLG	SB
Rick Aguilera	2	0	0	0	0	0	0	0	0	0				0
Wally Backman	6	18	4	6	0	0	0	1	3	2	.333	.429	.333	1
Gary Carter	7	29	4	8	2	0	2	9	0	4	.276	.267	.552	0
Ron Darling	3	3	0	0	0	0	0	0	0	1	.000	.000	.000	0
Lenny Dykstra	7	27	4	8	0	0	2	3	2	7	.296	.345	.519	0
Kevin Elster	1	1	0	0	0	0	0	0	0	0	.000	.000	.000	0
Sid Fernandez	3	0	0	0	0	0	0	0	0	0				0
Dwight Gooden	2	2	1	1	0	0	0	0	0	0	.500	.500	.500	0
Danny Heep	5	11	0	1	0	0	0	2	1	1	.091	.167	.091	0

(continued)	G	AB	R	H	2B	3B	HR	RBI	BB	SO	BA	OBP	SLG	SB
Keith Hernandez	7	26	1	6	0	0	0	4	5	1	.231	.344	.231	0
Howard Johnson	2	5	0	0	0	0	0	0	0	2	.000	.000	.000	0
Ray Knight	6	23	4	9	1	0	1	5	2	2	.391	.440	.565	0
Lee Mazzilli	4	5	2	2	0	0	0	0	0	0	.400	.400	.400	0
Roger McDowell	5	0	0	0	0	0	0	0	0	0				0
Kevin Mitchell	5	8	1	2	0	0	0	0	0	3	.250	.250	.250	0
Bob Ojeda	2	2	0	0	0	0	0	0	0	1	.000	.000	.000	0
Jesse Orosco	4	1	0	1	0	0	0	1	0	0	1.00	1.000	1.00	0
Rafael Santana	7	20	3	5	0	0	0	2	2	5	.250	.318	.250	0
Doug Sisk	1	0	0	0	0	0	0	0	0	0				0
Darryl Strawberry	7	24	4	5	1	0	1	1	4	6	.208	.321	.375	3
Tim Teufel	3	9	1	4	1	0	1	1	1	2	.444	.500	.889	0
Mookie Wilson	7	26	3	7	1	0	0	0	1	6	.269	.321	.308	3
TOTAL	7	240	32	65	6	0	7	29	21	43	.271	.330	.383	7

	G	ERA	W–L	SV	CG	IP	H	ER	BB	SO
Ron Darling	3	1.53	1–1	0	0	17.7	13	3	10	12
Bob Ojeda	2	2.08	1–0	0	0	13.0	13	3	5	9
Dwight Gooden	2	8.00	0–2	0	0	9.0	17	8	4	9
Roger McDowell	5	4.91	1–0	0	0	7.3	10	4	6	2
Sid Fernandez	3	1.35	0–0	0	0	6.7	6	1	1	10
Jesse Orosco	4	0.00	0–0	2	0	5.7	2	0	0	6
Rick Aguilera	2	12.00	1–0	0	0	3.0	8	4	1	4
Doug Sisk	1	0.00	0–0	0	0	0.7	0	0	1	1
TOTAL	7	3.29	4–3	2	0	63.0	69	23	28	53

1988 American League Championship: Boston vs. Oakland

BOSTON RED SOX

	G	AB	R	H	2B	3B	HR	RBI	BB	SO	BA	OBP	SLG	SB
Marty Barrett	4	15	2	1	0	0	0	0	1	0	.067	.125	.067	0
Todd Benzinger	4	11	0	1	0	0	0	0	1	3	.091	.167	.091	0
Wade Boggs	4	13	2	5	0	0	0	3	3	4	.385	.444	.385	0
Ellis Burks	4	17	2	4	1	0	0	1	0	3	.235	.235	.294	0
Dwight Evans	4	12	1	2	1	0	0	1	3	5	.167	.333	.250	0
Rich Gedman	4	14	1	5	0	0	1	1	2	1	.357	.438	.571	0
Mike Greenwell	4	14	2	3	1	0	1	3	3	0	.214	.353	.500	0
Spike Owen	1	0	0	0	0	0	0	0	1	0		1.000		0
Larry Parrish	3	5	0	0	0	0	0	0	0	2	.000	.000	.000	0
Jody Reed	4	12	0	3	1	0	0	0	2	1	.250	.400	.333	0
Jim Rice	4	13	0	2	0	0	0	1	2	4	.154	.267	.154	0
Ed Romero	1	0	0	0	0	0	0	0	0	0				0
Kevin Romine	2	0	1	0	0	0	0	0	0	0				0
TOTAL	4	126	11	26	4	0	2	10	18	23	.206	.306	.286	0

	G	ERA	W–L	SV	CG	IP	H	ER	BB	SO
Bruce Hurst	2	2.77	0–2	0	1	13.0	10	4	5	12
Roger Clemens	1	3.86	0–0	0	0	7.0	6	3	0	8

Appendix III

	G	ERA	W–L	SV	CG	IP	H	ER	BB	SO
(continued)										
Wes Gardner	1	5.79	0–0	0	0	4.7	6	3	2	8
Lee Smith	2	8.10	0–1	0	0	3.3	6	3	1	4
Mike Boddicker	1	20.25	0–1	0	0	2.7	8	6	1	2
Mike Smithson	1	0.00	0–0	0	0	2.3	3	0	0	1
Bob Stanley	2	9.00	0–0	0	0	1.0	2	1	1	0
TOTAL	4	5.29	0–4	0	1	34.0	41	20	10	35

OAKLAND ATHLETICS

	G	AB	R	H	2B	3B	HR	RBI	BB	SO	BA	OBP	SLG	SB
Don Baylor	2	6	0	0	0	0	0	1	1	2	.000	.125	.000	0
Jose Canseco	4	16	4	5	1	0	3	4	1	2	.312	.353	.938	1
Mike Gallego	4	12	1	1	0	0	0	0	0	3	.083	.083	.083	0
Ron Hassey	4	8	2	4	1	0	1	3	1	1	.500	.556	1.00	0
Dave Henderson	4	16	2	6	1	0	1	4	1	7	.375	.412	.625	0
Stan Javier	2	4	0	2	0	0	0	1	1	0	.500	.600	.500	0
Carney Lansford	4	17	4	5	1	0	1	2	0	2	.294	.294	.529	0
Mark McGwire	4	15	4	5	0	0	1	3	1	5	.333	.375	.533	0
Dave Parker	3	12	1	3	1	0	0	0	0	4	.250	.250	.333	0
Tony Phillips	2	7	0	2	1	0	0	0	1	3	.286	.375	.429	0
Luis Polonia	3	5	0	2	0	0	0	0	1	2	.400	.500	.400	0
Terry Steinbach	2	4	0	1	0	0	0	0	2	0	.250	.500	.250	0
Walt Weiss	4	15	2	5	2	0	0	2	0	4	.333	.333	.467	0
TOTAL	4	137	20	41	8	0	7	20	10	35	.299	.345	.511	1

	G	ERA	W–L	SV	CG	IP	H	ER	BB	SO
Dave Stewart	2	1.35	1–0	0	0	13.3	9	2	6	11
Storm Davis	1	0.00	0–0	0	0	6.3	2	0	5	4
Dennis Eckersley	4	0.00	0–0	4	0	6.0	1	0	2	5
Gene Nelson	2	0.00	2–0	0	0	4.7	5	0	1	0
Bob Welch	1	19.29	0–0	0	0	2.3	6	5	2	0
Rick Honeycutt	3	0.00	1–0	0	0	2.0	0	0	2	0
Curt Young	1	0.00	0–0	0	0	1.3	1	0	0	2
Greg Cadaret	1	27.00	0–0	0	0	0.3	1	1	0	0
Eric Plunk	1	0.00	0–0	0	0	0.3	1	0	0	1
TOTAL	4	1.96	4–0	4	0	36.7	26	8	18	23

1990 American League Championship: Boston vs. Oakland

BOSTON RED SOX

	G	AB	R	H	2B	3B	HR	RBI	BB	SO	BA	OBP	SLG	SB
Marty Barrett	3	0	0	0	0	0	0	0	0	0				0
Wade Boggs	4	16	1	7	1	0	1	1	0	3	.438	.438	.688	0
Tom Brunansky	4	12	0	1	0	0	0	1	1	3	.083	.143	.083	0
Ellis Burks	4	15	1	4	2	0	0	0	1	1	.267	.312	.400	1
Roger Clemens	2	0	0	0	0	0	0	0	0	0				0
Dwight Evans	4	13	0	3	1	0	0	0	1	3	.231	.286	.308	0
Mike Greenwell	4	14	1	0	0	0	0	0	2	2	.000	.125	.000	0

(continued)	G	AB	R	H	2B	3B	HR	RBI	BB	SO	BA	OBP	SLG	SB
Danny Heep	2	2	0	0	0	0	0	0	0	0	.000	.000	.000	0
Randy Kutcher	2	0	0	0	0	0	0	0	0	0				0
Mike Marshall	3	3	0	1	0	0	0	0	0	0	.333	.333	.333	0
Tony Pena	4	14	0	3	0	0	0	0	0	0	.214	.214	.214	0
Carlos Quintana	4	13	0	0	0	0	0	1	1	0	.000	.067	.000	0
Jody Reed	4	15	0	2	0	0	0	1	0	2	.133	.133	.133	0
Luis Rivera	4	9	1	2	1	0	0	0	0	2	.222	.222	.333	0
TOTAL	4	126	4	23	5	0	1	4	6	16	.183	.216	.246	1

	G	ERA	W–L	SV	CG	IP	H	ER	BB	SO
Mike Boddicker	1	2.25	0–1	0	1	8.0	6	2	3	7
Roger Clemens	2	3.52	0–1	0	0	7.7	7	3	5	4
Dana Kiecker	1	1.59	0–0	0	0	5.7	6	1	1	2
Jeff Gray	2	2.70	0–0	0	0	3.3	4	1	1	2
Tom Bolton	2	0.00	0–0	0	0	3.0	2	0	2	3
Larry Andersen	3	6.00	0–1	0	0	3.0	3	2	3	3
Jeff Reardon	1	9.00	0–0	0	0	2.0	3	2	1	0
Rob Murphy	1	13.50	0–0	0	0	0.7	2	1	1	0
Greg Harris	1	27.00	0–1	0	0	0.3	3	1	0	0
Dennis Lamp	1	108.00	0–0	0	0	0.3	2	4	2	0
TOTAL	4	4.50	0–4	0	1	34.0	38	17	19	21

OAKLAND ATHLETICS

	G	AB	R	H	2B	3B	HR	RBI	BB	SO	BA	OBP	SLG	SB
Harold Baines	4	14	2	5	1	0	0	3	2	1	.357	.438	.429	1
Lance Blankenship	3	0	1	0	0	0	0	0	0	0				1
Jose Canseco	4	11	3	2	0	0	0	1	5	5	.182	.412	.182	2
Mike Gallego	4	10	1	4	1	0	0	2	1	1	.400	.500	.500	0
Ron Hassey	2	3	0	1	0	0	0	0	2	0	.333	.667	.333	0
Dave Henderson	2	6	0	1	0	0	0	1	0	2	.167	.250	.167	1
Rickey Henderson	4	17	1	5	0	0	0	3	1	2	.294	.316	.294	2
Doug Jennings	1	1	0	0	0	0	0	0	0	0	.000	.000	.000	0
Carney Lansford	4	16	2	7	1	0	0	2	0	1	.438	.438	.500	0
Willie McGee	3	9	3	2	1	0	0	0	1	2	.222	.300	.333	2
Mark McGwire	4	13	2	2	0	0	0	2	3	3	.154	.353	.154	0
Jamie Quirk	1	1	0	1	0	0	0	0	0	0	1.00	1.000	1.00	0
Willie Randolph	4	8	1	3	0	0	0	3	1	0	.375	.444	.375	0
Terry Steinbach	3	11	2	5	0	0	0	1	1	2	.455	.500	.455	0
Walt Weiss	2	7	2	0	0	0	0	0	2	2	.000	.222	.000	0
TOTAL	4	127	20	38	4	0	0	18	19	21	.299	.399	.331	9

	G	ERA	W–L	SV	CG	IP	H	ER	BB	SO
Dave Stewart	2	1.12	2–0	0	0	16.0	8	2	2	4
Bob Welch	1	1.23	1–0	0	0	7.3	6	1	3	4
Mike Moore	1	1.50	1–0	0	0	6.0	4	1	1	5
Dennis Eckersley	3	0.00	0–0	2	0	3.3	2	0	0	3
Gene Nelson	1	0.00	0–0	0	0	1.7	3	0	0	0
Rick Honeycutt	3	0.00	0–0	1	0	1.7	0	0	0	0
TOTAL	4	1.00	4–0	3	0	36.0	23	4	6	16

1995 American League Division Series: Boston vs. Cleveland

BOSTON RED SOX

	G	AB	R	H	2B	3B	HR	RBI	BB	SO	BA	OBP	SLG	SB
Luis Alicea	3	10	1	6	1	0	1	1	2	2	.600	.667	1.00	1
Jose Canseco	3	13	0	0	0	0	0	0	2	2	.000	.133	.000	0
Mike Greenwell	3	15	0	3	0	0	0	0	0	1	.200	.200	.200	0
Bill Haselman	1	2	0	0	0	0	0	0	0	0	.000	.000	.000	0
Dwayne Hosey	3	12	1	0	0	0	0	0	2	3	.000	.143	.000	1
Reggie Jefferson	1	4	1	1	0	0	0	0	0	1	.250	.250	.250	0
Mike Macfarlane	3	9	0	3	0	0	0	1	0	3	.333	.300	.333	0
Willie McGee	2	4	0	1	0	0	0	1	0	2	.250	.250	.250	0
Tim Naehring	3	13	2	4	0	0	1	1	0	1	.308	.308	.538	0
Matt Stairs	1	1	0	0	0	0	0	0	0	1	.000	.000	.000	0
Lee Tinsley	1	5	0	0	0	0	0	0	1	2	.000	.167	.000	0
John Valentin	3	12	1	3	1	0	1	2	3	1	.250	.400	.583	0
Mo Vaughn	3	14	0	0	0	0	0	0	1	7	.000	.067	.000	0
TOTAL	3	114	6	21	2	0	3	6	11	26	.184	.254	.281	2

	G	ERA	W–L	SV	CG	IP	H	ER	BB	SO
Erik Hanson	1	4.50	0–1	0	1	8.0	4	4	4	5
Roger Clemens	1	3.86	0–0	0	0	7.0	5	3	1	5
Tim Wakefield	1	11.81	0–1	0	0	5.3	5	7	5	4
Mike Maddux	2	0.00	0–0	0	0	3.0	2	0	1	1
Mike Stanton	1	0.00	0–0	0	0	2.3	1	0	0	4
Zane Smith	1	6.75	0–1	0	0	1.3	1	1	0	0
Joe Hudson	1	0.00	0–0	0	0	1.0	2	0	1	0
Rick Aguilera	1	13.50	0–0	0	0	0.7	3	1	0	1
Rheal Cormier	2	13.50	0–0	0	0	0.7	2	1	1	2
Stan Belinda	1	0.00	0–0	0	0	0.3	0	0	0	0
TOTAL	3	5.16	0–3	0	1	29.7	25	17	13	22

CLEVELAND INDIANS

	G	AB	R	H	2B	3B	HR	RBI	BB	SO	BA	OBP	SLG	SB
Sandy Alomar	3	11	1	2	1	0	0	1	0	1	.182	.182	.273	0
Carlos Baerga	3	14	2	4	1	0	0	1	0	1	.286	.333	.357	0
Albert Belle	3	11	3	3	1	0	1	3	4	3	.273	.467	.636	0
Alvaro Espinoza	1	1	0	0	0	0	0	0	0	0	.000	.000	.000	0
Wayne Kirby	3	1	0	1	0	0	0	0	0	0	1.00	1.000	1.00	0
Kenny Lofton	3	13	1	2	0	0	0	0	1	3	.154	.267	.154	0
Eddie Murray	3	13	3	5	0	1	1	3	2	1	.385	.467	.769	0
Tony Pena	2	2	1	1	0	0	1	1	0	0	.500	.500	2.00	0
Herb Perry	1	1	0	0	0	0	0	0	0	0	.000	.000	.000	0
Manny Ramirez	3	12	1	0	0	0	0	0	1	2	.000	.143	.000	0
Paul Sorrento	3	10	2	3	0	0	0	1	2	3	.300	.462	.300	0
Jim Thome	3	13	1	2	0	0	1	3	1	6	.154	.214	.385	0
Omar Vizquel	3	12	2	2	1	0	0	4	2	2	.167	.286	.250	1
TOTAL	3	114	17	25	4	1	4	17	13	22	.219	.321	.377	1

	G	ERA	W–L	SV	CG	IP	H	ER	BB	SO
Orel Hershiser	1	0.00	1–0	0	0	7.3	3	0	2	7
Charles Nagy	1	1.29	1–0	0	0	7.0	4	1	5	6
Dennis Martinez	1	3.00	0–0	0	0	6.0	5	2	0	2
Julian Tavarez	3	6.75	0–0	0	0	2.7	5	2	0	3
Jose Mesa	2	0.00	0–0	0	0	2.0	0	0	2	0
Jim Poole	1	5.40	0–0	0	0	1.7	2	1	1	2
Paul Assenmacher	3	0.00	0–0	0	0	1.7	0	0	0	3
Ken Hill	1	0.00	1–0	0	0	1.3	1	0	0	2
Eric Plunk	1	0.00	0–0	0	0	1.3	1	0	1	1
TOTAL	3	1.74	3–0	0	0	31.0	21	6	11	26

1998 American League Division Series: Boston vs. Cleveland

BOSTON RED SOX

	G	AB	R	H	2B	3B	HR	RBI	BB	SO	BA	OBP	SLG	SB
Mike Benjamin	4	11	1	1	0	0	0	0	1	3	.091	.167	.091	0
Darren Bragg	3	12	0	1	0	0	0	0	0	5	.083	.083	.083	0
Damon Buford	3	1	2	0	0	0	0	0	0	0	.000	.500	.000	0
Midre Cummings	3	3	0	0	0	0	0	0	0	0	.000	.000	.000	0
Nomar Garciaparra	4	15	4	5	1	0	3	11	1	0	.333	.333	1.00	0
Scott Hatteberg	3	9	0	1	0	0	0	0	3	1	.111	.333	.111	0
Darren Lewis	4	14	4	5	2	0	0	0	1	3	.357	.438	.500	1
Trot Nixon	2	3	0	1	0	0	0	0	1	0	.333	.500	.333	0
Troy O'Leary	4	16	0	1	0	0	0	0	1	4	.062	.118	.062	0
Donnie Sadler	3	0	0	0	0	0	0	0	0	0				0
Mike Stanley	4	15	1	4	0	0	0	0	2	5	.267	.353	.267	0
John Valentin	4	15	5	7	1	0	0	0	3	1	.467	.556	.533	0
Jason Varitek	1	4	0	1	0	0	0	1	0	1	.250	.250	.250	0
Mo Vaughn	4	17	3	7	2	0	2	7	1	5	.412	.444	.882	0
TOTAL	4	135	20	34	6	0	5	19	14	28	.252	.327	.407	1

	G	ERA	W–L	SV	CG	IP	H	ER	BB	SO
Pedro Martinez	1	3.86	1–0	0	0	7.0	6	3	0	8
Bret Saberhagen	1	3.86	0–1	0	0	7.0	4	3	1	7
Pete Schourek	1	0.00	0–0	0	0	5.3	2	0	4	1
Derek Lowe	2	2.08	0–0	0	0	4.3	3	1	1	2
Jim Corsi	2	0.00	0–0	0	0	3.0	1	0	1	2
Tom Gordon	2	9.00	0–1	0	0	3.0	4	3	4	1
John Wasdin	1	10.80	0–0	0	0	1.7	2	2	1	2
Greg Swindell	1	0.00	0–0	0	0	1.3	0	0	1	1
Tim Wakefield	1	33.75	0–1	0	0	1.3	3	5	2	1
Dennis Eckersley	1	9.00	0–0	0	0	1.0	1	1	0	1
TOTAL	4	4.63	1–3	0	0	35.0	26	18	15	26

CLEVELAND INDIANS

	G	AB	R	H	2B	3B	HR	RBI	BB	SO	BA	OBP	SLG	SB
Sandy Alomar	4	13	2	3	3	0	0	2	1	4	.231	.286	.462	0
Joey Cora	4	10	2	0	0	0	0	0	3	2	.000	.231	.000	0

	G	AB	R	H	2B	3B	HR	RBI	BB	SO	BA	OBP	SLG	SB
(continued)														
Travis Fryman	4	13	1	2	1	0	0	0	3	4	.154	.312	.231	1
Brian Giles	3	10	1	2	1	0	0	0	1	4	.200	.333	.300	0
David Justice	4	16	2	5	4	0	1	6	0	1	.312	.294	.750	0
Kenny Lofton	4	16	5	6	1	0	2	4	1	1	.375	.412	.812	2
Manny Ramirez	4	14	2	5	2	0	2	3	1	4	.357	.471	.929	0
Richie Sexson	3	2	0	0	0	0	0	0	2	1	.000	.500	.000	0
Jim Thome	4	15	2	2	0	0	2	2	2	5	.133	.235	.533	0
Omar Vizquel	4	15	1	1	0	0	0	0	1	0	.067	.125	.067	0
Enrique Wilson	1	2	0	0	0	0	0	0	0	0	.000	.000	.000	0
TOTAL	4	126	18	26	12	0	7	17	15	26	.206	.303	.468	3

	G	ERA	W–L	SV	CG	IP	H	ER	BB	SO
Charles Nagy	1	1.12	1–0	0	0	8.0	4	1	0	3
Bartolo Colon	1	1.59	0–0	0	0	5.7	5	1	3	3
Dave Burba	1	5.06	1–0	0	0	5.3	4	3	2	4
Jaret Wright	1	12.46	0–1	0	0	4.3	7	6	2	6
Mike Jackson	3	4.50	0–0	3	0	4.0	3	2	1	1
Paul Shuey	3	0.00	0–0	0	0	3.0	3	0	1	4
Doug Jones	1	6.75	0–0	0	0	2.7	3	2	1	1
Jim Poole	2	0.00	0–0	0	0	1.0	1	0	1	2
Paul Assenmacher	3	0.00	0–0	0	0	1.0	2	0	0	2
Steve Reed	2	40.50	1–0	0	0	0.7	1	3	1	1
Dwight Gooden	1	54.00	0–0	0	0	0.3	1	2	2	1
TOTAL	4	5.00	3–1	3	0	36.0	34	20	14	28

1999 American League Division Series: Boston vs. Cleveland

BOSTON RED SOX

	G	AB	R	H	2B	3B	HR	RBI	BB	SO	BA	OBP	SLG	SB
Damon Buford	1	3	0	0	0	0	0	0	0	1	.000	.000	.000	0
Brian Daubach	4	16	3	4	2	0	1	3	0	7	.250	.250	.562	0
Nomar Garciaparra	5	12	6	5	2	0	2	4	3	3	.417	.562	1.08	0
Scott Hatteberg	1	1	1	1	0	0	0	1	0	0	1.00	1.000	1.00	0
Butch Huskey	2	5	0	1	0	0	0	0	0	1	.200	.200	.200	0
Darren Lewis	4	16	5	6	1	0	0	2	0	2	.375	.412	.438	1
Lou Merloni	3	6	1	2	0	0	0	1	1	1	.333	.429	.333	0
Trot Nixon	5	14	5	3	3	0	0	6	4	5	.214	.350	.429	0
Troy O'Leary	5	20	4	4	0	0	2	7	2	3	.200	.273	.500	0
Jose Offerman	5	18	4	7	1	0	1	6	7	0	.389	.560	.611	0
Donnie Sadler	2	2	1	1	1	0	0	0	0	1	.500	.500	1.00	0
Mike Stanley	5	20	4	10	2	1	0	2	2	3	.500	.545	.700	0
John Valentin	5	22	6	7	2	0	3	12	0	4	.318	.304	.818	0
Jason Varitek	5	21	7	5	3	0	1	3	0	4	.238	.273	.524	0
TOTAL	5	176	47	56	17	1	10	47	19	35	.318	.388	.597	1

	G	ERA	W–L	SV	CG	IP	H	ER	BB	SO
Pedro Martinez	2	0.00	1–0	0	0	10.0	3	0	4	11
Derek Lowe	3	4.32	1–1	0	0	8.3	6	4	1	7

(continued)	G	ERA	W–L	SV	CG	IP	H	ER	BB	SO
Ramon Martinez	1	3.18	0–0	0	0	5.7	5	2	3	6
Rheal Cormier	2	0.00	0–0	0	0	4.0	2	0	1	4
Bret Saberhagen	2	27.00	0–1	0	0	3.7	9	11	4	2
Rich Garces	2	3.86	1–0	0	0	2.3	2	1	3	2
Rod Beck	2	0.00	0–0	0	0	2.0	2	0	0	2
Tom Gordon	2	4.50	0–0	0	0	2.0	1	1	1	3
Tim Wakefield	2	13.50	0–0	0	0	2.0	3	3	4	4
Kent Mercker	1	10.80	0–0	0	0	1.7	3	2	3	1
John Wasdin	2	27.00	0–0	0	0	1.7	2	5	4	1
TOTAL	5	6.02	3–2	0	0	43.3	38	29	28	43

Cleveland Indians

	G	AB	R	H	2B	3B	HR	RBI	BB	SO	BA	OBP	SLG	SB
Roberto Alomar	5	19	4	7	4	0	0	3	2	3	.368	.409	.579	2
Sandy Alomar	5	14	1	2	0	0	0	1	2	6	.143	.235	.143	0
Harold Baines	4	14	1	5	0	0	1	4	2	1	.357	.438	.571	0
Wil Cordero	3	9	3	5	0	0	1	2	1	2	.556	.600	.889	0
Einar Diaz	2	1	0	0	0	0	0	0	0	0	.000	.000	.000	0
Travis Fryman	5	15	2	4	0	0	1	4	3	2	.267	.400	.467	1
David Justice	3	8	0	0	0	0	0	1	2	2	.000	.182	.000	0
Kenny Lofton	5	16	5	2	1	0	0	1	5	6	.125	.333	.188	2
Manny Ramirez	5	18	5	1	1	0	0	1	4	8	.056	.261	.111	0
Dave Roberts	2	3	0	0	0	0	0	0	0	2	.000	.000	.000	0
Richie Sexson	3	6	1	1	0	0	0	1	1	3	.167	.286	.167	0
Jim Thome	5	17	7	6	0	0	4	10	4	5	.353	.476	1.05	0
Omar Vizquel	5	21	3	5	1	1	0	3	2	3	.238	.304	.381	0
Enrique Wilson	3	2	0	0	0	0	0	0	0	0	.000	.000	.000	0
TOTAL	5	163	32	38	7	1	7	31	28	43	.233	.345	.417	5

	G	ERA	W–L	SV	CG	IP	H	ER	BB	SO
Charles Nagy	2	7.20	1–0	0	0	10.0	11	8	2	6
Bartolo Colon	2	9.00	0–1	0	0	9.0	11	9	4	12
Sean Depaula	3	1.80	0–0	0	0	5.0	2	1	3	5
Dave Burba	1	0.00	0–0	0	0	4.0	1	0	1	0
Paul Shuey	3	11.25	1–1	0	0	4.0	4	5	4	5
Steve Karsay	2	9.00	0–0	0	0	3.0	5	3	1	3
Steve Reed	2	30.86	0–0	0	0	2.3	9	8	1	1
Jaret Wright	1	22.50	0–1	0	0	2.0	4	5	1	1
Mike Jackson	2	4.50	0–0	0	0	2.0	2	1	1	1
Paul Assenmacher	1	27.00	0–0	0	0	1.0	5	3	0	0
Ricardo Rincon	1	40.50	0–0	0	0	0.7	2	3	1	1
TOTAL		9.63	2–3	0	0	43.0	56	46	19	35

1999 American League Championship Series: Boston vs. New York

Boston Red Sox

	G	AB	R	H	2B	3B	HR	RBI	BB	SO	BA	OBP	SLG	SB
Damon Buford	4	5	1	2	0	0	0	0	0	2	.400	.400	.400	1
Brian Daubach	5	17	2	3	1	0	1	3	1	4	.176	.222	.412	0
Nomar Garciaparra	5	20	2	8	2	0	2	5	2	2	.400	.455	.800	1
Scott Hatteberg	3	1	0	0	0	0	0	0	0	1	.000	.000	.000	0
Butch Huskey	4	5	1	1	1	0	0	0	1	1	.200	.333	.400	0
Darren Lewis	5	17	2	2	1	0	0	1	1	3	.118	.167	.176	1
Lou Merloni	1	0	0	0	0	0	0	0	1	0		1.000		0
Trot Nixon	4	14	2	4	2	0	0	0	1	5	.286	.333	.429	0
Troy O'Leary	5	20	2	7	3	0	0	1	2	5	.350	.409	.500	0
Jose Offerman	5	24	4	11	0	1	0	2	1	3	.458	.480	.542	1
Donnie Sadler	2	0	0	0	0	0	0	0	0	0				0
Mike Stanley	5	18	1	4	0	0	0	1	2	4	.222	.333	.222	0
John Valentin	5	23	3	8	2	0	1	5	2	4	.348	.400	.565	0
Jason Varitek	5	20	1	4	1	1	1	1	1	4	.200	.238	.500	0
Total	5	184	21	54	13	2	5	19	15	38	.293	.350	.467	4

	G	ERA	W–L	SV	CG	IP	H	ER	BB	SO
Kent Mercker	2	4.70	0–1	0	0	7.7	12	4	4	5
Pedro Martinez	1	0.00	1–0	0	0	7.0	2	0	2	12
Ramon Martinez	1	4.05	0–1	0	0	6.7	6	3	3	5
Derek Lowe	3	1.42	0–0	0	0	6.3	6	1	2	7
Bret Saberhagen	1	1.50	0–1	0	0	6.0	5	1	1	5
Rheal Cormier	4	0.00	0–0	0	0	3.7	3	0	3	4
Rich Garces	2	12.00	0–0	0	0	3.0	3	4	1	2
Tom Gordon	3	13.50	0–0	0	0	2.0	3	3	1	3
Pat Rapp	1	0.00	0–0	0	0	1.0	0	0	1	0
Rod Beck	2	27.00	0–1	0	0	0.7	2	2	0	1
Total	5	3.68	1–4	0	0	44.0	42	18	18	44

New York Yankees

	G	AB	R	H	2B	3B	HR	RBI	BB	SO	BA	OBP	SLG	SB
Clay Bellinger	3	1	0	0	0	0	0	0	0	1	.000	.000	.000	0
Scott Brosius	5	18	3	4	0	1	2	3	1	4	.222	.263	.667	0
Chad Curtis	3	6	1	0	0	0	0	0	0	2	.000	.000	.000	1
Chili Davis	5	11	0	1	0	0	0	1	3	4	.091	.286	.091	0
Joe Girardi	3	8	0	2	0	0	0	0	0	2	.250	.250	.250	0
Derek Jeter	5	20	3	7	1	0	1	3	2	3	.350	.409	.550	0
Chuck Knoblauch	5	18	3	6	1	0	1	3	0	.333	.429	.389	1
Ricky Ledee	3	8	2	2	0	0	1	4	1	4	.250	.333	.625	0
Tino Martinez	5	19	3	5	1	0	1	3	2	4	.263	.364	.474	0
Paul O'Neill	5	21	2	6	0	0	0	1	1	5	.286	.318	.286	0
Jorge Posada	3	10	1	1	0	0	1	2	1	2	.100	.182	.400	0
Luis Sojo	2	1	0	0	0	0	0	0	0	0	.000	.000	.000	0
Shane Spencer	3	9	1	1	0	0	0	0	1	6	.111	.200	.111	0
Darryl Strawberry	3	6	1	2	0	0	1	1	1	2	.333	.429	.833	0

	G	AB	R	H	2B	3B	HR	RBI	BB	SO	BA	OBP	SLG	SB
(continued)														
Bernie Williams	5	20	3	5	1	0	1	2	2	5	.250	.318	.450	1
TOTAL	5	176	23	42	4	1	8	21	18	44	.239	.313	.409	3

	G	ERA	W–L	SV	CG	IP	H	ER	BB	SO
Orlando Hernandez	2	1.80	1–0	0	0	15.0	12	3	6	13
Andy Pettitte	1	2.45	1–0	0	0	7.3	8	2	1	5
David Cone	1	2.57	1–0	0	0	7.0	7	2	3	9
Hideki Irabu	1	13.50	0–0	0	0	4.7	13	7	0	3
Mariano Rivera	3	0.00	1–0	2	0	4.7	5	0	0	3
Ramiro Mendoza	2	0.00	0–0	1	0	2.3	0	0	0	2
Roger Clemens	1	22.50	0–1	0	0	2.0	6	5	2	2
Allen Watson	3	0.00	0–0	0	0	1.0	2	0	2	1
Jeff Nelson	2	0.00	0–0	0	0	0.7	0	0	0	0
Mike Stanton	3	0.00	0–0	0	0	0.3	1	0	1	0
TOTAL	5	3.80	4–1	3	0	45.0	54	19	15	38

2003 American League Division Series: Boston vs. Oakland

BOSTON RED SOX

	G	AB	R	H	2B	3B	HR	RBI	BB	SO	BA	OBP	SLG	SB
Adrian Brown	4	2	0	0	0	0	0	0	0	1	.000	.000	.000	0
Johnny Damon	5	19	2	6	2	0	1	3	2	1	.316	.409	.579	2
Nomar Garciaparra	5	20	2	6	1	0	0	0	3	2	.300	.391	.350	1
Damian Jackson	4	5	0	0	0	0	0	0	0	2	.000	.000	.000	0
Gabe Kapler	4	9	0	0	0	0	0	0	0	3	.000	.000	.000	0
David McCarty	1	0	0	0	0	0	0	0	0	0				0
Kevin Millar	5	21	0	5	0	0	0	0	2	4	.238	.304	.238	0
Doug Mirabelli	2	4	2	2	1	0	0	0	0	2	.500	.500	.750	0
Bill Mueller	5	19	0	2	1	0	0	0	3	4	.105	.227	.158	0
Trot Nixon	4	10	1	2	0	0	1	2	1	3	.200	.273	.500	0
David Ortiz	5	21	0	2	1	0	0	2	2	7	.095	.174	.143	0
Manny Ramirez	5	20	2	4	0	0	1	3	3	7	.200	.304	.350	0
Jason Varitek	5	14	4	4	0	0	2	2	2	2	.286	.375	.714	0
Todd Walker	5	16	4	5	0	0	3	4	0	1	.312	.353	.875	0
TOTAL	5	180	17	38	6	0	8	16	18	39	.211	.290	.378	3

	G	ERA	W–L	SV	CG	IP	H	ER	BB	SO
Pedro Martinez	2	3.86	1–0	0	0	14.0	13	6	5	9
Derek Lowe	3	0.93	0–1	1	0	9.7	7	1	7	6
Tim Wakefield	2	3.52	0–1	0	0	7.7	6	3	3	7
John Burkett	1	6.75	0–0	0	0	5.3	9	4	2	1
Scott Williamson	5	0.00	2–0	0	0	5.0	2	0	3	8
Mike Timlin	3	0.00	0–0	0	0	4.3	0	0	0	5
Alan Embree	3	0.00	0–0	0	0	2.0	1	0	0	0
Byung-Hyun Kim	1	13.50	0–0	0	0	0.7	0	1	1	1
TOTAL	5	2.77	3–2	1	0	48.7	38	15	21	37

Oakland Athletics

	G	AB	R	H	2B	3B	HR	RBI	BB	SO	BA	OBP	SLG	SB
Eric Byrnes	5	13	2	6	1	0	0	2	0	5	.462	.462	.538	1
Eric Chavez	5	22	1	1	1	0	0	0	1	3	.045	.087	.091	1
Erubiel Durazo	5	21	3	5	2	0	0	3	3	4	.238	.333	.333	0
Jermaine Dye	4	13	2	3	0	0	1	3	0	2	.231	.286	.462	0
Mark Ellis	5	17	2	2	0	0	0	0	4	7	.118	.318	.118	0
Jose Guillen	4	11	1	5	1	0	0	1	3	2	.455	.571	.545	0
Scott Hatteberg	5	17	3	3	0	0	0	0	5	3	.176	.364	.176	0
Ramon Hernandez	4	15	1	3	0	0	0	2	2	1	.200	.333	.200	0
Terrence Long	4	8	0	2	0	0	0	0	1	3	.250	.333	.250	0
Billy McMillon	3	6	0	1	0	0	0	1	1	1	.167	.286	.167	0
Adam Melhuse	2	5	1	3	0	1	0	1	0	1	.600	.600	1.00	0
Frank Menechino	1	0	0	0	0	0	0	0	0	0				0
Chris Singleton	2	7	2	2	2	0	0	0	1	1	.286	.444	.571	1
Miguel Tejada	5	23	0	2	1	0	0	2	0	4	.087	.087	.130	0
TOTAL	5	178	18	38	8	1	1	15	21	37	.213	.310	.287	3

	G	ERA	W–L	SV	CG	IP	H	ER	BB	SO
Barry Zito	2	3.46	1–1	0	0	13.0	9	5	4	13
Ted Lilly	2	0.00	0–0	0	0	9.0	2	0	2	7
Tim Hudson	2	3.52	0–0	0	0	7.7	10	3	1	6
Keith Foulke	3	3.60	0–1	0	0	5.0	4	2	2	3
Steve Sparks	1	4.50	0–0	0	0	4.0	2	2	3	1
Ricardo Rincon	4	4.50	0–0	0	0	4.0	4	2	1	3
Chad Bradford	4	0.00	0–0	0	0	3.7	4	0	2	5
Rich Harden	2	13.50	1–1	0	0	1.3	2	2	2	1
Jim Mecir	1	0.00	0–0	0	0	0.7	1	0	1	0
TOTAL	5	2.98	2–3	0	0	48.3	38	16	18	39

2003 American League Championship Series: Boston vs. New York

Boston Red Sox

	G	AB	R	H	2B	3B	HR	RBI	BB	SO	BA	OBP	SLG	SB
Johnny Damon	5	20	1	4	1	0	0	1	3	3	.200	.304	.250	1
Nomar Garciaparra	7	29	2	7	0	1	0	1	2	8	.241	.290	.310	0
Damian Jackson	5	3	0	1	0	0	0	1	0	1	.333	.333	.333	0
Gabe Kapler	3	8	0	1	0	0	0	0	0	3	.125	.125	.125	0
David McCarty	1	1	0	0	0	0	0	0	0	1	.000	.000	.000	0
Kevin Millar	7	29	3	7	0	0	1	3	1	9	.241	.267	.345	0
Doug Mirabelli	3	7	0	2	0	0	0	0	0	2	.286	.286	.286	0
Bill Mueller	7	27	1	6	2	0	0	0	2	7	.222	.276	.296	0
Trot Nixon	7	24	3	8	1	0	3	5	3	7	.333	.429	.750	1
David Ortiz	7	26	4	7	1	0	2	6	3	8	.269	.367	.538	0
Manny Ramirez	7	29	6	9	1	0	2	4	1	4	.310	.333	.552	0
Jason Varitek	6	20	4	6	2	0	2	3	1	5	.300	.333	.700	0
Todd Walker	7	27	5	10	1	1	2	2	1	2	.370	.414	.704	0
TOTAL	7	250	29	68	9	2	12	26	17	60	.272	.326	.468	2

	G	ERA	W–L	SV	CG	IP	H	ER	BB	SO
Pedro Martinez	2	5.65	0–1	0	0	14.3	16	9	2	14
Derek Lowe	2	6.43	0–2	0	0	14.0	14	10	7	5
Tim Wakefield	3	2.57	2–1	0	0	14.0	8	4	6	10
Mike Timlin	5	0.00	0–0	0	0	5.3	1	0	2	6
Alan Embree	5	0.00	1–0	0	0	4.7	3	0	0	1
John Burkett	1	7.36	0–0	0	0	3.7	7	3	0	1
Bronson Arroyo	3	2.70	0–0	0	0	3.3	2	1	2	5
Scott Williamson	3	3.00	0–0	3	0	3.0	1	1	0	6
Todd Jones	1	0.00	0–0	0	0	0.3	1	0	1	1
Scott Sauerbeck	1	0.00	0–0	0	0	0.3	1	0	1	0
TOTAL	7	4.00	3–4	3	0	63.0	54	28	21	49

NEW YORK YANKEES

	G	AB	R	H	2B	3B	HR	RBI	BB	SO	BA	OBP	SLG	SB
Aaron Boone	7	17	2	3	0	0	1	2	1	6	.176	.263	.353	1
David Dellucci	3	3	2	1	0	0	0	0	0	1	.333	.500	.333	1
Karim Garcia	5	16	1	4	0	0	0	3	2	4	.250	.368	.250	0
Jason Giambi	7	26	4	6	0	0	3	3	4	7	.231	.333	.577	0
Derek Jeter	7	30	3	7	2	0	1	2	2	4	.233	.281	.400	1
Nick Johnson	7	26	4	6	1	0	1	3	2	4	.231	.286	.385	0
Hideki Matsui	7	26	3	8	3	0	0	4	1	3	.308	.321	.423	0
Jorge Posada	7	27	5	8	4	0	1	6	3	4	.296	.367	.556	0
Juan Rivera	2	2	0	0	0	0	0	0	0	1	.000	.000	.000	0
Ruben Sierra	3	2	1	1	0	0	1	1	1	0	.500	.667	2.00	0
Alfonso Soriano	7	30	0	4	1	0	0	3	1	11	.133	.188	.167	2
Bernie Williams	7	26	5	5	1	0	0	2	4	3	.192	.300	.231	0
Enrique Wilson	2	7	0	1	0	0	0	0	0	1	.143	.143	.143	0
TOTAL	7	238	30	54	12	0	8	29	21	49	.227	.299	.378	5

	G	ERA	W–L	SV	CG	IP	H	ER	BB	SO
Mike Mussina	3	4.11	0–2	0	0	15.3	16	7	4	17
Andy Pettitte	2	4.63	1–0	0	0	11.7	17	6	4	10
Roger Clemens	2	5.00	1–0	0	0	9.0	11	5	2	8
Mariano Rivera	4	1.12	1–0	2	0	8.0	5	1	0	6
David Wells	2	2.35	1–0	0	0	7.7	5	2	2	5
Jose Contreras	4	5.79	0–1	0	0	4.7	6	3	2	7
Jeff Nelson	4	6.00	0–0	0	0	3.0	4	2	0	3
Felix Heredia	5	3.38	0–0	0	0	2.7	0	1	3	3
Gabe White	2	4.50	0–0	0	0	2.0	4	1	0	1
TOTAL	7	3.94	4–3	2	0	64.0	68	28	17	60

2004 American League Division Series: Boston vs. Anaheim

BOSTON RED SOX

	G	AB	R	H	2B	3B	HR	RBI	BB	SO	BA	OBP	SLG	SB
Mark Bellhorn	3	11	2	1	0	0	0	0	5	4	.091	.375	.091	0
Orlando Cabrera	3	13	1	2	1	0	0	3	2	2	.154	.267	.231	0

(continued)	G	AB	R	H	2B	3B	HR	RBI	BB	SO	BA	OBP	SLG	SB
Johnny Damon	3	15	4	7	1	0	0	0	1	2	.467	.500	.533	3
Gabe Kapler	2	5	2	1	0	0	0	0	0	0	.200	.200	.200	0
Doug Mientkiewicz	3	4	0	2	0	0	0	1	0	0	.500	.500	.500	0
Kevin Millar	3	10	2	3	0	0	1	4	1	1	.300	.364	.600	0
Bill Mueller	3	12	3	4	0	0	0	0	1	1	.333	.385	.333	0
Trot Nixon	2	8	0	2	0	0	0	2	2	1	.250	.400	.250	0
David Ortiz	3	11	4	6	2	0	1	4	5	2	.545	.688	1.00	0
Manny Ramirez	3	13	3	5	2	0	1	7	1	4	.385	.375	.769	0
Pokey Reese	3	0	1	0	0	0	0	0	0	0				0
Dave Roberts	1	0	0	0	0	0	0	0	0	0				0
Jason Varitek	3	12	3	2	0	0	1	2	2	5	.167	.333	.417	0
Kevin Youkilis	1	2	0	0	0	0	0	0	0	1	.000	.000	.000	0
TOTAL	3	116	25	35	6	0	4	23	20	23	.302	.403	.457	3

	G	ERA	W–L	SV	CG	IP	H	ER	BB	SO
Pedro Martinez	1	3.86	1–0	0	0	7.0	6	3	2	6
Curt Schilling	1	2.70	1–0	0	0	6.7	9	2	2	4
Bronson Arroyo	1	3.00	0–0	0	0	6.0	3	2	2	7
Keith Foulke	2	0.00	0–0	1	0	3.0	2	0	1	5
Mike Timlin	3	9.00	0–0	0	0	3.0	3	3	1	5
Derek Lowe	1	0.00	1–0	0	0	1.0	1	0	1	0
Alan Embree	2	0.00	0–0	0	0	1.0	0	0	1	0
Mike Myers	2	27.00	0–0	0	0	0.3	0	1	1	1
TOTAL	3	3.54	3–0	1	0	28.0	24	11	11	28

ANAHEIM ANGELS

	G	AB	R	H	2B	3B	HR	RBI	BB	SO	BA	OBP	SLG	SB
Alfredo Amezaga	2	2	0	0	0	0	0	0	0	2	.000	.000	.000	0
Garret Anderson	3	13	1	2	0	0	0	0	0	3	.154	.154	.154	0
Jeff Davanon	3	10	1	2	0	0	0	0	2	1	.200	.333	.200	0
David Eckstein	3	12	2	4	0	0	0	0	0	1	.333	.385	.333	0
Darin Erstad	3	10	2	5	1	0	1	2	3	1	.500	.615	.900	0
Chone Figgins	3	14	0	2	0	0	0	0	0	5	.143	.200	.143	1
Troy Glaus	3	11	3	4	2	0	2	3	2	4	.364	.462	1.09	0
Vladimir Guerrero	3	12	1	2	0	0	1	6	2	4	.167	.286	.417	0
Casey Kotchman	2	1	0	0	0	0	0	0	0	0	.000	.000	.000	0
Dallas McPherson	3	9	0	1	0	0	0	1	0	4	.111	.111	.111	0
Ben Molina	3	6	0	1	0	0	0	0	0	2	.167	.167	.167	0
Jose Molina	2	3	2	1	0	0	0	0	2	0	.333	.600	.333	0
Curtis Pride	2	2	0	0	0	0	0	0	0	1	.000	.000	.000	0
Adam Riggs	2	1	0	0	0	0	0	0	0	0	.000	.000	.000	0
TOTAL	3	106	12	24	3	0	4	12	11	28	.226	.311	.368	1

	G	ERA	W–L	SV	CG	IP	H	ER	BB	SO
Bartolo Colon	1	4.50	0–0	0	0	6.0	7	3	3	3
Francisco Rodriguez	2	3.86	0–2	0	0	4.7	4	2	3	5
Kelvim Escobar	1	8.10	0–0	0	0	3.3	5	3	5	4
Brendan Donnelly	2	10.80	0–0	0	0	3.3	3	4	2	5
Jarrod Washburn	2	10.80	0–1	0	0	3.3	6	4	3	3

(continued)	G	ERA	W–L	SV	CG	IP	H	ER	BB	SO
Scot Shields	2	6.00	0–0	0	0	3.0	5	2	2	3
Kevin Gregg	1	0.00	0–0	0	0	2.0	3	0	1	0
Ramon Ortiz	1	4.50	0–0	0	0	2.0	2	1	1	0
TOTAL	3	6.18	0–3	0	0	27.7	35	19	20	23

2004 American League Championship Series: Boston vs. New York

BOSTON RED SOX

	G	AB	R	H	2B	3B	HR	RBI	BB	SO	BA	OBP	SLG	SB
Mark Bellhorn	7	26	3	5	2	0	2	4	5	11	.192	.323	.500	0
Orlando Cabrera	7	29	5	11	2	0	0	5	3	5	.379	.424	.448	1
Johnny Damon	7	35	5	6	0	0	2	7	2	8	.171	.216	.343	2
Gabe Kapler	2	3	0	1	0	0	0	0	0	0	.333	.333	.333	0
Doug Mientkiewicz	4	4	0	2	1	0	0	0	0	1	.500	.500	.750	0
Kevin Millar	7	24	4	6	3	0	0	2	5	4	.250	.379	.375	0
Doug Mirabelli	1	1	0	0	0	0	0	0	0	0	.000	.000	.000	0
Bill Mueller	7	30	4	8	1	0	0	1	2	1	.267	.333	.300	0
Trot Nixon	7	29	4	6	1	0	1	3	0	5	.207	.207	.345	0
David Ortiz	7	31	6	12	0	1	3	11	4	7	.387	.457	.742	0
Manny Ramirez	7	30	3	9	1	0	0	0	5	4	.300	.400	.333	0
Pokey Reese	3	1	0	0	0	0	0	0	0	1	.000	.000	.000	0
Dave Roberts	2	0	2	0	0	0	0	0	0	0				1
Jason Varitek	7	28	5	9	1	0	2	7	2	6	.321	.355	.571	0
TOTAL	7	271	41	75	12	1	10	40	28	53	.277	.344	.439	4

	G	ERA	W–L	SV	CG	IP	H	ER	BB	SO
Pedro Martinez	3	6.23	0–1	0	0	13.0	14	9	9	14
Derek Lowe	2	3.18	1–0	0	0	11.3	7	4	1	6
Curt Schilling	2	6.30	1–1	0	0	10.0	10	7	2	5
Tim Wakefield	3	8.59	1–0	0	0	7.3	9	7	3	6
Keith Foulke	5	0.00	0–0	1	0	6.0	1	0	6	6
Mike Timlin	5	4.76	0–0	0	0	5.7	10	3	5	2
Alan Embree	6	3.86	0–0	0	0	4.7	9	2	1	2
Bronson Arroyo	3	15.75	0–0	0	0	4.0	8	7	2	3
Curt Leskanic	3	10.12	1–0	0	0	2.7	3	3	3	2
Mike Myers	3	7.71	0–0	0	0	2.3	5	2	1	4
Ramiro Mendoza	2	4.50	0–1	0	0	2.0	2	1	0	1
TOTAL	7	5.87	4–3	1	0	69.0	78	45	33	51

NEW YORK YANKEES

	G	AB	R	H	2B	3B	HR	RBI	BB	SO	BA	OBP	SLG	SB
Miguel Cairo	7	25	4	7	3	0	0	0	2	4	.280	.419	.400	1
Tony Clark	5	21	0	3	1	0	0	1	0	9	.143	.143	.190	0
Bubba Crosby	1	0	1	0	0	0	0	0	0	0				0
Derek Jeter	7	30	5	6	1	0	0	5	6	2	.200	.333	.233	1
Kenny Lofton	3	10	1	3	0	0	1	2	2	3	.300	.417	.600	1
Hideki Matsui	7	34	9	14	6	1	2	10	2	4	.412	.444	.824	0

(continued)	G	AB	R	H	2B	3B	HR	RBI	BB	SO	BA	OBP	SLG	SB
John Olerud	4	12	1	2	0	0	1	2	1	1	.167	.231	.417	0
Jorge Posada	7	27	4	7	1	0	0	2	7	1	.259	.417	.296	0
Alex Rodriguez	7	31	8	8	2	0	2	5	4	6	.258	.378	.516	0
Gary Sheffield	7	30	7	10	3	0	1	5	6	8	.333	.444	.533	0
Ruben Sierra	5	21	1	7	1	1	0	2	3	8	.333	.417	.476	0
Bernie Williams	7	36	4	11	3	0	2	10	0	5	.306	.306	.556	0
TOTAL	7	277	45	78	21	2	9	44	33	51	.282	.371	.469	3

	G	ERA	W–L	SV	CG	IP	H	ER	BB	SO
Jon Lieber	2	3.14	1–1	0	0	14.3	12	5	1	5
Mike Mussina	2	4.26	1–0	0	0	12.7	10	6	2	15
Mariano Rivera	5	1.29	0–0	2	0	7.0	6	1	2	6
Tom Gordon	6	8.10	0–0	0	0	6.7	10	6	2	3
Esteban Loaiza	2	1.42	0–1	0	0	6.3	5	1	3	5
Javier Vazquez	2	9.95	1–0	0	0	6.3	9	7	7	6
Orlando Hernandez	1	5.40	0–0	0	0	5.0	3	3	5	6
Kevin Brown	2	24.30	0–1	0	0	3.3	9	9	4	2
Paul Quantrill	4	5.40	0–1	0	0	3.3	8	2	0	2
Tanyon Sturtze	4	2.70	0–0	0	0	3.3	2	1	2	2
Felix Heredia	3	0.00	0–0	0	0	1.3	1	0	0	1
TOTAL	7	5.30	3–4	2	0	69.7	75	41	28	53

2004 World Series: Boston vs. St. Louis

BOSTON RED SOX

	G	AB	R	H	2B	3B	HR	RBI	BB	SO	BA	OBP	SLG	SB
Bronson Arroyo	1	0	0	0	0	0	0	0	0	0				0
Mark Bellhorn	4	10	3	3	1	0	1	4	5	2	.300	.562	.700	0
Orlando Cabrera	4	17	3	4	1	0	0	3	3	1	.235	.381	.294	0
Johnny Damon	4	21	4	6	2	1	1	2	0	1	.286	.286	.619	0
Alan Embree	1	0	0	0	0	0	0	0	0	0				0
Keith Foulke	2	0	0	0	0	0	0	0	0	0				0
Gabe Kapler	4	2	0	0	0	0	0	0	0	1	.000	.000	.000	0
Derek Lowe	1	2	0	0	0	0	0	0	0	1	.000	.000	.000	0
Pedro Martinez	1	2	0	0	0	0	0	0	1	2	.000	.333	.000	0
Doug Mientkiewicz	4	1	0	0	0	0	0	0	0	0	.000	.000	.000	0
Kevin Millar	4	8	2	1	1	0	0	0	2	2	.125	.364	.250	0
Doug Mirabelli	1	3	1	1	0	0	0	0	0	1	.333	.333	.333	0
Bill Mueller	4	14	3	6	2	0	0	2	4	0	.429	.556	.571	0
Trot Nixon	4	14	1	5	3	0	0	3	1	1	.357	.400	.571	0
David Ortiz	4	13	3	4	1	0	1	4	4	1	.308	.471	.615	0
Manny Ramirez	4	17	2	7	0	0	1	4	3	3	.412	.500	.588	0
Pokey Reese	4	1	0	0	0	0	0	0	0	0	.000	.000	.000	0
Mike Timlin	1	0	0	0	0	0	0	0	0	0				0
Jason Varitek	4	13	2	2	0	1	0	2	1	4	.154	.267	.308	0
TOTAL	4	138	24	39	11	2	4	24	24	20	.283	.404	.478	0

	G	ERA	W–L	SV	CG	IP	H	ER	BB	SO
Derek Lowe	1	0.00	1–0	0	0	7.0	3	0	1	4
Pedro Martinez	1	0.00	1–0	0	0	7.0	3	0	2	6
Curt Schilling	1	0.00	1–0	0	0	6.0	4	0	1	4
Keith Foulke	4	1.80	1–0	1	0	5.0	4	1	1	8
Tim Wakefield	1	12.27	0–0	0	0	3.7	3	5	5	2
Mike Timlin	3	6.00	0–0	0	0	3.0	2	2	1	0
Bronson Arroyo	2	6.75	0–0	0	0	2.7	4	2	1	4
Alan Embree	3	0.00	0–0	0	0	1.7	1	0	0	4
TOTAL	4	2.50	4–0	1	0	36.0	24	10	12	32

St. Louis Cardinals

	G	AB	R	H	2B	3B	HR	RBI	BB	SO	BA	OBP	SLG	SB
Marlon Anderson	4	6	0	1	1	0	0	0	0	1	.167	.167	.333	0
Kiko Calero	1	0	0	0	0	0	0	0	0	0				0
Roger Cedeno	3	4	1	1	0	0	0	0	0	1	.250	.250	.250	0
Jim Edmonds	4	15	2	1	0	0	0	0	1	6	.067	.125	.067	0
Danny Haren	1	0	0	0	0	0	0	0	0	0				0
Jason Isringhausen	1	0	0	0	0	0	0	0	0	0				0
Ray King	1	0	0	0	0	0	0	0	0	0				0
Hector Luna	1	1	0	0	0	0	0	0	0	1	.000	.000	.000	0
John Mabry	2	4	0	0	0	0	0	0	0	2	.000	.000	.000	0
Jason Marquis	2	1	1	0	0	0	0	0	0	0	.000	.000	.000	0
Mike Matheny	4	8	0	2	0	0	0	2	0	3	.250	.200	.250	0
Yadier Molina	3	3	0	0	0	0	0	0	0	1	.000	.000	.000	0
Albert Pujols	4	15	1	5	2	0	0	0	1	3	.333	.412	.467	0
Edgar Renteria	4	15	2	5	3	0	0	1	2	2	.333	.412	.533	0
Al Reyes	1	0	0	0	0	0	0	0	0	0				0
Scott Rolen	4	15	0	0	0	0	0	1	1	1	.000	.059	.000	0
Reggie Sanders	4	9	1	0	0	0	0	0	4	5	.000	.308	.000	1
Jeff Suppan	1	1	0	1	0	0	0	0	0	0	1.00	1.000	1.00	0
So Taguchi	2	4	1	1	0	0	0	1	0	2	.250	.250	.250	0
Julian Tavarez	1	0	0	0	0	0	0	0	0	0				0
Larry Walker	4	14	2	5	2	0	2	3	2	2	.357	.438	.929	0
Tony Womack	4	11	1	2	0	0	0	0	1	2	.182	.250	.182	0
TOTAL	4	126	12	24	8	0	2	8	12	32	.190	.261	.302	1

	G	ERA	W–L	SV	CG	IP	H	ER	BB	SO
Jason Marquis	2	3.86	0–1	0	0	7.0	6	3	7	4
Jeff Suppan	1	7.71	0–1	0	0	4.7	8	4	1	4
Danny Haren	2	0.00	0–0	0	0	4.7	4	0	3	2
Matt Morris	1	8.31	0–1	0	0	4.3	4	4	4	3
Ray King	3	0.00	0–0	0	0	2.7	1	0	1	1
Woody Williams	1	27.00	0–0	0	0	2.3	8	7	3	1
Jason Isringhausen	1	0.00	0–0	0	0	2.0	1	0	1	2
Julian Tavarez	2	4.50	0–1	0	0	2.0	1	1	0	1
Cal Eldred	2	10.80	0–0	0	0	1.7	4	2	0	2
Kiko Calero	2	13.50	0–0	0	0	1.3	2	2	4	0
Al Reyes	2	0.00	0–0	0	0	1.3	0	0	0	0
TOTAL	4	6.09	0–4	0	0	34.0	39	23	24	2

2005 American League Division Series: Boston vs. Chicago

Boston Red Sox

	G	AB	R	H	2B	3B	HR	RBI	BB	SO	BA	OBP	SLG	SB
Alex Cora	1	0	0	0	0	0	0	0	0	0				0
Johnny Damon	3	13	2	3	1	0	0	0	1	4	.231	.286	.308	0
Tony Graffanino	3	12	0	3	2	0	0	0	0	0	.250	.250	.417	0
Adam Hyzdu	1	0	0	0	0	0	0	0	0	0				0
Alejandro Machado	1	0	0	0	0	0	0	0	0	0				0
Kevin Millar	2	3	0	1	1	0	0	1	0	1	.333	.333	.667	0
Doug Mirabelli	1	2	0	0	0	0	0	0	0	0	.000	.000	.000	0
Bill Mueller	3	11	0	0	0	0	0	0	1	2	.000	.083	.000	0
Trot Nixon	3	11	1	3	0	0	0	1	1	1	.273	.333	.273	0
John Olerud	3	7	0	2	1	0	0	0	2	0	.286	.444	.429	0
David Ortiz	3	12	2	4	2	0	1	1	0	3	.333	.333	.750	0
Manny Ramirez	3	10	2	3	0	0	2	4	2	0	.300	.417	.900	0
Edgar Renteria	3	13	1	3	2	0	0	0	1	1	.231	.286	.385	0
Jason Varitek	3	10	1	3	0	0	0	1	0	2	.300	.300	.300	0
TOTAL	3	104	9	25	9	0	3	8	8	14	.240	.295	.413	0

	G	ERA	W–L	SV	CG	IP	H	ER	BB	SO
David Wells	1	2.70	0–1	0	0	6.7	7	2	0	2
Tim Wakefield	1	6.75	0–1	0	0	5.3	6	4	1	4
Jonathan Papelbon	2	0.00	0–0	0	0	4.0	2	0	0	2
Matt Clement	1	21.60	0–1	0	0	3.3	7	8	0	0
Jeremi Gonzalez	1	15.43	0–0	0	0	2.3	2	4	1	0
Chad Bradford	2	0.00	0–0	0	0	1.3	1	0	0	1
Bronson Arroyo	1	18.00	0–0	0	0	1.0	2	2	2	1
Mike Timlin	1	9.00	0–0	0	0	1.0	1	1	0	1
Mike Myers	1		0–0	0	0	0.0	0	0	1	0
TOTAL		7.56	0–3	0	0	25.0	28	21	5	11

Chicago White Sox

	G	AB	R	H	2B	3B	HR	RBI	BB	SO	BA	OBP	SLG	SB
Geoff Blum	1	1	0	0	0	0	0	0	0	0	.000	.000	.000	0
Joe Crede	3	9	2	1	0	0	0	1	1	1	.111	.200	.111	0
Jermaine Dye	3	10	1	2	0	0	0	0	1	2	.200	.273	.200	0
Carl Everett	3	11	2	3	0	0	0	0	0	0	.273	.273	.273	0
Willie Harris	1	1	0	1	0	0	0	1	0	0	1.00	1.000	1.00	0
Tadahito Iguchi	3	12	1	3	0	0	1	4	0	3	.250	.250	.500	0
Paul Konerko	3	12	3	3	0	0	2	4	0	1	.250	.250	.750	0
Timo Perez	1	1	0	0	0	0	0	0	0	0	.000	.000	.000	0
A.J. Pierzynski	3	9	5	4	2	0	2	4	1	0	.444	.500	1.33	1
Scott Podsednik	3	11	3	3	1	0	1	4	1	1	.273	.333	.636	1
Aaron Rowand	3	10	3	4	2	0	0	2	1	1	.400	.455	.600	1
Juan Uribe	3	10	4	4	1	0	1	4	0	2	.400	.400	.800	0
TOTAL	3	97	24	28	6	0	7	24	5	11	.289	.324	.567	3

	G	ERA	W–L	SV	CG	IP	H	ER	BB	SO
Jose Contreras	1	2.35	1–0	0	0	7.7	8	2	0	6
Mark Buehrle	1	5.14	1–0	0	0	7.0	8	4	1	2
Freddy Garcia	1	5.40	1–0	0	0	5.0	5	3	4	1
Orlando Hernandez	1	0.00	0–0	0	0	3.0	1	0	0	4
Bobby Jenks	2	0.00	0–0	2	0	3.0	1	0	1	1
Cliff Politte	1	0.00	0–0	0	0	1.0	1	0	0	0
Neal Cotts	1	0.00	0–0	0	0	0.3	0	0	0	0
Damaso Marte	1		0–0	0	0	0.0	1	0	2	0
TOTAL		3.00	3–0	2	0	27.0	25	9	8	14

Chapter Notes

CHAPTER 1

1. *When Boston Won the World Series*, by Bob Ryan, page 27.
2. "Series of Games: Killilea Will Soon Confer with Dreyfuss Regarding Boston-Pittsburgh Match," by Tim Murnane, *The Boston Globe*, September 1, 1903.
3. *When Boston Won the World Series*, by Bob Ryan, page 94.
4. *The Glory of Their Times*, by Lawrence Ritter, page 81.
5. *When Boston Won the World Series*, by Bob Ryan, page 140.
6. *The Boston Globe*, October 9, 1903.
7. *When Boston Won the World Series*, by Bob Ryan, page 157.
8. *Total Baseball*, sixth edition, by John Thorn, et al, page 2002.

CHAPTER 2

1. *Before the Curse*, by Troy Soos, page 157.
2. *Baseball: A Film By Ken Burns*.
3. *Before the Curse*, by Troy Soos, page 139.
4. *Before the Curse*, by Troy Soos, page 139.
5. *Baseball: A Film By Ken Burns*.
6. "Sox Champions on Muffed Fly," *The New York Times*, October 17, 1912.

CHAPTER 3

1. *Baseball: A Film By Ken Burns*.
2. "Fans Flock to City, and Many Fail to Get Tickets," *The New York Times*, October 9, 1915.
3. "Wilson Watches Red Sox Win," *The New York Times*, October 10, 1915.
4. Red Sox World's Best Ball Team," *The New York Times*, October 14, 1915.
5. "Red Sox World's Best Ball Team," *The New York Times*, October 14, 1915.
6. "Series Was Hard Fought," *The New York Times*, October 14, 1915.
7. "Series Was Hard Fought," *The New York Times*, October 14, 1915.

CHAPTER 4

1. "Speaker Has Not Agreed," *The New York Times*, April 10, 1916.
2. www.baseballlibrary.com
3. www.baseballlibrary.com
4. *Spring Training Handbook*, by Joshua R. Pahigian, page 115.
5. *The Curse of the Bambino*, by Dan Shaughnessy, page 25.
6. *Baseball: A Film By Ken Burns*.
7. "Brooklyn Downs Red Sox in First Contest at Home," by Hugh Fullerton, *The New York Times*, October 11, 1916.
8. "Red Sox Are Again World's Champions, Defeating Dodgers," *The New York Times*, October 13, 1916.
9. "Red Sox Are Again World's Champions, Defeating Dodgers," *The New York Times*, October 13, 1916.

CHAPTER 5

1. "Ruth Collapses in Tonsillitis Attack," *The Boston Globe*, May 21, 1918.
2. "Sore with Barrow," *The Boston Post*, July 4, 1918.
3. "Babe Ruth Quits Red Sox," *The Boston Herald and Journal*, July 4, 1918.

4. "Cleveland Ball Park Will Close," *The Boston Globe*, July 21, 1918.
5. *The Boston Globe*, July 20, 1918.
6. "Baker Gives Baseball Till Sept. 1 to Wind Up Season," by Arthur Sears Henning, *The Chicago Daily Tribune*, July 27, 1918.
7. "Father of Babe Ruth Is Killed," *The Boston Post*, August 26, 1918.
8. *The Chicago Tribune*, September 5, 1918.
9. "Breaks of Contest Against Cub Team," *The Chicago Tribune*, September 8, 1918.
10. "Ruth May Try Comeback," *The New York Times*, September 8, 1918.
11. *The Year the Red Sox Won the Series*, by Ty Waterman and Mel Springer, page 237.
12. "Barrow Says, 'All Over,'" *The Boston Herald and Journal*, September 10, 1918.
13. *Before the Curse*, by Troy Soos, page 160.
14. "Harry Hooper Saved the Situation," *The Boston Post*, September 11, 1918.
15. "The Last Say," *Chicago Tribune*, September 12, 1918.
16. "The Last Say," *Chicago Tribune*, September 12, 1918.
17. "It May Have Been the Last Title, But it Was Hardly the Best," by Bob Richardson, *The Boston Globe*, October 22, 2004.

Chapter 6

1. *My Turn at Bat*, by Ted Williams with John Underwood, page 118.
2. *My Turn at Bat*, by Ted Williams with John Underwood, page 124.
3. *The Curse of the Bambino*, by Dan Shaughnessy, page 64.
4. *My Turn at Bat*, by Ted Williams with John Underwood, page 124.
5. "Red Sox to Keep Williams," *The New York Times*, October 10, 1946.
6. "Noisy Celebration Marks Cards' Record-Equaling Batting Feat in Boston," by James P. Dawson, *The New York Times*, October 11, 1946.
7. "Noisy Celebration Marks Cards' Record-Equaling Batting Feat in Boston," by James P. Dawson, *The New York Times*, October 11, 1946.
8. "Noisy Celebration Marks Cards' Record-Equaling Batting Feat in Boston," by James P. Dawson, *The New York Times*, October 11, 1946.
9. "Noisy Celebration Marks Cards' Record-Equaling Batting Feat in Boston," by James P. Dawson, *The New York Times*, October 11, 1946.
10. "'Atom Ball Pitch' Baffled Cards in Fifth World Series Game," by James P. Dawson, *The New York Times*, October 12, 1946.
11. "'Atom Ball Pitch' Baffled Cards in Fifth World Series Game," by James P. Dawson, *The New York Times*, October 12, 1946.
12. *Major League Baseball Productions Presents: 2004 World Series*.
13. *Major League Baseball Productions Presents, 100 Years of the World Series*.
14. *Faith Rewarded, The Historic Season of the 2004 Boston Red Sox*.
15. *My Turn at Bat*, by Ted Williams with John Underwood, page 129.
16. *The Curse of the Bambino*, by Dan Shaughnessy, page 69.
17. "Curse Reversed," by Jeff Idelson, *National Baseball Hall of Fame and Museum, 2005 Yearbook*, page 38.
18. *The Curse of the Bambino*, by Dan Shaughnessy, page 68.

Chapter 7

1. *Summer of '49*, by David Halberstam, page 7.
2. *Summer of '49*, by David Halberstam, page 5.
3. *Red Sox vs. Yankees: The Great Rivalry*, by Harvey Frommer, page 162.
4. *The Curse of the Bambino*, by Dan Shaughnessy, page 81.
5. "McCarthy Sorry for Players' Sake; DiMaggio Lauds Bearden's Work," by Roscoe McGowen, *The New York Times*, October 5, 1948.
6. "McCarthy Sorry for Players' Sake; DiMaggio Lauds Bearden's Work," by Roscoe McGowen, *The New York Times*, October 5, 1948.
7. *The Curse of the Bambino*, by Dan Shaughnessy, page 83.

Chapter 8

1. *The Impossible Dream Remembered*, by Ken Coleman and Dan Valenti, page 45.
2. *The Impossible Dream Remembered*, by Ken Coleman and Dan Valenti, page 100.
3. *The Impossible Dream Remembered*, by Ken Coleman and Dan Valenti, page 127.
4. *The Impossible Dream Remembered*, by Ken Coleman and Dan Valenti, page 216.
5. "Two Other Red Sox Follow Example," by Dave Anderson, *The New York Times*, October 5, 1967.
6. "Lonborg in 'Utter Agony' after Javier's Double Spoiled Bid for No-Hitter," by Dave Anderson, *The New York Times*, October 6, 1967.
7. *The Impossible Dream Remembered*, by Ken Coleman and Dan Valenti, page 230.
8. *The Curse of the Bambino*, by Dan Shaughnessy, page 102.
9. *Major League Baseball Productions Presents: 100 Years of the World Series*.
10. *The Impossible Dream Remembered*, by Ken Coleman and Dan Valenti, page iii.

Chapter 9

1. *The Long Ball*, by Tom Adelman, page 46.
2. www.baseballlibrary.com
3. "Hard Life of Charley Finley," by Red Smith, *The New York Times*, October 5, 1975.

4. "Boston Rally Downs A's 6–3," by Murray Chass, *The New York Times*, October 6, 1975.
5. *The Long Ball*, by Tom Adelman, page 197.
6. "A's and Finley Hail their Conquerors," *The New York Times*, October 8, 1975.
7. "A's and Finley Hail their Conquerors," *The New York Times*, October 8, 1975.
8. *The Curse of the Bambino*, by Dan Shaughnessy, page 119.
9. *The Curse of the Bambino*, by Dan Shaughnessy, page 121.
10. *The Long Ball*, by Tom Adelman, page 237.
11. *The Wrong Stuff*, by Bill Lee, page 137.
12. *The Curse of the Bambino*, by Dan Shaughnessy, page 123.
13. *Official Baseball Rules*, page 19.
14. *Major League Baseball Productions Presents: 100 Years of the World Series*.

Chapter 10

1. *Red Sox vs. Yankees: The Great Rivalry*, by Harvey Frommer, page 38.
2. *All Roads Lead to October*, by Maury Allen, pages 109–110.
3. www.baseballlibrary.com
4. *Red Sox vs. Yankees: The Great Rivalry*, by Harvey Frommer, page 43.
5. *The Curse of the Bambino*, by Dan Shaughnessy, page 139.
6. *The Curse of the Bambino*, by Dan Shaughnessy, page 139.
7. *A Day of Light and Shadows*, by Jonathan Schwartz, page 32.
8. *A Day of Light and Shadows*, by Jonathan Schwartz, page 35.
9. *The Curse of the Bambino*, by Dan Shaughnessy, page 146.
10. *A Day of Light and Shadows*, by Jonathan Schwartz, page 40.

Chapter 11

1. *One Strike Away*, by Dan Shaughnessy, page 59.
2. "The King of K's Roger Clemens Breaks Major League Record with 20 Strikeouts," by Steven Krasner, *The Providence Journal*, April 30, 1986.
3. *One Strike Away*, by Dan Shaughnessy, page 84.
4. "That Clinches it: Red Sox Rap Blue Jays, Wrap up East," by Larry Whiteside, *The Boston Globe*, September 29, 1986.
5. "That Clinches it: Red Sox Rap Blue Jays, Wrap up East," by Larry Whiteside, *The Boston Globe*, September 29, 1986.
6. *One Strike Away*, by Dan Shaughnessy, page 196.
7. "Henderson Savors Deliverance," by Michael Madden, *The Boston Globe*, October 13, 1986.
8. "Henderson, Backup Center Fielder, Takes Center Stage After Armas' Injury," by Gene Wojciechowski, *The Los Angeles Times*, October 13, 1986.
9. "Clemens, Red Sox, Bombard Angels 8–1," by George White, *The Houston Chronicle*, October 16, 1986.
10. *One Strike Away*, by Dan Shaughnessy, page 241.
11. *One Strike Away*, by Dan Shaughnessy, page 241.
12. *Major League Baseball Productions Presents: 100 Years of the World Series*.
13. *One Strike Away*, by Dan Shaughnessy, page 11.
14. "Curse Reversed," by Jeff Idelson, *National Baseball Hall of Fame and Museum, 2005 Yearbook*, page 38.

Chapter 12

1. "Evans Balks at Talk of Move: He has Angry Words about Benzinger," by Ron Borges, *The Boston Globe*, May 31, 1988.
2. *The Curse of the Bambino*, by Dan Shaughnessy, page 182.
3. "OC Woman Hits Boggs with Suit," by Donald Skinner, *The Orange County Register*, June 4, 1988.
4. "Rice Suspended by Red Sox after Run-In with Morgan," *The Chicago Sun-Times*, July 22, 1988.
5. "Rice Suspended by Red Sox after Run-In with Morgan," *The Chicago Sun-Times*, July 22, 1988.
6. "Red Sox to Keep Morgan for at least Rest of Year," by Mark Vancil, *The Minneapolis Star Tribune*, July 21, 1988.
7. "Canseco Leaves Strong Impression on Red Sox," by John Weyler, *The Los Angeles Times*, October 6, 1988.
8. "A's Get a Whiff of Victory," by Larry Whiteside, *The Boston Globe*, October 6, 1988.
9. "Canseco Leaves Strong Impression on Red Sox," by John Weyler, *The Los Angeles Times*, October 6, 1988.
10. "Canseco Leaves Strong Impression on Red Sox," by John Weyler, *The Los Angeles Times*, October 6, 1988.
11. "Boston Skipper All But Admits Playoff Over," by Bill Sullivan, *The Houston Chronicle*, October 7, 1988.
12. "A's Rally on Homer Spree; Red Sox Angry About Key Call," by Bruce Bursma, *The Chicago Tribune*, October 9, 1988.
13. "Brown Defends Kaiser's Call," by Larry Whiteside, *The Boston Globe*, October 10, 1988.
14. "Red Sox Swept Away in the End; The A's Beat a Beaten Club," by Leigh Montville, *The Boston Globe*, October 10, 1988.
15. "Red Sox Swept Away in the End; The A's Beat a Beaten Club," by Leigh Montville, *The Boston Globe*, October 10, 1988.
16. "The Talent Gap was Too Great," by Dan Shaughnessy, *The Boston Globe*, October 10, 1988.
17. "The Talent Gap was Too Great," by Dan Shaughnessy, *The Boston Globe*, October 10, 1988.

Chapter 13

1. "Buckner Released," *The Orlando Sentinel*, June 6, 1990.

2. "Clemens' Message Produces Brawl as Red Sox top Indians," *The Houston Chronicle*, June 4, 1990.
3. *The Curse of the Bambino*, by Dan Shaughnessy, Epilogue, page 213.
4. "Sox Answer Call to Arms: Gorman Deals Bagwell for Astros Reliever Andersen," by Nick Cafardo, *The Boston Globe*, September 1, 1990.
5. *The Curse of the Bambino*, by Dan Shaughnessy, Epilogue, page 214.
6. "Stone's Single Throws Red Sox Back into First," by Peter Schmuck, *The Baltimore Sun*, September 29, 1990.
7. "Morgan Magic Almost Spooky on Wild Night," by Tom Slater, *The Toronto Star*, September 29, 1990.
8. "Sox Come Through in a Clinch," by Nick Cafardo, *The Boston Globe*, October 4, 1990.
9. "A's Trounce Red Sox in Opener, 9–1: Clemens' Effort Goes for Naught as Boston Bullpen Gets Pummeled," by Dan Shaughnessy, *The Boston Globe*, October 7, 1990.
10. "Sox Stumble to Brink, A's Win 4–1: Now It's All Over But the Pouting," by Dan Shaughnessy, *The Boston Globe*, October 10, 1990.
11. "Morgan Shrugs Off More Criticism from Players," by Steve Fainaru, *The Boston Globe*, October 11, 1990.
12. "Sox Stumble to Brink, A's Win 4–1: Now It's All Over But the Pouting," by Dan Shaughnessy, *The Boston Globe*, October 10, 1990.
13. "Stewart Raps Morgan for Letting Ace Pitch," by Steve Fainaru, *The Boston Globe*, October 10, 1990.
14. *The Last Commissioner*, by Fay Vincent, page 173.
15. "Toss-Out and Knockout: Clemens Ejected in Second Inning of A's 3–1 Win," by Steve Fainaru, *The Boston Globe*, October 11, 1990.
16. "Toss-Out and Knockout: Clemens Ejected in Second Inning of A's 3–1 Win," by Steve Fainaru, *The Boston Globe*, October 11, 1990.
17. *The Last Commissioner*, by Fay Vincent, page 173.

Chapter 14

1. "Sox Never Spun Out of Control: They Danced to the Top Despite Player Shuffling," by Nick Cafardo, *The Boston Globe*, October 1, 1995.
2. *Commissioners: Baseball's Midlife Crisis*, by Jerome Holtzman. Total Sports: New York, page 280.
3. *Commissioners: Baseball's Midlife Crisis*, by Jerome Holtzman. Total Sports: New York, page 281.
4. "Belle's HR Bat Ruled OK," by Todd Jones, *The Cincinnati Post*, October 4, 1995.
5. "Belle's HR Bat Ruled OK," by Todd Jones, *The Cincinnati Post*, October 4, 1995.

Chapter 15

1. "Grand Opening: Mo Puts on Grand Show, Slam Lifts Sox in Ninth Over Seattle," by Tony Massarotti, *The Boston Herald*, April 11, 1998.

2. "Wild Season Earns Four Stars," by Michael Gee, *The Boston Herald*, September 25, 1998.
3. "Breakthrough: Vaughn, Sox End Droughts with a Bang," by Gordon Edes, *The Boston Globe*, September 30, 1998.
4. "Final Daze: Curious Moves Lead to Sox' Elimination," by Tony Massarotti, *The Boston Herald*, October 4, 1998.

Chapter 16

1. "Hard Feelings Spill Over for Williams to Mop Up" by Dan Shaughnessy, *The Boston Globe*, August 15, 1999.
2. "Garciaparra Sidelined by Wrist Injury," by Howard Ulman, *The Associated Press*, February 28, 2001.
3. "Indians beat Sox in 9th," by Tom Withers, *Austin American Statesman*, October 7, 1999.
4. "Pedro's Problems Continue; Sox Ace Struggles to Toss Ball Before Game," by Tony Massarotti, *The Boston Herald*, October 10, 1999.
5. "The Ins and Outs of Shortstop Wrist Still Hurting, Garciaparra is Unable to Lend a Hand," by Mark Blaudschun, *The Boston Globe*, October 10, 1999.
6. "Monster Numbers on Sox' Frightening Display of Offense Left Indians Shaken," by Mark Blaudschun, *The Boston Globe*, October 11, 1999.
7. "Slammin' The Door: Heroics of Martinez, O'Leary Get Sox over Threshold," by Gordon Edes, *The Boston Globe*, October 12, 1999.
8. "Slammin' The Door: Heroics of Martinez, O'Leary Get Sox over Threshold," by Gordon Edes, *The Boston Globe*, October 12, 1999.
9. "Sudden Impact: Williams's Blast in 10th Finishes Sox After They Drop Ball in Seventh," by Gordon Edes, *The Boston Globe*, October 14, 1999.
10. "Red Sox Cast Net for Scalpers," by Will McDonough, *The Boston Globe*, October 16, 1999.
11. "Crash Landing: Rocket Fizzles Out in Postseason Again," by Dan Shaughnessy, *The Boston Globe*, October 17, 1999.
12. "Help Is Not on the Way: Men in Blue Left Red-Faced by MLB," by Steve Fainaru, *The Boston Globe*, October 19, 1999.
13. "Red Sox and Fans Lose It: Yankees Win Big; Second Umpire Concedes Error; Debris Rains on Field," by Dan Shaughnessy, *The Boston Globe*, October 18, 1999.
14. "Red Sox and Fans Lose It: Yankees Win Big; Second Umpire Concedes Error; Debris Rains on Field," by Dan Shaughnessy, *The Boston Globe*, October 18, 1999.
15. "Insight from Williams, Sox Manager Blows Off the Comments of Blustery Yankee Owner," by Gordon Edes, *The Boston Globe*, October 19, 1999.

Chapter 17

1. *The Ultimate Baseball Road-Trip*, by Josh Pahigian and Kevin O'Connell, The Lyons Press, page 6.

2. "Up Next: Boston Red Sox," by Marc Topkin, *St. Petersburg Times*, April 15, 2003.

3. *The Possible Dream: How the 2004 Red Sox Reversed History*, by Vin Femia, Chandler House Press, page 26.

4. "Dissecting the Marlins-Sox Blowout One Year Later," by Christopher Young, *The Boston Phoenix*, June 21, 2004.

5. "Great Escape," by Gordon Edes, *The Boston Globe*, October 5, 2003.

6. "A Hair Raising Experience," by Gordon Edes, *The Boston Globe*, October 4, 2003.

7. "Muscle Strain Sidelines Hudson: Bar Incident Might be Culprit," by *Susan Slusser, San Francisco Chronicle,* October 6, 2003.

8. "Muscle Strain Sidelines Hudson: Bar Incident Might be Culprit," by *Susan Slusser, San Francisco Chronicle,* October 6, 2003.

9. "Five Outs Away," by Tom Verducci, *Sports Illustrated*, October 11, 2004.

10. *Red Sox vs. Yankees: The Great Rivalry*, by Harvey Frommer and Frederic J. Frommer, Sports Publishing LLC., page 23.

11. "Embarrassment Really Hits Zimmer," by Jackie MacMullan, *The Boston Globe*, October 13, 2003.

12. *Red Sox vs. Yankees: The Great Rivalry*, by Harvey Frommer and Frederic J. Frommer, Sports Publishing LLC., page 27.

13. "Ex-Yankees Accepting Probation for Roles in 2003 Bullpen Brawl," *DailyRecord.com*, October 27, 2004.

14. "Even Money, Wakefield Deposits a Win in the Bank as Sox Tie Series," by Gordon Edes, *The Boston Globe*, October 14, 2003.

15. "Five Outs Away," by Tom Verducci, *Sports Illustrated*, October 11, 2004.

16. "Five Outs Away," by Tom Verducci, *Sports Illustrated*, October 11, 2004.

17. "Five Outs Away," by Tom Verducci, *Sports Illustrated*, October 11, 2004.

Chapter 18

1. "The Recap," by Dan Shaughnessy, *Finally: The Red Sox are the Champions after 86 Years*, Triumph Books, page 88.

2. *Faith Rewarded, The Historic Season of the 2004 Boston Red Sox.*

3. *Faith Rewarded, The Historic Season of the 2004 Boston Red Sox.*

4. *Faith Rewarded, The Historic Season of the 2004 Boston Red Sox.*

5. *Faith Rewarded, The Historic Season of the 2004 Boston Red Sox.*

6. "Dark Days Have Hit the Road," by Dan Shaughnessy, *The Boston Globe*, August 27, 2004.

7. *Faith Rewarded, The Historic Season of the 2004 Boston Red Sox.*

8. "Schilling Keeps Eye on Ankle," by Bob Hohler, *The Boston Globe*, October 7, 2004.

9. *Keep the Faith, The Official Major League Baseball & Boston Red Sox 2004 World Series Championship Commemorative Magazine*, Dunfey Publishing Company, page 71.

10. *Faith Rewarded, The Historic Season of the 2004 Boston Red Sox.*

11. "Fits and Starts," by Bob Hohler, *Finally: The Red Sox are the Champions after 86 Years*, Triumph Books, page 36.

12. "Talking Doesn't Get It Done," By Thomas Boswell, *The Washington Post*, October 14, 2004.

13. *Keep the Faith, The Official Major League Baseball & Boston Red Sox 2004 World Series Championship Commemorative Magazine*, Dunfey Publishing Company, page 77.

14. *Faith Rewarded, The Historic Season of the 2004 Boston Red Sox.*

15. *Faith Rewarded, The Historic Season of the 2004 Boston Red Sox.*

16. *Faith Rewarded, The Historic Season of the 2004 Boston Red Sox.*

17. *Keep the Faith, The Official Major League Baseball & Boston Red Sox 2004 World Series Championship Commemorative Magazine*, Dunfey Publishing Company, page 83.

18. *Faith Rewarded, The Historic Season of the 2004 Boston Red Sox.*

19. "Student's Death Raises Questions about Boston Police Use of Force," By Denise Lavoie, Associate Press, October 22, 2004.

20. *Faith Rewarded, The Historic Season of the 2004 Boston Red Sox.*

21. *Faith Rewarded, The Historic Season of the 2004 Boston Red Sox.*

22. *Major League Baseball Productions Presents: 2004 World Series.*

23. "Magic # 1," By Bob Hohler, *Finally: The Red Sox are the Champions after 86 Years*, Triumph Books, page 27.

24. *Major League Baseball Productions Presents: 2004 World Series.*

25. "Thank You, Millions Turn out to Salute Red Sox for a Season to Remember," by Brian MacQuarrie, *The Boston Globe*, October 31, 2004.

26. *Faith Rewarded, The Historic Season of the 2004 Boston Red Sox.*

Chapter 19

1. "Damon Makes a Strong Pitch for Timlin," By Nick Cafardo, *The Boston Globe*, July 7, 2005.

2. "Trade Bait Ramirez wants out, which doesn't surprise Lucchino," by Chris Snow, *The Boston Globe*, July 29, 2005.

3. "Nightmare Inning Puts Sox on Brink," by Dan Shaughnessy, *The Boston Globe*, October 6, 2005.

Bibliography

The following reference sources were invaluable to the author's research:

PERIODICALS

The Associated Press
The Austin American Statesman
Baseball America
The Boston Globe
The Boston Herald
The Boston Phoenix
The Boston Post
The Boston Record and American
The Dayton Daily News
The Houston Chronicle
The Los Angeles Times
The New York Daily Record
The New York Post
The New York Times
The Orange County Register
The Orlando Sentinel
The Ottawa Citizen
The Portland Press Herald
The Providence Journal
The St. Petersburg Times
The San Francisco Chronicle
Sports Illustrated
USA Today
The Worcester Telegram & Gazette

BOOKS

Adelman, Tom. *The Long Ball: The Summer of '75 — Spaceman, Catfish, Charlie Hustle, and the Greatest World Series Ever Played*. New York: Little, Brown, 2003.

Allen, Maury. *All Roads Lead to October: Boss Steinbrenner's 25-Year Reign Over the New York Yankees*. New York: St. Martin's, 2000.

Bryant, Howard. *Juicing the Game: Drugs, Power, and the Fight for the Soul of Major League Baseball*. New York: Viking, 2005.

Canseco, Jose. *Juiced: Wild Times, Rampant 'Roids, Smash Hits, and How Baseball Got Big*. New York: Regan, 2005.

Coleman, Ken, and Dan Valenti. *The Impossible Dream Remembered: The 1967 Red Sox*. Lexington, Massachusetts: Stephen Greene, 1987.

Femia, Vin. *The Possible Dream: How the 2004 Red Sox Reversed History*. Worcester, Massachusetts: Chandler House, 2004.

Finally: The Red Sox Are the Champions after 86 Years. Chicago: Triumph, 2004.

Frommer, Harvey, and Frederic J. Frommer. *Red Sox vs. Yankees: The Great Rivalry*. Champaign, Illinois: Sports Publishing, 2004.

Halberstam, David. *Summer of '49*. New York: Avon, 1989.

Holtzman, Jerome. *Commissioners: Baseball's Midlife Crisis*. New York: Total Sports, 1998.

Keep the Faith: The Official Major League Baseball and Boston Red Sox 2004 World Series Championship Commemorative Magazine. Boston: Dunfey, 2004.

Lee, Bill, with Dick Lally. *The Wrong Stuff*. New York: Viking, 1984.

National Baseball Hall of Fame and Museum, 2005 Yearbook. Cooperstown, New York: National Baseball Hall of Fame and Museum, 2005.

Official Baseball Rules. St. Louis: The Sporting News, 1995.

Pahigian, Joshua, and Kevin O'Connell. *The Ultimate Baseball Road-Trip.* Guilford, Connecticut: Lyons, 2004.

Pahigian, Joshua R. *Spring Training Handbook.* Jefferson, North Carolina: McFarland, 2005.

Ritter, Lawrence S. *The Glory of Their Times.* New York: Macmillan, 1966.

Ryan, Bob. *When Boston Won the World Series.* Philadelphia: Running Press, 2003.

Schwartz, Jonathan. *A Day of Light and Shadows.* Guilford, Connecticut: Lyons, 2003.

Shaughnessy, Dan. *The Curse of the Bambino.* New York: Penguin, 1990.

Shaughnessy, Dan. *One Strike Away: The Story of the 1986 Red Sox.* New York: Beaufort, 1987.

Soos, Troy. *Before the Curse: The Glory Days of New England Baseball: 1858–1918.* Hyannis, Massachusetts: Parnassus Imprints, 1997.

Thorn, John, and Peter Palmer. *Total Baseball.* Sixth Edition. New York: Total Sports, 1999.

Vincent, Fay. *The Last Commissioner: A Baseball Valentine.* New York: Simon & Schuster, 2002.

Waterman, Ty, and Mel Springer. *The Year the Red Sox Won the Series: A Chronicle of the 1918 Championship Season.* Boston: Northeastern University Press, 1999.

Williams, Ted, with John Underwood. *My Turn at Bat: The Story of My Life.* New York: Simon & Schuster, 1969.

WEB SITES

www.baseballlibrary.com
www.baseball-reference.com
www.boston.com
www.dailyrecord.com
www.espn.go.com
www.facts.com
www.redsoxdiehard.com
www.retrosheet.org

FILMS AND ALBUMS

Baseball: A Film By Ken Burns. Florentine Films, 1994.

Faith Rewarded, The Historic Season of the 2004 Boston Red Sox. Produced by the Boston Red Sox and NESN, 2004.

The Impossible Dream. Narrated by Ken Coleman, 1967.

Major League Baseball Productions Presents: 100 Years of the World Series; Celebrating a Century of Championships. Produced by Major League Baseball Productions, 2003.

Major League Baseball Productions Presents: 2004 World Series. Produced by Major League Baseball Productions, 2004.

Index

Aase, Don 115
Abad, Andy 188
ABC 128
Aberdeen, Lord 30
Adair, Jerry 87, 89, 95
Adams, Margo 138, 144
Affirmed 116
Aguilera, Rick 124, 134, 157, 159
Aldine Hotel 35
Alexander, Grover Cleveland 33, 34, 35, 36, 37
Alicea, Luis 155, 159, 160
Allen, Maury 116
Allietta, Bob 100
Alomar, Roberto 173
Alomar, Sandy 159, 161, 166, 177
Altrock, Nick 4
Ames, Red 21
Anaheim Angels 201–204
Anaheim Stadium 124
Andersen, Larry 148, 151, 152
Anderson, Brady 137, 139
Anderson, Garret 202
Anderson, Sparky 102, 106, 107, 109, 111, 112
Andrews, Mike 86, 93, 94, 95, 96
Armas, Tony 123, 127, 128
Armas, Tony, Jr. 162
Armbrister, Ed 109, 111, 113
Arroyo, Bronson 195, 200, 201, 206, 209, 211, 213, 218
Assenmacher, Paul 160
Astrodome 122
Avery, Steve 164

Backman, Wally 124, 131, 132, 133, 135
Baerga, Carlos 158, 161
Bagby, Jim 72
Bagwell, Jeff 148, 171
Baines, Harold 148, 152, 153, 154, 175

Baker, Frank 20
Baker, Newton 51, 54
Baker Bowl 32, 33, 35, 38
Ballafant, Lee 69
Bancroft, Dave 33, 35, 36, 37, 38
Bando, Sal 102, 103
Barber, Turner 58, 60
Barfield, Jesse 148
Barnett, Larry 109, 110
Barrett, Marty 123, 125, 127, 129, 130, 132, 135, 136, 138, 140, 141, 143, 144, 150, 151, 153, 154
Barrow, Edward 52, 53, 58, 59, 60, 62
Barry, Jack 34, 35, 37, 38, 41, 42, 51, 52
Bauer, Hank 88
Baylor, Don 120, 123, 128, 129, 130, 131, 134, 136, 140
Bearden, Gene 80, 81, 82, 83, 84
Beaumont, Ginger 6, 8, 10, 11
Beazley, Johnny 68
Beck, Rod 178, 181
Becker, Beals 23, 32
Bedient, Hugh 17, 19, 20, 23, 24, 27, 28, 29
Belinda, Stan 157
Bell, Gary 87, 88, 90, 94, 96
Belle, Albert 158, 159, 160
Bellhorn, Mark 204, 205, 209, 210, 211, 213
Bench, Johnny 102, 106, 107, 109, 112
Bender, Chief 29
Beniquez, Juan 103, 104, 110, 112
Benjamin, Mike 163
Benz, Joe 19
Benzinger, Todd 137, 138, 139, 142, 143, 145
Berardino, Dick 154
Berry, Charlie 80
Berry, Ken 89

Bickford, Vern 84
Billingham, Jack 103, 107
Blue, Vida 100, 102, 104
Boddicker, Mike 139, 143, 149, 150, 151, 152, 153
Boggs, Wade 122, 123, 125, 126, 127, 129, 132, 134, 135, 136, 138, 140, 141, 142, 143, 144, 145, 148, 149, 150, 152, 153
Bolton, Tom 147, 148, 150, 151
Bonds, Bobby 99
Bonham, "Tiny" 64
Bonilla, Bobby 156
Boone, Aaron 186, 196, 197
Boone, Bob 124, 125, 126, 127, 129
Borbon, Pedro 102, 112
"Born in the U.S.A" 185
Bosman, Dick 102
Boston Americans 3–16
Boston Braves 30, 31, 78, 84
Boston Daily Record 67
Boston Garden 121
Boston Globe 4, 5, 6, 13, 16, 54, 146, 153, 156, 206
Boston Record and American 97
Boston Marathon 52
Boston Red Sox: (1903) 1, 3–16, 25, 27, 56, 217; (1907) 3; (1911) 18; (1912) 1, 17–28, 67, 217; (1913) 29; (1914) 30; (1915) 1, 29–39, 40, 45, 48, 170, 217; (1916) 1, 40–50, 57, 170, 217; (1918) 1, 51–62, 63, 131, 217; (1945) 63; (1946) 1, 2, 63–77, 78, 210; (1948) 1, 78–84, 168; (1962) 148; (1967) 1, 85–98, 165, 210; (1974) 99; (1975) 99–114, 210; (1978) 2, 115–119; (1986) 1, 120–136, 147, 174, 175; (1988) 137–145; (1990) 146–154; (1995) 2, 155–161, 187; (1997) 162, 180; (1998) 162–169, 170; (1999) 2, 170–182, 221; (2003) 183–197,

273

198, 221; (2004) 2, 13, 175, 198–215, 216, 217; (2005) 216–222
Boswell, Thomas 141
Boudreau, Lou 64, 66, 80, 82, 83
Boyd, Dennis "Oil Can" 120, 121, 122, 123, 126, 129, 130, 132, 136, 138, 140, 147, 217
Bragg, Darren 164, 169
Bransfield, Kitty 7, 8, 11
Braves Field 33, 36, 37, 45, 50, 84
Brazle, Al 68, 72
Brecheen, Harry 68, 69, 70, 74, 75
Briles, Nelson 90, 94
Brinkman, Joe 166, 167
Brock, Lou 90, 93, 94, 96, 98
Brockton, Mass. 19
Brooklyn Robins 43–50
Brosius, Scott 178, 181
Brown, Bobby 144, 160
Brown, Kevin 147, 206, 209, 210
Brown, Mace 72
Brown, Mike 123
Brown, "Three Finger" 29
Brunansky, Tom 147, 149, 150, 153
Bruschi, Teddy 217
Buckner, Bill 1, 17, 123, 126, 127, 128, 129, 131, 132, 134, 135, 136, 147, 150
Buehrle, Mark 219, 220
Buford, Damon 164, 179
Burba, Dave 164, 165, 167, 173, 175
Burgmeier, Tom 117
Burkett, John 185, 189, 194, 195
Burkhart, Ken 69
Burks, Ellis 137, 139, 140, 142, 143, 150, 151, 152, 154
Burleson, Rick 102, 103, 104, 105, 106, 107, 109, 110, 112, 113, 114, 116, 117, 119, 124
Burns, Ed 36, 38, 39
Burns, Todd 150
Burton, Jim 113
Busch Stadium 94, 212, 214
Bush, "Bullet Joe" 52, 53, 55, 57, 59, 60, 62
Bush, Homer 171
Buzhardt, John 87
Byrne, Tommy 81
Byrnes, Eric 187, 188, 190

Cabrera, Orlando 200, 202, 205, 206, 207, 210, 211, 212, 216
Cadaret, Greg 143
Cady, Hick 22, 23, 24, 25, 26, 34, 37, 41, 50, 52
Cairo, Miguel 206, 209
Caldwell, Ray 18, 31
Caldwell, Slim 41
California Angels 124–130
Camden Yards 164
Cameron, Mike 218
Candelaria, John 124, 126, 127, 130
Canseco, Jose 124, 140, 141, 142, 143, 144, 150, 152, 153, 155, 157, 159, 160, 161
Carbo, Bernie 102, 109, 112, 113, 117
Carew, Rod 100, 101
Carlton, Steve 90, 95, 121, 150
Carrigan, Bill 23, 29, 35, 36, 38, 39, 41, 42, 43, 44, 45, 47, 48, 49

Carroll, Clay 102, 106, 113
Carter, Gary 124, 132, 133, 134, 135, 136
Case, George 64
Castro, Fidel 101
Cater, Danny 120
CBS 141
Cepeda, Orlando 90, 94, 96
Cerone, Rick 138, 147
Chalmers, George 33, 37, 38
Chamblis, Chris 118, 119
Chance, Dean 89
Chase, Hal 29
Chavez, Eric 186, 187, 188
Cheney, Larry 45, 46
Chesbro, Jack 6
Chicago Cubs 55–62
Chicago White Sox 219–222
Chunichi Dragons 183
Cincinnati Reds 102–103, 106–114
Clark, Al 181
Clark, Tony 209
Clarke, Fred 6, 8, 11, 12, 13, 14
Clemens, Debbie 121
Clemens, Roger 120, 121, 122, 123, 125, 127, 128, 130, 131, 132, 133, 135, 136, 138, 140, 142, 143, 147, 148, 149, 150, 151, 153, 154, 155, 156, 157, 159, 162, 163, 170, 171, 172, 173, 180, 186, 187, 192, 193, 195, 196
Clement, Matt 216, 218, 220
Cleveland, Reggie 101, 102, 104, 106, 111
Cleveland Indians 81–84, 157–161, 164–169, 173–177
Cobb, Ty 19, 20, 100
Coffee, Jack 55
Coleman, Ken 85
Collins, Eddie 20
Collins, Jimmy 4, 5, 10, 11, 13, 14, 16
Collins, Ray 20, 22, 25
Colon, Bartolo 163, 164, 168, 173, 174, 176, 177, 202
Colosi, Nick 106
Comiskey Park 31, 53, 56
Concepcion, Dave 102, 106, 107, 109
Cone, David 171, 178, 179
Conigliaro, Tony 87, 88, 89, 90, 99, 100, 101
Conley, Gene 148
Contreras, Jose 195, 200, 219, 220
Coombs, Jack 45, 46, 48, 49
Cooney, Terry 126, 154
Cooper, Cecil 101, 102, 104, 105, 106, 107, 110
Cooper, Scott 148
Copley Plaza Hotel 60
Cora, Joey 168
Corbett, Doug 127
Cordero, Wil 174
Cormier, Rheal 161, 170, 174, 178, 179
Correnti, Chris 196
Corsi, Jim 163, 164, 184
Costas, Bob 135
Crandall, Doc 21, 22
Cravath, Gabby 32, 34, 35, 36, 37, 38, 39

Crawford, Carl 184, 220
Crawford, Steve 128, 129, 131, 132, 134
Criger, Lou 4, 8, 11, 13, 14
Cronin, Joe 63, 67, 69, 71, 72, 74, 78
Crowley, Terry 110
Cubbage, Mike 189
Cubs Park 56
Culberson, Leon 74, 76, 77
Cummings, Midre 163, 169
Curse of the Bambino, The 146
Cutshaw, George 44, 45, 46, 48, 49, 50

Damon, Johnny 188, 189, 190, 191, 193, 195, 199, 200, 201, 202, 204, 207, 208, 210, 211, 213, 218, 221, 222
Darcy, Pat 103, 111, 112
Dark, Alvin 103, 104, 105
Darling, Ron 124, 130, 131, 133, 134, 136, 156
Daubach, Brian 157, 170, 172, 173, 174, 175, 177, 178, 183
Daubert, Jake 44, 46, 48, 49
Davis, Chili 172
Davis, Ron 122
Davis, Storm 140, 142
Deal, Charlie 57
DeCinces, Doug 124, 126, 127, 129
Delaware River Shipbuilding League 51, 53
Deloc, Ike 148
Demaree, Al 33
Demeter, Don 87
Dent, Bucky 2, 119
Devore, Josh 21, 24, 26, 27, 28
Dickson, Murry 68, 70, 71, 75, 76
DiMaggio, Dom 63, 64, 67, 69, 70, 71, 74, 75, 76, 77, 79, 81, 82, 83, 84, 217
DiMaggio, Joe 81, 116
Dinneen, Bill 4, 5, 8, 11, 12, 13, 15, 16
Dobson, Joe 67, 72, 74, 79, 80
Doby, Larry 83
Doerr, Bobby 63, 64, 67, 68, 71, 72, 74, 75, 79, 80, 81, 82, 83, 96, 97
Doheny, Ed 6, 10
Donahue 138
Donnelly, Brendan 157
Donovan, Patsy 18
Dougherty, Patsy 4, 5, 8, 12, 13
Douglas, Phil 56, 59, 60, 62
Downing, Brian 124, 125, 126, 127, 129
Doyle, Denny 100, 103, 105, 106, 107, 109, 111, 112, 113
Doyle, Larry 21, 24, 25, 26
Drago, Dick 101, 104, 105, 107, 109, 112
Dreisewerd, Clem 72
Dreyfuss, Barney 5, 13, 16
Dropkick Murphy's 13
Dubuc, Jean 58
Dunn, Jack 29, 30
Dunn, James 54
Duquette, Dan 155, 156, 162, 163, 170, 171, 180, 198

Durazo, Erubiel 186, 187, 190
Dusak, Erv 74
Dye, Jermaine 189, 190, 219, 220
Dyer, Eddie 68, 71, 72, 76
Dykstra, Lenny 131, 132, 134, 136

Easler, Mike 120
Eastwick, Rawly 102, 107, 109, 111, 112
Ebbets, Charles 48, 50
Ebbets Field 45, 48, 67
Eckersley, Dennis 115, 116, 118, 140, 141, 142, 143, 144, 145, 150, 151, 152, 163, 164 167, 171, 184, 217
Eckstein, David 204
Edmonds, Jim 213
Egan, Ben 30
Egan, Dave 67
Ellis, Mark 187
Embree, Alan 183, 187, 190, 191, 192, 195, 196, 210, 213
Emerson College 210
Emmel, Paul 188
Engle, Clyde 25, 27
Epstein, Theo 183, 184, 185, 198, 199, 200
Esasky, Nick 146
Escobar, Kelvim 202
Eshelman, Vaughn 156
Evans, Dwight 99, 102, 103, 106, 109, 110, 112, 113, 116, 120, 121, 123, 126, 128, 129, 130, 132, 134, 135, 136, 137, 138, 140, 142, 143, 144, 145, 150, 152, 217
Evans, Jim 154
Everett, Carl 219
Exposition Park 6, 11

Fainaru, Steve 153
Farrell, Charley 4, 13
Federal League 29, 30, 31, 39, 44
Felix, Junior 149
Feller, Bob 64, 80, 81, 83
Fenway Park 17, 19, 22, 23, 25, 26, 29, 31, 33, 40, 41, 52, 54, 55, 60, 61, 62, 64, 65, 66, 67, 68, 70, 71, 73, 78, 79, 80, 81, 83, 85, 87, 88, 89, 91, 93, 96, 100, 101, 103, 112, 116, 117, 118, 121, 123, 132, 133, 138, 141, 143, 148, 151, 155, 157, 161, 163, 164, 166, 167, 171, 172, 173, 175, 180, 181, 183, 184, 185, 188, 191, 199, 205, 211, 213, 215, 216, 217, 219, 221
Fernandez, Alex 149
Fernandez, Sid 124, 134
Ferris, Hoby 4, 7, 10, 14, 15
Ferriss, Dave 63, 64, 70, 71, 75, 78, 79, 81
Fingers, Rollie 102, 104
Finley, Charlie 100, 102, 104
Fischer, Bill 135
Fisk, Carlton 99, 100, 101, 102, 103, 104, 106, 107, 109, 110, 111, 112, 113, 114, 116, 119, 170, 171, 217
Fitzgerald, John "Honey Fitz" 22, 26, 30, 60
Flack, Max 56, 57, 58, 60, 61, 62
Flaherty, Pat 5
Fletcher, Art 22, 23, 24, 25, 26

Fletcher, Scott 149
Flood, Curt 90, 93, 94, 98
Florie, Bryce 172
Ford, Whitey 59, 87
Fort Myers, Fla. 155
Fossum, Casey 198
Foster, George 102, 106, 107, 109, 110, 112
Foster, Rube 30, 31, 32, 33, 35, 36, 38, 39, 41, 42, 43, 48, 52
Foulke, Keith 189, 199, 201, 202, 207, 208, 209, 210, 211, 212, 213, 216, 218
FOX 200, 208
Fox, Chad 183
Foy, Joe 87, 88, 95, 96, 98
Franco, John 156
Francona, Terry 198, 199, 200, 202, 204, 206, 207, 209, 212, 220
Frazee, Harry 50, 52, 53, 54, 61, 62, 63, 146
Freeman, Buck 4, 5, 7, 8, 12, 13, 14, 15, 16
Frick, Ford 67
Fryman, Travis 164, 168, 174

Gainer, Del 38, 47
Galehouse, Denny 79, 80, 82, 83, 84, 168
Gallego, Mike 144, 152, 154
Galt, Mrs. Norman 35
Garagiola, Joe 69, 70, 71, 72, 74, 75
Garces, Rich 164, 174, 176, 181
Garcia, Freddy 219, 221
Garcia, Karim 193, 194
Garcia, Richie 126
Garciaparra, Nomar 162, 163, 164, 165, 166, 167, 168, 169, 171, 172, 173, 174, 175, 176, 177, 179, 180, 181, 185, 187, 188, 189, 190, 192, 195, 199, 200
Gardner, Larry 20, 22, 23, 24, 25, 28, 34, 36, 41, 42, 43, 46, 47, 48, 49, 50, 52
Gardner, Wes 120, 143, 147, 148
Garland, Jon 219
Garner, Phil 102, 103
Gedman, Rich 121, 122, 126, 127, 128, 129, 130, 131, 135, 136, 141, 142, 143, 144, 145
Geronimo, Cesar 102, 106, 109, 110, 112, 113, 114
Giambi, Jason 186, 192, 196
Giambi, Jeremy 183
Gibson, Bob 90, 91, 93, 94, 97, 98
Gibson, Kirk 120, 145
Gibson, Norman 4, 5
Gibson, Russ 88, 90
Glaus, Troy 204
Gooden, Dwight 124, 131, 132, 134, 165, 166, 167
Goodman, Billy 79, 81
Gordon, Joe 82, 83
Gordon, Tom 162, 163, 164, 165, 167, 168, 169, 172, 179, 180, 205, 206, 207, 208
Gorman, Lou 120, 137, 138, 139, 146, 147, 148, 152
Gossage, Rich "Goose" 115, 118, 119

Graffanino, Tony 221, 222
Gray, Jeff 148, 149, 151
Greenberg, Hank 63
Greenwell, Mike 131, 135, 137, 138, 139, 140, 142, 143, 144, 145, 148, 150, 153, 156, 157, 159, 161
Grich, Bobby 126, 127, 128, 129
Griffey, Ken 102, 106, 109, 110, 111, 112, 113
Griffin, Doug 100
Griffith Stadium 42
Gruber, Kelly 123
Guerrero, Vladimir 204
Guidry, Ron 116, 117, 118, 119
Guillen, Jose 190
Guillen, Ozzie 149, 219, 221
Gullett, Don 103, 106, 111, 113
Gutteridge, Don 72, 74

Haefner, Mickey 67
Hall, Charley 20, 26
Hamilton, Jack 88
Hanson, Erik 156, 157, 160
Harden, Rich 187, 188
Hargrove, Mike 159, 163, 167, 168, 174, 175, 176
Harper, Moxie 53
Harrelson, Ken 89, 93, 96, 98
Harrington, John 163, 170, 198
Harris, Bucky 81
Harris, Greg 148, 149, 150, 151, 152, 153
Harris, Mickey 64, 67, 70, 74, 78, 79
Harvard University 18, 19
Hassey, Ron 143
Hatteberg, Scott 162, 164, 169, 182, 190
Heep, Danny 131, 149
Hegan, Jim 83
Henderson, Dave 123, 124, 128, 129, 130, 132, 134, 136, 140, 141, 142, 144, 151, 153
Henderson, Rickey 150, 152
Hendrick, George 127
Hendrix, Claude 56, 59
Henke, Tom 149
Henriksen, Olaf 23, 27, 35, 48
Henry, John W. 183, 198, 199, 200, 217
Heredia, Felix 195
Hernandez, Angel 192
Hernandez, Keith 124, 131, 132, 135
Hernandez, Orlando 178, 181, 182, 207, 221, 222
Hernandez, Ramon 186, 187, 188, 190
Herrman, August 55
Hershiser, Orel 158, 160
Herzog, Buck 22, 23, 24, 25, 26
Heydler, John 55
Higgins, Pinky 68, 69, 70, 72, 74, 76
Hill, Ken 158, 159
Hillenbrand, Shea 183, 185
Hilltop Park 18, 19
Hoblitzel, Dick 30, 32, 34, 35, 36, 37, 38, 41, 42, 45, 46, 47, 49, 52, 53
Hobson, Butch 116, 117, 119, 155, 217

Hoerner, Joe 96
Hollenden Hotel 138
Hollocher, Charlie 56, 59, 60, 62
Holt, Jim 105
Holtzman, Ken 102, 103, 105
Honeycutt, Rick 141, 144, 150, 154, 184
Hooper, Harry 17, 22, 24, 27, 31, 32, 34, 35, 36, 37, 38, 39, 41, 43, 46, 47, 48, 50, 52, 54, 55, 56, 57, 58, 60, 61
Horn, Sam 147, 217
Horton, Tony 87
Hosey, Dwayne 157, 159, 160
Hot Springs, Ark. 18, 40, 52
Howard, Elston 87, 88, 90, 96
Howry, Bobby 183
Howser, Dick 88, 116, 117, 122
Hrabowski, Al 116
Hriniak, Walt 140
Hudson, Tim 186, 187, 189, 190
Huff, Aubrey 218
Hughes, Dick 90, 93, 96
Hughes, Tom 4, 5, 9, 10, 11
Hughson, Tex 66, 67, 69, 71, 74, 75, 78
Hunter, Jim "Catfish" 99, 100, 101, 103
Huntington Avenue Grounds 1, 3, 4, 7, 8, 9, 10, 14, 15, 18, 25
Hurst, Bruce 120, 122, 123, 125, 126, 128, 130, 131, 133, 134, 135, 136, 138, 140, 141, 144
Huskey, Butch 182
Hutchinson, Fred 80

Iguchi, Tadahito 221
Irabu, Hideki 180

Jackson, Damian 190, 192
Jackson, Joe 19, 20, 51, 53
Jackson, Mike 164, 165, 167, 168, 169
Jackson, Reggie 102, 104, 115, 116, 117, 118, 119, 124, 125, 126, 127
Jacobs Field 165, 174, 177
James, Chris 147
Janvrin, Hal 41, 46, 47, 49, 50
Japanese League 183, 221
Javier, Julian 93, 98
Jefferson, Reggie 155, 161, 164
Jefferson, Stanley 147
Jenks, Bobby 220, 221, 222
Jeter, Derek 178, 179, 180, 182, 186, 196, 199, 205, 206, 209, 216
Johnson, Ban 6, 40, 54, 55
Johnson, Darrell 107, 109, 110, 111, 112, 113
Johnson, Davy 132, 133
Johnson, Earl 69, 70, 75
Johnson, Nick 192, 193, 196
Johnson, Randy 163, 216
Johnson, Walter 19, 20, 29, 41, 42
Johnston, Jimmy 45, 47, 49
Jones, Dalton 89, 94, 96
Jones, Doug 147, 165
Jones, Jake 78, 79
Jones, Ruppert 125, 127, 130
Jones, "Sad Sam" 40, 52, 53, 55, 60, 62

Joyner, Wally 124, 125, 126, 127
Juiced 142
Justice, Dave 167, 168

Kaiser, Ken 142, 143, 144
Kaminiecki, Scott 156
Kapler, Gabe 188, 191, 192, 201, 213
Keating, Ray 31, 41
Keltner, Kenny 64, 82, 83
Kenmore Hotel 84
Kennedy, Brickyard 12
Kennedy, Kevin 155, 156, 159, 160, 161, 162, 163
Kennedy, Pres. John F. 22
Kerrigan, Joe 174, 175
Kiecker, Dana 148, 150, 151, 152
Killebrew, Harmon 89
Killefer, Bill 39, 57, 58, 59, 60
Killilea, Henry 5, 6, 8, 16
Kim, Byung-Hyun 185, 187, 190
Kim, Wendell 168
Kinder, Ellis 78, 79, 80, 83
Kinney, Walt 59
Kirby, Clay 103
Klinger, Bob 75
Klink, Joe 150
Knabe, Otto 57
Knight, Ray 1, 124, 131, 134, 135, 136
Knoblauch, Chuck 178, 179, 181, 182
Konerko, Paul 219, 220, 221
Kramer, Jack 78, 79, 80, 81
Kurowski, Whitey 68, 69, 71, 72, 74, 75

LaChance, George 4, 8, 10, 11, 12, 15
Lake, Eddie 63
Lake Erie 122
Lamabe, Jack 96
Lamp, Dennis 140, 151
Landis, Kenesaw Mountain 30, 31, 39
Lannin, Joseph 29, 39, 40, 41, 50
Lansford, Carney 140, 141, 142, 143, 144, 154
Larkin, Barry 171
LaRussa, Tony 141, 142, 150, 152, 183, 184
Leach, Tommy 6, 7, 11, 12, 13, 14
League Park 66
Ledee, Rickey 179
Lee, Bill 100, 101, 102, 107, 113, 117, 118
Leever, Sam 6, 8, 13
Lemon, Bob 80, 83, 84, 89, 115, 117, 118, 161
Leonard, Dutch 30, 32, 33, 36, 37, 41, 43, 49, 52, 53, 55, 62
Leskanic, Curtis 206, 207
Lewis, Darren 165, 166, 167, 169, 175, 176, 178
Lewis, Duffy 17, 19, 20, 21, 22, 23, 28, 32, 34, 35, 37, 38, 41, 42, 45, 46, 47, 49, 50, 51, 62
Lidle, Cory 157
Lieber, John 205, 206, 208
Lilly, Ted 188
Lindblad, Paul 102, 105

Little, Grady 183, 184, 187, 190, 192, 196, 197, 198
Lloyd, Graeme 171
Loaiza, Esteban 204, 208
Lofton, Kenny 158, 159, 160, 165, 167, 168
Logan Airport 88, 101, 106, 213
Lonborg, Jim 85, 87, 88, 89, 90, 91, 93, 95, 96, 97, 98
Long, Terrence 190
Looney, Brian 156
Louis, Joe 73
Lowe, Derek 162, 164, 167, 168, 172, 174, 175, 177, 178, 185, 187, 188, 189, 190, 192, 194, 201, 202, 204, 207, 209, 210, 213, 216, 217, 218
Lucas, Gary 128
Lucchino, Larry 195, 201, 215, 217, 218
Luderus, Fred 33, 34, 35, 36, 38, 39
Lyle, Sparky 120
Lynn, Fred 99, 100, 101, 103, 104, 105, 107, 109, 110, 111, 112, 113, 114, 116, 117, 119
Lyon, Brandon 183, 198
Lyons, Steve 122

Maas, Kevin 148
MacFarlane, Mike 155, 160, 161
Macha, Ken 189
Mack, Connie 4, 31, 33
Macon, Ga. 4
Maddux, Mike 159
Mahay, Ron 156, 157
Mann, Les 56, 57, 59, 60, 62
Marion, Marty 69, 72, 74, 75
Maris, Roger 90, 93, 94, 95, 96, 98
Marlborough, Ma. 4, 13
Marquard, Rube 19, 21, 23, 25, 45, 46, 49
Marquis, Jason 213
Marshall, Mike 148, 150
Martin, Billy 115, 116, 117
Martinez, Dennis 158, 159
Martinez, Pedro 2, 162, 163, 164, 165, 168, 169, 170, 171, 172, 173, 174, 175, 176, 177, 180, 184, 185, 186, 187, 190, 192, 193, 194, 195, 196, 199, 200, 201, 202, 203, 205, 206, 207, 208, 210, 212, 216, 218
Martinez, Ramon 170, 173, 175, 178, 179
Martinez, Tino 179, 180
Mathewson, Christy 21, 23, 24, 27, 28
Matsui, Hideki 186, 192, 193, 195, 196, 205, 206, 208
Mattingly, Don 123
Mauch, Gene 124, 126, 128
Maxvill, Dal 98
May, Lee 99
Mayer, Erskine 33, 35, 38
Mays, Carl 32, 41, 42, 43, 45, 46, 48, 52, 53, 55, 56, 58, 60, 61, 62
Mazeroski, Bill 112
McAleer, James 17, 18, 25, 29
McBride, Tom 69, 71, 76
McCarthy, Joe 78, 79, 83, 84, 168

McCarver, Tim 94, 98
McCaskill, Kirk 124, 125, 126, 129
McClelland, Tim 149, 192
McCormick, Moose 22
McDermott, Mickey 79
McDowell, Oddibe 122
McDowell, Roger 124, 134, 136
McEnaney, Will 102, 107, 112, 113, 114
McGee, Willie 148, 152, 160
McGraw, John 16, 20, 21, 24, 28
McGreevey, Mike 5
McGwire, Mark 140, 142, 143, 150, 151, 152, 153, 171
McInnis, Stuffy 52, 54, 55, 57, 58, 62
McLain, Denny 87
McMahon, Don 87
McMillon, Billy 187, 190
McNally, Mike 47
McNamara, John 120, 121, 122, 123, 124, 125, 127, 128, 129, 131, 132, 133, 135, 136, 137, 138, 139
Mele, Sam 80
Melhuse, Adam 190
Mendoza, Ramiro 181, 182, 183, 206
Mercker, Kent 173, 176, 178, 181, 182
Merkle, Fred 21, 22, 23, 24, 25, 26, 27, 28, 46, 49, 56, 57, 58, 60, 61
Merloni, Lou 157, 175, 176
Mesa, Jose 158, 160
Metkovich, "Catfish" 63
Meyers, Chief 21, 22, 25, 26, 27, 44, 46
Mientkiewicz, Doug 200, 213
Millar, Kevin 157, 183, 184, 185, 188, 192, 195, 196, 199, 200, 202, 204, 206, 207, 208, 211, 212, 220
Miller, Damian 157
Miller, Frank 53
Miller, Otto 47, 48
Miller, Rick 217
Mirabelli, Doug 188, 203, 211
Mitchell, Fred 57, 58, 59, 62
Mitchell, Kevin 135
Monbouquette, Bill 148
Moret, Roger 100, 101, 102, 104, 110, 112, 113
Moore, Donnie 126, 127, 128, 129
Moore, Mike 150, 152, 153
Moore, Terry 70, 72, 74
Moran, Pat 32, 36, 38, 39
Morgan, Bill 172, 208, 211
Morgan, Joe (Hall of Fame player) 102, 106, 107, 110, 111, 112, 113
Morgan, Joe (Red Sox nanager) 137, 139, 143, 144, 147, 149, 151, 153, 217
Morris, Jack 120
Morris, Matt 211, 212
Morton, Guy 53
Moses, Wally 71, 72, 75
Mowrey, Mike 44, 46, 47, 48, 50
Mueller, Bill 183, 185, 187, 188, 190, 192, 195, 196, 200, 205, 206, 211, 212, 213
Mulder, Mark 186
Munger, George "Red" 71, 72
Munson, Thurman 116, 118, 119, 170

Murnane, Tim 4
Murphy, Rob 151
Murray, Eddie 158, 159, 160
Murray, Matt 156
Murray, Red 21, 22, 23, 24, 25, 26, 27
Musial, Stan 68, 69, 70, 71, 72, 74
Mussina, Mike 186, 191, 194, 196, 204, 205
Myers, Hy 45, 46, 47, 49
Myers, Mike 202

Naehring, Tim 148, 156, 159
Nagy, Chuck 158, 160, 161, 164, 167, 173, 174, 175, 177
Narron, Jerry 127
National Commission 55, 56, 60, 62
NBC 135
Nelson, Gene 142, 143, 150, 184
Nelson, Jeff 182, 193
Nettles, Graig 101, 118, 119
New York Daily News 142
New York Giants 21–28
New York Highlanders 17, 18, 20
New York Mets 3, 124, 130–136
New York Times 28, 45, 116
New York Yankees 115–119, 173, 177–182, 186, 191–197, 204–210
Newhowser, Hal 67, 80
Newman, Jeff 167
Newsom, Bobo 64
Newswatch 141
Niehoff, Bert 34, 35, 36, 37, 38, 39
Nilson, Dave 157
Nipper, Al 120, 121, 122, 123, 133, 134, 136, 137
Nixon, Otis 155
Nixon, Trot 175, 176, 180, 182, 188, 194, 195, 196, 199, 204, 206, 213, 221
Nolan, Gary 103, 109, 111
Norman, Fred 103, 110
North, Billy 103, 105
Nunamaker, Les 41

Oakland A's 102–106, 140–145, 150–154, 186–190
Oakland Coliseum 143, 187
O'Brien, Buck 17, 18, 19, 20, 23, 25, 26
O'Brien, Jack 12
O'Connell, Dick 87, 88, 100, 115
Odom, "Blue Moon" 100
O'Farrell, Bob 57
Offerman, Jose 170, 171, 175, 176, 178, 180, 181, 182
Ojeda, Bobby 120, 124, 132, 135
O'Leary, Troy 156, 157, 159, 164, 168, 169, 173, 177, 180, 182
Olerud, John 206
O'Loughlin, Silk 23
Olson, Ivy 44, 46, 47, 48, 50
O'Neil, Paul 178, 179
Oquendo, Jose 212
Ordonez, Maggilo 199
Orlando, Johnny 76
Orosco, Jesse 124, 133, 134, 136
Orr, Bobby 217
Ortiz, David 183, 185, 188, 189, 190, 192, 195, 196, 201, 202, 204, 205, 207, 208, 210, 211, 212, 213, 218, 219, 221
Ortiz, Luis 155
Orza, Gene 199
Owen, Spike 121, 123, 125, 127, 129, 130, 132, 134, 137, 139

Paige, Satchel 80
Palmer, Jim 101, 118
Pape, Larry 20
Parent, Freddy 4, 5, 8, 11, 12, 13, 15, 16
Parker, Dave 142, 143
Parnell, Mel 79, 80, 83, 84, 168
Parrish, Larry 121, 140
Partee, Roy 69, 74, 76
Paskert, Dode 34, 35, 36, 37, 38, 56, 57, 58, 60
Pavano, Carl 162
Pena, Tony 2, 147, 150, 153, 158, 159, 160, 187
Pennock, Herb 31
Penthouse 138
Pepitone, Joe 88
Perez, Tony 102, 106, 107, 109, 110, 111, 112, 113
Pesky, Johnny 1, 17, 63, 64, 65, 67, 68, 69, 70, 71, 72, 74, 75, 76, 77, 79, 83, 123, 157, 213, 217
Petrocelli, Rico 88, 90, 93, 96, 98, 100, 101, 104, 105, 107, 108, 111, 112, 165, 217
Pettis, Gary 125, 126, 127, 129, 130
Pettitte, Andy 180, 181, 186, 192, 195
Pfeffer, Jeff 45, 46, 48, 49, 50
Phelps, Ed 15
Phelps, Ken 121
Philadelphia Phillies 33–39
Phillippe, Deacon 6, 7, 8, 9, 10, 11, 12, 13, 14, 15
Phillips, Tony 143
Pick, Charlie 57, 58, 59, 62
Pierzynski, A.J. 220, 222
Piniella, Lou 118, 119
Pittsburgh Pirates 3–13
Plantier, Phil 149
Podsednik, Scott 219, 220, 221
Pole, Dick 101
Pollet, Howie 68, 69, 70, 72, 74
Polo Grounds 21, 31, 32, 52
Poole, Jim 156, 159
Portugal, Mark 170, 172
Posada, Jorge 182, 186, 193, 195, 196, 206
Pujols, Albert 212, 213

"Q" 189
Quantrill, Paul 207
Quigley, Ernie 47
Quinn, Robert 62, 63
Quinones, Rey 122, 123
Quintana, Carlos 147, 150, 152
Quirk, Jamie 151

Ramirez, Manny 158, 164, 167, 168, 173, 174, 183, 185, 187, 188, 189, 190, 192, 193, 194, 195, 198, 199, 200, 201, 202, 204, 205, 207, 208, 210, 211, 212, 213, 218, 221
Randolph, Willie 118, 153

Rapp, Pat 170, 172, 180
Raschi, Vic 81
Reagan, Pres. Ronald 135
Reardon, Jeff 146, 149, 152
Reed, Jody 137, 139, 140, 141, 142, 144, 150, 152, 154
Reed, Rick (player) 168
Reed, Rick (umpire) 178, 181
Reese, Pokey 210
Remy, Jerry 100, 115, 116, 119
Renteria, Edgar 211, 212, 213, 216, 221, 222
Rettenmund, Merv 110
Reyes, Al 172
Reynolds, Allie 80
Rice, Del 70, 74
Rice, Jim 99, 100, 101, 103, 104, 116, 118, 119, 122, 123, 127, 128, 129, 130, 131, 133, 134, 136, 137, 138, 139, 140, 141, 142, 143, 144, 147, 217
Ricketts, Dave 96
Rincon, Ricardo 175, 187, 189
Ritchey, Claude 7, 8, 10, 13
Rivera, Luis 150, 152, 153
Rivera, Mariano 178, 179, 180, 181, 192, 193, 194, 195, 196, 197, 200, 204, 205, 206, 208
Riverfront Stadium 109
Rivers, Mickey 118, 119
Rixey, Eppa 33, 38, 39
Roberts, Dave 200, 207, 208, 217
Robidoux, Billy Jo 147
Robinson, Frank 89
Robinson, Wilbert 43, 44, 45, 46, 49
Rodriguez, Alex 199, 206, 209
Rodriguez, Francisco 202
Rodriguez, Frankie 157
Rohr, Billy 87, 88
Rolen, Scott 212, 213
Rollins, Rich 90
Romero, Ed 136
Romine, Kevin 139, 141
Rose, Brian 163, 172
Rose, Pete 102, 107, 109, 110, 111, 113, 114
Rowand, Aaron 220
Royal Rooters 5, 6, 11, 12, 14, 15, 21, 22, 25, 26, 27, 37, 48
Rudi, Joe 102, 104
Ruhle, Vern 101
Ruppert, Jake 62
Russell, Bill 217
Russell, Rip 68, 69, 76
Ruth, Babe 1, 4, 30, 31, 32, 35, 40, 41, 42, 43, 45, 46, 47, 48, 52, 53, 54, 55, 56, 57, 58, 59, 60, 62, 63, 131, 146, 181, 205
Ryan, Ken 157
Ryan, Mike 88, 90
Ryan, Nolan 121, 171
Ryba, Mike 72

Saberhagen, Brett 162, 163, 164, 167, 172, 174, 175, 177, 180
Sadler, Donnie 169
Sain, Johnny 84
St. Louis Cardinals 1, 67–77, 90–98, 210–215

Sambito, Joe 121, 123, 129, 136
San Francisco Chronicle 142, 189
Sanchez, Rey 183
Sancta Maria Hospital 88
Sanderson, Scott 150
Sanford, Maine 4
Santana, Rafael 132, 136
Santiago, Jose 89, 90, 91, 93, 94
Sauerbeck, Scott 185, 192
Schang, Wally 52, 58, 59, 60, 62
Schilling, Curt 139, 198, 199, 200, 201, 202, 204, 205, 207, 208, 209, 211, 212, 213, 216, 218
Schiraldi, Calvin 1, 120, 123, 127, 128, 129, 130, 131, 134, 135, 136, 137
Schoendienst, Red 68, 69, 71, 74, 91
Schofield, Dick 125, 126, 127, 129, 130
Schourek, Pete 168
Scioscia, Mike 204
Scott, Dale 181
Scott, Everett "Deacon" 30, 34, 35, 37, 41, 46, 47, 48, 50, 52, 57, 58, 62
Scott, George 86, 88, 90, 93, 94, 95, 96, 98, 116, 117, 119
Seaver, Tom 100, 121, 122, 123, 133
Sebring, Jimmy 8, 10, 16
Seerey, Pat 64, 66
Sele, Aaron 155, 156
Selig, Bud 16, 155, 195
Sellers, Jeff 138
Seton Hall University 157
Sewell, Rip 64
Sexson, Richie 173, 174
Seymour, Richard 217
Shafer, Tillie 23
Shannon, Mike 94, 95, 98
Shaughnessy, Dan 146
Shea Stadium 101, 131, 135
Shean, Dave 52, 55, 57, 59, 61, 62
Sheffield, Gary 199, 206, 209
Shibe Park 31, 54
Shore, Ernie 30, 31, 32, 33, 34, 35, 37, 38, 41, 42, 43, 45, 46, 49, 50, 51, 62
Shorten, Chick 48, 50
Shuey, Paul 169, 174, 176
Sierra, Ruben 194, 210
Singleton, Chris 187, 190
Singleton, Ken 99
Sixty Minutes 142
Slaughter, Enos 1, 68, 69, 70, 71, 72, 74, 76, 77, 85
Slocumb, Heathcliff 162, 163
Smith, Lee 137, 140, 142, 143, 144, 146, 147
Smith, Red 116
Smith, Reggie 88, 89, 94, 95, 96
Smith, Sherry 45, 46, 47
Smith, Zane 157, 158, 159, 160
Smithson, Mike 138, 140, 147
Snelgrove, Victoria 210
Snodgrass, Fred 17, 21, 24, 25, 26, 27, 28
Soriano, Alfonso 186, 193, 194, 196
Sorrento, Paul 160, 161
Sosa, Jorge 184

Sosa, Sammy 149, 171
Sotomayor, Sonia 155
Souchock, Steve 81
South End Grounds 3
Sparks, Steve 189
Speaker, Tris 17, 19, 20, 21, 22, 23, 24, 26, 27, 28, 31, 32, 34, 35, 36, 37, 38, 39, 40, 41, 43, 53
Spence, Stan 79, 80, 83
Spencer, Shane 157
Sports Illustrated 218
Sportsman's Park 19, 69, 76
Springsteen, Bruce 185
Sprowl, Bobby 118
Stahl, Chick 4, 5, 10, 12, 13, 14, 16
Stahl, Jake 18, 20, 22, 23, 24, 25, 26, 27, 29
Stange, Lee 90, 94, 96
Stanley, Bob 1, 117, 118, 119, 121, 123, 125, 129, 130, 131, 132, 135, 136, 140, 143, 145, 147
Stanley, Mike 164, 168, 169, 174, 175, 176, 177, 180, 182
Stansbury, Jack 53
Stanton, Mike 182
Stapleton, Dave 128, 129, 136
"Star Spangled Banner" 56
Statler Hotel 66
Stefero, John 123
Steinbach, Terry 142, 151, 154
Steinbrenner, George 115, 116, 117, 148, 181, 195, 200, 204
Stengel, Casey 43, 45, 46, 48, 49, 50
Stephens, Vern 78, 79, 80, 81, 83
Stephenson, Jerry 94
Stevens, Julia Ruth 181
Stewart, Dave 140, 141, 144, 148, 150, 151, 153, 154
Stewart, Sammy 121, 122
Stock, Milt 35, 36
Stone, Jeff 149
Strawberry, Darryl 124, 134, 135
Strunk, Amos 52, 55, 58, 61
Stubing, "Moose" 129
Sturze, Tanyon 205
Sullivan, Haywood 115
Sullivan, Marc 122
Suppan, Jeff 185, 212
Sutton, Don 124, 126, 127, 130

Tannehill, 11
Tartabull, Jose 87, 89
Tavarez, Julian 158, 160, 161, 210, 211
Taylor, Charles 6, 13, 16
Taylor, James 217
Tebbetts, Birdie 78, 80, 83, 84
Tejada, Miguel 186, 188, 189, 190
Tenace, Gene 102, 105
Tesreau, Jeff 21, 24, 26
"Tessie" 12, 13, 14, 48
Teufel, Tim 131
Thomas, Chester "Pinch" 41, 47, 48, 52
Thomas, Fred 40, 55, 58, 59
Thomas, George 94, 96
Thomas, Gorman 121, 122, 123
Thome, Jim 158, 159, 161, 164, 165, 167, 173, 174, 175

Thompson, Gus 12
Tiant, Luis 100, 101, 102, 103, 104, 106, 107, 110, 111, 112, 118, 217
Tiger Stadium 100
Tillotson, Thad 88
Timlin, Mike 183, 187, 189, 190, 191, 192, 193, 196, 202, 204, 207, 218
Tinker, Joe 29
Tinsley, Lee 157
Todd, Jim 102, 103, 105
Torre, Joe 171, 180, 182, 191, 196, 205, 206
Torrez, Mike 99, 115, 116, 117, 118, 119
Trammell, Alan 137, 147
Tresh, Tom 87
Truman, Pres. Harry 63
Tschida, Tim 181
Tyler, Lefty 56, 57, 58, 59, 61, 62

University of Texas 121
Urbina, Ugueth 183
Uribe, Juan 220, 221, 222
US Cellular Field 220

Valentin, John 156, 157, 159, 160, 163, 164, 165, 166, 167, 168, 169, 174, 175, 176, 178, 180, 181
Van Egmond, Tim 156
Varitek, Jason 162, 164, 173, 175, 176, 182, 187, 188, 190, 192, 194, 195, 200, 205, 206, 208, 209, 211, 212, 213, 215, 216, 221, 222
Vaughn, Hippo 56, 57, 58, 59, 60, 62
Vaughn, Mo 156, 157, 159, 160, 161, 162, 163, 164, 165, 166, 167, 169, 170, 171, 173
Vazquez, Javier 206
Veach, Bobby 53
Veil, Bucky 8
Vincent, Fay 148, 154
Vizquel, Omar 159, 160, 161, 163, 168, 177

Wagner, Hal 64, 78
Wagner, Heinie 22, 23, 24, 27, 57
Wagner, Honus 6, 7, 8, 12, 13, 14, 15, 16
Wakefield, Tim 156, 157, 159, 160, 161, 164, 165, 167, 172, 185, 187, 191, 192, 194, 195, 196, 197, 201, 206, 207, 208, 210, 211, 217, 221
Walker, Harry 72, 74, 75, 76
Walker, Larry 171, 211, 212, 213
Walker, Tillie 41, 42, 43, 46, 47, 48, 52
Walker, Todd 183, 187, 188, 189, 190, 191, 192, 193, 194, 195
Wallace, Dave 196
Walsh, Jimmy 47
Warhop, Jack 31
Wasdin, John 167, 175
Washburn, Jarrod 201, 202, 204
Washington, Claudell 102, 103, 104, 105, 147
Washington Post 141
Waslewski, Gary 87, 96
Waterbury, Con. 4
Watergate 116
Watson, Allen 182
Watson, Bob 194
Weaver, Earl 101
Weiss, Walt 143, 144, 151, 152
Welch, Bob 140, 143, 150, 152
Welke, Bill 188, 190
Welke, Tim 159
Wells, David 171, 186, 194, 216, 218, 220, 221
Werner, Tom 217
West, Joe 207
Wheat, Zack 44, 45, 47, 48, 49, 50
White, Roy 119
Whiteman, George 55, 57, 58, 59, 60, 61, 62
Whitted, Possum 39
Wilfong, Rob 125, 129
Wilhelm, Hoyt 164
Williams, Bernie 163, 170, 178, 192, 196, 205, 206, 208
Williams, Billy 102, 105
Williams, Dick 85, 87, 88, 94, 96, 97, 107
Williams, Jimy 162, 164, 168, 169, 171, 172, 174, 175, 177, 180, 181
Williams, Matt 171
Williams, Paul 193
Williams, Ted 63, 64, 65, 66, 67, 69, 70, 71, 72, 75, 76, 78, 79, 80, 81, 82, 83, 85, 134, 171
Williams, Woody 211
Williamson, Scott 185, 187, 188, 189, 190, 191, 192, 194, 195, 196
Willis, Ron 93
Willoughby, Jim 109, 110, 113
Wilson, Art 23, 26
Wilson, Enrique 193, 196
Wilson, Mookie 131, 135
Wilson, Pres. Woodrow 35
Winfield, Dave 148
Winter, George 4, 5
Winter Haven, Fla. 99, 120
Wise, Rick 100, 101, 102, 105, 109, 111, 112
Witt, Mike 124, 125, 128
Womack, Tony 211
Wood, Smoky Joe 17, 18, 19, 20, 21, 22, 23, 24, 25, 26, 27, 28, 31, 32, 41
World War I 51, 54, 55
World War II 33, 63
Wortman, Chuck 60
Wright, George 121
Wright, Jaret 165, 175
Wright, Jim 117
Wrigley Field 56
Wyatt, John 87, 90, 96

"Yankee Doodle" 14
Yankee Stadium 64, 80, 87, 116, 163, 172, 179, 192, 209, 210, 218
Yastrzemski, Carl 85, 87, 88, 89, 90, 91, 93, 94, 96, 98, 99, 100, 101, 102, 103, 104, 105, 106, 107, 109, 110, 111, 112, 113, 114, 116, 118, 119, 165, 171, 217
Yawkey, Jean 115, 135, 138
Yawkey, Tom 63, 78, 90, 101, 114
Yerkes, Steve 22, 24, 25, 27, 28, 29
York, Rudy 63, 64, 65, 67, 68, 69, 70, 71, 72, 74, 75, 76, 78
Young, Cy 1, 4, 5, 7, 8, 11, 12, 14, 16

Zeider, Rollie 60
Zimmer, Don 103, 112, 117, 118, 186, 193, 194
Zito, Barry 186, 187, 188, 190
Zuber, Bill 72

www.ingramcontent.com/pod-product-compliance
Lightning Source LLC
Chambersburg PA
CBHW081545300426
44116CB00015B/2759